Praise F

Greg May is a **dy**... ... disciples of Jesus Christ! His **laugh-out-loud** book pushes tension out the door and opens it wide for forgiveness and healing. Greg is a **brilliant artist** creating unique word pictures. He's also **bold**, not holding back for sensitive "religious" ears, and often stepping on his own toes. And he is **profound**, scoring high on hitting the bull's-eye on spiritual matters.

– Anne Chancey Dalton
author of *Jeremiah A. Denton, Jr: Vietnam War Hero*

Greg May's writing is delightfully irreverent and truthfully trashy. It's a beautiful blue collar view that always makes heavy weight topics seem digestible without ever losing the gritty truth of what we need to wrestle with as Christ followers.

– Lee Baker, Worship Arts Pastor
Northstar Church, Panama City, FL

Greg May has had a special place in my life ever since he was my childhood youth minister. His commitment to making disciples of Jesus Christ is lived out everyday. I am delighted to have Greg's devotional book as a part of my life. These pages are filled with fatherly advice, homespun wisdom, hilarious stories, heart-felt admonishment, and reassuring encouragement. Starting your day with Holy Scripture, bold coffee, and *Crewed Awakening* will jolt you awake to a new life in Christ.

– Dr. Geoffrey Lentz, Associate Pastor
First United Methodist Church, Pensacola, FL

We contemplate, we muse, and we ponder. We struggle and sometimes kneel, frustrated before a mighty God because we feel ashamed. Disgraced by internal thoughts and prayers. Thinking God can't handle an attitude that resembles something less than perfect. Thinking we just can't pull off the "put together" air of the Sunday morning church pew; we pull away. As humans we isolate from our Creator because we think He doesn't understand us.

Greg May's *Crewed Awakening* is a refreshing invitation back to reality. It invites us to return to our Savior's feet, and it teaches us to be genuine in front of a God who truly already knows us completely. Insightful.

Poignant. Reflective. Authentic. I always come away from this devotional feeling as I should feel—like a real-life human, in the hands of a very gracious God.

– Leah Taylor, Worship Leader, Coastline Calvary Chapel Gulf Breeze, FL, http://www.leahtaylorministries.com/

Crewed Awakening is the fruit of a man who spends time with the Lord. He captures everyman's life experience. Greg May is able to fashion into words the struggles, joys and pain of just plain living. His honesty makes you identify with him and each devotional becomes your experience and awakening, and even your answer from God. Sometimes, the answer is a startling awakening that makes you know just how real God is and how much He loves and cares for you. Greg is able to be human and at the same time to lift you to new levels of spiritual awareness.

I have known Greg May for about twenty years as his pastor, watched him become a committed Christian, a disciple and then a disciple-maker. He became a part of our ministry team and served as youth pastor. He was and is a wonderful friend. I had the privilege of watching him become a godly man and husband.

Crewed Awakening comes out of this well of experience. Greg is like an artesian well that flows daily with life giving fresh water for the thirsty. You will read and re-read this devotional guide--for it truly is a guide.

– Perry M. Dalton, retired United Methodist Pastor

You will enjoy meeting Greg May and his beloved "crew": wife, Hannah and their three sons in *Crewed Awakening*. Greg loves life, people and God. But what makes Greg May special is that he is a great storyteller. He can take everyday things in life and lift them up as wonderful insights into his large, humorous soul.

He invites you to join him on his US Postal route and meet the "crazies" and the dogs he failed to dodge. He takes you for rides in his truck with his boys and his pet dog, Louie. He will tell you fish tales, baseball stories and why he loves "Westerns". You will read of his love for old people on his route and for the starving teen who walked into his church youth meeting from off the street.

Greg is not afraid of being transparent in revealing his faults and failings, for he sees God's loving kindness in the mundane places of life where we all live. Pretty soon, you'll be hooked on his fishing line for God.

Crewed Awakening is real. I know. I knew Greg before he had time to sit at a computer.

– Linda Smith, former youth director and fan of Greg May

When working in youth ministry, one is constantly scouring for new youth devotionals and materials. We want anything that brings truth, is relevant and captures their attention. Believe me, it's no easy task. I had been looking for weeks for a new Summer Discipleship program for our young men. However, when the day we were to start rolled around, I still had no material. Desperate, I printed out a couple copies from a devotion that Greg used in his blog earlier that day, and passed them out. I don't even know what I was expecting......but they got it. I was floored. The devotion was on a complicated truth, but the simplicity of the explanation, combined with Greg's life story did the trick. I think this is the greatest compliment I could give. Don't get me wrong, I'm 32 and I constantly get something out of what God puts on his heart. Yet, when you can write where adults are touched and middle school boys get it, then you have something truly special.

– Erin McClellan, Youth Director
Pine Forest United Methodist Church, Pensacola, FL

Crewed Awakening
Not Your Every Day Devotional for Every Day

Greg May

Energion Publications
Gonzalez, FL
October, 2012

Copyright © 2012, Greg May
All Rights Reserved

Unless otherwise marked, Scripture quotations are from the New International Version Bible. Copyright © Zondervan Corporation. 1973, 1978, 1984, 2011. Used by Permission.

Cover Design: Nick May

ISBN10: 1-938434-14-5
ISBN13: 978-1-938434-14-3
Library of Congress Control Number: 2012951588

Energion Publications
P.O. Box 841
Gonzalez, FL 32560
www.energionpubs.com

DEDICATION

This book is dedicated to the love of my life, Hannah May.
You started all of this with that Father's Day gift in 2008.
Thank you! I love you!

Acknowledgments

Thanks Mom and Dad for being there from start to finish.

Thank you to my sons Ben, Ryan and Nick, who loved and tolerated me as I efforted to raise them, when all along God was using them to grow me up.

Thanks to my anointed teacher Linda Smith and my example of a loving "discipler" Terrie Taylor. These two are truly the "Show and Tell" of fulfilling The Great Commission.

Thank you Perry Dalton, who always had my back when we were in ministry together or I would have been wounded continually in battle.

Thank you to that group of kids in the 90's (grown adults now) who lived out their faith in front of me and I saw what it was to grow "in wisdom and stature, and in favor with God and men". You know who you are, everyone of you, thank you!

Thanks to Kevin, my prayer partner in the tough times.

Thank you Preston and Jeanette, true friends and fellow servants through thick and thin.

Thanks Jody and Henry, for taking a chance in publishing this book.

Thank you every one of you who helped, encouraged, supported, and prayed for me. All of your names would fill another book, but everyone of you are close to my heart.

Introduction

My desire and motive for writing this book is to show God at work in a real way in "everyday life." We can and should read His Word (The Bible). It is "living and active," not to mention timeless. And if we will look, we will see Him writing daily on the pages of our lives. In some small way, this is my attempt to share with the reader what God has shown me on the pages of the book of my life.

For example, He has shown me the importance of pure motives. Had I written a book even a few years ago, my reason would have been to see what it could profit the writer. Now I write this book in hopes of it profiting the reader.

I pray that if you do not know Jesus, this book would encourage you to consider Him becoming your Lord and Savior. If you already know Him, I pray that you will be seeing Him in your everyday life as you catch a glimpse of yourself in these pages.

My hope is not that you totally agree with everything I have written, but that you are provoked to seriously ponder the things of God; the God who personally writes on the pages of your life, every single day.

This is my testimony telling of how God has brought all of the streams of my life together for His purposes:

Crewed Awakening

Psalm 37:4 says: "Delight yourself in the Lord and He will give you the desires of your heart." When I first read this verse I had a "Let's Make a Deal" mentality. My motive was to get the desires of my heart, not delighting myself in the Lord. I am now seeing how God means for this to work in my own life.

As far back as I can remember, I have loved fishing, the sea, and as I got older, boats. I remember as a small boy fishing with my grandfather, standing in shallow streams in Washington State, catching rainbow trout and putting them in a fish basket. I also remember as a small pirate fishing here on the Gulf Coast with my other grandfather. He would give me his cane pole and put a little piece of bait on the small hook and I would tirelessly catch one pinfish after another, all while drinking coffee with him out of his thermos. I recall the day I caught a 13-inch white trout (a monster at the time) while fishing with my dad. I cannot tell you how many Saturday nights, during my teen years, I spent on the Three Mile Bridge with my friends fishing the night away. Then there was the time with my dad fishing in a way too small boat, in way too turbulent water, but we truly caught the monster that day! I have taken my own sons fishing, bringing back memories of good times together. Those were the days!

I spent many hours of my formative years in a pool hall. It was my favorite hangout because everyone knew me and many of us truly cared about one another. There was this unbelievable level of openness and trust. We would shoot pool, play cards, eat together and lean on each other when necessary. Sticking together through thick and thin, and there was a plenty of both. Those were the days!

In the past I have spent my fair share of time as a volunteer bartender, in my home and others. Alcohol aside, it was always nice to spend time together with friends and share our life experiences. Those were the days!

Cheers is one of my all time favorite TV shows. It was often kooky and had a little to much hormonal overload from Sam. However it was a place where "everybody knows your name." Who doesn't want to be where everybody knows your name?

What does this have to do with Psalm 34? Please receive this as boasting in the Lord and not myself. I have been seeking God, trying to delight myself in Him, not as a means to get the desires of my heart but just to know Him more. Well, well, guess what. That's right, the desires of my heart.

He is bringing so many of the streams of my past together. He made me the way that I am. The personality He gave me is being aligned with His will to be used for His glory. It is amazing to me to look back at my life and see what He has been up to all along. The gates of hell cannot prevail against Him. The only thing that can screw this up would be my disobedience. (Pray for me to know and do His will at every step).

So what's up? Tomorrow Greg's Fishin Hole takes the next step. The opening of a place where we can come together and share life. A place where we can be there with one another and for one another. A place where we can play, pray, laugh and cry. Where everybody knows your name, and I pray it will be a place where everybody knows His name. A place where God will get the glory. These are the days!

First Things First   January 1

For the 59th straight morning, I got up and went to the table with my computer to write this morning's thoughts in my blog. Soon after I sat down, an uneasy realization of distance between me and God came over me. It wasn't a feeling of His total absence. It was more like I had moved Him out, but only next door. You know, where He would be handy if I needed Him.

This had happened so painlessly I hadn't even noticed. Like laughing gas at the dentist office, you're laughing so hard you can't feel the dentist ripping the tooth out of your face! But then the numbness wears off, the hole in your jaw is sore and you can't chew anything!

For more than two years (prior to starting my blog) I had gotten up almost every morning and spent time with God in prayer and reading His word. Those two years, for me personally, were hard times filled with long days. They were not bad, just long and hard. In fact, as far as my personal relationship to God is concerned, it was the best two years of my life! I learned and experienced dependence on Him as my Lord.

So where did this realization of distance come from? I think it all started about 59 days ago when I started writing the blog. To be sure, God has been faithful every single day to give me something to say and share. So He didn't move away from me. Personally, my blog has been a wonderful way for me to testify of what God is doing and has done in my life. So writing the blog isn't causing the separation.

What is it then? It's not what I started that is the cause of this feeling of distance between me and God. It's what I stopped! I stopped meeting Him every day. I prayed less and less and I read His Word less and less. The growing distance between me and God was being numbed by me placing a higher priority on writing a blog than on my time and relationship with Him.

This morning the numbness wore off and the distance became a sore spot. I realized that I want that closeness to God that I had in those tough two years. In fact, I want to be even closer! Closer than a brother. That's what it's all about – relationship to God, not *religion* about God.

Anyway, I believe He still wants me to keep on with the "Watering Hole," I'll just be writing it after we meet every morning.

P.S. I wrote this over a year ago. It's working. God is real and good. He's real good! If you don't know that, try Him. I dare you!

No Parking   January 2

More than half of the deliveries on my route are mounted. The route I just moved from was almost totally mounted. Mounted means that the delivery is made to a curbside box, which allows me to pull up to the mailbox and deliver the mail without exiting my truck. This gives me the ability to make the most possible deliveries in the time allotted.

The biggest aggravation to this type of delivery for a mailman is when people park their cars, or place their yard trash and garbage cans in front of their mailbox. This forces the driver to stop, turn off the engine, place the vehicle in park and set the emergency brake before exiting the truck and making the delivery. A time consuming act as well as an aggravation.

I understand how it is difficult for yard maintenance guys with trucks and trailers to not block a box. Sometimes roofers have several big trucks and moving vans are huge. I get it when a box is blocked in those cases. But I can't tell you how often the cars I know belong to the homeowner are parked right up against their mailbox! To add to the aggravation, their driveway is empty! My terminology for these blockers of their own boxes is "jerks," which is a recently upgraded term from what I used to call them!

One more added point of grief is how often these cars blocking the boxes have a church sticker proudly displayed on them! Enough said.

Even in this frustration at work, God is at work in me. Several days in a row as I approached this particular box on my route that had the same cars blocking two mailboxes. As I approached these boxes the other day, another car pulled up into the empty driveway. A lady got out and slowly meanders over towards me. About then my patience was wearing out. Not only had they blocked these boxes for days, but she was taking her sweet time in coming over to get her mail from me! Then it happened.

She said she was sorry for the boxes being blocked. To which I replied (in a joking voice, but meaning it): "Yeah, you guys are killing me here."

Then she said that she had been in a terrible car accident (hence her slow walk towards me to get her mail). She also told me that her daughters had come down to take care of her. That was why there were so many cars there for days.

It was choice time for me. I could just say that it was OK about the cars, or just blow it off and still be aggravated, or I could show some genuine concern. So, all I did was ask her how she was doing and she lit up! When I showed concern for her situation, instead of beefing at her about how her daughter's parking messed me up, I made a friend, not an enemy.

Maybe something is finally changing in me. He is at work, hard at work as far as changing me, but something is changing. Something that I could never do on my own! Thank you, Jesus!

If anything blocks our routine, maybe we should stop, get out and see if God's up to something. Maybe He wants us to make a delivery that really matters.

Where Has All the Carbon Paper Gone
January 3

Last night I had to fill out some forms in duplicate. I figured it would make sense to go to the nearby drugstore and grab some carbon paper. This would save me half the time of filling out these forms. I went to two nearby stores and neither had carbon paper. Where has all the carbon paper gone? Has it gone the way of the rotary phone? The cloth diaper (good riddance)? The bad gum in baseball cards? One-on-one discipleship?

By far and away, one-on-one discipleship is the biggest failure of the church today! It has been fumbled by us, and the enemy has picked it up and run the other way for what seems to be a sure touchdown.

We will not succeed in "raising them up in the way they should go" (children or disciples), by just having them in Sunday school and listening to a preacher an hour a week (if that often). Those are good things, but are not the totality of making disciples. That is what He commissioned us to do; make disciples.

I have seen (a few) people who are wonderful at making disciples. They are great "carbon paper." What makes them so successful? Are they smarter than everyone else? Richer? Cooler? More likable or outgoing? Nope. They are willing to give of their time. That's their best trait.

Many of us are willing to give a little of our spare time to a project at church. However, we often would much rather give our money than our not-so-spare time. But that's what it will ultimately require; total availability to others.

That's the way Jesus showed us to disciple. He *lived* with those guys (His disciples) for years. He was available to them, teaching and demonstrating the everyday walk of a godly man. They weren't carbon copies of Him, but they were carbon copies of His message.

I have dropped the ball in this area before because of my own selfishness with my time. But it isn't really my time, is it? So, I'm praying again: "Lord, if You desire it, show me if there is someone willing to have me share what You have shown me. Maybe we could leave a few of Your copies around here for the next generation."

The Deck January 4

My last two days off, as well as a few evenings after work, I have been rebuilding a deck on the side of my house. Several years ago, when we first built it, I seem to remember my dad and Ben saying we should do this or that to make it more stout. I was in a bit of a hurry and wanted to get it built and start enjoying it. Well, after several years it sagged in places and warped in others. It now had to be repaired and reinforced.

When I took the old deck boards off, it was easy to see the problem. I had not made the structure (framing) underneath strong enough to support the load of the deck boards and the traffic of people.

I replaced and repaired the old framing underneath. I also put in a lot more support to the framing. It took quite a bit more time preparing the structure underneath (the foundation for the deck) than it did to put the new deck boards on top of the framing.

However, if you came by and looked at it now, you would only see the deck floor and not all the new and reinforced framing underneath.

Outwardly it looks a lot like the old deck, but underneath is a whole new strength.

This is similar to what God does in our lives when we allow Him to come in and rebuild us. He changes the foundation that we stand on. When He enters our lives His strength is now our support and we won't sag, crumble, warp and then be blown away. Even when we face trials or troubles and we are seemingly blown apart, His "foundation" stands and we can rebuild on it because He is unmoved.

He is the concrete foundation that is still there after the storm. He is the Rock that is not washed away. After a storm, or just years of being out in the weather of the world, we may look a little different on the outside (like when I need a haircut and a shave). But on the inside, underneath this flesh, I am not moved because my foundation is strong. I'm standing on the Rock!

"Therefore everyone who hears these words of mine and puts them into practice is like a wise man who built his house on the rock. The rain came down, the streams rose, and the winds blew and beat against that house; yet it did not fall, because it had its foundation on the rock. But everyone who hears these words of mine and does not put them into practice is like a foolish man who built his house on sand. The rain came down, the streams rose, and the winds blew and beat against that house, and it fell with a great crash." – Matthew 7: 24-27

Who's Lost Here Anyway, Bozo   January 5

I spend most of my workday on the street. Several times a week people will pull up alongside me and ask for directions. Unless they are UPS, Fed Ex (YES! they stop and ask me) or jerks, I will send them correctly on their way. Yesterday was an example of the latter personality.

I was sitting at a traffic light on my way back to the station when this elderly man and woman pulled up beside me. He rolled down his window and asked for directions to his destination.

I told him "Turn right here..."

"No," he interrupts, "I was told to stay on this street!"

I feel the hair going up on the back of my neck as I think: "Who's lost here anyway, Bozo?" I told him: "If you do stay on this street you won't get there!"

"Oh," was his brilliant response.

I then informed him, "If you insist on staying on this road, then go ahead and go straight until it dead ends about half a mile ahead. Then turn right and go another mile to the north and turn right at the next traffic light. All that would take about ten minutes travel time. Then you will be right back where you would be if you just turn right here like I told you and go up this street for about thirty seconds! Your destination is about two minutes east of that point!"

So, my short tirade ends and I wait to see which way he's going to go when the light changed. Twelve minutes or two and a half minutes. What's it going to be? The light turned green and off he went straight up the street, the long way! Resisting the temptation to chase him down and continue my tirade, I turned left and went on my way.

I'll bet some of you are thinking the lesson here is patience, kindness to our fellow man, and not letting your anger cause you to sin. Maybe it should be, but not this time.

Actually, my question here is: "To God, are we like the man in the car asking directions?" Thankfully, God will not call us Bozo when we argue, disobey instructions, and disrespect Him. He may discipline us, but more often than not, that discipline and correction will come in the form of natural consequences for not doing something the way he told us.

The man did have the good sense to realize I might know the quickest, easiest and best way for him to get to his destination. I did. I told him. He chose to go his own way. Maybe my tone of voice had a little to do with his decision to not follow my directions.

Anyway, even when we have the good sense to ask God what direction to go, do we follow His instructions? Do we interrupt Him and argue? Do we follow the instructions of someone else? Do we flat out disobey when we know exactly what He said and that what He said is the right way to go?

Shouldn't we follow the directions of the One who knows the best way to get to where we're going? Besides, if we're the ones asking for directions, who's lost?

Ruined   January 6

I was just watching a re-cap show of the Alaska Experiment. These four groups of people had gathered together to share their experiences of being sent into the Alaskan Wilderness (with few provisions) to live for three months. The things they were able to do and learn to do in those most difficult conditions were amazing!

They had to hunt, fish, cut wood, hike, and scavenge, among many other things, all while being alert to the dangers around them, which included: bears, wolves, ice covered mountainous terrain, and sub-zero temperatures.

The distractions of the world were gone and they had focused on the most important thing in their lives, which was making provisions for their very survival.

During the discussion at the post-show get together, one man said the strangest thing to get used to after coming back to the world was the noise, busyness, and hustle bustle of life. Another person spoke of his will being broken, realizing who you are and then going to the next level. Then, when asked if they would endure it all again, everyone of them immediately said "Yes."

Two of them are going back for good. It sounds as if they have been ruined and will settle for nothing less than the constant adventure, now that they have had a taste. All of these individuals have been changed through this event. Two of them have been changed seemingly forever. They just can't settle for coming back to the everyday world.

So, when we ask ourselves as believers "What is my focus for my survival?" Do we quickly reply, "Oh, of course, it's Jesus," or do we think of the price it will cost? Because (spiritually speaking) we are going to have to learn to hunt, fish, and cut wood in tough conditions while being on the alert for the wolves.

I think back to taking youth groups to camp where there would be no TVs, iPods, phones, radios, or hustle bustle of life. The focus was on one's relationship to Christ. These were great times of getting closer to God by setting the things of the world aside and putting our focus on Him who we say we depend on for our survival. We would have that "spiritual mountaintop" experience. We are often broken at events like these and are taken to a higher level. We experience a closer walk with

God. We like it and we would go back again. But if we are not ruined, then when we get back to the everyday world, the busyness of life will draw us away. The closeness to God will become distance.

How do we stay ruined? By keeping our focus on the Lord. Get away with Him as much as possible. Not just every event, but everyday more and more! Make Him first priority all of the time.

I have been reading the Bible, praying, and listening to Him more consistently for a good while now and I can say that even in the challenges of this earthly wilderness, He is with me and He is the provision for my survival.

I think I am being ruined!

"Do not store up for yourselves treasures on earth, where moths and vermin destroy, and where thieves break in and steal. But store up for yourselves treasures in heaven, where moths and vermin do not destroy, and where thieves do not break in and steal. For where your treasure is, there your heart will be also...

So do not worry, saying, 'What shall we eat?' or 'What shall we drink?' or 'What shall we wear?' For the pagans run after all these things, and your heavenly Father knows that you need them. But seek first his kingdom and his righteousness, and all these things will be given to you as well." – Matthew 6:19-21,31-33

Think Of Jerks More Highly Than Myself
January 7

For most of us, if we are going to be truthful, there are a few people in our lives that just grate on us. In my case, it is mostly people that I frequently run into related to my work. Customers that seemingly wait daily by their mailbox just to complain to me (about the whole world, not just junk mail) or hit me with the original line: "Keep the bills." Jerks, whiners and pains in the butt with a crappy outlook on life who just have nothing better to do than complain! Do you know some?

I have written before about my often lack of a Christ-like attitude towards them. I am trying, and seem to be doing better, but some of them are tougher to tolerate (much less, deal with) than others, if you know what I mean. There are a few of them that I will try to avoid if at all possible. For instance, if I am at the store taking my break and one of the most whiny of the complainers pulls up, it's break-time over and to be continued at another (more peaceful) location.

That's exactly what happened the other day. I was just chillin in the A/C of the convenience store, when the biggest whiner on the route pulls in. He pulled up at the other end of the store from my truck and so I made a break for it. Sometimes I get away, but not this time. I begin to rearrange the load in my truck while I pretended to listen to him babble.

"Hey, have you seen or delivered any of those sweepstakes envelopes, any at all? I have sat at my computer for hours filling out one after another of those entry forms. They keep telling me I am successfully entered for this prize and that prize but I haven't won a thing! Well, have you seen or delivered any of those; huh?"

Fighting off my "auto smart aleck mode" to tell him he's wasting his time and is only going to win an offer for magazine subscriptions and a one-of-a-kind plastic spoon Christmas ornament, I just reply, "Nope."

He then says: "Well it didn't cost me anything but my time, and my time is not worth anything anyway."

I think but don't say: "Well mine is." Then I reply: "I have to get moving." And I am gone! Annoyance over at minimum expense.

As I thought about this encounter, I realized that it is a sad thing for him to think his time is worth nothing. Sadder still is that I think my time is more valuable than his.

In Ephesians and Colossians, Paul tells us to: "...make the most of every opportunity...". Epic fail on that encounter, Greg!

It occurs to me that the reason I may not be having success at "making the most of every opportunity" is that I am more concerned about my need for a change in my attitude than for someone else's need to be heard. In other words, I am more concerned about my improvement rather than being an uplifting influence on someone else.

Funny how God works sometimes. My self improvement could be better achieved through my encouragement and service to others.

Fear The Sore Butt   January 8

Got fear? I'm not talking about being fearful of everything around us. I'm talking about "fear of God."

First of all, what is "fear of God"? We can really get some varying opinions on this question! Some will say it is a reverent respect for God. That is most assuredly a big part of it, but if we think that is all there is to it, are we possibly avoiding part of what the fear of God should be for us?

I have a healthy dose of respect for my dad. But as I was growing up, there was also the fear, as the old saying goes, that "he brought me in and he can take me out." Yep, there was a, he can and will, if he deems necessary, punish me kind of expectation in my mind. When he caught me doing something wrong, "Gee, I really respect you, Dad," is not what came to my mind first! It was more like, "Oh crap, I'm in it now! How long will it be before I can sit down on my sore butt?"

In many ways, that "fear of the sore butt," was a deterrent from doing wrong in my father's eyes.

When should we experience the "fear of God"? I often experience the fear of God after I have committed some sin. I ask Him for mercy, but I fear the Righteous Judge.

Proverbs says, "the fear of the Lord is the beginning of wisdom." James said, "ask for wisdom and not doubt." I say, "coming by wisdom and fear of the Lord by trial and error is no fun!" I think our best option is to walk in the fear of the Lord always (before sin), thereby not encountering necessary discipline of a loving Father.

Proverbs 16:6: "...through the fear of the Lord a man avoids evil." Think ahead. Fear the spiritual sore butt!

I'm Pissed — January 9

Go ahead, tell me you have never been so angry you just wanted to fight. Sure you haven't! OK, maybe you haven't, but I have and was angry enough to fight just the other night. Someone said something and it hit a raw nerve in my flesh! It was all I could do to not blow a fuse and go off like a bomb! Emotionally it felt like I was slamming on brakes in the rain. Was I going to hit something before the anger train came to a halt as I had many times in the past?

Now I know a lot of Scripture I could have leaned on and advice I could have given to someone else in the same situation. I've done just that in the past. Knowing the right words to say can be helpful but applying Scripture and sound advice while going through some aggravation or tough time is another matter. It's like James is standing there casually leaning on a light pole saying: "Don't just read the Word, do what it says."

Right about then is when my flesh wants to say: "Just take it down the street to another light pole dude, 'cause somebody's lights are about to go out here!"

Thankfully the light didn't go out. In fact, that night and the next morning His light got brighter. Here's the conversation we had. We both said only a few things over several hours, with me left to think about His answers in between my responses.

Greg: "OK God, why do I have to put up with that? I'm going along happy and having a great time talking about good times and then someone has to be a smart ass! I mean it, I'm pissed!"

God: "Uh-huh."

Greg: "Well! What do I do here?" (I really wanted to let the other person have it! I'd been working on my coming tirade for hours. I was still fuming!)

God: "Forgive them."

Greg: "Say what? Didn't you see that?! They made an ass out of me!"

God: "Just forgive them."

Then it occurs to me that the one who is telling me to forgive them is the same one that was hanging on a cross with nails in His hands and feet, asking His Father to forgive the ones who nailed Him up there! All of a sudden my grievance seems awful petty.

Greg: "OK Lord, I'll forgive 'em."

God: "And ask them to forgive you. Offer no excuses, explanations or reasons for your behavior. Just ask for their forgiveness."

Greg: "But I...Yes, Lord."

I did. It could not have ended better. Yep, He's right there even in the tough times.

Jesus said, "Father, forgive them, for they do not know what they are doing." And they divided up his clothes by casting lots. – Luke 23:34

Who Are Those Guys   January 10

In the movie *Butch Cassidy and the Sundance Kid,* these bandits, portrayed as happy-go-lucky guys, seemed to have the world by the tail. They had the pretty lady, as much money as they wanted and seemingly could go and do what ever they desired. They made up their own rules as they went along. Butch even changed the rules during a fight so as to defeat his foe and continue his control of the gang. He and his crew were in control of their world. Nothing and no one had the power to stop them. Or so they thought.

The train company they continually robbed, hired (empowered) an elite band of lawmen and trackers to find Butch and Sundance and bring them to justice. The best line in the movie is spoken when the outlaws have been running from this posse for quite a while. They stop for a moment to look back and see that this posse is not ordinary, but relentless and one of the outlaws ask in amazement and with trepidation: "Who are those guys?"

The same kind of thing happens in the Book of Acts. There was this group of guys seemingly in control of the Jewish religious world and they made up their own rules to enforce as they went along. This was a religious council called the Sanhedrin, made up of Pharisees (Sundances) and Sadducees (Butches). They thought they had won a shootout with this Sheriff named Jesus. Although He had challenged them, in their minds He was dead, or so they thought.

But Jesus had empowered His posse to continue His work and that did not sit well with the Sanhedrin. Two of the leaders of the Jesus' posse, named Peter and John were arrested by the Sanhedrin. Peter and John boldly stood before these religious rulers and witnessed to Jesus' life, death, resurrection and deity.

The Sanhedrin told them to shut up about Jesus. Peter and John told them that was not going to happen. Somewhere along in this exchange of gunfire, the Sadducees and Pharisees had to wonder: "Who are these guys?" The answer is in Acts 4:13:

When they saw the courage of Peter and John and realized that they were unschooled, ordinary men, they were astonished and they took note that these men had been with Jesus.

The thing is, these ordinary men were now walking in the power of an extraordinary God and from here on the Jesus posse will grow and spread, until our Sheriff comes riding back into town! Want to ride along?

Heroes Of Our Heroes — January 11

I went to visit with my grandmother yesterday. She lives in another town about 125 miles away. I had not seen her in quite a while. She's closer to 100 than 90 now but is still able to take pretty good care of herself.

My aunt checks on her regularly and along with my parents tend to her needs as necessary, such as taking her to get groceries, doctor visits and financial assistance. My mom has a good heart in doing this and though my dad and aunt act as if they're the parents now and not the child, they have good hearts when it comes to taking care of their mother.

Also yesterday, I was at church in the same town with my in-laws. My wife's mom is now getting up in age to where she requires assistance to take care of herself. One of my nephews has taken care of her almost exclusively for a while now. He has a totally unselfish heart toward his grandmother. The wife of another nephew demonstrated her good heart as she walked my mother-in-law out to her car, assisting her into the car and with putting her drops in her eyes for her.

I know a lady at my workplace who spends a lot of her time caring for her mother. She does it with little help and no complaining.

I know a young lady (in her twenties) who is taking care of her elderly grandfather. In the prime of her life she is putting many of her desires on the back burner to care for this man. I admire her more than she can imagine!

This is as it should be, but too often is not the case.

I know a many more examples of people who care for their elderly loved ones if at all possible. Our elderly loved ones are the people who cared for and raised us for probably more years than we will have to care for them. We should not shuck them aside like an old pair of shoes and then run to see them when our consciences need a rescue.

Besides, in many cases, these elderly loved ones are the ones who prayed us through all the crap we got ourselves into as young people. Hold on to them! Their wisdom is endless, their smile is priceless and we owe them more than we have time to repay.

God bless you, heroes of elderly loved ones. Your reward awaits you!

Thank you Aunt Margie, Mom, Dad, Bobby, Priscilla, Barbara, Kayla and all of you unnamed here, who care for those who cared for us.

Done Or Still Working On It   January 12

One thing I don't like about my job is the sense that it is never truly completed. What I mean is, after a long day of delivery, I return to the shop to see the next day's deliveries already beginning to pile up. It may sound corny, but I like the feeling of a job well done! You know, finished, completed, and tangible.

For instance I like to say: "Greg, you did a great job on that deck! Why don't you get a big glass of tea and sip on it – in the shade, on your new deck? It's done, enjoy it!"

When I used to work construction, I loved starting on an empty lot and then a year or two later walking away from a completed new school or hospital. It was a feeling of a completion that was rewarding. Now on to something else. But that's not the way it works with everything in life.

My parents used to tell me that I would have to work at being married. As a young man I would blow that one off in a hurry, saying: "No problem, if we're in love it'll be easy." Did anyone else hit about 25 or 30 years old and realize your parents are pretty wise after all? Anyway, I'm not just talking about marriage, but all relationships.

Relationships are our jobs that are never completed, but there are rewards. The receiving of love, for example. The two greatest commandments are relational: Loving God and loving others. That's our job. Do you need some work in some of your relationships? I'll bet we all do. A relationship is not a job we finish. It's the job we should always be doing.

After writing this I feel as though my desire for completion of a task or job, so that I can move on to something else, is for me a fleshly desire for something. And although working at a relationship is open ended, it is rewarding. Besides, aren't we all looking to love and be loved?

Clean And In Good Working Order   January 13

When I was about twelve I got my first real gun for Christmas. It was a bolt action .22 caliber rifle with a scope. I remember that it felt so much heavier than a BB gun. It was the real deal.

Later, I lived next to a pond that was surrounded by a lot of overgrown brush, and beyond that, open pasture. It was a great place to shoot my rifle. I would zero in on a moccasin's head sticking up out of the water and decapitate it with one shot.

Another cool thing about having a gun was taking care of it. My dad bought me a cleaning kit especially made for my type of rifle. The kit included a rod with a wire brush on the end. It was the perfect size for a .22 rifle barrel. I would put a little oil on the brush and push the rod with the brush on it up and down the barrel. This process would clean out all the residue and dirt, leaving the barrel clean and in good working order. I would also disassemble working parts of the gun. I would clean them with a cloth and a light coat of oil to keep those parts in working order.

My son Ryan is a gun guy. He will take his guns apart completely to clean them so they will be ready at the next opportunity to go shooting.

Sometimes I feel like my old .22 rifle before a good cleaning. I can get all clogged up with selfishness, pride, and all sorts of sin. When this happens I am not able to function as best I can as a weapon for God in the Kingdom. I have to allow the "gun owner" to clean me out so that I can work to my maximum potential.

It should be our desire and goal to please God by staying clean (not sinning) while doing His will in the Kingdom. But the truth is, we are fallible and we will mess up. That's when we should go to the one with the perfect ability to clean us and render us completely serviceable again. We should ask to be cleaned as often as necessary. If we continue trying to work while becoming more and more clogged up, we become less and less useful, even to the point of backfiring.

Having said that, even backfiring can be repaired. However, it could take more time to get us back to peak performance.

If we confess our sins, He is faithful and just and will forgive us our sins and purify [cleanse] us from all unrighteousness. – 1 John 1:9 (my addition)

Just Waiting   January 14

Matthew 24:36-25:46

The world encourages us and our flesh seeks to fulfill the notion that we should put ourselves first in all things we undertake. Look out for number one, etc. God's plan is the opposite. He says that we should all be servants, "thinking of others more highly than ourselves."

Jesus says that we are to love God with all our heart, soul and mind. He also says to love our neighbor. These are the two greatest commandments. If we do the first, the second will follow. He calls us to serve and Jesus showed us how to do that in the life He lived.

Our flesh might say, "I'm ready, I've saved, I'm good. I've got mine, I'll just go on cruise-control and coast into Heaven."

I've read stories and seen TV shows that chronicle hunting trips and mountain climbs. The first thing that people do when they are going to undertake such an expedition is to locate and hire a guide. Someone who knows how to prepare for the trip and how to get there. The guide is a servant. He is the person with the knowledge of where to go and how to get there successfully.

In the movie *Jeremiah Johnson*, he was ask to guide a rescue party to some lost travelers in snow covered mountains. He was their guide. He knew the way to get the rescue party into the area.

I think we can all place ourselves into one of two categories here. We are either a guide or someone who needs to be rescued out of the storm. Unfortunately, many of the *guides* are just sitting in the cabins waiting for the winter to pass.

What Jesus is saying here is that there are people (souls for the Kingdom) out there in the snow. In deep snow, even blizzards of life where they can't see and don't know which way to go. If we are a guide, sitting in a warm cabin, He wants us to get off our butts and get out there and show the lost the way to the cabin.

Even if I am a guide, all safe in my own salvation, I wouldn't want to be sitting with someone and be taken up, while the one I was sitting with looks up with eyes that say "Where are you going?"

Been There...Didn't Do That   January 15

I used to ride motorcycles quite a bit. For a short period of time it was my main mode of transportation. However, riding dirt bikes on the trails in the woods was by far the most fun. My friends and I would race through the woods that surrounded a nearby lake. We got to the point that we seemingly knew every twist and turn of those trails.

The motorcycle I had at the time was called an "enduro", meaning a dirt bike that was equipped with lights, mirrors and such that made it street legal. On one occasion a friend and I borrowed my dad's dirt bike for a ride through the woods. We headed for our favorite trails for a race around the lake.

I got out front and we began zipping through the woods. I headed into a sand-banked turn at high speed. I had been around this turn hundreds of times. Except this time, instead hitting the gas hard and digging in as I rounded the embankment, I hit the gas, dug in and went flying over the the hill and down into the woods.

I landed well, but at high speed there was no way I was going to avoid all those trees. I hit a pine tree so hard it bent the forks on the front of my motorcycle. That was a serious impact! I thank God my head didn't hit that tree or another one as I flew over the handlebars to a relatively soft landing in the leaves.

I looked up to see my friend who was behind me (he must have caught the rut I made) go flying by me. His face caught a limb and it peeled him right off my dad's motorcycle. He was none the worse for wear and the only damage to Dad's bike was a busted chain.

As I write this, I am reminded of times in the Bible when men of God, instead of seeking God as to how to handle a situation each time, did something the same way as they had done successfully in the past. For example, battle strategies that had proved victorious before were unsuccessful the next time.

We need to seek God's will at every turn in our lives, even if we've been there before. He has reasons for doing things differently. It could be the way that one person was reached is completely different from how another will come to the Lord.

I just went hard into that turn like every time before. This time the result was not the same. Worse yet, someone following me was caught up in it and went down with me. He could have paid a very high price! For our own sake, for the sake of others and for His Kingdom, let's be sure we know where He wants us to go and how to get there each time.

Beyond The Harvest January 16

When I was about eleven years old, I went with my sister to visit our grandmother in Washington state. She lived in a small town surrounded by wheat fields that seemed to stretch out as far as the eye could see.

I remember riding on a combine with a friend of Grandmother's while he was harvesting his wheat. It seemed as if I was on a giant lawnmower as we cut down these endless fields of grain. A large truck stayed alongside us as we harvested the field, receiving the grain as the combine separated it from the stalks. That would be the last I would see of that grain. Unless it somehow showed up as a loaf of bread at my table later. So it must have gone through some process to get from harvested grain to useful bread.

I believe that we as a the Church have dropped the ball when it comes to processing "the harvest." For instance, an evangelist comes to town for revival services or a person comes to the Lord through some special service or even a television broadcast. They confess their faith, become believers and we tell them to join a Bible-Believing church and get involved. OK, that's wonderful. Salvation is first and most important but not the completion of the Great Commission.

Jesus said to "go and make disciples." I am not down on Sunday School or small groups, I just believe that they are not enough to make disciples. Discipling someone requires more than an hour or two on Sunday or a single block of time at some special event, even though these times are wonderful.

I know that some men and young people are reading this right now and are rightly screaming at me, "Yea Greg, you dropped the ball when you were discipling me!" I will address you guys a little further along here, but that is exactly why I believe God has me writing this story. I've dropped the ball with you and it has happened to me as well.

I believe that Jesus is our example of what we are to do with the "harvest of souls." We are to disciple them like He did those that were with Him. By allowing new believers into our daily lives and living out our lives in Christ before them. Yes, with all our flaws and mistakes in our everyday lives. How else will they learn and see the grace, mercy and forgiveness of our God?

So why don't so many of us carry out this part of the Great Commission to "go and make disciples?" Speaking from my own experience, I would say that I have an attitude that my time is my own. This attitude is not one that "loves my neighbor as myself" or "thinks of others more highly than myself." We are often more protective of our time than even our money.

My first Youth Director position was at a church that had only a few youth when I was hired. During the first finance meeting I attended I ask for $6000 for a youth budget! I thought this would indicate to me their commitment to building the Youth Department. No sweat! Money seemed to be no object. My next question was who could go with the Youth Group and me to camp that summer? You could have heard a pin drop!

That is not a knock on them. Many of us are like that. It takes time and work to process a harvest.

I was watching a wildlife program earlier tonight showing a grizzly bear coming out of hibernation with her new cubs. The narrator explained that these cubs would spend the next three years of their lives at their mother's side. The cubs would observe and learn how to live and survive by her example. That's about how long those guys hung around with Jesus, isn't it?

Got three years?

Matthew 28:18-20, 22:34-40

P.S. If you're one of the guys I dropped the ball with, and you know who you are, I ask you to forgive me. If you want to give it another shot, well maybe I've learned my time is not my own.

Foggy Water   January 17

A couple of weeks ago Ryan and I began establishing an aquarium in The Fishin Hole. He already had a tank, so we ordered some covers for the top, bought a filter, the necessary water chemicals, and of course some fish. Everything seemed to be cruising along just fine. Ryan was dilligent to check the water everyday for ph, chlorine and all that necessary "get the tank ready" work. He knows about this stuff. He worked at a pet store and in particular, the fish department. Suffice to say, he got the fish tank going for me and I kind of tried to take it from there. You know, feed the fish and ... well ... feed the fish. Anyway, it seems that I have not learned enough to be in charge of the fish tank yet.

Three or four days ago I noticed that the water was getting foggy. Several possible causes came to mind and so I did a quick fix. Well, how often do quick fixes usually work? Answer: Yesterday I found the catfish floating at the top of the tank. Time to call in the expert. So, I'll talk to

Ryan today. It will take more effort to make the long term fix, but he'll know what to do. Maybe he will show me and I can do it, or he may have to do it himself if it's more than I can handle.

Is this the way we are with God sometime? He will help us establish something. It could be our faith, family, work, church, someone we're discipling or any number of things that we seek Him out for His help and guidance. Then slowly, we move out on our own, doing more and more things our way. The water becomes foggier and foggier. Obedience to Him shifts to control by us.

None of us will ever learn enough to be in control of our own lives and have a good godly outcome. The wonderful thing about God is that when the water of our lives gets foggy, He can show us the "permanent fix" for clearing it up. Sometimes He will show us what to do and as we are obedient the waters clear. In some cases He may just clear the water for us. Either way, we need to stay close to Him and let the One who knows what to do be in control.

Oh yeah, sometimes, just because He loves us, He may do a miraculous quick fix that's permanent! He IS God. He can do that!

Fastest Lesson Ever — January 18

As a boy, a teenager, and into my young adult years, I enjoyed watching prize fights. I knew all of the heavyweight boxers of the day (Ali, Frazier, Foreman, Norton, Young and an upstart named Holmes).

In my teens I could see that the prize money was going higher and higher. I thought, I can do that! I didn't mind fighting when necessary and I was pretty good at it too.

One year several of us in the neighborhood planned to get boxing gloves for Christmas. We all got them and immediately made a plan to have several matches. The "Main Event" would be me and Big Mike. I couldn't wait. Mike was a big guy but was pleasant and easy going. He would be an easy mark because of his lack of speed. I was going to knockout the biggest kid in the neighborhood! I was Ali; he was Frazier or Foreman.

Well, if you know anything about boxing, you know that it is not the same as fighting. Boxing is a sport, a talent, a learned art and skill. Fighting is war, anger, vengeance, destruction and is survival driven.

I was pretty good at fighting because I would do what ever it took to subdue the other guy and be able to walk away. If things were not going well in a fight I would throw sand in their eyes, kick'em, bite'em or get a big stick and clobber'em!

After the early matches on the "Card," it was time for the Main Event. I was stoked, I couldn't wait! Somebody said: "Ding" and I moved straight at Mike. I was Ali (fast and elusive); he was Frazier and Foreman (big and strong).

The first punch of the match landed flush on my nose! Snot flew out of my face and my eyes watered so much I couldn't see! I felt like Frazier and Foreman had both hit me! That was the only punch of that fight, I lost by TKO. That was my only boxing match ever!

Pride goes before the fall! It all happened in the same moment for me!

Sometimes it takes us a lifetime to learn lessons; sometimes only moments. Lesson learned: "Greg, you're not a boxer! And by the way, don't mess with Big Mike!"

Scripture references too numerous to mention!

Don't Eat The Azaleas — January 19

Just a few days ago I cut back an azalea bush in my front yard. It had grown very large and was taking up a large portion of the yard. Azaleas are very common in this area of the country. They are beautiful as they bloom for a short time when the weather starts to warm up here in March and April.

Part of my route at work is in a somewhat rural area. People have large gardens, horses, chickens, goats and so on. One day I saw a new sign on a fence where I had seen children feeding some goats in a small pasture. The sign read: "No azaleas, poisonous." There were azaleas near the fence that kids would feed the friendly goats when they came to the fence. I know of another pasture on my route where the owner fenced off a few azalea plants to keep his goats from eating them.

Azaleas are toxic to goats (and other livestock) and will make them very sick and can kill them. Goats will feed on the azaleas readily.

Sometimes we can be like these goats. Some things look good to us, taste good to us and in our case some things (as opposed to goats and azaleas) may even be useful to us, yet be poisonous to our soul and spirit.

For instance, we may enjoy (consuming) sin for a season, but it will have it's negative effects. Continued abuse of drugs, alcohol, and sexual sin will lead to terrible physical consequences. Other lifestyles of unwise consumption, like over spending or using credit cards to get things can leave us in an awful hole of debt that tears at our mental state, as well as our pocketbook. And there are the things that can be useful if used correctly such as computers, phones, TV, etc, as long as we consume them without them consuming us.

When we become consumed and addicted to things, we are no different than the goats eating the azaleas. We should completely cut down or fence off our "spiritual azaleas." They look pretty, but they can be deadly! Watch what you eat.

Don't Go Numb   January 20

When I worked on jets, we often used safety wire. The idea was to put safety wire through a hole in the bottom of a bolt after placing a nut on the bolt. This would keep the nut from coming off and going through a running engine which could cause serious damage or injury.

One day while taking a break at a table in the hangar, a friend was wrapping safety wire around his finger. He wrapped it about half way down his finger as we talked. As he casually unwrapped the wire from his finger he could see that the end of the wire had gone into his finger!

We ask him: "How did you do that? Doesn't that hurt?"

"It does now, but I didn't feel a thing when it went in!

As he wrapped the wire tightly around his finger it numbed his finger, we supposed. Anyway, he tried to pull it out and it would not budge. He was in some pain at this point. We tried pliers; no go! That wire was in the bone! They got it out at the ER!

Sin can be like that safety wire. We can just be playing around with it a little bit. A little lie on the taxes, a little bigger one the next time and then, OOPS! We owe more dough, or maybe off to jail we go! It could be speeding down the road for just a short distance. We do it all time and we're OK. OOPS again! A hefty ticket, or a child runs out in front of us and we can't stop soon enough.

Seemingly getting away with sin can numb us to the point that we don't feel it is having an affect on us. Then when it gets exposed (unwrapped) it causes guilt, pain and suffering and separation. It may require some serious (spiritual) ER time.

"Lord, show me where I'm numb to sin. I know some of the spots already. Please forgive me and unwrap from me the sins that numb me."

Can't Remember What Not To Do   January 21

I'm glad I didn't live in Old Testament times. I would have been continually bringing sin offerings (lambs, rams, bulls and whatever) to the priests. The priest would have been fat and my pastures would have been empty! I know, sin offerings were specific and what was to be done with them and what offerings could or could not be eaten were specified. I just said "fat priest and empty pastures" for a little humor.

Anyway, there may have been some confusion for the regular guy on what to sacrifice when, how to do it, who could eat it and how to dispose of remains that weren't sacrificed.

The same could be said for the commandments and teachings of God, if we look at them as a list of things we're not supposed to do. Sure, there are only Ten Commandments, but there are teachings in the Word about what is sin for one and not the other (ex. what to eat or not eat and in front of who). There are many teachings and instructions of Jesus including: thought life, motives, judging others, etc. I can't remember all that!

But I can remember these two commands: "Love the Lord you're God with all your heart and with all your soul and with all your mind" and "Love your neighbor as yourself. All the Law and the Prophets hang on these two commandments." If we keep these two commandments we will naturally keep the rest of the commandments.

Trying to live out the Christ-like, godly life is not an endless list of what not to do. It is a short list of who to be.

Hearing that Jesus had silenced the Sadducees, the Pharisees got together. One of them, an expert in the law, tested him with this question: "Teacher, which is the greatest commandment in the Law?"

Jesus replied: "'Love the Lord your God with all your heart and with all your soul and with all your mind.' This is the first and greatest commandment. And the second is like it: 'Love your neighbor as yourself.' All the Law and the Prophets hang on these two commandments." – Matthew 22:34-40

Answer To A Friend   January 22

Do you ever wonder what God is up to when He puts you in places, situations and people's lives. A couple of years ago I took a part time job to help pay for my son's college and hopefully pay off some financial debt. During the time I had this job I met and worked with some fun and truly amazing people. I may not see them very often now but I will always consider them among my best friends.

One man in particular became a close friend. We worked together, rode home together, we spent time together outside of work and he even employed my sons for a while. We talked about life and each of our struggles. He attended my son's wedding. He is a smart man with a good heart and a friend I know I could count on in a pinch.

The other day, on my blog site, I ask the question: "What do you expect from Jesus?" This friend's response was: "The question is not what I expect from Jesus but what does Jesus expect from me? And the answer is: ????"

Answers to my friend:

If your question is: What does He want from me? Then the simple answer is: Everything; your life, meaning living it for Him the best you can. He will help. He also wants you to trust Him with everything you have and try to obey Him. He will supply the power for you to be able to do this.

If you mean by *expect*, what does He want you to *do* to earn your way to Him and into Heaven, to be saved? Well, you can't work your way in. He will give you that for free! You just ask. By admitting we are sinners and acknowledging that He is the only way to the Father.

Jesus answered, "I am the way and the truth and the life. No one comes to the Father except through me." – John 14:6 Believing that He died on the cross as the one and only sacrifice for our sins and by asking Him to come and live in us and through us. This the way to be saved. We can't work, earn or do enough good deeds to get to Him, it's free.

For it is by grace you have been saved, through faith—and this not from yourselves, it is the gift of God— not by works, so that no one can boast.
– Ephesians 2:8-9

You know me, dude. You and I both know I have flaws, lots of them. That's why I need Jesus and that's why I ask Him to live in and through me. I pray you would have Him, too.

Bump In the Road   January 23

Every once in a while God brings us through a *test* or situation in our lives to show us how far He has brought us. I don't believe He tests us so He can see how we're doing. I'm pretty sure He already knows what's truly in us, being that He's omniscient. We are the ones who need to know where we are in our walk with Him.

Surprisingly, at my young age, I sometimes get a new pain here, a bump there, and a scratch or cut that looks worse than it used to and takes a little longer to heal. When these have come up lately I would pray and ask God to take the pain away or heal this or that and He has! I am less and less surprised at what He does as my faith in Him grows, but I am more and more amazed!

Several months ago, I had a bump come up on my knee. At the time it was about the size of a BB. I laid my hands on the little bump and prayed for its demise, but to no avail. What's this, Lord? My prayers had been working so well! No faith drop off, no unconfessed sin, what's up?

A couple of weeks ago, the bump got bigger. It was now the size of a pea. OK, I figured it was time to see the doc. I know God works through doctors all the time. Faith is required there too if that is the way God wants to work. I made the appointment.

I'll write more later about the actual visit to the doctor and what God showed me there. However, what I want to share here is how God has grown me. As you read the rest of this be sure I am boasting about His work, not my own courage.

I don't know about you but when a "bump" or something comes up on my leg, my flesh wants to expect the worst. My flesh does not want to let it go. It will broadcast the worst case scenario all through my being over a bullhorn.

In the past, that week between getting the appointment with the doctor and the actual visit would have been hell for me and probably the people around me. Especially after I found another suspicious spot on my other leg. It was different this time. Although my mind was aware of the possibilities, I was NOT afraid, worried, or freaked out. I was totally at ease, peaceful and full of trust in God of whatever the outcome would be. I didn't even tell anyone until after the doctor visit. Maybe next time I'll tell someone to pray for me.

God has shown me that He has brought me this far; that I can trust Him for my own health and well being and that no man or devil can ultimately trump His will. Yet there is still more road to travel here because I know I need to learn to trust Him for the salvation and well-being of those I love, and that is even harder than trusting Him for mine.

Doc's Office – Bump In The Road Part 2
January 24

I had found the spot on my other leg between the time I made the appointment and the actual visit. When the doc came in and looked at both spots, he was immediately more concerned with the new spot. He sprayed (froze/burned) the new spot and said that would take care of it.

Then he moved on to the bump on my knee. Long story short, he diagnosed three possibilities.

One was kind of unappealing in which a cyst grows into the joints and nerves. The second possibly a little less aggressive and the third would basically be a harmless, possibly becoming an unsightly growth. Each scenario could be dealt with but of course I would choose the easiest, most painless option.

Anyway, he wanted to drain some fluid from the bump to make a sure diagnosis. I told him to go ahead. He comes back in with three needles. Now I am about to hear things I don't want my doctor to say. No.1: "I'm going to deaden the area with this shot so that the bigger needle, I am going to use to drain the fluid, won't hurt as much." That little needle was bending as it went in, which made me think this may not be as much fun as watching some *ER* show on TV. After he put the bigger needle in, he was obviously having difficulty drawing anything out. He had told me that if it was the harmless kind of bump, the fluid inside would look like motor oil. He finally got a small amount of fluid out and it looked more like vanilla cream. No.2 (What you don't want your doc to say) "Well I've never seen that before. We'll have a culture done on that to identify it."

God is using this in my life to show me how far He has brought me. I know that God is good. He has brought me to the place that I can trust Him with things that appear uncertain in my life. I can trust Him because He has not just a good plan, but the best plan for my life. What I have to do is trust Him and obey His guidance to see His best plan for me.

If you get right down to it, if we really believe what we say we believe, what's the worst that could happen? I could beat you guys to Heaven? That's just a question to make us measure our faith, not a declaration of my departure. Paul said: "For to me, to live is Christ and to die is gain" (Philippians 1:21). Don't be afraid. BE ALIVE!

The Cyst Buster – Bump In The Road Part 3
January 25

While the doc was explaining treatment scenarios for each possible diagnosis, he told me of the old time remedy for these bumps. He said: "Back in the day, they used to take a Bible and whack the bump in an attempt to bust it and cause it to drain and heal." I guess a Bible was the biggest, heaviest book to clobber a cyst with in that day. I'm going to have to Google that one!

Anyway, I just thought that was appropriate. I mean, here I am, this "analogous Christian blog writer" (oops, labeled myself), who has this "thing" in my leg and I want it out. He has stuck a needle in this bump and hardly got anything out of it. It's like sin! A secret sin or a habitual sin. We allow it in (fun for a season), our flesh wraps around it and does not want to let go! We may even try to (drain it), defeat and dispose of it ourselves. But only the forgiveness offered by God can separate that sin (poison inside) from us.

When I was a small boy I dreaded going to the doctor. Sometimes I was ill, sometimes it was for some vaccination, but it always seemed there was a needle involved. The Bible shows us how to "get well" spiritually and stay that way. It's the medicine that our Lord (Spiritual Physician) offers us to guide us into spiritual good health. We can take the medicine after we have been ill for a period of time, or we can take the medicine as a daily vaccine to keep us from yielding to the temptation "bug."

The point is, He can heal us either way. It just seems that avoiding illness in the first place is a great idea. So lets be in the Word. It is our weapon of offense against the enemy. It's "the cyst buster" (bet you've never heard it called that). The Word will show you straight to the Great Physician and He'll fix you up. No line! No waiting!

The Results Are In   January 26

The results are in. The fluid from the bump on my leg is harmless and the spot on my other leg has been rendered harmless. I thank God for His healing and protection. I also thank all of you who were praying for me during this "bump in the road." I am truly humbled and blessed to know that you have taken your time to pray for and encourage me. Thank you! God Bless you!

In everything we go through, we will get to the point that "the results are in." The results will manifest themselves in two categories. There will be spiritual results and there will be physical results. To gain all the wisdom and knowledge we can, we need to take notice of both the spiritual and physical outcomes.

If we are concerned only with the physical, natural, earthly outcome to a situation, we may be operating out of fear or lack of faith that doesn't seek God or allow Him to move in the situation. If there is an undesirable outcome in the natural to the situation, we may be left broken and hopeless.

If we concern ourselves with only the spiritual outcome, i.e, sitting on our butts doing nothing, refusing to go to a doctor thinking, "I'll just sit here and let God handle it," we may be operating in disobedience. We may be living in a sluggard mentality and the physical result could be devastating.

"Pray as though everything depended on God. Work as though everything depended on you" - Saint Augustine

Commit to the Lord whatever you do, and your plans will succeed. – Proverbs 16:3

The physical outcome in my "bump in the road?" Good health, praise God!

The spiritual outcome to my "bump in the road"? No fear of man or the enemy and a real trust in Him. Praise God!

Are We At Our Duty Station   January 27

The process of becoming a soldier in the military has a lot in common with becoming a soldier in God's Army.

I was recruited when I was 18 years old. The recruiter told me about all the wonderful things, people and places that I would encounter. He left out some of the not so wonderful things. However, three squares a day, room and board, a little travel and a paycheck sounded pretty good to a kid with no marketable skills, outside of flipping burgers and mowing some grass. I signed up and was off on my adventure.

First stop was basic training, where I was shown the importance of discipline and obedience to those over me. I saw how things went much smoother when my squad did things the way we had been instructed. I also learned the consequences for lack of discipline and being disobedient.

Tech school was next. This was where I learned the basic skills for doing my job. I was to work on airplanes, particularly the sheet metal and frame areas of the aircraft. I learned what many tools were used for and the most efficient and effective way to repair damage and do general maintenance.

Upon completing tech school, I was assigned to my duty station. This is where I received specific, on the job training, for the actual aircraft I would be assigned to work. The learning never stopped because there was always a new challenge. It was always important to do the job correctly.

Thankfully, someone experienced was always there to advise me or a technical manual was available to tell me how to proceed. Even when I became one of the trainers and had a question or doubt, it was beneficial to check the manual and get the advice of a more experienced mechanic. It could mean the difference between a successful mission or a tragedy.

There are similarities to this in the Kingdom. A wonderful teacher taught me the three E"s. We are to "Evangelize, Establish, and Equip" others to work in the kingdom.

Evangelize: Recruit for God's Army by offering people the love of Christ as demonstrated in what He did for us, dying on the cross, paying for our sin and His resurrection in defeat of sin and death.

Establish: Teach them the importance of discipline and obedience to God by telling and showing them how God has been faithful to us and others since creation. As well as truthfully sharing what has been or could be the cost and consequences of disobedience.

Equipping: Investing of ourselves (discipling) into their lives by showing and telling the way to live a godly life. Also by teaching them from and showing them how to use the manual (Bible). And always being available for counsel, comfort and instruction when needed.

Then Jesus came to them and said, "All authority in heaven and on earth has been given to me. Therefore go and make disciples of all nations, baptizing them in the name of the Father and of the Son and of the Holy Spirit, and teaching them to obey everything I have commanded you. And surely I am with you always, to the very end of the age." – Matthew 28: 18-20

Baggage Claim   January 28

Whenever you travel on a bus or an airline you must check your luggage. This baggage is supposed to stay in the luggage compartment until your arrival at your destination. The things one might need along the way are to be taken on board in some sort of carry-on bag.

However, this has not been my personal experience. No matter how much I encouraged, threatened, begged or bribed, luggage staying stowed or checked was not the case on any trip with a youth group or ball team. It might be a chartered bus or a caravan pulling trailers but the inevitable words would spew forth: "I need to get into my suitcase". These needs have included wallets, clean shirts, makeup and assorted toiletries. After a short discourse of: "You should've … " and "Didn't we tell you … " we the leaders would relent and open the trailers or cargo bay and let the culprits get to their baggage.

This seems to always lead to one or more others (realizing their need) to get into their baggage while we're at it. It's amazing how this scene repeats itself every trip!

I'll bet you've seen this at an airport. A family greets a loved one at the arrival gate and it goes something like this: Hug, hug, kiss, kiss, lets get to the baggage claim. Many of us put way too much importance on our stuff, our baggage. By the way, if an airline loses your luggage they pay for it and you get new stuff!

Spiritually speaking we should go ahead and take our carry-on bag (our prayers, gifts, talents, and service, etc) as we board the flight as followers of Jesus. But, as for our "checked baggage" (our sin, desire to do our own will, etc) we need to leave these in the cargo hold of forgiven sin. Lets not stop the journey dead in it's tracks to dig into our baggage of the past and bring out the old stuff. Going into our baggage may take others back through their baggage as well.

Instead, check your baggage for good, as you fly with Jesus. Know this, He WILL lose your "baggage" as far as the east is from the west and He will give you all new stuff!

... as far as the east is from the west, so far has he removed our transgressions from us. – Psalms 103:12

The Hell With Things   January 29

I was just sitting here thinking about how my desires have changed over the course of my life. I was thinking about how my desires and presumed needs crowded out the really important and godly things of this life. My life has had this battle of "things I want" versus "times that are good." Personally, it has been a no holds barred fight to the death. Things I want has been winning for so long I didn't even realize the battle was still going on.

The first things I remember wanting were cowboy pistols (dual holster). Then it was a boat for the tub (with the wind up motor). Then a tricycle, bicycle, a real gun (rifle), a car, motorcycle, house, truck, a real boat, a bigger house, a nicer car and it goes on and on. It was like potato chips. I couldn't eat just one and the bag was never empty. I'd quench that thirst with a drink from a credit card, a loan or a second job and then, "more chips please!" I got every one of those things, and they got me! More specifically, the enemy had me in a whirlwind of stress and debt. The things started to matter less and less, as the short term joy from them turned into long term chains. I wanted my freedom back. I wanted the Good Times again.

As opposed to the things, the effect of the times that were good is happiness that occurs with every remembrance of the times spent with someone. As I look back on the good times in my life it always involved time spent with people. My memories of good times include: playing with a train set with my dad; or playing catch with him in the back yard; fishing with him or one of my grandfathers; playing dominoes at Grandmother's and eating Oreos and milk at her house; playing cards with Mom and hearing her sing in church, times in the neighborhood making homemade ice cream or pizza; taking my sister to cheerleading practice and the times going with her through surgeries and healing; the cold nights coming out of the movies with Hannah Pooh; the ball games and the fishing with my sons; the boat rides with my new daughter and grandchildren. The list goes on and on!

Where am I going with this? The Bible is full of relationships. Man to God and man to man. There were people in the Bible who were filthy rich and those who were dirt poor. But what made their spirit thrive was their service and love for God and one another.

We know (spiritually) that he who dies with Jesus in his heart wins. Some say (in the flesh) that he who dies with the most toys (things) wins. I say he who dies with the most loved ones and friends coming to heaven behind him wins.

I think I'll go see Grandmother this weekend. She wants to have a barbeque because the last one is such a great memory to her.

Knowing And Not Doing — January 30

Over the years I have read and studied a lot of the Bible. It is really the best read and study for life. It is fresh and new every time I open it because my life is in a different place every time I read the Word. I have come across and studied under many knowledgeable teachers. What I'm saying here is that there are a lot of folks out there with a boatload of Biblical knowledge of how we as believers and followers of Jesus are supposed to live out our lives.

I was looking at a list of small groups that the church I attend is offering. As I have been going through this process I believe that God is showing me something about myself and He wants me to take a step out in faith and obedience.

After quickly looking over the options of small groups (around 30-40) I narrowed it down to the Bible study type groups, picked out the one with the most convenient time and registered for it. I never gave a second thought to the other groups (fun groups, focused subject groups, prayer groups, service groups etc).

There is nothing wrong with any of the other type of small groups. I think we all need to have knowledge of His Word, a prayer life, specific knowledge of subjects we are interested in and possibly called to and opportunities to serve others.

It is in the serving others (particularly the homeless and needy) that I have been avoiding His call to serve. There, I wrote it right out loud! Now I'm not only accountable to God, but to every reader of this story. A part of me wants to backspace right here and now!

I have felt and known this calling was here for quite a while. How many times and ways do things need to be confirmed before we step out in obedience. How long do we argue with God as if we might have a better plan!

I was reviewing the list of small groups a few days ago and realized the time for the Bible study group I had signed up for was 7 a.m. not 7 p.m. That won't work. There are however a couple of service groups to the homeless and needy I could join.

It really is good for us to have knowledge of God and His instruction for our lives. But what good are His instructions if we don't follow them? What good is our knowledge if we don't apply it to our lives? What good is our knowledge of God if we keep it to ourselves? What good is it if we know everything there is to know about God and His Kingdom (especially His love) but don't tell or show it to anyone?

Knowing and not doing...what a waste!

If anyone, then, knows the good they ought to do and doesn't do it, it is sin for them. – James 4:17

Lessons Learned January 31

I write a lot about things I do and the things that happen to me. Usually I have done something wrong, goofy or without prior thought of the possible outcome and consequences of my decision. Therefore, more often than not, a lesson is learned by me that I can share with others in hopes they will not have to learn a lesson for themselves. One true mark of wisdom is learning from other's mistakes, thereby not having to suffer the consequences of making the mistakes ourselves.

One of the reasons God teaches us lessons is so that we might change our ways and our character to be more like Him and to carry out His will in our lives. I have learned a lot of lessons in this life. Not a single one of these lessons do me any good unless I put what I have learned from them into practice. That's what I am about to share with you now.

I said all that in hopes that you will not receive what I am about to write as pride in myself or bragging on what I may have done right. Instead, please receive this as boasting about my God and what He has done and is doing in me. I would be a hopeless mess without Him!

Yesterday I bought an old truck. I needed to move and haul some stuff and I needed something to pull the boat. The little car I have been driving can do neither of these things.

After learning some good lessons about stewardship of money and some hard lessons about debt and it's "choking chains," I was diligent and patient about finding a good deal. I paid cash for the truck and got what I needed without having to finance it and pay monthly payments. Lesson learned... lesson applied...good outcome. So far, so good.

Then, just like school (this life is Kingdom School you know), the next test pops up. Title transfer and truck insurance. On the title I can write any amount I want for the purchase price and lower the amount of tax I will have to pay. Nobody, I mean nobody (on earth) would know the difference. You know people get over paying those taxes by doing this all the time! It crossed my mind, but it wasn't the temptation it would have been in the past. I wrote in the exact amount I paid for the truck.

Then, transferring the insurance; the bigger test. This one will cost a lot more. If I just tell one little lie, I could save a nice chunk of change. I told the truth. Some would ask: "Why did you do that?" Answer: Lessons learned. God is my source. I know He will supply all my needs. Some would say it's a little thing. No, it is not!

Jesus said, "Whoever can be trusted with very little can also be trusted with much, and whoever is dishonest with very little will also be dishonest with much. So if you have not been trustworthy in handling worldly wealth, who will trust you with true riches?" – Luke 16:10-11

God doesn't need to test us so He can see what we will do. God allows us to be tested so we can see what He can do when we obey. Trust Him. Do it His way!

What My Mom Never Said — February 1

First, a little fun. Some things she did say: "Don't cross your eyes, they'll get stuck like that!" Or, "How would you like me to knock you into the middle of next week?" (Could have advantages, knowing the future). She didn't really say those. Here's some she did say: "Who do you think you are?" (I thought we knew that one, Mom). "Stop licking your sister's face!" And the one all moms say: "Put on clean underwear, you may be in an accident." (Mom, if I'm in an accident it won't matter if my drawers *were* clean!)

I've been thinking about my mom quite a bit lately. It would be hard to prove it by the way I forgot to call her the other day (her birthday). Smooth move, Greg! Anyway, I called today and wished her "Happy Birthday." I groveled and she was gracious not to rake me over the coals. Instead, she was genuinely happy I called, late or not.

So, where does a heart of unconditional love like that come from anyway? Well that's a no-brainer! The woman is a gift from God! How does she maintain that level of love? That's the question.

I have spent most of my single life pursuing what I wanted without concern for anyone else's welfare. Then, in my married lifetime, I still tried to figure out how to get my way as much as possible. Lately God has been working on me to think of others first. Maybe that's where I started thinking about Mom and what she didn't say.

I always knew my mom wanted the best for her family (my dad, my sister and me). She would work long and hard at her job and then take care of us at home. To this day she has the spirit of a loving caretaker and servant. She serves in several capacities at her church. Right now she is patiently nursing Dad back to health after shoulder surgery.

Then there were my teen years, when my dad was working out of town for long periods of time. I probably should have been kicked out for being such an jerk; instead she persevered and brought me through.

The Word says to bring a child up in the way he should go and when he is old he will not depart from it. Well Mom, I am just a little older and am now seeing your example of putting others ahead of yourself. Thanks, I love you!

Oh yeah, what my mom never said; I never heard her say: "What about me?"

The Good, The Bad And The Uncertain
February 2

Do you remember having to get used to someone else's driving habits? I mean you had to ride with them, and it was probably their car, so you weren't behind the wheel. You were not in control.

As a child I really wasn't concerned with my parents' driving habits. I couldn't see over the back seat anyway. When I got older, riding in the front seat more often and being able to see over the dash, I became more conscience of the need for good driving habits. It is necessary to drive safely because the consequences for unsafe driving can be fatal. With this awareness comes the desire, for me at least, to be the one behind the wheel (in control).

In my Christian walk, I say I want God to be in control of my life; behind the wheel, so to speak. Yeah, easier said than done. It seems (to me anyway) when things are going good, it's easy for me to let God be in control. It would be like riding with my son when he got his restricted license, as long as we were on an abandoned road somewhere that he could race down at ten miles an hour. I could get back behind the wheel easy enough.

However, if things are going bad in my life then I want to take control. As if I'm riding along again with my son, the new driver, and we come to a major highway that I'm afraid for him to drive on, then I would get behind the wheel, taking control.

An even harder time for me to let God be in control is a situation where there may be uncertainty. For sake of this discussion, I will define a *bad* situation in life as one in which we can take control ourselves (for better or worse, usually worse if we are not trusting God). I'll define an *uncertain* situation as a bad situation that we cannot take control at all, whether we trust God or not; like the first time you give that sixteen year old the keys to drive off alone. You just have to pray and trust God or be a fear-filled, emotional train wreck.

Why trust God? Because He has always been faithful. I rode a many a mile on the highways with my dad when our work would take us out of town. He just about always drove. My first recollections of riding with him up and down the highways had some scary moments with me pushing on the phantom brake pedal on the passenger side of the truck as he began to pass a slower car on a two lane road. But the more I rode with him, the safer I felt because he always got us to our destination safely.

Are there going to be "car wrecks" in our lives? Yep. But even through those, especially in those times of uncertainty, if we believe what we say we believe, then God is ultimately in control. Trust God in every situation.

P.S. I drive for a living. I see all kinds of dangerous driving everyday. The new danger is texting while driving. I have seen the deadly results of this practice. If you text while driving, STOP IT! For everyone's sake.

Walking The High Wire   February 3

Have you ever been to the circus? I used to like to go as a kid. The lions, tigers and bears were always pretty cool, though I never got to see them eat anyone. The other trained animals were OK, but I can only stand to watch horses prance around for so long. The clowns were sometimes funny, but an elephant stopping the show to take a dump is a whole lot funnier.

The reason for me to go to the circus was to see the high wire acts and the men on the flying trapeze. Now that was cool! They would walk or run on a high wire. Sometimes they would jump up in the air and land right back on the wire. And those guys on the trapeze would swing back and forth, then let go and fly through the air doing flips, then latching on to the other guy's legs, arms or an empty swing. Awesome!

The catch was, running the length of the tent underneath the high wire and trapeze was a net, to catch the performers if they missed their prescribed landing zone. Sometimes there was another net underneath the first one.

I really can't remember one of the trapeze or high wire entertainers falling during the act, but they would often end the performance by diving into the net below. You realize there are probably many other ways to get hurt doing this kind of act that don't include falling off the wire or swings. Given that, I never expected anyone to get hurt or severely injured because there was a net there to catch them.

Where I work (my second job), we have an "order picker." We often use it to get heavy merchandise down off of shelves 25 feet in the air. It raises a 4 ft. square platform into the air on which a person is standing. Then the employee takes merchandise off the high shelf and along with the merchandise, rides the platform back down to the floor.

There is a harness I wear while working on the order picker. This harness has a strap that is hooked to the moving part of the platform so that while I am harnessed in and hooked up, I could not fall. If I did step off the platform I would be dangling safely in the harness only a few feet below the platform.

The other day I was using the picker, and while taking some merchandise off the platform on the floor, I unhooked the strap from the picker. This enabled me to walk around and put up the merchandise. Then I got back on the picker and went up for more goodies to bring down, forgetting to re-attach the strap to the picker. It took my breath away for a second when I realized I was 25 feet up in the air lifting heavy equipment and my safety strap was not hooked to the picker.

Without Jesus, our lives are like not having my safety strap hooked into the order picker. Without the grace and mercy of God we are like those circus performers working without a net. Jesus is where we "hook" our lives to be in relationship to God, and as long as we stay hooked in, we will not fall.

Then there are times when we unhook ourselves (sin), but the nets of the grace and mercy of our Lord catch us. He forgives us and we are restored back to the platform of a relationship with Him.

This world (circus tent) is often full of clowns and wild animals and sometimes it stinks. It seems as if life is sometimes a high wire act at dangerous heights. Let's walk through life hooked into Jesus, trusting His salvation, grace, and mercy.

It Just Needs To Be Said February 4

This life can often seem like we are walking on a high wire or we are high above the ground dangerously swinging from one trapeze to another.

God has placed the nets of mercy, grace and forgiveness below the high wire of life to catch us when we fall. Then He places us back up on the wire to continue our walk, like we place our children back on the bicycle from which they have just fallen. Hopefully, prayerfully, when we come to that place on the wire where we fell the last time, with God's help, we will have the balance to navigate it successfully.

Now, although intentionally jumping off the high wire of life (intentional, blatant sin, premeditated with the thought in mind of seeking forgiveness later) can still be caught in God's nets, this should not be our mindset. We should certainly not go off sinning because the nets are below us. We should instead make every effort in obedience to God to keep our balance!

What I'm saying is that the "grace, mercy and forgiveness nets" of God are not a *free pass* for us to sin. His grace, mercy, and forgiveness is a pass of sorts, given to us freely, but it was far from free for Him. Our forgiveness cost Him His only Son, Jesus.

So if we love Him and appreciate the price He paid for those nets, maybe we should trust Him up on the "high wire" and diligently try to keep our balance.

Romans 5:12-6:3

Made In The Shade   February 5

When it gets right down to it, all we need for this earthly life is food, clothing and some sort of shelter. Everything else is gravy! No, I do not want to live with just these bare essentials, but it is all we need.

Most of us here in the U.S. have it "made in the shade." For instance, I figure I am in the middle of the middle class in our country. My income is more than some and less than many others. I have a little three bedroom house (with a mortgage), two decent cars, etc. I think I'm pretty close to the average Joe. Many are worse off than me, many are better off.

Having said that, if you are reading this story on your internet connected computer, you are likely to be as well off as me or better. This story is aimed at us. The middle class and up in our society, particularly the believers in this group.

By "made in the shade," I mean that we have everything we need and more; seriously! We take so much for granted. I have heard it come out of my own mouth! I need a bigger house, truck, boat, paycheck, piece of property and on and on. Those are wants, not needs. I am not discounting that God wants to bless us, instead I am trying to show how incredibly blessed we already are!

I wonder how having it made in the shade affects how much faith we have or how much faith we think we need? I mean, how much faith does it really take for you and me to believe for our next meal? How much faith do we have to exercise for a comfortable, dry place to spend the night? How much faith do we really expend to believe our kids will be healed of the measles, mumps, or the flu. Do we really have to stretch out in faith to believe God for the clothing of our families? I doubt there is a big "yes" to any of those questions.

To put this in perspective, let's think about most of the world's population outside of the middle and upper classes here in the U.S. Many of the people on this earth do have to pray, exercising their faith, believe God for their next meal, some shelter for the night, clothing and healing for illnesses.

The necessities for life will not come to many of them short of intervention by God. That's trusting Him! Believing He will come through for us when there is no other way to get our needs met except for the hand of God.

So, is there a place, time or circumstance that the prosperous believer (that's who we are) can step out of "the shade" in faith, and trust God to come through for us as we obey Him?

Made In The Shade – Part 2　　　February 6

If we are in this comfort zone of having it made in the shade, perhaps we need to exercise our faith. Exercise does make us stronger, right?

The first thing to point out here is a proposed course of action that we as the believers with financial resources should consider. As the Bible tells us, take care of the poor, needy, widows and orphans. We could be putting some of our time, money and resources into acquiring and delivering food, clothing, shelter and the love of God to those in need. We could share our "shade" with them, so to speak. As a result of our stepping out in faith, or spending our money and time helping others, we will see God bless and take care of us. This would strengthen our faith to help others even more.

The second thing I should mention here is a word of caution. We could get way too comfortable in the shade! It feels good to our flesh to lay around in the shade. It is good to rest and Sabbath, but I am speaking of a lifestyle of lazy selfishness.

In Daniel chapter four, King Nebuchadnezzar (king of the known world at the time) has a dream of a great and massive tree. As the interpretation of the dream comes forth from God through Daniel, it is revealed that King Nebuchadnezzar is this tree. The tree is representative of Nebuchadnezzar's power, wealth, authority and greatness. The world is his oyster! He doesn't need anything or anybody. He's the man!

This dream is God's warning to him about his pride in particular, but this man has the fate of others in his hands as well! When Nebuchadnezzar not only refuses to repent, but claims he is his own source, God takes him down several notches! God cut down the tree! Nebuchadnezzar had it made in the shade. Now there is no shade!

I'm not saying that God is going to make someone insane, eat grass like cattle, make their hair long and their fingernails be like claws on a bird. But He does have a way of bringing humility upon the lazy and proud. God can cut down the tree. He can take away the shade. He could plant the tree in someone else's yard who is willing to share the shade with those who need a break from the heat.

Possum Christians   February 7

While traveling down the highway one afternoon my dad commented: "That's not a very good place to take a nap". We were passing by some "road kill." There was some chuckling at his comment (not me of course) as we cruised by the site of the possum homicide.

It got me to thinking about how a possum will play dead in hopes of avoiding a predator. I've seen them do it (on TV); they will just lay there as they are pushed, pulled, and poked.

I'm afraid as Christians we may do this same act. We play like we're "dead in sin" just to blend in with the world so as to not be bothered by the "predators." Who are the predators? Those who would make fun of us or persecute us in some way, or the Devil who may try to come against us if we live out our faith. Sometimes, even with God's poking and prodding us to come to life, it's just easier to go with the flow of the world. Plus, we certainly won't be bothered by Satan if we just lie there and are no threat to him.

In a western I used to watch on TV, this cowboy had stopped at a house where he thought an outlaw may be hiding. He ask the woman there where the outlaw had gone. The woman said: "I can't tell you, he'll kill me!" To which the cowboy replied: "Lady, you're afraid of the wrong man!"

Jesus is our example. He is not the "possum of Judah!" He is the "Lion of Judah!" So what are we afraid of? Who are we afraid of? Man? The Devil?

When Jesus was sending out the twelve, He told them they would be flogged and arrested. Then He said: *"Do not be afraid of those who kill the body but cannot kill the soul. Rather, be afraid of the One who can destroy both soul and body in hell."* – Matthew 10:28

Are we maybe afraid of the wrong person?

But Words Will Never Hurt Me   February 8

Ephesians 5:1-4 includes: Be imitators of God...live a life of love, just as Christ loved us (sacrificially)...among you there must not be... coarse joking, which (is) out of place, but rather thanksgiving.

"Sticks and stones will break my bones, but words will never hurt me." That little rhyme is a great lie from the pit of hell! Here is a subject I know a little something about. As more people at my work place are reading these blogs and devotionals I write, I do expect, deservedly so, some ribbing on this subject. In fact, there may be some real grief if they have been the target of some of my "coarse joking."

Simply put, coarse joking is "cut downs," "dissing," "humor," and the like, that hurts or puts someone down, making them the butt of the joke. Why do we do it? Well, I can speak to why I have done it. Insecurity is one reason. By putting others down, it might seem to me that I am raising myself up. Another reason is that others might see it as funny, unfortunately many people do, and thereby; I receive the approval of others.

So while I'm at it, if you have been hurt by words that have come out of my mouth please forgive me. If you want to call me out on it, OK.

I will be glad to apologize in person. If you hear me do it again, please do call me out on it.

There it is: the confessional devotional. God wants us to lift others up, not put others down.

It requires a heart change. Jesus said: *"For out of the overflow of the heart the mouth speaks."* – Matthew 12:34

Hope That Will Not Disappoint   February 9

We all know people who have lost loved ones. We have seen those in anguish over what to make of death in this life. In any case, the loss of a loved one is usually an emotional train wreck. Often when those who have lost someone are not believers they seem to look for some hope to latch on to and see them through that loss.

I knew a man who was having a hard time with his sister's death. In talking with him I told him that if we believe what we say we believe, your sister is healed and with the Lord in heaven. I've never seen him again. I think of him and wonder how he's doing.

Seven years ago I got a call that a close friend of my son had passed away after a long illness. It hurt the whole family because the families were close too. We had spent so much time together in ballparks, church, and the older brothers and sister know each other well.

As much as it wrecked my son and our family, I can't imagine the emotion his family felt. I can't fathom losing a son. But in all of this loss and sadness, this young man's entire family was a testimony to everyone else. His funeral was a celebration of life because his resurrection is a defeat of death.

Someone else's Son died to make this young man's eternal life the reality it is today. How'd you get through that, Father? Letting your Son die for others. That's God's love for us, letting His Son die for our life.

I imagine many of us could die for people we love. But how many of us would let our son die for others? Not me.

That's where the family of this young man draws their faith, hope and love from, His sacrifice! Where does our hope come from?

Yesterday there was another celebration of this young man's life! Tributes and videos, prayers and celebration.

Beat the drum loudly, James! We'll see you soon!

Beyond Gotcha   February 10

Wednesday it rained here all day. At one point it was pretty rough with lightning, tornado warnings and driving rain. I was out on my route in the midst of it all day. As a delivery guy who delivers to the same locations and people every day, it is truly my desire to keep them happy by providing them good, reliable service. Yet no matter how hard I try, it just doesn't always work out that way.

When I am delivering a package and no one is home, I will leave it in a dry, relatively secure location as long as it does not require the recipient's signature for delivery. Wednesday I had a package I could have left at the address but there was absolutely no cover to leave it under where it would stay dry.

In the past, I have left packages anywhere I could so that the customer would not have to make the drive to our office and spend the time in line to pick it up. I have left parcels under steps, house trailers, carports and even in patrons unlocked cars. Then I would leave them a note in their mailbox to let them know where I left their package. Almost all of them are very appreciative.

Back to Wednesday. With nowhere to leave this parcel, I left a notice for the customer to come pick it up. Thursday my boss gets a phone call from an irate lady who says I didn't leave her package at her house. In the pouring rain, it would have been soaked! I had gotten out and knocked on the door. There was no answer so I left a notice which is proper procedure. She had not bothered to call first or read the notice that gives the address of the office at which she could pick up her parcel. Instead, she had walked a couple of miles to the wrong office to try to pick up her package.

Now that's not funny! Well it is to me, maybe not to her. My first reaction to the call was, "Gotcha Grumpy, that's what you get." Sometimes we enjoy seeing a whining, unsatisfiable grump get what we feel like's coming to them. That could be the end of the story. Or maybe not. Maybe there is something more to her anger. Maybe there is a person in need of something we could give. Maybe they need prayer, a kind word, a listening ear or maybe they need someone to demonstrate how much better kindness can be than anger and bitterness. Maybe I'll see her today. Maybe I'll let you know what happens, depending on how good of a witness I end up being.

Cleaning Out The Stuff — February 11

I've been thinking about doing a little fixing up around the house. However, some questions have presented themselves as obstacles, such as: "Where are my tools and do I have the materials I need?" I keep all my stuff in one place; on my property, somewhere. So I say to myself: "The stuff I need is probably in the garage somewhere." This revelation brought on the prospect of a garage cleaning project before I would be able to move on to the fix-up project. "Ah, but where am I going to put the stuff that I clean out of the garage that I want to keep? I know, I'll put it in the shed. Uh oh, that means I have to clean out the shed first!"

Well, it all needs doing so I got started yesterday. I got the shed cleaned out and put most of the outdoor kinds of stuff like grills, mowers, and shovels in the shed. It's real clean and organized and I found a lot of stuff I am going to need for the fix-up projects while cleaning out the shed!

Today it was on to the garage. This will be a much more demanding task. It has been a cabinet shop, a movie production room and a jet ski repair garage. All good causes that I supported, but I am looking forward to having my garage again. Today I made some shelves, hung up my fishing gear and got started organizing my tools. Again I found a lot of the stuff I will need to work on my fix-up projects.

Cleaning out *stuff* is not always easy. Maybe you're like me, I pile all the crap I don't need right in there with the stuff I do need; into the garage, the shed, and don't even get me started about my dresser! The crap we don't need hinders, blocks and blinds us from the things we do need.

Sin does the same thing in our walk with God. It hinders, blocks and blinds us from getting to the things we need. It will hinder our relationship to Him. It will cause our witness to be ineffective to the lost. It will steer our hearts toward compromise. That is what spiritual compromise is, letting sin into the places God wants to dwell.

Judges speaks to this issue. The people of God sinned (compromised) by worshiping the gods of other nations (putting things in the places God wants to dwell). Judges also shows there are consequences for sin while there is blessing for obedience.

So Lord, please forgive my compromises (piling sin in where You want to dwell). Show me where I have done this and if I am doing it now. Clean out these places in me leaving only the things I need, the things of You.

Got Friends — February 12

Yesterday I'm rolling along on my route and a woman comes out and hands me her outgoing mail. She is pleasant, asks how I'm doing, asks me to take her mail, says thank you and I drive off. This is a common, daily occurrence with many of my patrons on the route. However, when I am coming back up the other side of the street, she comes barreling back out right at the truck! I think, "uh-oh complaint time."

Instead she runs out into the street and comes toward the window on the other side of my truck. This causes me to stop right in the middle of the road! She sticks her head in the window and starts telling me about how her husband had committed suicide about six months ago and that she moved here to be near her sister.

This kind of stuff happens to me a lot out on my route. It makes me wonder if they read the sign on my truck that says "U.S. Mail," or once I get inside of the truck, does the sign change to "Shrink On Wheels." You would probably be amazed at how many people come out to meet me at their mailbox and just start spilling their guts! I guess it probably happens to other delivery people too. My flesh wants to say, "You know, I just don't need this, I've got enough worries and troubles of my own."

The difference in my troubles and theirs may be that I have some place to take mine. I have a wife that's willing to listen, a friend who can keep a confidence and a God that I can leave my troubles at His feet. But others may have none of these. In their desperation to have someone to talk to, they may view me as a guy who is kind of anonymous and therefore relatively safe to confide in. Some, I know, are just plain lonely!

We all want and need friends. Not just a crowd of friends, but those close few who we can really count on. Have you got one? Are you one?

Shouldn't we all be one? Instead of wishing we could find one, shouldn't we seek to become one?

Shouldn't we also seek the Friend who "sticks closer than a brother" (Proverbs 18:24)?

Memories Of The Daytona 500   February 13

I like stock car racing! Big tracks, small tracks, and even road courses. I remember the one time I went to the Daytona 500. My dad was a construction superintendent and he was building a hotel very close to the track. We pulled past the long lines of cars waiting to get into the parking lots and parked inside the fence of the construction site. I asked him if we could sell parking in there but he said there were too many liability issues. We could have made a mint!

We locked the car inside the gate and proceeded to make the short walk to the track. Of course it was February and it was a cool morning in Florida. My uncle was walking just in front of me along the side of the road. He had his jacket zipped up and his hands in his pockets. All of a sudden it was as if he disappeared. He went down like he was shot! He had tripped over a small sign about four inches high that said: "Keep Off The Grass." He should have, well, stayed off the grass. He had crashed, face-first with no hope of getting his hands out of his pockets to brace his fall. The only thing that came out of his pocket was a load of coins. It was an ugly scene, and really funny! I tried the best I could to make sure he was OK before I busted out laughing. I don't think I made it!

Watching a race in person, at these speeds, was amazing. You just don't get the feel of how fast they are moving by watching on TV. Seeing these guys go past you bumper to bumper at nearly 200 mph makes you hold your breath. If anyone of them makes a mistake, it's going to be a mess, a dangerous mess!

We were sitting right at the exit of the pits at turn one with a great view. I remember Donnie Allison and Richard Petty coming out of the pits side-by-side during a green flag pit stop. Amazing!

What are my memories from this year's 500? I spent part of two days with my parents. Eating, talking and laughing. I visited with my grandmother and my aunt who have been such a big part of my life. I watched as my nephew and his son got baptized. I saw old friends and other relatives that I know and love, and I met some new ones. I was blessed in more ways than I can write here! It was a great Daytona 500 weekend and I didn't even see a car race!

Car races are cool, but I think I had my priorities right for this weekend.

P.S. Did anybody DVD the race?

Can You See Him Now — February 14

Often we can look back and see where God has been at work in our lives. Much of my writing falls into this category. However, I really love realizing God at work in the present.

A few weeks ago I began looking at the story of Joseph. I wondered why I was being led there and decided to share the story and some thoughts with the Men's Group at The Fishin' Hole. I figured, OK that's why God wanted me to look at this story.

But there's more. Sunday a close friend of mine tells us about going to his church and hearing about Joseph. He said he feels like Joseph in a lot of ways, as he is going through a bitter divorce. Joseph's story seemed to give him a glimmer of hope in a seemingly hopeless situation.

Then there's more! A blogger friend writes that she has be reading about Joseph this week and talks about how God worked in Joseph's apparently hopeless situation.

Yep, there's still more. Then my friend writes me this: "Greg, tell me some about Joseph. I know you are studying it."

My reply was Romans 8:28 *And we know that in all things God works for the good of those who love him, who have been called according to his purpose.*

Joseph's life is a perfect example of God turning what was meant for evil into His purposes for good. Joseph was his father's favorite son. This was obvious to his brothers and they were very jealous. They were jealous enough to want to kill him, but they settled for selling him into slavery and telling their father he had been killed.

I imagine Joseph was pretty angry at the time himself, but he was stuck. So he turned to God, not man, or any desire he may have had for revenge. He trusted God even through slavery and prison.

Through events in his life, God freed him from slavery and prison and made him governor of all Egypt. Somewhere along the line he forgave his brothers. That's when he really became free, on the inside, in his spirit.

Unforgiveness, not forgiving someone who has done us wrong, will burn in our gut like salt in a wound. The only remedy is to forgive the person that has wronged us and turn our situation over to God. He can work it all out for good.

Besides, our unforgiveness only makes us bitter, and we get consumed by anger and rage. I know it's not easy, but forgive the person like Joseph forgave his brothers, and move on with God's guidance. Then you will be free of your anger and God will work it all together for good!

WOW! Can you see Him working now?!

Close One   February 15

We've watched those rescue or emergency shows that tell a story of someone being saved from certain death. Maybe it was mountain climbers injured and stranded in a blizzard high on a mountain. Possibly it was someone terribly injured in a car wreck who recovers against impossible odds. Maybe it was a story of someone trapped under tons of rubble from an earthquake.

Often, when the survivors are interviewed following their rescue or miraculous recovery, they speak of how their priorities have changed and how they will live their life from now on because of their experience. It seems that the busyness of their lives and whatever things they were chasing (money, fame, fortune, power) are no longer important compared to loving their family and friends and helping others in need or crisis.

Many of us have been in a "close one." I remember racing with a friend of mine one night. We were in two little cars. My future wife was riding with me and my sister was riding in my friend's car. Don't freak out when you read this part, Mom. We were wide open as we approached this "T" intersection. The whole area was wooded, except for an old abandoned bar across the intersection. We waited way too long to try to stop. My friend sailed his car to the right, into the woods short of the intersection and then across the street, barely missing an oncoming car. They hit nothing, not a scratch! I was approaching the intersection as fast as he was, with that bar across the street directly in my path! There was no way I was not going to crash into that building. Just by reflex I turn the car sideways. We stopped at the stop sign! We didn't even cross the street, much less hit the building! Miraculous is the only explanation.

We drove home a little slower.

I know we were spared that night, all of us. Things in our lives could have changed forever in an instant. I think that God sometimes uses events like this to make us think about and realize what the really important things are in this life. By His grace, He saved us from disaster, no doubt about it. It's a scary memory, but when I think back on the awful outcome it could have had, it makes me appreciate the things that are really important. It changes my priorities.

Have you had a "close one?" If the memory of it has faded, think back on it for a moment and let it encourage and remind you of what's really important.

A Disciple Encounters Discipline   February 16

I have never been crazy about corrective discipline. No matter who was dishing it out to me! It was usually Mom, Dad, or maybe a grandmother or grandfather. Yet they all used discipline to "bring me up in the way I should go!"

My first run in with discipline that I remember, was my grandfather coming down the middle of the street after me. I was just a toddler who had gone for a walk! I figured if I stood in the middle of the big road, I could get a closer look at the semi-trucks coming out of the pea cannery down the street. He didn't agree.

Grandmother would make me go pick the switch she was going to use on me; a terror all to itself.

Mom would beat me with a broom, not really (family joke).

Dad had a piece of leather he kept around his waist for such occasions.

And my other grandfather, although never abusive, you just knew better than to piss him off!

Truthfully, I'm not so crazy about self-discipline either. I don't have it in so many areas that I could surely use it. One place however, that I have made good progress is reading the Word and spending time in prayer. I had to ask God to help me in this regard. It really came about as a result of being at the end of my rope in a certain area of my life.

You know how we go to God in times of trouble. That's what I did. "Woe is me God, rescue me again!" I had been here before. I stayed in the Word and prayed more consistently, just like in troubled times in my past. Previously, as God brought me through some "trial of life," I would gradually ease up reading the Word and ease up on the prayer life, thereby easing up on my relationship to Him.

This time it was different. Maybe it was genuine gratitude for His rescue, or His working in me, but I stayed the course. I continued consistent in reading of the Word and time in prayer. Some other trials have come along, but they were so much easier to endure and get through. Anxiety, worry and stress were replaced with faith, endurance and peace. Knowing He is there in the midst of my ordeal takes me through to victory.

It occurs to me, to be a good disciple, it is necessary to have good spiritual self-discipline.

Consequences — February 17

This week, God willing, there is going to be a milestone victory in my life. In the next few days, except for my house, I will pay off the last of my financial debts. I will be debt free. Praise God! I imagine some are saying: "How did you do that?" Well that's another story, or even a face-to-face testimony. God did some awesome things throughout this time of my financial struggles.

What I do want to say is that there will be consequences for our actions. Good consequences for good actions and bad consequences for bad actions. Before we take any action, we should take into account the consequences that are sure to follow.

If I go out and burn up the credit card by buying everything I want, there will be a cost, a poor set of consequences. Over spending brings on debt I can't handle. Next, I juggle other bills that get further behind. Then comes the creditor's harassment , and it only gets worse.

King David (1Samuel 16-1 Kings 2) committed many sins. However he knew the forgiving nature of God. His confession to God was true and his repentance was real. He desired, he needed and he received God's forgiveness. But the awful consequences for his actions were still there.

I read a quote that said: "Too often we would rather avoid the consequences than experience the forgiveness". Yep, I'm guilty of feeling that way sometimes. Which way would you rather have it? Does it really make a difference? Before you answer, think about this. Two criminals were crucified with Jesus. Hanging on their crosses, suffering the consequences for their actions, one insulted Jesus and the other spoke for Jesus. He received forgiveness. Jesus told the one who spoke for Him: "Today you will be with me in paradise." Yeah, it makes a difference. I'll take the forgiveness.

Hit The Road   February 18

When I was 10 to 15 years old my friends and I spent a lot of time playing in the streets of our neighborhood. We would play ball, race bikes and play games in these short streets that provided the large play area that we required. For instance, if you hit a home run in someone's back yard, you had to go two houses down and challenge Rover just to get the raggedy ball back! Our street was relatively safe, as long as we were aware when a car would occasionally come down the road. We didn't play in the nearby four lanes or any thoroughfares in the area because we knew the obvious danger.

As we got older and got our licenses, we did venture out on the four lanes and fast lanes of the city. Sometimes we would treat these much more dangerous streets as if they were our own personal playgrounds. As a teenager I was in several minor fender benders and one or two not so minor crashes. I was never in a reckless mode when I was in an auto accident. However, I was in several near hit scenarios when I was showing off and being reckless. It was certainly God's grace that protected me in those situations. Any one of those close calls could have resulted in injury or death of my friends, relatives, people in other cars and myself. Not to mention damage to vehicles and property.

Nevertheless, our daily lives require us to go out into these busy streets to accomplish needed tasks such as going to work, school, the grocery store and much more. It would be much easier and safer for us just to stay home inside our safe house. It would even be easier and safer to stay on our own street than to venture out into the highways. But if we don't go out onto the busier streets we limit what we can gain in life.

The same principles apply in the Kingdom. It's sure easier to play it safe. Stay in our house (comfort zone) and don't venture out. But if we don't venture out, we will have little effect and witness for the Lord.

It's even easier to stay on our own street (in our own realm such as our church or small close knit group of like thinking, affirming friends).

While we can learn some things in the safer streets, we won't get far in the Kingdom, in an outreach sense, by staying in the house or in our safe circles on our street. We'll probably get in a fender bender or two (be rejected, lose a friend maybe), but God will be our seat belt and airbag. Our emotions will recover.

Jesus said to: "GO and make disciples." He didn't say: "Wait until they come down our street," did He?

Caught In A Storm   February 19

I remember seeing old movies, maybe a western or a depression era film, where people are traveling across the open plains in a covered wagon or a slow moving Model T and run into these horrendous dust and sand storms. The storms would be blinding and very dangerous; so much so, that to continue on during the storm would most certainly cause the travelers to wind up lost, injured or dead.

Life's storms can come from any direction. We can be overrun by clouds of dust and sand resulting from our own poor choices, friends or loved one's poor choices, events that are seemingly no fault of our own or anyone else's including issues of the economy, wars, illness, death and all sorts of strife.

Often our first reaction to being caught in a life storm is to fight through, but if we are blinded by the dust, we cannot see our own way through the storm. Whether we could have avoided it or not, once the storm is upon us it is then time to seek shelter. Our shelter from life's storms should be our literal Savior, Jesus. He knows which way the wind is blowing and we should go to Him when we find ourselves caught out in life's bad weather. He can address the storm and show us the way out.

Oh yeah, back to whether we could have avoided the storm or not. God always knows which way the wind is blowing and which way it's going to blow. The best action to avoid potential storms is to always be in communication with the "Weather Maker." He can show us ahead of the storm, how to totally avoid it or the best way through it, before we are caught in it and blinded.

As they sailed, he fell asleep. A squall came down on the lake, so that the boat was being swamped, and they were in great danger.

The disciples went and woke him up, saying, "Master, Master, we're going to drown!" He got up and rebuked the wind and the raging waters; the storm subsided, and all was calm. "Where is your faith?" he asked his disciples.

In fear and amazement they asked one another, "Who is this? He commands even the winds and the water, and they obey him." – Luke 8:23-25

A Golf Lesson　　　　　　　　　　　February 20

The night before last, I was watching *Feherty* on TV. Feherty was a pro golfer and now does announcing for professional golf tournaments. A while back he began to host this show in which he spends a day with sports' celebrities, mostly golfers. He interviews them not only about their sport, but about their life in general. His manner of interview and his accent using Irish slang is not only amusing, but down right funny.

While spending time with these celebrities Feherty is able to give us a glimpses into the real lives of these sportsmen. It seems the more time he spends talking and doing things with them, the more they open up and share about themselves. Nevertheless, I was not expecting what happened on the show when he spent time with Tom Watson.

As they sat at a picnic table in the middle of Tom's huge barn, Feherty began to share about Tom's friendship to him and how he was there for him as he battled alcoholism. This relationship affected Feherty's life immensely. A relationship that may have saved his life. He had earlier said "I knew I was dying."

I don't think anything can affect us as profoundly as relationships with other people. We were made for relationships, to God and men.

"Teacher, which is the greatest commandment in the Law?"

Jesus replied: "'Love the Lord your God with all your heart and with all your soul and with all your mind.' This is the first and greatest commandment. And the second is like it: 'Love your neighbor as yourself.' All the Law and the Prophets hang on these two commandments." – Matthew 22: 36-40

I am becoming more and more aware of the value of spending time with God and with people instead of chasing after the things of this world. Sure, there will be some relationships where there is pain, that's the risk. There will also be relationships of love and encouragement that will lift us up like nothing else is able to do. Good relationships (to God and man) will be what keeps us going in the toughest of times.

Building real relationships also affords us the opportunity to be the encourager and be there for others in their tough times. We are simply foolish if we think or act as if we don't need true friends, especially during hard times.

Spend time with God. Spend time with others. Invest yourself in relationships. It could save your life. It did mine.

Dreamer   February 21

I remember as a little boy having dreams that I could fly. These dreams would happen very often and would be incredibly realistic! I would be able to run, take off, and fly effortlessly. The view was unbelievable as I cruised the skies! It was usually during the flight portion of the dream that I would wake up. Needless to say, I was more than a little upset! I recall trying to go back to sleep really quick in hopes of resuming my flight.

I had two dreams last night. In one dream I was fishing with a friend. I dream in "comedy mode" sometime. For instance, in this dream we were fishing in what seemed to be a shallow retention pond, catching fish that wouldn't live in fresh water. Anyway, we were beginning to catch some nice ones. Of course it was during this feeding frenzy of redfish that I woke up. Aahhhh!

On the other hand I have dreams from which I am very glad to wake up. Unfortunately, I too often dream of things going stupidly wrong at work (comedy/aggravation mode). I have dreamt of falling asleep on my lunch break, then waking up after dark with half my route left to finish! I'm am always relieved and even excited to wake up from dreams like these!

Which brings me to last night's second dream. For whatever reason, I found myself out on my route with only the second portion of the route in my possession (loaded in a grocery cart). The dream is a series of misadventures as I search frantically (unsuccessfully) for the missing grocery cart of mail containing the first half of my route. I was almost in a fight, nearly ran over some kids and even broke a window trying to go in the side door of a department store! Thankfully, I finally woke up, tired before my day ever began!

Although I very much prefer life going so great it feels like a dream of soaring high above any potential problems of life, I know it won't stay that way forever this side of Heaven. But I am thankful and praise God for those wonderful times. And I am also very thankful that He is with me when life seems like an uncontrollable bad dream with no end of difficulties in sight. I know that if I stay with Him (He said, I will never leave you or forsake you), He will wake me up from the bad dream, bringing me His peace, relief and more times of soaring high above the obstacles of this life.

Are We Good Tenants Of The Vineyard
February 22

"Listen to another parable: There was a landowner who planted a vineyard. He put a wall around it, dug a winepress in it and built a watchtower. Then he rented the vineyard to some farmers and moved to another place. When the harvest time approached, he sent his servants to the tenants to collect his fruit.

"The tenants seized his servants; they beat one, killed another, and stoned a third. Then he sent other servants to them, more than the first time, and the tenants treated them the same way. Last of all, he sent his son to them. 'They will respect my son,' he said.

"But when the tenants saw the son, they said to each other, 'This is the heir. Come, let's kill him and take his inheritance.' So they took him and threw him out of the vineyard and killed him.

"Therefore, when the owner of the vineyard comes, what will he do to those tenants?"

"He will bring those wretches to a wretched end," they replied, "and he will rent the vineyard to other tenants, who will give him his share of the crop at harvest time."

Jesus said to them, "Have you never read in the Scriptures:

*"'The stone the builders rejected
has become the cornerstone;
the Lord has done this,
and it is marvelous in our eyes'?*

"*Therefore I tell you that the kingdom of God will be taken away from you and given to a people who will produce its fruit. Anyone who falls on this stone will be broken to pieces; anyone on whom it falls will be crushed."*

When the chief priests and the Pharisees heard Jesus' parables, they knew he was talking about them. They looked for a way to arrest him, but they were afraid of the crowd because the people held that he was a prophet.
– Matthew 21:33-46

In this passage Jesus is exposing the hearts and plans of the chief priest and the Pharisees to kill Him, as Israel had done in the past to the prophets. They wanted the "vineyard" for themselves. They were jealous of Jesus because the people listened to Him, followed Him, and believed Him. The religious leaders wanted their status and unchallenged leadership back.

As believers we would not say in words that we want Jesus out of the picture so we could be the "religious leader" of our own lives.

Verse 43 says: *"Therefore I tell you that the Kingdom of God will be taken away from you and given to a people who will produce its fruit."*

Jesus is saying that we as tenants (serving believers) in His vineyard (the Kingdom) are to produce fruit (go and make disciples). We are not to just keep the produce from the vineyard to ourselves. Instead we are to share it with others. Let's not just keep Jesus selfishly to ourselves on the inside and live like we want on the outside. Behaving in that way would make us our own "religious leader". If we do that, no one will ever meet the owner of the vineyard.

Dirty Diapers   February 23

What are the greatest invention of our time? Internet? Cell Phones? A/C? Nope! The greatest invention of not just our time but of all time is – disposable diapers! I remember my mom and grandmother changing cloth diapers of someone who will remain nameless. OK, it was my sister. Anyway, they would often prick their fingers when changing her baby diaper, but that wasn't the worst of it, if you know what I mean!

The real mess was dealing with that dirty diaper after it was removed. Cheryl would be clean and smelling like baby powder, but somebody had to deal with the mess. I know some of you are saying: "Gross, Greg! Great Christian devotion!" But this was a real dilemma for me, even as a small boy. I think I was emotionally scarred for a while. I was four and I had already decided there would be no kids for me! NO WAY!

Healing for my scars came the day that I first saw a TV commercial for disposable diapers. It was OK now to seek out a girlfriend and no longer be in the chains of "poopaphobia."

Now I'm going to get a little gross again to make a point. The Bible speaks of us and sacrifices as a pleasant or pleasing aroma to God. Yet sin has a stench to Him. In Greg words, "sin must smell like crap to Him."

In the Old Testament, sin was dealt with through ceremonial animal sacrifice and it took time and effort (like cleaning a dirty cloth diaper). Nowadays God has paid the price (sacrifice) through Jesus and He separates our sin (crap) from us as far as the east is from the west. It's analogous to bringing the boys home from a day at the beach. You know what they did in those diapers sleeping in the car on the way home! To the backyard we'd go and I'd yank off that dirty diaper, throw it away, hose their butts off and they were good as new!

I know this sounds simplistic, and frankly it is for us. Trust, believe, repent and ask forgiveness. For Jesus, not so easy, He died on the cross so we could be "hosed off" by His blood. For the Father not so easy either, watching His Son crucified. The cost was the ultimate price to clean up our crap. That's how much He loves us.

...as far as the east is from the west, so far has he removed our transgressions from us. – Psalm 103:12

Can You Hear Him Now   February 24

When I was a boy and my dad was trying to instruct me and I argued with him over the issue, he would say: "Boy, you're broadcasting, but you're not tuning in."

Another saying along the same lines is: "That's why God gave you two ears and one mouth." Which implies we should listen twice as much as we talk.

As I was praying this morning, making MY request to God in an almost routine manner without much thought, I was halted. It was as if God was saying my dad's words to me in His voice: "You're broadcasting, but you're not tuning in. Could you just stop, be still and listen?"

I was all about getting through my "holy routine." I have to get moving. I have to get a shower. I have to get dressed for work. I have to get something to eat. I have to go, go, go! Busy, busy, busy!

All the while the Creator of the universe wants to speak to me. Good going, Greg!

I was like the guy who just keeps talking and doesn't hear a thing the other person is trying to say. What if the other guy is trying to tell me my house is on fire or not to walk out in front of that speeding truck? I better learn to listen more and better.

I'll ask God to help me with that, as soon as He's finished talking to me.

P.S. I wonder if they'll get it when I show up for work hungry and smelly, in wrinkled clothes?

The Jigsaw Puzzle   February 25

When I was in the Air Force, I knew this guy whose hobby it was to put together jigsaw puzzles. He had gotten to the place where he would find a beautiful puzzle, put it together and then mount it on a piece of finished wood. Once the puzzle was clear-coated onto the wood, he would hang it on a wall in his home. It was as attractive as any painting or picture.

The other day I started thinking about how our lives are like jigsaw puzzles and God is the puzzle maker. God gives us this puzzle and has us put it together. His perfect plan (the picture the puzzle will turn into) for our lives, has already been painted on the lid of the box. We have to follow that picture to make our lives into what He designed them to become.

Puzzles (lives) are different. Some are harder to put together than others. Some seem difficult, intricate and hard to figure out. Others look simple and easy to put together. Either way, the trick is to follow the designer's plan. We have to look at the plan (the lid).

The plan for our lives (the lid) is painted in the Bible and looked at in prayer. The putting together of the puzzle (our lives) is guided by the

Holy Spirit. Still, sometimes it seems to be difficult to match the pieces together.

For instance, the top of the puzzle may be pieces of all blue skies and every piece looks the same. This may discourage us into thinking we will never see the "blue skies" in our lives. Yet we must keep at it by trying to understand what piece fits where. One way we can start is to establish what we know to be right. We know there are pieces to the outside of the puzzle. We can start at the edges of the puzzle where the outside pieces are straight. These pieces hold the whole puzzle together.

These outside or edge puzzle pieces in our lives that hold us together are our trust in Christ for our salvation and His direction. Once we have these outside pieces in place, He will begin to show us "the lid of the box" and where and when to place the inner pieces of our lives.

This will result in the picture (our lives) becoming what He designed us to be. We then will have become a beautiful picture for others to see, as God displays us as His artwork.

What Do I Do Now   February 26

As a youth leader in the past, I have had many a high school graduate come to me and ask: "What do I do now? Go to college? Major in what? Get a job? Go in the mission field?" Some of these young people were literally in a "frantic panic"! They were trying to decide what they were going to do for the rest of their lives at a very young age for such a decision!

I may not have always known the best and most godly advice to give in a given situation, but in these cases I would tell them this: "Of course pray and ask God for guidance, then rest in the confidence that He made you who you are to be. What you do will come from who you are (being) in Him. If you are being who you are in Him, you will as a result, do what He would have you to do."

I often have to remind myself that the most important thing is my relationship to God. Like any relationship we want to have, we must put forth effort on our part to maintain and improve it. If I love someone I will do nice things for them, such as acts of kindness and service. As a parent it is nice to see my children doing nice things for me, but most of all I want their love.

We can do all kinds of things, but they must be with right motive in our hearts. We are capable of doing things just to get something for ourselves. We can do religion or be in a relationship with our God. If we are being who God made us to be, our motives will be pure and what we do will glorify Him.

Where did this blog come from today? I got up this morning wondering what God wanted me to DO today. His answer was a question. Could we just hang out and BE together for awhile?

Take It To The Mechanic   February 27

Hannah and I did a little road trip the other day in my old truck. My road trips in old trucks are rarely without some peculiar incident. This trip was no exception.

The day had been without incident until we were almost home. As we came back into town, the truck started cutting out. The closer we got to the house, the worse it got; stalling a couple of times. We barely made it to the house before the truck quit running.

After the long day, I decided the truck would be tomorrow's project. The next day I went out, cranked the truck and it ran all afternoon without so much as a hiccup! Although there is something in that motor that caused it to run so terribly, I couldn't figure it out and therefore I couldn't fix it.

I'll probably end up taking it to a trusted mechanic who can diagnose and repair the problem.

We can do the same thing in our spiritual lives.

For instance I know there are plenty of times in my own life that I am not running on all cylinders. I could be ill, lazy, selfish, wanting my own way, maybe tricked by the enemy or just angry to name a few reasons I'm not running smooth.

Often I don't have a clue what the source of the problem is or how to fix it. I do know who the most trustworthy "Mechanic" is in these times. God can diagnose the problem and He does have the tools and the ability to fix it right.

Sometimes we are spiritual "shade tree mechanics" that think we can fix our motors ourselves. Often we make matters worse by trying to fix it ourselves. We may even think we have it fixed only to see the problem reappear as a more intense situation. Eventually we end up going to God with the problem after we have prolonged the matter, probably making it worse!

Other times we think we should try to fix the problem ourselves because it will cost too much to take it to the mechanic. Truth is, it may cost a lot, but it will be fixed right so that our motor will be running smooth again.

When our motor isn't running on all cylinders, lets take it to the Mechanic right off the bat. He can fix it right the first time.

Me First! Me First! February 28

Read Matthew 20:1-16 (First!)

First is usually the best, most desired place in this world. Who remembers the name of the fifth guy who walked on the Moon, even though his achievement was as amazing as the first? First place is where you find the champions in sports. What do you get for fourth place? Second is first loser; that's how the world thinks. Thank God that's not how it is in the Kingdom!

That is what Jesus is telling us in this passage. He's saying that His grace is sufficient for all and He loves us all the same. Did you ever picture yourself at the marriage supper of the Lamb? To my flesh it might seem..."well, I've been serving God a long time. I think I'll take a seat here close to the head of the table." Only to be told by the "angelic bouncer" to get up and go sit at the other end of the table. Then watch him give that good seat to some mass murderer who truly repented right before he was executed!

Another way I look at this is family. I had my first son for over four years before the second one came along. But as soon as that second one arrived I instantly loved him as much as the first. Same thing when the third baby was born. I instantly loved him as much as the older sons. At some stages in life, being first might mean pioneer or wisdom or more skills, but in the Kingdom it doesn't mean first on the love meter.

Interference   February 29

I remember in my late teens CB radios were all the rage. We would talk on them for hours to almost anyone who would listen. Sometimes reception was good, other times there was considerable interference.

I had a friend who had a power booster he would attach (illegally) to his CB and be able to communicate over long distances. When you think about it, this was a selfish act on his part because when he keyed up his CB with his boost attached, he drowned out any nearby CB. This boosted interference would even affect neighborhood TV reception! His actions produced interference in others' ability to receive their desired communications. Not to mention just plain ticking people off!

As believers, do we do the same think to other people? Do we try to turn up our own perceived "power boost" (what we think others should hear), to impose our will on them? Good intentions or not, are we then causing "interference" in their reception of God's messages to them of what His will is for their lives?

This is a dangerous place! Sure, when it comes to our young children and those who can no longer decide or care for themselves, then decisions need to be made for them. Yet way too often people (believers included) try imposing their will into others lives. If we do this, then we can be causing interference in someone's reception of God's will for their lives.

We say we have surrendered our will to God? Shouldn't we surrender others' will to God too, instead of trying to get them to surrender their will to us?

Smooth Sailing   March 1

I love "Smooth Sailing!" That's what I call it when everything is going just the way I want. There are all kinds of Smooth Sailing!

There is "physical" smooth sailing, such as being out on the boat when the water is calm so that the bow slices through the water with ease.

There is mental and emotional smooth sailing. The bills are paid, our loved ones are well, and the stress levels are low.

Then there is spiritual smooth sailing. All seems well with God, prayers answered and the devil must be bothering someone else for the time being. Thank you Lord, keep it right here on this heading; I'm loving it!

I suppose many of us come to God expecting, hoping and certainly wanting smooth sailing the rest of our earthly lives. We soon find out that although our eternity is certain and that in His strength, grace and mercy we can get through troubled waters, the problems of this life are going to come our way.

The waters of my life have had a slight chop to them for the last couple of weeks. Nuisance stuff mostly, but requiring my attention enough to require some navigation. Including computer malfunctions, extra long workdays for weeks on end, unexpected bills and a few other aggravations.

I expect many of you are saying: "That's not problems and trials, you big baby, listen to this … ," and you could give me a real list. I know, because every time I think about my little problems, God seems to send people across my path with real problems. People needing comfort after losing a loved one, food or shelter, physical healing or in real financial trouble. God starts telling me to count my blessings, quit my whining over my situation and then pray for and help these people.

Funny how that works. I end up getting blessed in the process.

Ship Of Faith   March 2

Just another thought about smooth sailing. It appears to me that some people can get through the "choppy, rough and even stormy seas of life" with much greater ease than others. I think there are a couple of reasons for this.

One is their ability to navigate in rough waters. The other is the size of their "boat or ship."

When I am in my boat and find myself in choppy seas, the safest way to navigate and keep my boat upright is to go forward, straight into the waves. If I try to turn the boat in high seas I could get swamped and sink. If I try to run from the waves, I could be overtaken by large waves, or nose in over the front of a breaker and sink that way.

My boat is rather small in comparison to most of the ones I see when I'm out on the water. I may have problems in my boat in a 3 or 4 foot chop because my boat is only 16 feet long. However, that 55 footer cruising by has little problem with this size chop in the water. Yet where a 55 footer may have trouble in rougher seas, an aircraft carrier would hardly notice until hurricane force winds are in play.

In the storms of life we need the Lord to be our Navigator, guiding us through the rough seas as we turn into the wind and face them head on.

Secondly we need as big of a Ship of Faith as we can get, to ride the storm out. The bigger the ship, the smoother the ride through the storm.

No storm is fun, but the bigger the ship, with the right Navigator, the smoother the sailing will be.

Stick' em Up — March 3

There is this wonderful lady who works on my route. She is getting close to retirement age but still has a lot of feistiness. She takes care of her husband, her home, and holds down a full time job. She is strong, independent, dependable, and has a touch of a banty hen's demeanor. Yet deep down, she's caring, considerate and desires what's fair and best for all.

A few nights ago her house burned down. Now out of a place to stay, she is faced with depending on others. This goes contrary to every fiber of her strong, tough, and independent nature. She was basically forced to surrender her independence and trust others for her needs.

I think it's this way for many of us. We have an independent nature. Maybe it's pride. Maybe it's not trusting others. Maybe it's truly believing our way is the best way or even the only good way. Maybe it's living in a free country and we don't want to relinquish our freedom.

If we are in combat and we have no option but to surrender, we raise our hands, we are then captured and are no longer free. We are subject to the actions of our captors. We have lost our freedom!

In the Kingdom, we are captives until we surrender. Captives to sin. We spiritually put our hands up surrendering our lives to God. In that surrender, we are set free and are no longer captive to sin.

It doesn't take a brain surgeon or fifty years of reading the Bible to see that sin can burn our house to the ground. If you're a prisoner of sin, stick 'em up! Surrender is the way to freedom!

The Little Red Truck   March 4

I got my delivery truck back from maintenance yesterday. They had done some body work on it where there were some scratches and small dents. It really looks as good as new on the outside. You wouldn't know it by looking at the outside, but the inside is all scratched up and dirty and the motor has 160,000 miles of wear and tear.

Also yesterday, I went and looked at a little red truck that is for sale. It is not exactly what I want. At first glance it was old and beat up. It was not the size I had in mind. But I decided to take it for a ride anyway. I got in and cranked it up. It sounded good. I shifted it into gear and it went in smoothly. I hit the gas, and the power surprised me as I spun the wheels pulling away. It's no show truck in appearance, but its heart and soul is well tuned!

That's the way it is in this world when it comes to people. We place way too much value on outward appearances rather than the inner man. We look up to someone because of their beauty or maybe their money, possessions or talents. Only to find out later that their true character is phony, ugly or without good foundation. The Lord told Samuel (when he was about to anoint one of Jesse's sons to be king), *"The Lord does not look at the things man looks at. Man looks at the outward appearance, but the Lord looks at the heart."* – 1 Samuel 16:7

Last night I saw a little boy on TV whose face and body had been disfigured as a result of disease. He was pretty much confined to a wheelchair. He no longer looked anything like his pictures taken prior to the onset of his illness. Yet inside him burned a little boy's desire for adventure. He wants to go camping and play pirates. That's who he is, not what our eyes see. He is the heart that God sees.

"Lord, I would rather run good and look like the old truck than be looking good and broken down on the side of the road of life. Change my heart so that it pleases you because I know that what is in my heart will eventually come to the surface and be exposed. Amen."

That'll Leave A Mark   March 5

You've seen it on blooper shows or even done it yourself. Strolling down the sidewalk enjoying conversation with a friend or looking at someone dressed funny and *Wammo!* right into that light pole. Dazed and staggering like a drunk, you try to regain your composure as the knot raises on your head. Your friend, assuming you will be alright, wisecracks: "That'll leave a mark!"

I remember each one of the "crew," when they were just young sailors, earning their marks. The oldest was brought home once by the neighbor, bleeding all over his white shirt and pants, as a result of a crash on a concrete pad. The next one, after crashing into the toilet or tub, telling me at the hospital he was "OK now," and wanted to go home (as they approached him with shots and stitches in hand). He couldn't see his eyelid hanging down over his swollen eye. I also remember the youngest running towards me hollering, with a nosebleed from a baseball he didn't see coming. The other night I was washing dishes (yes I was), and broke a glass, cutting my finger nearly to the bone! That'll leave a mark.

These events are all too common in our lives and they do leave a mark. Some marks are on the inside of us as memories we will never forget. Some marks are on the outside of us in the form of a scar, that will always be there on our bodies, to remind us of what happened.

Just the other day I went to the funeral of a friend of mine. Jim was a mighty man of God and is with the Lord as I write this about him. You can read about Jim's witness to me in "The Phone Call I Should Have Made" (July 18).

Another friend of mine sent me an e-mail, since the funeral, that had this line: "Can't seem to understand why such a good man is taken and why it is that so many wicked men with wicked hearts seem to thrive on....doesn't make sense to me." I have been thinking about this a lot this week.

Maybe God is giving the wicked more time. Maybe He is giving the godly an "early out" of this world. Although I don't have the entire answer to this question, I do know this: We will all be taken. And at the moment we are taken, the destination has already been determined.

Jim chose his destination a long time ago. His being taken is going to leave a lot of marks. Emotional marks on his loved ones and friends who will miss him terribly. But he also leaves Kingdom marks on many of us, marks that will always be a witness to us in our walk with the Lord. The Kingdom marks he has left on us will no doubt find their way down to those on who we leave marks. Be sure of this: We will leave a mark. The question is, what kind of mark are we leaving?

Follow my example, as I follow the example of Christ. – I Corinthians 11:1

No Mercy   March 6

When I was about twelve, a new family moved in across the street. There were two boys in this family. I guess they were maybe ten and eight years old. The ten year old was kind of big for his age and the eight year old, kind of small.

They had a cousin who would come visit fairly often. He was around twelve and he was a huge guy, bigger than any of us in the neighborhood. He was a mean, nasty bully. I remember him coming over to go trick-or-treat with us one Halloween. We were walking down the street near the curb when he spotted a frog in the road. Without any hesitation, he jumped up in the air above that frog and splattered it halfway across the street when he landed on it. I must admit it sounded funny but it was a gross sight!

Every time he came over, he would somehow intentionally hurt his eight year old cousin. He would cream him while tackling, push him down, slap him or just plain beat up the little guy. The ten year old would try to help his little brother but to no avail. Even when the parents were told of an incident, their response was some sort of, "boys will be boys, let them work it out."

Finally one day I had seen enough and I had the upper hand. The huge cousin started in on the little guy in my next door neighbor's back yard. We were over there shooting my neighbor's new BB gun, a really cool rifle that would fire with every pump if you held the trigger down. I had the BB gun in my hands when he started pounding on the little guy. I told him to leave him alone. As he turned and came at me screaming, "What are you going to do about it?" I responded with three rounds right in his chest from about six feet. He fell backwards through a lawn chair and hit the ground. I stood over him and informed him that if he didn't leave the little guy alone I would show him how well I could use the other end of the rifle.

By the way, the BB's didn't go in him, but they did leave three really cool looking bee sting-like marks on his chest. However, I think it was the prospect of meeting the butt end of that gun that convinced him to lay off his cousin.

He didn't visit much after that day. The older brother told me that when his cousin's parents told him they were coming over, the bully just said he wanted to stay home and watch TV.

Mercy   March 7

So after yesterday's story, "No Mercy" (read it), maybe you're saying: "OK, what's the rest of this story?" Here it is.

Around the same time in my childhood we used to take a shortcut through the woods to a pond where we would fish and play. A group of us went down there this one particular day and heard gunshots on and off. We didn't think too much of it at first because we had heard people shooting guns in those woods from time to time. We went right on playing.

When we came out from under the little bridge, and went up on the dirt road, I was staring right down the barrel of a rifle. It was pointed right at my face and the guy behind the trigger was not a happy camper.

I don't know why he was angry. I didn't ask! We told him we didn't do anything, we were just playing under the bridge. We were at his mercy. After a few moments he just made a short wave with his rifle indicating which direction for us to leave. We were gone!

Someone told us later that a kid had been shot up there earlier that day. I don't know if that guy was the shooter or if he was looking for the shooter. He didn't shoot us though.

I guess I almost always think of mercy in terms of being the recipient of it. When we receive mercy it costs us nothing. If I have wronged someone (anything from hurting their feelings to committing a crime against them) and they do not retaliate, take revenge or seek justice, and then forgive me, it cost me nothing!

But to give mercy we must be in possession of mercy. We possess mercy when someone has wronged us. Once we realize we are in possession of mercy, we are then in a position to decide whether to extend that mercy to the person who hurt us; to be merciful to them or not.

Also, giving mercy most often cost the giver something. When someone wrongs us it can hurt deeply! It can cost money, possessions, friendships and in awful cases, loved ones.

Jesus said: "Blessed are the merciful, for they will be shown mercy." – Matthew 5:7

At the beginning of mercy is forgiveness for someone who has wronged us. At the end of mercy is freedom for the "mercy giver" from carrying around hate, anger, and unforgiveness.

Have mercy.

Spiritual Diet March 8

A couple of years ago I went on a diet (lifestyle change in eating). I lost seventy pounds! I went from 265 down to 195. My doctor cut my BP meds, I stopped snoring, I had tons more energy, wasn't sleepy and generally felt much healthier.

After being on this diet for a while, the results were obvious to others. My achievement was impressive to them. More and more people came and ask me how I was losing the weight. They were listening to my answer because they could see the positive results. I had credibility on the subject because I had successfully achieved a goal.

How did I do it? First I got a book (actually Hannah did, and she prepared the meals). Anyway, we read it and followed it. We memorized some of it, so as to know what to have when eating out or for lunch at work, etc. This lifestyle of eating got down in us and the results were not only good for us, but obvious to others. They could see it could be done as they observed the change it made in me.

It wasn't good enough just to have the book. It wasn't good enough to just read it. It wasn't good enough to just understand the book. It wasn't even good enough to memorize it. I could only achieve the results it promised by putting its words into action and living them out!

It's the same with the Word of God. The Bible can be the instrument of change in our lives. But for us to be changed for the good, we must stay on the "diet" of having the Book, reading it, understanding it, memorizing it, and then putting its words into action in our lives.

Soon others will see the real and obvious change in our lives. We will have the credibility of living out this wonderful change. Then others will ask, "How did you do this?" And we can show them.

Do not merely listen to the word, and so deceive yourselves. Do what it says. – James 1:22

Spiritual Diet (Continued) — March 9

What is more impressive than going on a diet and losing weight? Being disciplined enough to keep the weight off by not "backsliding" into old eating habits and physical inactivity.

How about the guy on the TV commercials who lost all that weight (over 100 lbs, I'm pretty sure) and just ran in and finished a marathon! Now that's impressive! That will inspire others to do likewise.

These kind of results will require the discipline to continue eating right and staying the course. Discipline is not what my flesh wants. It wants a boatload of Oreo's and milk in front of the TV! But Proverbs says, "fools despise wisdom and discipline." Ouch!

To the point. Physically speaking, I "backslid." I have been putting the hurt on Oreo's, holiday goodies, second helpings (just because it tasted good), and then working out by anchoring down my couch. Forty of the seventy pounds I previously lost have been found hanging over my belt buckle!

I obviously cannot stay physically fit without discipline. It's back to the diet. I pray I will not have to diet again after this time but instead will stay disciplined so as to stay healthy and productive.

The same goes for our spiritual fitness. It takes discipline. All good relationships take continued effort and that goes for our relationship to God, too.

The recommended diet is as follows: Consume the Word and live it, along with prayer and obedience. If we stay disciplined (stick to His recommended diet), we will be plenty strong in His power to finish this race. Not to mention an inspiration to others as a witness of Christ's Word being truth.

Who's Really The Time Bandit   March 10

I remember going to my first finance meeting at a church that I had just been hired as the Youth Director. Having no idea at the time what churches starting out with so few youth might typically budget for their program, I just decided to ask for money to cover everything. Later in ministry at other churches, I found out that typically youth programs were given considerably less in comparison to what I was asking at the first church I served.

Anyway, in that first meeting I ask for $6000. No one even blinked! After only minimal discussion I was given $5000 for a program starting with only three youth! I of course had a vision of the group growing and going to camps and doing all that youth stuff. So in that meeting, right after their approval, I casually ask: "Would anyone like to go and help me out at youth camp this summer." You could have heard a pin drop! No takers! Zip, zero, nada!

I think a lot of us are this way. I would much rather give some money to something than my time. I truly struggle with this issue in my life. For instance I have given money to homeless shelters, but I haven't worked a day in one.

When someone comes to me wanting some of my time, my flesh thinks of them as a "Time Bandit." (The name of a crab boat on one of my favorite TV shows). Most men I know will tell you that they would rather not loan someone their tools or their truck. I am of that opinion. But you let someone ask me to help them move, at least my flesh would like to say, "I'm sorry, but I have some plans (sitting on my butt watching a ball game). How about I let you use my truck?" That's spiritually disgusting, huh?

Or let me be laying on the couch, being selfishly lazy, and Hannah Pooh asks me to do this or that, (especially rub her feet) and I may truly go off in the flesh! Sadly, we are often harsh to the ones we love the most, but that's another devotion.

So, should we tithe our time like we do our money? Even more, should we give our time over and above a tithe? I've lost several rounds in this fight within myself, but with God's help I've won some too. And I suspect there are many more rounds in this fight. But just like any other fight, it's not over until the bell rings.

Scripture references too numerous to mention ... you know: "think of others more highly than yourself," serve, serve, serve ...

Toe Nailed   March 11

As I got out of the rack this morning and was putting on my britches in the dark, I kicked my left leg through and busted my toe upside the steel bed rail. It hurt alright, but not more than any other stubbed toe. Upon further review, in the light of the bathroom, I had a loose toenail with blood coming out from underneath.

I figured since the blood is coming out from the loose toenail it won't build that throbbing pressure up underneath the nail that I would later have to relieve by use of some medieval method (hot needle etc).

This is the way we look at things sometimes, is it not? We let a fingernail build pressure to an absurd point before opening that bad boy up so it can heal. We wait until a painful tooth is causing abscess misery before we go to the dentist.

I once had a infected bump on my leg that was nasty looking! A big red bump with a giant yellow core in it! It looked like a giant zit and it hurt like mad! I finally went to the doctor and he did just what I was afraid of: he got his sterile pliers out and literally yanked that core out! I came up off of the table with tears in my eyes as he pulled the core out. I told him he better have gotten it because that was his first and last attempt!

I could go on and on about waiting until I couldn't stand it anymore, the stress of some financial pressure, or the anguish of some mental hurt, the shame of hurting someone else, or the conviction of some sin I committed. Anywhere along the path to complete misery over some situation, a moment of pain, humility, confession or asking for forgiveness, and misery could have been relieved long ago.

Just like a hot needle through a smashed toe nail, it may hurt for a instant, but the relief and peace is certainly worth it.

The Devil's weapon is fear. Fear of a little pain. Fear of what people will think. Fear of facing who we really are.

Wherever your pressure may be, I say: "Stick a hot needle in the fear of man and the Devil's plans, relieve the pressure. Freedom feels great!"

Just Routine   March 12

I woke up this morning at my regular time and hit the snooze button. I'm not usually a snoozer, but I hit it two or three times this morning. However, I must have missed it on the final attempt, resulting in my waking up an hour later than usual. Right off the bat my routine was messed up.

OK, I can hear some of you now. Routine! I don't want a routine! I want to be spontaneous and free!

I'm not talking about a routine that is bondage. Routines can be very bad. We could routinely use drugs, get drunk, drive too fast, be lazy, and selfish. That can lead to bad things happening.

There are also good, beneficial, disciplined routines such as having a basic schedule and order of doing things. Having a good disciplined routine (meaning we actually use it) will actually free up more of our time that we can use spontaneously.

A friend once told me to keep a calendar. I told him I was busy enough without writing down everything I needed to do! He said no, what will happen is you will see all the blank spots in the calendar, which is the free time you really have. I tell you it works!

The Bible tells us to be good stewards, of our time as well as our money. I'll bet most of us make a much more concerted effort to budget our money than our time. I believe that when it comes to the things of the Kingdom, what we do with our time is every bit as important as what we do with our money.

P.S. It's March, calendars are cheap this time of year.

One Of Those Days   March 13

As I began to think about the day ahead of me, I started trying to figure out how I might navigate the possible obstacles that may come my way. I am looking forward to having dinner with some friends tonight.

But yesterday I had to work really late so I am trying to figure out how I might avoid that happening again today. Some options might be to talk to the boss (who truthfully may have no options of his own), maybe skip or cut short my lunch or breaks. You get the idea. Anyway, the old saying: "It's going to be one of those days," came to mind. That saying has a negative, "throw in the towel and still take the beating" kind of connotation to it.

However, the next thing that came to mind was that it doesn't have to have that meaning. I started thinking about the good days. Not in order or rank of importance, but just the order they came to mind. The days with my grandfathers fishing, one on a dock of a bay, the other standing in a stream in the Northwest. Playing catch with Dad. The birth of each of my children. The moment on the beach when Hannah said "yes." The salvation of each of my sons. Sitting with my granddaughter Ella on the balcony. Ben and Brianna's wedding. Fishing with Ryan just the other day when we limited out. Nick's book release. I could just keep writing as more and more "days" come to mind.

Some great days are planned and some God just drops in your lap as a blessing. Thank you, Lord!

Maybe today is going to be "One of those days"!

Character Wreck   March 14

I saw a fender bender the other day as I was taking my lunch break at a convenience store. One young guy who had just been in the store trying to buy smokes without an ID hurried out, and backed into this lady in a beat up old car.

Watching through the glass from inside the store, this is how the incident played out in my mind. It was like watching a silent movie. You kind of know what's going on but you really don't get the exact story.

The young fellow who is in a hurry backs into the lady and puts a few new scratches on her old beat up car. The young guy jumps out, looks at the damage and assures the lady that it's minimal and heads back to his car. The lady then pops out of her jalopy, holding her side as if she's hurt. Yeah, sure! It was a bump, not a collision! Anyway, she begs to differ with the young man's assessment of the damage. She starts to rail at him. Then it gets better! He takes off!

The manager of the store decides to go out and check on the situation. She comes back in a few minutes later and calls to report the accident. Soon a deputy shows up to investigate. I can only imagine what he's thinking: "You have got to be kidding! I've got to spend an hour writing up a bump in a parking lot for a lady faking an injury, in a clunker that looks like it was in a train wreck before the guy hit her!"

As the officer begins to investigate the incident, a young man who saw the accident walks up and hands the officer a piece of paper with the tag number of the perp and begins to tell the deputy what he saw. This young witness had stayed around the entire time just to help out. Why? All I could figure was that he thought it was the right thing to do.

Obviously the guy that backed into the lady should not have fled the scene. There may have been more to his leaving than just no ID. And though I write this with some cynicism, the probability is that the lady was faking her injury (just an honest opinion). And there is no way there was enough damage to file insurance. Also, just for the record, I wouldn't blame the deputy if he was frustrated with the whole situation.

After reflecting on the whole incident, I came away with the conviction that one's character really matters.

The guy that left the scene and the lady faking an injury were examples of poor character. But the young guy who stayed around, for no other reason than it was the right thing to do, was an example of good character. He had nothing to gain. In fact it cost him his own time. But he did what he thought was right anyway. A little thing? Yes, maybe. But after thinking about it, I was impressed and challenged to try to be of better character with more integrity. That way I will become someone who does the right thing, just because it is the right thing to do!

Good character or integrity = Doing the right thing, even if you're the only one who's going to know about it.

To do what is right and just is more acceptable to the Lord than sacrifice. – Proverbs 21:3

Cooking In The Rain   March 15

I have this picture of myself holding an umbrella while cooking on the grill in the rain. Strange the lengths a fellow will go to prepare something good. I wanted some grilled food and I was willing to "weather the storm" to have it.

God will go to great lengths to prepare us for something good as well. But, are we willing to weather a storm, if need be, to allow Him to prepare us for His will in our lives?

It has been my experience that when I find myself in a comfort zone, I should look under my boat seat because I am about to be blown out of the water! I'll give you a personal example.

I was cruising along in life with steady wind and following seas. I was so *comfortable* I had become a couch potato. Then it started to happen. Hannah called me one afternoon distraught over her work situation. I heard God say, "Ask her if she wants to quit her job." Without a second thought I did just that! At that same time Nick was about to leave for college and I had just bought a truck and a boat. You see where this is going; more dinero going out than is coming in, and in nothing flat my comfort zone is nuked!

So I get up off my spiritual couch and jump into God's lap, just like He planned it, because I am now in a situation I cannot fix. That is what He wants me to know: that He is my source and that I am to depend on only Him.

During this time, the story of Shadrach, Meshach and Abednego came to me and so I said to God: "You are able to deliver me from this, but even if You do not, I will not bow to this; You are my God." God has given me real peace and joy right in the midst of this time and has been working in me and through me in mighty ways that will have to be shared in another post.

I guess it will take a little more "cooking" until I am "done". Until then I'll weather the storm because He is cooking up something good.

If we are thrown into the blazing furnace, the God we serve is able to deliver us from it, and he will deliver us from Your Majesty's hand. But even if he does not, we want you to know, Your Majesty, that we will not serve your gods or worship the image of gold you have set up. – Daniel 3:16-18

Easier Said Than Done　　　　　　　March 16

Just yesterday I had two people I love and care about tell me of difficult times they are going through. I have just come through some difficulties myself. Truthfully, my reaction to test or trials is: "Why God? Why me, God? I know what I'm supposed to do here. Why do I need to go through a test if I already know how I am supposed to respond to a situation like this?"

When I am going through some trial of faith or obedience, I often end up in the book of James. If books of the Bible had nicknames, James would be called: "Easier Said Than Done." Check out these pearls of wisdom. (That's sarcasm speak for "I don't want to hear this again!"):

Consider it pure joy (uh-huh, sure) *my brother, whenever* (not if) *you face trials of many kinds, because you know that testing of your faith develops perseverance. Perseverance must finish its work so that you may be mature and complete, not lacking anything* (getting all that I need and knowing that I have it in Christ Jesus, I like that). – James 1:2-4 (my additions)

How about this one?

Do not merely listen to the Word, and so deceive yourselves. Do what it says. (More of the "easier said than done"!) – James 1:22 (more of my additions)

James is just loaded with this stuff!

But when I get past the "woe is me" or "why God" sarcasm, whining, and yes, even genuine crying out to Him to get me through again, I get: "It is easier said than done, Greg. You may know what you are supposed to do in this test, but are you going to do it?" We are taught things not just so we know them, but so we will use them. The real use for what we have been taught is to live it out. That's what makes us stronger and more mature in our faith. A teacher teaches children math so they can add, English so they can speak, and the alphabet so they can read. The students use this knowledge. They are not just acquiring it to store up for the sake of knowledge. It's like being in a gym and seeing weights sitting on the floor. We know lifting them can make us stronger, but we actually have to lift them to get stronger.

One more thing. We often go through things so that we can be a genuine help to others who may go through the same things later.

And we know that in all things God works for the good of those who love Him, who have been called according to His purpose. – Romans 8-28

If I am going through a tough situation I want the counsel of someone who can say truthfully: "I know how you feel and I know what you're going through. Let me pray with you and tell you how God brought me through my situation."

Lifting weights isn't easy, but it makes you stronger. Going through tests and trials isn't easy. In fact, it's hard. It sucks! But it makes you stronger. Persevere and receive all you need, and know that you have it in Christ Jesus!

Business Is About To Pick Up   March 17

There is a saying: "Business is about to pick up!" which means things are about to change, get moving, get exciting, or get busy.

Sometimes in our lives we feel like we just hit a wall or get obstructed in some way. Other times, maybe it's just a feeling (or leading) that a change in direction or purpose is in order.

Still other times we may just get comfortable with a successful routine and start living life on cruise control. It's been my experience that God doesn't want me on cruise control!

To the point. Slowly, at first, things began to pick up as one of my sons and his family made a major decision to move. With a baby on the way and obstacles to climb and avoid, they followed what God is showing them. My other two sons are also making big decisions about their futures. My wife is right now in the midst of the culmination of her efforts in ministry that will take some sort of turn today! I personally see things coming over the horizon at me.

Years ago I would have felt overwhelmed by the thought of having to navigate all of this life change in and around me. Not anymore! As I look back, I can see where God has used things in my past to prepare for these things now. I am not afraid. This is an adventure! Comfort and peace comes from knowing that He has taken me through every single situation in my life, no matter how hard, lengthy and tiring the situation became.

Another comfort to me is that each of my sons, my daughter-in-law, my wife and I are trying to follow God's leading in our lives. He knows where He is taking us and the best way to get us there. What is there to fear? I'm excited and expectant that He will give us and show us "more than we could ask or imagine." I feel like a kid on Christmas morning, not knowing what's under the tree but knowing it's going to be good!

It just doesn't get any better than this!

The Crazy Lady   March 18

There is a lady on my route that I call the "Crazy Lady." A worldly diagnosis would be that she is certifiably nuts!

From the time I got this route, our relationship has gone from one of contention (her cussing and spewing at me about how sorry I was), to acceptance and tolerance of me (as she perceived me to be following her instructions), to full blown adoration and praise (as she now views me correctly, the greatest delivery man on the planet).

Nowadays she will come scootin' out of the house in her black hair wig. It will be flopping in the breeze with plenty of her real gray hair sticking out from underneath. She'll bring me a "goodie" to the mailbox or sometimes just leave something in the box for me.

This goodie could be a can of soda, but usually it is an unusual treat; for instance, a cup of juice (How long has that been in the box and what's really in it?), an open container of store bought muffins (with half of them missing), but the best was the most recent. I pulled up and opened the mailbox to find a baggie with something inside of it wrapped in a paper towel. I opened it up to find a large, single (homemade, I think) muffin inside. It looked OK, but as I had opened the baggie, the strong odor of mothballs attacked my nostrils! It smelled exactly like it does when I take a package to her door and she opens the screen, and WHAM, mothballs!

It tasted kind of dry and gave me cotton mouth. No! I didn't eat it, but Louie (our Basset Hound) did drink a lot of water after it!

Anyway...

How did I go from the worst to the greatest in her eyes? I think I did it right – by accident!

At first I was fine with her discontent, she's nuts and I don't like her either. Then, later her husband died and I figured we didn't both need to be jerks, so I was intentionally more sympathetic towards her. Finally, being the softy that I am, I began to be kind and listen to her ramblings a minute each time I saw her, instead of hitting the gas and running for it. It is truly amazing how people's demeanor can change if we just answer their (often annoying) cries for attention.

Whoops, I just realized how much I cry out for attention. I also realized how much I like it when someone really does pay attention to me. I don't think I like this story. It exposes me! Never mind this story everyone, don't read it!

Yesterday, the Crazy Lady told me she's moving soon. I'm going to miss her. Who's going to pay attention to me out there now?

From Crazy To Lunacy   March 19

I've written about the "Crazy Lady" on my route and how she thought that everyone was stealing her packages. She would cuss and scream at me, telling me that she was surrounded by thieves. The short version is that with God's help I was able to navigate her eccentric behavior and avoid losing my composure when dealing with her. Well, she finally moved a couple of weeks ago. I felt like it was a reward from Heaven, not having to deal with her anymore.

Not so fast! I'm hoping that this is God's sense of humor. But very near or on the day she moved out, a raging lunatic moved in another house on my route! The first moment this guy saw me, before I said anything, he began insulting me and my employer saying we're no good, overpaid and don't do our jobs. I thought: *"It's nice to meet you too. Do you happen to know a crazy woman that wears a black wig half way off her head?"*

The other day as I was driving by his house, he screamed at me. Screamed, not yelled! I backed up. He had evidently called to have a package redelivered. Unfortunately I had no knowledge of this as the clerks had not distributed the package to me. I tried to apologize, but to no avail. He began to berate me again. As he continued my patience wore completely off, so I pulled away. He continued to scream insults. I slammed on the brakes and popped off my seat belt. I not so kindly, informed him that I was not going to entertain any more of his personal insults directed at me. I meant it and was willing to enforce it at this point. He shut up.

As I drove around the corner I became aware that God might be at it again. Maybe He's at work on my temper. Maybe He wants me to pass along the mercy and grace He has given me. Maybe He wants me to pray for my new enemy. Not three blocks away from the incident, I began to laugh as I saw how God was at work in me.

I had finally passed the test of the "Crazy Lady." Now on to the "Lunatic." The growing never stops.

Hold On — March 20

My son text'd me last night and said we should go golfing. When I read that, it took me back to the first time I ever took him golfing.

We had just finished a hole and were riding in the golf cart to the next tee. The cart path had a hairpin turn as we approached the tee box. Having a little fun driving the cart, I just zipped around the turn. My dad, in the cart behind us, started shouting something. As I turned my head to see what he wanted, Ben was no longer in my cart, but instead was rolling through the rough! When I had taken that hairpin turn, I had slung him right out of the cart! I just assumed he was holding on as I turned.

He was unhurt physically, but I figured he would not want to go golfing with me anymore! If he did, he would probably want to drive the golf cart this time for his own safety. Not to get even, but I would hold on in the turns anyway.

When they had finished eating, Jesus said to Simon Peter, "Simon son of John, do you love me more than these?"

"Yes, Lord," he said, "you know that I love you."

Jesus said, "Feed my lambs."

Again Jesus said, "Simon son of John, do you love me?"

He answered, "Yes, Lord, you know that I love you."

Jesus said, "Take care of my sheep."

The third time he said to him, "Simon son of John, do you love me?"

Peter was hurt because Jesus asked him the third time, "Do you love me?" He said, "Lord, you know all things; you know that I love you."

Jesus said, "Feed my sheep." – John 21: 15-17

Jesus told Peter to feed and take care of His (followers) sheep. As believers, that is what we are supposed to do. We are to (teach) feed them and care for them. As disciplers, we are to tend to them, watching that they stay in the flock and not get lost in the "rough" of the world just because we get inattentive in our shepherding. We are to make every effort to make sure they are holding on to Jesus.

Maybe I have let a few sheep slip off into the rough. I think I'll look them up and make sure they're still holding on to Jesus.

Lures Of Temptation — March 21

One of my favorite ways of fishing is using a lure. A lure is basically any piece of fake bait. For instance a plastic shrimp not a real shrimp, or a fake fish not a real one. I don't know, maybe the fun of it is in outsmarting the fish, saving on bait, not having to bait the hook over and over again, less smelly bait or some combination of these reasons. You usually stay busy using a lure too, not just sitting around waiting for a bite to come along.

Top water lures are some of the most fun because as you retrieve the lure you can often see the fish follow it and hit it ferociously, then the battle is on! I wonder what the thought process must be for a hungry fish that spots what he thinks is a delicious supper swimming by him. Some phrases from commercials come to mind of animals with uncontrollable hunger like: "I'm cuckoo for Cocoa Puffs!" or "Bacon, bacon, bacon!"

Anyway, as soon as he takes a big bite on that lure he knows he has made a big mistake and instinctively tries to free himself from the hook. Sadly, I see where I sometimes swim right up to the "lure of temptation" and take a big bite, like a dumb mackerel.

It really doesn't matter who it is throwing the lure our way; our own sinful desires, someone else's anger, or the devil. The lures are coming into the waters we swim in; work, home, school, and even church, wherever we're spending our time. The lures of temptation can look like: quick money, instant happiness (alcohol, drugs, etc), power over others, personal success at other's expense, the blame game, laziness and on and on.

Here comes a lure and we bolt towards it, latch on as hard as we can and have a mouth full of hooks poisoned with fake satisfaction. Why? Maybe because we haven't had a decent meal of the real Bread of Life lately. Maybe it was our own gluttony for more of the wrong food. I know there are far too many times I will eat a bowl of ice cream or some cookies when I am slap full! I mean that spiritually as well as physically.

What do we do when we have a mouthful of hooks? Ask the Great Fisher of Men to forgive us, stop wiggling (repent) and let Him unhook us. Sometime the soreness from the hook lingers and will keep us away from the lures for awhile. But the best way to avoid being tempted by the lures is to be full of the true bread, the real food that satisfies.

Fair And Right...Same Thing?   March 22

I usually get up around 5 am every morning. I get some coffee and then pray and write a blog. I routinely do this at the kitchen table. This morning is different. Hannah pops up a few minutes before me and decides to make herself breakfast (in the kitchen obviously), then eat it watching TV in the living room immediately adjacent to my kitchen table "writing throne"! This isn't fair to me! I have a routine! She's causing me to be terribly inconvenienced! This is disrupting to me! This is not fair to me! Whaaaaa!!!

According to God however, my reaction to this invasion of my space is incorrect. Jesus said that we are to love our neighbor as ourselves, and she's more than a neighbor! He further says this is one of the greatest commandments. He explains that if we obey this command and love God as we should, we will be in obedience to all of His commands and directions.

The Bible tells us to think of others ahead ourselves. This, God views as right. Man would say it's not fair!

In Matthew 20, Jesus tells the parable of the workers in which the workers hired at the end of the day are paid as much as the workers who labored all day. This also, God views as right. But it's not fair!

This morning I suppose I had an opinion that fair and right are the same thing. I imagine a lot of us have this concept as a settled truth in our minds. That's flawed "flesh thinking." Man's view says everything should be fair. God says everything should be right, and He determines what is right.

Fair can be cold, unfeeling, selfish and unforgiving. But what is right in God's eyes offers His grace, mercy and love. So, what will it be: fair or right? Whichever way we want this applied to us is the way we should apply it to others. Besides, isn't that only fair, or right?

Fishing In The Right Spot — March 23

We once lived on a small lake (big pond is more like it). Anyway, one day when I came home from work, two of my sons were all excited about their day's catch. They had caught two very nice bass. After congratulating them, I ask them to tell me the secret to their success.

They informed me that they had caught their fish with my cast net. How they threw that large, heavy cast net is beyond me. Neither of them was grown at the time. And how they threw it into that pond and not tear it up on tree stumps is another mystery. The thing is they wanted to catch fish, so they went after them.

Now I am no expert on fresh water fishing but I do know it is illegal to use a cast net in fresh water! I'm not sure if they really got the idea of how much I may have been fined or whatever, but they did understand not to fish again for bass using a cast net.

Now having told that slightly humorous tale of illegal fishing, they at least knew where to fish. First and most obvious, fish are in the water. Second fish are often around structure; a bridge, boat dock, tree stumps and the like. Third, you have to go to them. The fish are not likely to swim over and jump in your boat or jump up on dry land next to you and surrender.

Those are principles we believers should know and use in evangelism (fishing for men). We know where the fish (lost) are. They are out in the water (the world). They are not in the boat (the church). They are out there around the bridges, boat docks and tree stumps (work, recreation and business places) that we frequent in our own daily lives.

So church, you and me (not the building), we're the boat. Let's go to where they are and in love, offer them Jesus. While we're at, let's make sure they know they can come to Him anytime, anywhere (meaning just as they are, right where they are). Because Jesus is just like all fishermen, He catches His fish before He cleans them.

Effective In the Kingdom — March 24

I am convinced that we cannot be effective in the Kingdom without growth in our own lives through the disciplined study of God's Word.

It seems to me that the enemy, if he is unable to keep us from being saved, would as his second option, desire for us to be ineffective as believers, thereby thwarting the will of God for us to further His Kingdom.

It is as if we were at our favorite amusement park standing in line for our favorite ride. We have our ticket and we are waiting for our turn to get through the gate to the ride. Others are gathering around, frantically looking for the ticket salesman. They are trying to buy a ticket to get into the gate, but to no avail. They have no idea that the tickets are free or how to get them! We know where the "Ticket Man" is but we are not about to get out of line (our comfort zone) and show them where He is, besides, we have our ticket.

The enemy knows we are saved, but to those without a ticket, we may as well not be saved. We would be useless in the Kingdom! How do we become more and more effective in and for the Kingdom? Obedience to God and His Word.

Obedience to His Word requires the knowledge of what He says to us in His Word. Sounds elementary, doesn't it? What to do is not hard to understand. It is the willingness and discipline to follow through in attaining the knowledge of the Word. He wants us to obediently apply His Word to our lives as His witnesses. Study, disciplined study. We need to make a focused, committed, daily, unstoppable effort to get His Word into our hearts, mind and character. This effort will produce the boldness, knowledge, discernment and desire to jump out of line and take them straight to the Ticket Man, who has already paid for all the tickets.

Do not merely listen to the word, and so deceive yourselves. Do what it says. Anyone who listens to the word but does not do what it says is like someone who looks at his face in a mirror and, after looking at himself, goes away and immediately forgets what he looks like. But whoever looks intently into the perfect law that gives freedom, and continues in it—not forgetting what they have heard, but doing it—they will be blessed in what they do. – James 1:22-25

Are We Safe March 25

My favorite line from *The Lion, The Witch and the Wardrobe* is in response to the question asked about Aslan, "Is he safe?" The answer was: "Course he isn't safe. But he's good." That is how I view our God.

He is good, and yes, He is full of grace and mercy. He is also just and righteous. You don't have to read very far in the Bible to figure out that there are consequences for sin and disobedience. So where has the "fear of God" gone?

I believe in large part the church has been subdued by the "fear of man." It just seems easier to go with the flow, not upset the apple cart, and to be approved by men and not rejected. Wasn't our Savior despised and rejected. I'm not saying we should go out and tick people off so as to get rejected. I'm saying we should try to live our lives as the Lord leads us, and not be surprised by rejection of men.

We can easily be *safe* Christians. We can know the Word, but if we're not living it, then we are playing it *safe* to gain the approval of men. We're just staying off the radar so we don't become a target of rejection. We can easily live in the safety of man-pleasing flesh because it has little risk or danger of rejection. You can talk about church or even your God.

Yet if you start living by the Spirit and obeying God's word, all of the sudden the road of man's acceptance becomes very slippery. Go ahead and mention your personal relationship with Jesus and that no one comes to the Father but by Him and you could be spinning out of the *fear of man* into a rejection train wreck! On the other hand, you could be showing someone with an accepting heart the love of God and the way to salvation. Is it worth the risk?

There is absolutely a sea of souls out there living to please men in hopes of gaining their acceptance and approval. Are we as believers just going to cruise by them in our safe ship of salvation or are we going to be a lifeboat offering to throw them the Life Preserver and pray they accept Him? Be careful how you answer this one. It is not *safe*. These rescue attempts are often very dangerous as there are high seas, heavy winds of anger and rejection in these waters.

Acts 4:1-21

Do It Over — March 26

I really enjoy watching a good game of football. And although I am amazed at how many calls the referees get wrong or miss, the replay rules have really slowed down the pace of the game. For instance, the score can be close and a team is moving the ball. Momentum is on their side, the excitement is building and then – a guy catches a pass near the sidelines. The opposing coach throws his challenge flag and it's, "Stop everything while we take five or ten to see if the receiver stayed in bounds." Aaaahhh! Sometimes you can go to the bathroom and hit the kitchen for a chicken leg and a glass of tea before they make their decision!

When I was a kid, we had our own Replay Rules. If during a baseball game in the neighborhood a dispute broke out over say a hit ball being fair or foul or a close call for out or safe, we would simply "do it over." If we were playing football and an argument breaks out over out of bounds or if a pass was complete or not, just "do it over." No long delays, no rules discussion, just forget it and do it over. I can't tell you how many times we would just do it over.

"Do it over" was the greatest rule ever made! We didn't keep fighting and arguing, we would just do it over and keep playing.

Wouldn't it be great if we lived life by the Do It Over Rule? If your spouse does something you don't like or if you offend him or her, just forget it and do it over, like it never happened. Or there is a business dispute and someone wants to sue someone else, forget it and just do it over. We have an dispute with our parents, just forget it and do it over.

Easier said than done, right? But we do have an example to follow. Surely God desires for us to "stay in bounds." Yet we have wronged, sinned against, and in so many other ways let God down. But Jesus hung there on a cross and in different words He said: You know, I'm going to just forget it, go ahead and do it over. And, if we are truly repentant, He says that to us as many times as we need it.

Go ahead, Do It Over!

Come On In For Sin   March 27

Temptation seems like a door that the Satan leaves unlocked. He may use sly tactics to get us to the door but, truthfully, we can often see it as clearly as if a sign on the door said: "Come On In For Sin."

In the Garden, just before He was arrested, Jesus told the disciples: "Watch and pray so that you will not fall into temptation" (Matthew 26:41). If I did this I would no doubt have fewer sins for which I would have to ask His forgiveness. Preventive prayer you might say.

Satan will tempt us at our weakest point. "The spirit is willing, but the body is weak." We all know our flesh's weak link. We should be aware, prayed up and on watch, at the enemies point of attack.

Our comfort should come in these:

We have One (Jesus) who has been tempted in every way, just as we are, yet was without sin. – Hebrews 4:15

Because He Himself suffered when He was tempted, He is able to help those who are being tempted. – Hebrews 2:18

We should also remember this:

No temptation has seized you except what is common to man. And God is faithful; He will not let you be tempted beyond what you can bear. But when you are tempted, He will also provide a way out so that you can stand up under it. – 1 Corinthians 10:13

Right now, before we are tempted, we should ask God to keep us from falling into temptation. Also ask Him to strengthen us at our weak points. When it comes to temptation, He has been there without falling. He knows the way out, so He can guide us through, if we will follow Him.

Wide Open In First Gear — March 28

Do we spend too much time in the drive-thru? Is that a contradiction in terms? Most of the world that I live in seems to be running wide open in first gear! If you don't know what I mean, think about putting your car in first and staying on the gas without shifting into second and third. The engine is working as hard and as fast as it can, but not really getting as far down the road as it should, using all that energy.

Advanced countries (U.S. for example) have become obsessed with quick. I understand managing our time wisely. But I do not believe that the quicker we do things automatically shows we are good stewards of our time. From the Kingdom perspective, I think the wisest, most productive, fruitful, rewarding and joyful thing we can do with our time is spend it in relationship with God and those He puts in our life.

Think about your favorite meal. Does it come out of your oven at home after careful preparation or through the drive-thru window, as you rush alone to your next chore?

I remember as a little boy it seemed my family always had a home-cooked dinner together. Looking back, I loved those times and appreciate the family bond those dinners help to build.

I realize that our families can be spread out and have different schedules, but if we can manage our time for quickness, we can certainly manage it for some time together. For that matter, we probably have friends that would like a home-cooked meal more than stopping by the drive-thru to get something on the way home, to eat alone.

Of course this is not just about eating. It's about spending our own time where, and more importantly with whom it will really matter in the long run.

Spending time with God will give us faith, hope, love, strength and closeness to Him. Spending time with others will give them these things from Him through us, not to mention we're getting more ourselves.

Spending our time at Kingdom speed is like shifting the gears in your car. Shifting to a higher gear may seem like the engine isn't running as hard, but we're getting a lot further down the road.

The Dream Of God's Protection   March 29

I can't remember more than five dreams I've had in my life that I would say were from God. But the other night I had one of those dreams. I hesitate even to post it here because of it's content. I also have second thoughts about telling this story because when I hear people say God told me such and such, frankly, I'm skeptical. Especially when it is someone I don't know. But it is what it is, so here's the dream.

My son and I were in a car going up a hill on a four lane highway. I was driving. As we crested the hill several cars come right at us (going the wrong way) in our lanes. There is no time to react; the front car hits us head on. It is a very hard lick at highway speeds. However, we are still moving forward, I think the other car went over the top of us after the collision.

My initial reaction, after realizing we were still moving, was to avoid the rest of the oncoming traffic. As I frantically ask my son if he is OK, I instinctively swerve to the right to get off the road but it is a steep hillside that is certain disaster. I jerked the steering wheel the other direction, back onto the roadway, missing the oncoming traffic in the near lane and crossing into the far lane that is now miraculously clear of vehicles!

I now quickly glance over to my son to see that he is stunned and has some cuts, but no critical wounds. In the rear view, I can see that I have also sustained similar but non-critical wounds. We make our way off the highway and end up slowly coasting through an upscale neighborhood. (What's that about? Future reward? Heaven?)

When I woke up, God spoke into my spirit and said: "He can't even knock you guys out, much less take you out."

You see, my son and I have been "going through the wringer" lately. God was showing me that when He protects us, the enemy can't take us down. Maybe we didn't have the armor on (Ephesians 6:10-18) quite tight enough, or maybe sometimes soldiers get wounded even with their armor on; whatever, we were protected!

Something else came to me and was confirmed when I told my son about the dream. When we crossed back into the traffic to the far lane, that wasn't a normal reaction, but it saved us.

Trust in the Lord with all your heart and lean not on your own understanding; in all your ways acknowledge Him, and He will make your paths straight. – Proverbs 3:5-6

Moving Up The Food ChainMarch 30

One of the bigger, ongoing battles I personally come up against in my flesh is the desire for the approval of man. I've wanted to be "The Man", "The Boss", "The Leader" or "The Pastor," just to name a few. I believe these can be good and honorable desires if we have the right heart, motives and calling to these positions. The trouble for me has often been my desires and motives were often based (at least partly) on pleasing man to advance myself in their eyes and move up on the earthly "food chain."

Sometimes this has resulted in a pat on the back, a raise in pay or position, material gifts, etc. This is about what we can expect from our efforts in our own power. Give a fleshly effort here on this earth and get a fleshly reward here on earth, where it's going to stay when we go. And we will go!

My latest confrontation with "wanting to be somebody" was recently when a pastoral job came open at a church. I have held church staff positions in the past, but I think God had to work overtime to make "all things work together for good" in those situations because of a lot of my fleshly efforts.

On a previous occasion when I was offered a staff job in a church, I prayed about it and declined, but some of that was a fleshly decision, although is was better in that instance for that particular church that I not take the position. They hired the right person.

In this instance, I quickly filled out and sent in the preliminary application (believing there was some urgency on the church's part). However, after praying and seeking God on the matter and trying to view the needs of this church for this position, it became clear that I am not "The Man" for this position.

I don't believe God judges us on how high up we are on man's "food chain." I believe He wants us in the position that best uses the gifts He gave us to accomplish His will in the kingdom. That means the pressure is off to fight my way up some ladder of importance in man's eyes. The pressure being off is a real relief and it allows me to focus on where He is leading me. Not to mention that I like and feel comfortable where He is leading me because I will be using the gifts He gave me. I pray I will always be seeking Him and not a position.

Pop 'em   March 31

O.K., answer truthfully! Aren't there times when someone says something about you that makes you want to pop 'em right in the mouth? They may tell someone something you told them in confidence. Maybe they're telling lies about you. Possibly they're just a jerk picking a fight. These are the times the "two-hit solution" comes to my mind. I hit them, they hit the floor. Problem solved? Not really.

What would God say in situations like this? "Turn the other cheek!" What! Yes, it is for Him to handle, to vindicate us, to correct or avenge as He sees fit. Yet, for me, one of the hardest things in life is to leave a personal assault on me in the hands of someone else, even God. I want justice and I want it immediately! Funny, isn't it, that when I mess up, I want mercy. When someone messes with me, I want justice.

In many, many of the Psalms, David ask God to rescue him from those who seek to kill and overthrow him.

For instance, David knew for many years He was going to be Israel's King. Though he was chased by Saul (who was trying to kill him) and even though David had several opportunities to kill Saul, he left it to God to deliver him.

Again, when his son Absalom was chasing him, David left his situation in God's hands. David was king and probably could have raised an Army and slaughtered Absalom. Instead David sought God for his rescue.

Time after time, when someone came against David personally, he sought God for vindication and deliverance. When David trusted God in his predicament, God came through for him.

When I think back over the times I let God handle attacks on me personally, the results were always better than when I took matters into my own hands.

Besides, sometimes the "two hit solution" backfires and there are two more hits, if you know what I mean!

HOWEVER

There are those times when I believe we should go ahead and "pop'em in the mouth" as many times as it takes to stop the oppressor! The correct time to do this is in defense of others, especially those who cannot defend themselves against their attackers.

Instances like this can be seen when people verbally assault others, in physical abuses and all- out wars. In these cases it is not only right, but godly, to go to the aid of the victims. This aid we offer could be prayerful, verbal, financial, or physically forceful to the extent necessary to stop the assault.

Why do I think that "turning the other cheek" is right and godly when we are personally attacked while advocating "busting the cheek" of someone else's attacker? Because that's the way Jesus lived. He took all the abuse His attackers could dish out without turning them to dust! He "turned the other cheek" right on through the cross and His death. That's when Satan thought he had us. That's when Jesus came to our defense; saving us when we couldn't save ourselves. He came right up out of that tomb and busted Satan right in the mouth!

Ice Cream And Coffee — April 1

Opening day of Dixie Youth Baseball was always a fun day for me. I think the boys liked it too. Anyway, it was the first day of baseball for them. On the first Saturday in April, every team would have a game. The ballpark was buzzing with activity.

Besides baseball, there were all kinds of carnival type booths with games and prizes. There were concession stands everywhere, selling all sorts of food, drinks, and candy. All these concessions and game booths were sponsored by individual teams so as to raise money for teams expenses in the coming season. It took a good piece of change to fund a team for several months and Opening Day fund raising was a big part of covering those expenses.

Just prior to Opening Day, each team would draw a number and choose what kind of booth or concession they wanted to host Opening Day. This was done so as not to duplicate effort (twelve hamburger stands would spread the money kind of thin).

One year, a team had an Ice Cream stand. It was a nice day and they sold popsicles and ice cream cones like they were free! Right then I said to myself: "If I ever draw a low number for Opening Day concession, we're selling ice cream!"

Well, well, I drew #1 the next season. I was fired up! Our team bought a boat load of ice cream to sell. We were going to raise a whole season worth of money in one day!

Not exactly. The night before Opening Day it snowed! In North Florida! We didn't sell five popsicles the next day but the team selling donuts and coffee made a killing. Maybe consulting a weather forecast a week in advance would have benefited me a little.

I can think of occurrences in the Bible where men of God (ex: Moses striking the rock) decided to do something the same way as before (without asking God) because that's the way it worked the last time.

We need to be sure of this: We need to seek God for guidance. He may want us to get the same result as in a previous situation by using a different method. His reasons may not be known to us, only Him. But in all situations He will be faithful. We need only to seek Him and obey Him.

So Bright I Couldn't See The Light   April 2

    Have you ever used a "scanner," aka, a "hand held barcode reader"? I carry one of these electronic marvels with me on the job every day. I have to scan all sorts of items, including packages, deliveries requiring signatures, and certain designated locations along my route. By the way, we delivery personnel have been assured that scanning these "certain" locations is not being done to keep track of us but to insure quality service. Yeah, right!

    Anyway, these scanners shine a green light when you mash the trigger. The idea is to aim the green light at the barcode and it will "beep" when it reads the barcode. The beep lets you know the scanner has stored the information.

    It was very bright outside today and as I scanned one of the location barcodes, it didn't beep. Immediately the thought came to me that, *"it's so bright I can't see the (green) light."* Only "green" was not part of the phrase that came to mind, just, *"it's so bright I can't see the light."* This phrase put me into what I now call "spiritual decipher mode."

    I am going through some difficult situations in my own life right now and God is using them to teach me many things. Is that the way it is a lot of the time? God has to get our attention because when things are going good, we act as if we don't need Him as much. That's the way it was for me.

    I had a big house and so much money I didn't even use a budget (that's sorry stewardship), and I had it under control. I was on "spiritual cruise control." The things of this world were going great for me. My world was "so bright I couldn't see the Light."

    So the Lord, in His love for me, slapped the "shade glasses of humility" on me and dimmed my "bright world!" I emphasize, " in His love for me." He is the perfect Father and "He disciplines those He loves." So if our world seems bright right now lets be sure to put on the shades (cloak) of humility because if we don't He just might set us down and put 'em on for us.

    And have you completely forgotten this word of encouragement that addresses you as a father addresses his son? It says, "My son, do not make light of the Lord's discipline, and do not lose heart when he rebukes you, because the Lord disciplines the one he loves, and he chastens everyone he accepts as his son." Endure hardship as discipline; God is treating you as his children. For what children are not disciplined by their father? – Hebrews 12:5-7

The Feed Store   April 3

I really like the idea of life in a small farm town. I've never lived in one, but the idea of a hard working, moral, love thy neighbor kind of community just appeals to me deep down in my core. Some will say it's fantasy, but I think they're out there somewhere.

You've seen movies with this kind of setting. The farmers meet at the feed store. They talk and spend time together in an unrushed way. They drink a cup of coffee and catch up on each others lives. They will joke and laugh. They have things to do, but they always have time for a friend or a neighbor. They care and will help one another. They encourage each other and share information and knowledge about farming, such as how to prepare the soil, what's good to plant, how to take care of a crop while it grows and then how to harvest it.

I see the local church as the "feed store" and the church members as the "farmers." It's good to go to the feed store and see friends, fellowship with them, be encouraged and learn how to be a better farmer. The deal is we can't just stay at the feed store and expect to be able to harvest a crop. The inside of the feed store won't provide very a large field for harvest. We might have an indoor plant growing a little fruit over by the window, but that's hardly a good harvest. We, as godly farmers, should take what we learn at the feed store to our own fields to plant, nurture and harvest a crop.

Jesus said : "The harvest is plentiful but the workers are few." – Matthew 9:37

That has got to be some of the saddest words to come out of Jesus' mouth.

The feed store is a great place, but does it really do any good to learn how to grow a crop and then never go work in the field?

Pass The Torch   April 4

On opening day of the 2010 Major League Baseball season in Atlanta there was a "passing of the torch." Hall of Famer Hank Aaron threw out the ceremonial first pitch to rookie phenom Jason Heyward. This act expressed the hopes of fans, players and owners of the team. It was an exciting time for the Braves with optimism renewed, thanks in no small part to arrival of this talented young man.

Jason obviously has God-given gifts, but along with those gifts someone has already passed the torch on to him in the areas of knowledge, strategies and honing his physical skills to be able to play the game of baseball so well. Someone has taken their own time to train him how to best use his gifts and talents.

We all can pass a torch. We need a fire to pass and we need to be willing to spend the necessary time with someone to pass the torch on to them.

The Word of God is the knowledge and instruction we need to live a life pleasing to God. A simplistic analogy would be that the Bible is the "textbook for life." But it always helps to have a teacher to guide us through the textbook. A good teacher knows what is in the textbook and how to apply that knowledge correctly to achieve the best results.

If you want to develop your gifts and talents, get the Textbook and seek out a Teacher. Be bold and ask them (challenge them) to guide you.

If you are a teacher (you know who you are), pass the torch. One torch can start a lot of fires.

And the things you have heard me say in the presence of many witnesses entrust to reliable men who will also be qualified to teach others. – 2 Timothy 2:2

Out On The Route   April 5

For the most part I like my job. I go in to work at 7:30 am. I usually case up mail for about two hours, then the rest of the day I am out on the street delivering mail. I personally enjoy being outside and moving around throughout the day.

I actually remember when I was younger, having not had my license very long, thinking, "I'd like to have a job that I can just drive around all day." I guess I was thinking more along the lines of being a truck driver like Sonny Pruitt. Remember that TV show *Moving On*? Yes, you do!

Anyway, I have over 800 possible deliveries a day. This affords me the opportunity to meet, talk to and get to know a lot of different people. I deliver to all sorts of "characters," young and old, rich and poor, down to earth people, and a few, I swear, are from outer space! I have been cussed at and praised, smiled at and been given ugly stares. My day is rarely boring.

Two particular characters come to mind. Both, I assume, are retired, because they are always home. Hardly a day goes by that they don't meet me at their mailboxes. Truthfully, these are the guys I love to avoid.

The first one, we will call "H". He must watch out his window for me every morning, because as I turn around at the end of the block to head back up his side of the street, "H" is on his way out the door. I have gotten to the point that I will separate his mail at the end of the street, just so I could hand it to him on the way by. I'll give him the customary, "How ya doin?" "Here's your mail". "See ya tomorrow," hit the gas, and I'm outta there!

He usually manages to get out one of the two most original comments a mailman ever hears; "Just gimme the checks," or "Keep the bills!" In days gone by, I have been so inclined as to tell people spewing these original comments at me to, "Go turn your stinkin AC off if you don't like the electric bill!" But now, having a Christian attitude, I hand off the mail and hit the gas.

The other guy, we will call "Q". "Q" is on the afternoon side of my route and is a strange fellow, who also likes to talk. Usually, he wants to give me the daily gossip in a list of complaints about the neighbors or how the street crew screwed up the ditch in front of his house. These two characters may sound amusing to you, but at my daily expense!

Well, you'll never guess what happened as I whined about these characters to myself in my thoughts the other day. That's right, God started talking to me.

He says, "Hey Greg, don't you get two breaks each day?"

"Yes, God."

"One in the morning?" He says.

"Yes, God," I reply.

"One in the afternoon?"

"Yes, God."

He says, "These guys just want to talk. You could talk to them, be their friend, pay them some attention, tell them about Me. Don't you remember that Great Commission sermon you preached?"

"Ouch," I reply.

Do you know, I used to see those guys almost every day. I haven't seen either one of them since God said that to me about a week ago?

"God, I'm sorry. I pray I haven't missed an opportunity while I was avoiding them."

...to be continued...I pray...

The Comfort Zone   April 6

Did you ever get to a place in your walk with God that you said, "This will do."? What I mean is, did you or have you come to a place to spiritually set up camp, and figure on making it permanent? Right here is good. This is enough God for me. I can handle this and like it too. Spiritually, life becomes easy, safe, predictable, with no risk because we have it down to a fine, manageable art. There is no risk because there is no real need to trust God. It's the spiritual rut. In "Christian-ese" we call it our "Comfort Zone."

It's where ministry goes to die. It may have not started out that way. You may have come from a previous Comfort Zone. Wasn't the trip worth it? As we walk with God, we strengthen our faith as we trust and obey Him, and as a result of that obedience we see Him work in our lives and the lives of others.

It's not like you have to leave where you are (sometimes you may) or stop what you're doing. It's more like spreading out spiritually, growing into more of what God has for us and more of what He is calling us to do.

Faith is like a muscle; it's not going to grow unless you work it out. Once we've gotten all we can get out of lifting a certain amount of weight, then that's as much as the muscle is going to grow. Is it time to put on a little more weight to our "spiritual barbells"?

So, have you been feeling safe but bored in your walk with God? Have you felt Him tugging at you to come along with Him a little further. There are new adventures of service for God and closeness to Him, if we will just go with Him. It takes an added measure of faith and trust in God to to leave a comfortable place. But isn't that what it will take to grow?

So, go on and get! He knows where He's taking you. Besides, He's going with you!

The Perfect Ending to the Perfect Game   April 7

There have been less than thirty perfect games thrown in all Major League Baseball history. Last week the third perfect game of this season was thrown. This has never happened three times in one season. However, there will only be two in the record books (barring another one later this year).

A perfect game in baseball is a most rare event. It only occurs when no batters on one team reach base throughout an entire game. No hits by the batters, no walks by the pitcher, no errors by the fielders, 27 up, 27 down. It's better than a shut out, it's better than a no hitter; no single game accomplishment is better. It's perfect!

The other night there was such a game. Perfect to this point; with two out in the ninth inning, Armando Galarraga gets the twenty-seventh batter to hit a ground ball to the first baseman who fields and throws to Galarraga covering first. The batter is clearly out. Perfect Game! Oops! No! The umpire, Jim Joyce calls the batter safe! The place goes bonkers, he was clearly out. In "Baseball Heaven," this is a terrible sin! "Baseball Earth" wants justice now!

Instead, what happens? The umpire reviews the video of the play and confesses he missed the call; the batter was out. The umpire is truly distraught and no doubt wishes he could take the call back, but he can't. Later, Galaragga (the pitcher) forgives the umpire publicly!

Yet the call will not be changed and the record books will not record this perfect game. A tragedy in the history of baseball? Or a "perfect" example of the healing power of forgiveness.

Hope or Fear, It's a Choice   April 8

While delivering mail to a house one morning I noticed the front door had been kicked in. It was obvious; a big shoe print, a busted door jamb and wood splinters everywhere. With the possibility that the intruder was still inside, I delivered the mail normally. I then returned to my jeep and went to call the police.

The police dispatcher ask if I could observe the house until the officer's arrival to see if anyone came out. I positioned myself a block away behind a house and waited. In just a few minutes the officer arrived. I met her at the house as she proceeded inside (with her gun drawn). She ask me to wait at the door in case the intruder was still there and got by her.

Ideas of this giant burglar (like the cartoons when I was a kid) go through my head. I was thinking: "Sure, I'm supposed to stop this monster that is able to get by a trained officer with a gun! Great!" Anyway, she clears the house and comes out. The thief is gone with some electronics, jewelry and probably cash.

Now I have been in scarier situations than that, but for some reason I was rattled pretty good. I was fearful maybe, that a gun was already out and that I may face an unknown adversary unarmed. I'm talking about the fear that we let grip us that squeezes out our hope. Fear often rears its head in a time of testing of our faith. Yet we need to hold to our hope in Christ and not be chained by fear.

I know in the flesh this is easier said than done. But if we ask Him to give us the power not only to not fear, but instead be filled with hope and believe what we say we believe, then as followers of Christ, whatever the outcome in any situation, He will take care of us. Whether, in natural terms, that outcome is good (no burglar coming out the door), or not so good as in getting run over or beat up by an escaping intruder, or even as terrible as a death. No matter what, if we trust in Jesus and believe what we say we believe, He is faithful and will take care of us.

Satan wants us to be full of fear. Jesus wants us to be filled with hope. It's all in who we choose to follow. The giver of hope or the author of fear.

A Verbal Mugging — April 9

So I wrote a blog about loving our neighbor and showing others the love of Christ. Then I blew a fuse at my boss the next afternoon. Perfect!

I got back off of my route in plenty of time to make it home and get ready for my men's group that was coming over to my house. We're going to grill some food, eat, talk about life, study a little of the Word, and pray together. It seemed as if the timing would work out fine and that was a relief, after having to work past 6pm the day before. But no!

I returned to the office, got checked in and prepared to go home for the day. Then the boss tells me he wants me to go back out and help someone else on their route! I haven't been sent back out after returning for the day in months. Not to mention there were people junior to me who had returned that he could send out instead. For reasons that only make sense to him, he wanted me to go.

I proceeded to verbally light him up! Aw yeah, there it was, a perfect example and testimony of showing the love of God to my fellow man! During my tirade, I informed him that I had plans for company to be coming over to eat at my house. I didn't mention it was for a Bible study! I left that part out, realizing that I was not behaving like someone who was making any effort to follow what the Bible said about how to behave in this type of situation.

There are people at my work who know that I am trying to follow Jesus. Some read my blog. I have told them that I want any change in me to be real, not some fake piety that is not real. They see my screw-ups, and they happen more often than I want them to happen. Still, I refuse to be a hypocrite and act as if I am perfect. I am not. That's the big reason I need Jesus. I'm sorry for the way I handled that situation and I pray I do better the next time.

Having said that, I believe people need to see not only people behaving in a Christ-like manner, but they also need to see and know that believers are far from perfect. Believers need the love, grace, mercy and forgiveness from God as much as anyone else. Just because we are believers doesn't mean we have it all together. Those that portray they have perfection down or think that they are better than others are fakes and are doing the kingdom a disservice of hypocrisy; that does nothing but turn non-believers away!

People need to see that God loves us and will forgive us. He is a God with a hug, not a hammer, if we will only fall into His arms.

Number 12   April 10

When I was in my late teens and early twenties, my friends and I played a lot of golf. We knew the people quite well at one particular course where we often played. On weekends on which they required tee times, they would allow us to go off the back nine at the crack of dawn. We would finish the back nine before our front nine tee time and thereby be able to play 27 holes that day.

One particular Saturday morning, we were on the tee at number 12 by about 6:45 am, it's a short Par 3 of about 150 yards. It was a straight, unobstructed shot to a flat green with a extreme slope falling off one side of the green. We were playing for real score. No mulligans (taking shots over).

I stepped up and hit a beautiful high shot that looked as if it was going straight for the hole. Our excitement built while the ball was in flight as we anticipated the coolest shot in golf, the "Hole in One." I had never made a hole in one. I still haven't.

The ball did come down right into the cup and then bounced out very high, hitting on the green once before trickling slowly, tragically down that steep slope into the heavy grass below. I must confess that back in that day, at that moment, I was inventing new cuss words to scream at the top of my lungs. I probably woke up everyone in the houses surrounding the green at number 12! I made a bogey 4 on the hole where my tee shot had bounced out of the hole.

The rest of the day went great. I hit plenty of great shots that day and creamed my friends. But winning the game isn't the memory I take away from that day, and that's just wrong thinking on my part.

In my daily life, I do this way too often. I dwell on the things I did wrong (sin and mistakes) instead of keeping my eye on the prize so as to be victorious in the end, when the "game" of life on this earth is over.

It's the enemy's plan to try to focus us back to what we have done wrong; things that we obviously can't go back and change or take a mulligan on.

It is God's plan however, to provide us forgiveness for our sin and give us healing and a way of correcting and moving beyond our mistakes.

Lets not dwell on what went wrong, but persevere on to the next place He sends us. Lets keep our eyes on the prize, because what matters is who we belong to at the end of the game, not how many bad shots we hit or bad breaks we encountered.

With our God, we don't need a mulligan!

Expose The Cover Up — April 11

The Lord does not look at the things man looks at. Man looks at the outward appearance, but the Lord looks at the heart. – 1 Samuel 16:7

OK, don't tell anybody this, but when I was a young teenager, I could grow these monster zits. They would have a nice red color with a yellow peak that looked like a volcano of snot was about to erupt all over my mug! This story gets better. I would try to keep some kind of zit cream around to dry them up and more importantly, cover them up. This cream had a flesh color to it like women's makeup. I would cake this stuff on trying to cover up zit mountain. And if I ran out of the zit medicine, yep, I slipped into Mom's makeup stash and got myself some coverage!

People often wear makeup to make their appearance more pleasing to others and themselves. This ranges from a slight bit of makeup to blend skin tones to the ridiculously caked on rainbow of colors that looks like someone was hit in the face with a four year old's birthday cake! The point is this; many of us want to cover up what we perceive as our flaws. Makeup is a tool used by many to cover up these perceived imperfections.

Phony Christianity and religiosity is the makeup of today's Pharisee. I've worn this makeup too! It is available in many shades (as in shady and fake). Some of the more popular shades are: "More Holy Than Thou," "You'll Never See Me Sin," "I See Your Sin," and the hottest shade sold out of the back of the truck, "You're Going To Hell!"

I have the desire to be who God wants me to be, but it will certainly take His power to make the changes in me for that change to be real. I will mess up along the way (some zits will pop up), but even in that, others will see the Love, Grace, and Mercy of my Lord. So, I won't wear any more religious makeup. And I'm not going to be faking it!

Testimony Is The Name Of My Truck   April 12

When God does something in her life, Hannah says she had a "God moment." This entire truck buying experience has been a "God event" for me!

From the availability of the funds, to the knowing it was specifically to be spent on a truck, to the waiting for the right truck, to only looking at the two trucks we looked at Monday (physically going to see and drive them) and having the (God-given) patience to wait a month or more to get the right truck – it was a "God month!"

When we got in to test drive the truck Monday, the radio was on a Christian radio station. Ryan and I both noticed that as well as how kind the gentleman was who was selling the truck. He was patient and answered all of our questions.

Yesterday we went to pick up the truck. When we were all done with the business, and we were getting in the truck to leave, I mentioned to him that I wrote blog and that I had written about my experiences of that Monday. I told him the name of the site if he would like to read my story. He did. This is his reply:

Greg,

I'm so glad that you are happy with your new truck. As we discussed, it was my father's pride and joy and it was sad for us to let it go. I remember the day he drove to Mississippi to pick it up – he was so proud when he got back with it. Unfortunately his health didn't let him enjoy it for long but even in his last months, whenever one of his friends would come pick him up to get him out of the house, he would insist that they drive him in his shiny red pickup.

I told you today that my venture to Florida has been one of great faith and tremendous blessings. I moved over here last February for a new job and lived the first week in a hotel that I really couldn't afford. After my first week I had to move into a place that I was literally sick to my stomach all night due to the environment I was in. I prayed that night that I would find a decent temporary home until my family would move over in the next few months. The next morning, one of my coworkers received a call from someone who was looking to rent a garage apartment at a very reasonable cost. During the next few months, we searched for a permanent home and had almost given up hope when one Saturday morning we started out to look at a long list of homes that were overpriced and under-kept and we happened upon a sign on the side of the road. We called the owner and set up a meeting the next day and were amazed to find that it was within our price range and much nicer than we had ever expected. He had just put the sign out the morning we saw it! We are now in a great neighborhood with wonderful Christian neighbors and know that the Lord has provided for us once again.

I am so happy to know that you attribute finding my dad's truck to be a part of God's design. The loss of our father last month has been difficult to deal with but I know that he is looking down from above and very proud that its purchase has become a part of your witness to others.

Take care (of yourself and the truck),
Thank you, and God bless!

If a truck ever had a name, this one is TESTIMONY!

Checking In Or Checking Out   April 13

In some western movies, when the sheriff was trying to keep peace in a rowdy town, he would make the cowboys check their guns at his office when they rode into town. Then they could pick up their weapons as they left town because the cowboys would be need their guns for hunting and protection.

We also check our coats as we go inside a fancy restaurant. We check our luggage prior to boarding an airplane. But, when we leave the restaurant, we pick up our coats and put them on because it's cold outside. After the plane lands we retrieve our luggage so we are able to change clothes on our trip.

The sheriff realized the cowboys needed their guns when they left town, not in the saloon. We need our coats outside in the cold because it rarely snows inside a restaurant. We need our luggage after the plane ride, not in our laps in a little airplane seat.

So, what are the "weapons, coats and luggage" of the Christian going out into the world today? The Word (in our hearts and in a book), our testimony, our faith, our salvation, our character, our attitude, our love for God and others, just to mention a few.

Unfortunately, I'm afraid it appears to the world that we have it backwards. That we as Christians put on our weapons, coats and luggage as we enter church on Sunday. Then as we leave church we check all our weapons, coats and luggage of our Christianity at the door on the way out! Left there to be picked up for an hour next Sunday.

This is just what the devil wants us to do. If we're going to call ourselves believers, just let it be for an hour a week, then go around "unarmed" the rest of the time!

No, if we are going to hunt (evangelize), share our coat (comfort others), or use our luggage (the gifts and talents He has given us), then we don't check them on the way out of church. We take them with us! We're going to need them out there.

Finally, be strong in the Lord and in his mighty power. Put on the full armor of God, so that you can take your stand against the devil's schemes. For our struggle is not against flesh and blood, but against the rulers, against the authorities, against the powers of this dark world and against the spiritual forces of evil in the heavenly realms. Therefore put on the full armor of God, so that when the day of evil comes, you may be able to stand your ground, and after you have done everything, to stand. Stand firm then, with the belt of truth buckled around your waist, with the breastplate of righteousness in place, and with your feet fitted with the readiness that comes from the gospel of peace. In addition to all this, take up the shield of faith, with which you can extinguish all the flaming arrows of the evil one. Take the helmet of salvation and the sword of the Spirit, which is the word of God. And pray in the Spirit on all occasions with all kinds of prayers and requests. With this in mind, be alert and always keep on praying for all the Lord's people.
– Ephesians 6:10-18

Unity...Really — April 14

This subject is where "theologians lock horns like deer out in the woods and wallow around until they die." (A.W. Tozer, *The Attributes of God: A Journey into the Father's Heart*. Christian Publications. 2003.)

A friend posted this quote of Tozer. I loved it and it got me to thinking.

Many years ago I went with a group of people to a debate. I won't mention the subject, so as not to create the debate here, but suffice to say it was over a difference in theology that certainly will not matter in the Kingdom long-term. The participants in the debate were two men of God that many would recognize.

The discussion was cordial enough as it got underway with each man giving his views on the subject. They were almost calm as each responded to the other's view. As they progressed into defending their positions the air went from almost calm to almost tense. The verbal exchanges that followed were intense! At this point the moderator was able to interrupt the combatants and wisely noticed that we were out of time and stopped the fight, I mean, closed the meeting.

I walked out of there wondering what just happened. Two men of God lost their cool in front of an auditorium full of people. I suppose many of the Christians in the room walked out of there pondering the same things I was thinking about, such as: "That display was not a good witness to anyone. It was divisive to the Church. Is this the picture we want to portray to the world? Is the world thinking that Christians run off at the mouth about loving one another and their leaders can't even get along in public?"

It is important to know what we believe. However, it is much more important to know who we believe in and follow His example. The divisiveness in the Church over theology that will change nothing in the Kingdom is like a zit the size of a quarter on our nose. It's gross, it's ugly, everybody sees it, and if we don't clear it up it's going to bust all over us! As Christians we have the same loving, caring, living and active God, no matter what our theology or denomination! Let's act like it!

Love Exam   April 15

Put a check in the blanks beside the attributes of Love you extend to others.

LOVE...

Is Patient __

Is Kind __

Does Not Envy __

Does Not Boast __

Is Not Proud __

Is Not Rude __

Is Not Self Seeking __

Is Not Easily Angered __

Keeps No Record Of Wrongs __

Does Not Delight In Evil __

Rejoices With The Truth __

Always Protects __

Always Trust __

Always Hopes __

Always Perseveres __

Now apply your results to these categories:

Parenthood __

To Parents __

To Spouse __

Other Loved Ones __

Friends __

Poor __

Needy __

Widows __

Orphans __

Lost __

Enemies __

Yeah, I took my own survey ... I don't want to talk about it!

If "love never fails," then why don't we always use it?

Grab 'em   April 16

Isolation is a dangerous and effective tool of the enemy. Divide and conquer. Satan likes to take a perceived or real offense, feeling of self-doubt, insecurity, feeling of not being loved or cared about and other negative emotions to isolate us from one another. He wants to break up our support of one another by any means, even by trying to confuse us about our faith.

To think that we can be all we can, in and for the Kingdom, while we are on this earth, without the support of other believers is plain foolishness!

I can hear it now: "All I need is Jesus. I'm good. I can make it to heaven. All I have to do is hang on and wait it out."

OK, fine. Sit in your box and wait it out!

But answer me this: What does it mean when the Word tells us to not forsake meeting together? What about loving our neighbor? What about "as iron sharpens iron, one man sharpens another"? What about different parts of the body working together as Christ would have us to work? I could go on and on.

If this sounds a little harsh, well good! The enemy has me ticked off about this and it's our own fault! Yes, ours! Those that isolate themselves and those of us who do not or have not reached out to the isolated.

Plainly said, we as believers need to get off our collective butts and reach out to each other. If you're isolated, reach out. If you know of someone isolated, reach out to them. Grab on to each other with the love of Christ and get free from the isolation of the enemy.

Got friends, brothers and sisters? Grab 'em!

Easy, Or Dangerous   April 17

Years ago, my son and I had driven quite a ways to go do some surf fishing at a favorite spot. As we were on our way, the weather was changing from clear, to cloudy and windy. By the time we arrived and got setup, the surf was churned up and the water was brown.

Most days like this don't hold much promise for surf fishing. However, we had driven about twenty miles and so decided to stay and wet a line anyway.

Somewhat to our surprise, we were catching quite a few Whiting. These were not the Pompano we had originally hope to catch, but Whiting are pretty good tasting fish. We started a stringer to keep the fish we caught. We staked it on the beach and threw the other end, with our catch, back into the surf.

We were steadily adding to our catch until we noticed some visitors hanging around our stringer. Out of the surf appeared two 7-8 foot sharks who wanted a share of our catch. Well, that was not happening!

At their first appearance, I simply pulled the stringer of fish out of the surf and up on the beach. When I thought they had left I put the stringer back into the surf to keep the fish alive and fresh. They had not left and this scene repeated itself several times. Each time I returned the stringer to the surf the sharks came back for another shot at a meal. Then I decided to pull the stringer almost all of the way out of the water. The sharks would have to beach themselves to get to our catch now. Well, they tried! The two sharks would actually come partially out of the surf and take a shot at the stringer and ride out on the next wave. I kid you not!

There must have been a lot of Whiting swimming around in that brown surf that day. We were catching a lot of them and the sharks were obviously in there after them. But what seemed to be the easiest and biggest meal to these sharks was probably the most dangerous and life-threatening to them. If they beach themselves, they'll die one way or another. They'll die out of the water or my son and I will get them for supper!

I can be like those sharks sometimes. I know that I have seen a car, house or boat I wanted and I could have it, if I just stick my neck out a little ways to get it. In the times I have stuck my neck "out of the water" to get something I know I shouldn't, I've ended up in a tight, even dangerous position of not being able to "breathe" very well.

God does indeed want to bless us. His blessing us is Him doing the provision and the giving, not us taking what we want or think we need because it appears easy to take. He sees the big picture and the pitfalls that await us when we find ourselves going after things because we are greedy, lustful, or just too lazy to gain a blessing His way.

What appears to be the easy way is often a trap of the enemy.

Eat The Spinach — April 18

My first (TV) hero was none other than Popeye The Sailorman. He was almost always in a conflict of some sort with the bad guy, Bluto. The struggle between the two was usually over the affections of Popeye's girl, Olive Oyl. In each episode Bluto would gain the upper hand and it would seem all was lost, even Olive Oyl. That is until Popeye would find his way to a can of spinach. Eating a can of spinach would, of course, give Popeye superhuman strength. He would then use his new found strength to clobber Bluto, rescue Olive and sail away into the sunset to live happily until the next episode.

As a little sailor man, I of course had to try this out for myself. I think it was my grandmother who provided me with a can of spinach. I ate it cold right out of the can, like my hero. I didn't eat spinach again for forty years!

Seriously, in this life we face struggles of some sort almost daily, just like Popeye. And we all search for a way to cope with and conquer the "Bluto" in our lives. Sometimes we try all kinds of stuff to cope. We try the "ice creams" of the world; such as alcohol, gambling, drugs, self-abuse, etc. Yet there's no victory, we haven't conquered Bluto. The only way to conquer Bluto is to eat the spinach.

Thankfully, in God's Kingdom, spinach comes in three great flavors: God, The Bible and godly counsel. That's right! When we are faced with the struggles of this life we should go get ourselves a can of neopolitan spinach. You can eat it in any flavor first, but it seems best to eat the whole can. It may even taste different from what you're used to eating, but isn't that the point. Besides, you know it's good for you.

Go to God in prayer, seeking His guidance. Read His Word, the Bible. Seek out those men and women of God that you know have been eating their "spiritual spinach" for a long time. I dare you to try a can! In fact, it should be a part of our daily diet. Then we'll be strong anytime Bluto comes along.

The Walk Off Homer   April 19

In the last inning of a baseball game, the most exciting ending for me is the "Walk Off Homer." It happens when the game is tied or the home team is behind and they win the game in their last at bat, when one of their players hits a home run, winning and ending the game.

That's it! It's over, the end, the good guys win!

I have been reading some Psalms of late, where David has prayed to God asking not if, but how much longer before, the Lord has victory over his enemies. The Bible tells of those who, in this life, prosper while not following God, or even flying in the face of God. They become rich and powerful, even evil and destructive.

In our flesh, it may seem that we are defeated and that our enemies have overcome us, and they may well have us down, in the flesh. But the game is not over, until our last at bat. In the bottom of the ninth of each of the believers' lives, and at the end of this world, Jesus Christ will come to the plate and be our last batter. And He will (because He already has) hit death, hell and the grave right out of the park!

That's it, it's over, the new beginning, the good guys win! And there's not one thing the devil or any other evil can do about it! Hallelujah! I'm going to the Tailgate Party in Heaven! See you there?

Got Wisdom   April 20

How about the line from the teacher: "What can we learn from this?" I think that is a question we can ask ourselves as we read the Word of God. Do we apply what we learn from reading the Word? That's another good question. I believe we have a lot more knowledge than we are using

Sometimes we just don't seem to learn. We continue to make the same mistakes over and over again. My mistake is often running my mouth, trying to be funny by picking on someone to the point I have obviously gone overboard.

Other times we do learn from our mistakes. I once left the plug out of the boat as we launched it at the ramp. We launched it, tied it to the dock and pulled the truck to a the parking area. We got some things out of the truck and strolled back to the waiting boat, which now had about eight inches of water in it! Some boat captain! I almost sunk my boat and never left the dock!

Then there are times we learn from others' mistakes. My dad and I were changing drum brakes on my first car. He was rescuing me by helping because I didn't have a clue how to do a brake job. There is a special tool for pulling a very tight spring off of these old style brakes, but it was rather expensive and he thought he could do it with a pair of pliers, as he had done on past brake jobs. He clamps down on the release mechanism for the brake spring with all his might. Then the pliers fly off cracking him in the forehead and it's off to the ER. I have never done my own brake job again!

I've heard it said that not learning from our mistakes is stupid. And that learning from our mistakes is smart. But that learning from someone else's mistakes is wisdom.

It's obvious that if we don't learn from our mistakes, we will commit them over and over again. Along with this behavior, the negative consequences will also continue. If we learn from our mistakes, we will only suffer the consequences one time. If we learn from others' mistakes, we don't have to suffer the consequences. In fact, we could see and hear what the consequences might be, thereby providing a deterrent to making the same mistake over again.

This is just another reason to read the Word. Read it to gain wisdom by learning from others' mistakes. Read the Bible to see the consequences for wrong actions. Read it to see the blessings for obedience. Choose the path of Wisdom. Read it! Apply it!

Maintain The Motor — April 21

I have a nearly new four-stroke outboard motor on my boat. It runs like a top, fast, quiet, and doesn't miss a beat. That is as long as I maintain it and keep it clean on the inside. Part of the maintenance is to pour a fuel treatment in to keep the additives (ethanol) in the gas from clogging the fuel injectors. If those injectors get clogged it's $300 to repair them. When I get back from a fishing trip, I have to hook up the water hose to the motor and run it for a while to flush out the saltwater. Saltwater will damage the motor if it is not washed out after every trip.

This is a crazy analogy I know, but if we look at my boat motor as my relationship to God and the fuel injectors as my spirit that hears from Him, we can see the need to keep ourselves as clean as possible on the inside.

I could easily just wipe off the outside of the boat motor and it would appear to be in great shape. People could be deceived into thinking it is running great. Like a fake smile on our face and pretending to everyone that everything is OK.

However, for our spiritual life to be in good working order, we need to keep the inside of the "motor" clean. We should be regularly reading the Bible (the fuel additive) to keep any build-up of the devil's influence (ethanol) from interfering with the free flow of our relationship (fuel) with God. And yes, it is easier on the motor to run it in freshwater (God's presence), but we do have to go out of the River of God into the ocean of this world and motor around in the saltwater. We will then, without doubt, get some saltwater inside our motor. If that saltwater (the influences of the world) is allowed to remain in our motor it could lead to corrosion (sin) that will cause our motor to run poorly. The remedy is, as quickly as possible, flush out the inside of our motor to keep it in the best working order. Get back in the freshwater, the Living Water, (God's presence) and flush out all that saltwater of the world. Pour some additive (the Word) into the fuel and get ready for the next voyage.

Fair Or Right...Something's Changing   April 22

I hesitate writing blogs along the lines of personal victories for fear of sounding prideful or "bragadocious." However, I hesitate more not writing about personal victories because if I don't, then God won't get any glory for them and the enemy has kept a fruitful testimony quiet. So, I will tell and believe that you will receive this as bragging on God and not anything in me except what He has changed.

Where I work I get an annual allotment of sick leave. I don't call in sick unless I am sick. I know from experience how blessed I am to have sick leave and how it has kept me paying bills when I had surgery, a broken elbow and a torn up ankle. Wasting sick leave could be potentially costly.

Having said that, a few years ago I had taken vacation time and during that time off I was ill for several days. It is possible to change annual leave (vacation time) to sick leave after the fact. But it had been an aggravating process as I had gone through it before just to change one day of AL for SL. As a result both leave accounts had gotten messed up and it took months to straighten out!

Anyway, after this last time of illness on vacation time I decided not to go through that aggravation of changing the leave around. I came to the conclusion it would just be easier to call in sick on some days in the future instead of taking vacation time. I planned on doing this until I "got even" on the account for my lost vacation time.

Until the other day I had not gotten around to putting this decision into action. My parents were coming into town on short notice. Too short for me to get annual leave. So I figured this would be a good time to get one of my vacation days back. Members of my family were asking me if I was off that day and I told them I had not decided. They knew what that meant.

Maybe it was just me, but the look in their eyes when I gave that response seemed to say: "I'm watching to see what you do here." It was almost as if my integrity was about to get adjusted one way or another. That was the man side of the situation.

The question on the God side of the situation was: "Are you getting it about loving others? Do I care about everyone at work enough to not call in sick?" Not all of them as much as I should, some of them have and will do it to me. But if I call in sick I am forcing others to carry my load that day. That is just not right in most anyone's eyes.

From my side, it would probably be "fair" for me to call in sick. But it would not be "right." I believe God wants us to do what is right in His eyes even when it's not fair in our eyes.

We had a great time as a family the night before with Mom and Dad. Then I went to work the next day. I missed being with them that day, but I feel like I did the "right" thing.

Something's changing.

I'll Fix It Myself   April 23

OK ladies, have you ever been in a car that your man is driving when he gets lost? You know the conversation.

You say: "Are we lost?"

He says: "No."

You say: "Why don't we stop and ask for directions?"

He says: "I'm not lost!"

Although I have never been lost myself, I think I understand how the poor guy must feel.

Guys are fixers. If something is broken (mechanically, physically, financially, emotionally, spiritually), it doesn't matter what's wrong, we can fix it! "No, I don't want your help, honey. I'll fix it myself."

A little "man secret" here, ladies. We might call a buddy for some help in a real pinch, but you won't know it. Asking for help just goes against our DNA! "No honey, I didn't call Ralph over to help me lift the freezer, he was just driving by and thought he would stop and say hello."

We (guys especially) don't like to ask for help. When we do ask for help, it will be someone we know who will come through for us in a pinch. Someone we trust.

David had someone like that. It seemed as if David stayed in a pinch. His life was always on the line. Bears, lions, enemy armies, a son and a king all tried to kill him. Psalms is full of prayers that David cried out to God for his rescue and deliverance. David knew God. He knew God would come through for him as He had so many times in the past. He trusted God, and God rescued him continually.

We need to know God personally. We need to trust Him and ask Him to help us fix what's broken in our lives. He is trustworthy. We'll see Him come through for us time and again. He loves us as much as He loved David. He will rescue us too!

The Lord is my rock, my fortress and my deliverer; my God is my rock, in whom I take refuge, my shield and the horn of my salvation, my stronghold. – Psalm 18:2

Consumers And The Consumed — April 24

In the natural, a consumer is a person who buys some product and uses that product as he sees fit. The product, a tool for example, is designed for a specific purpose. You drive a nail with a hammer, not a putty knife. You cut a board with a saw, not a piece of sandpaper. However, many of us have used a knife blade for a screwdriver or a wrench to drive a nail just because the wrong tool was handy. Some correct uses for products we consume might be: a house for shelter, a car for transportation, food to eat, clothes to wear, electricity for power, water to drink...etc.

There are all sorts advertising and marketing sources we can use to help us decide what products to consume. Magazine articles rate products. There are sale papers, catalogs, and Internet to see the choices and prices as well as TV and radio ads to entice us to purchase all kinds of goodies.

We consume in the natural out of need or desire. It is the consumer's choice, not the product's decision. But in the spirit realm it is God or Satan who will be the consumer and you and I are the products that will be consumed. The difference is, in the spiritual, the product has the choice of who will be the consumer and how we will be used by that consumer. The advertising and marketing efforts in the spiritual world for the services of the products are more intense than any sales meeting on earth.

God provides us sources to guide us into making the right choices. These choices are no less than life and death. When we read and study His word, pray and follow the leading of the Holy Spirit, we can make the right choices in obedience and be used for what we were designed. We can do all things through Christ who strengthens us (Philippians 4:13) and if we show our love for God through our obedience, we can be in His presence (John 14).

The enemy on the other hand will use any means possible to consume us to the point of being used up for his evil purposes. Temptations that seem to be used by the devil on men include: work, sexual temptations, things that *have* to get done, TV, busyness...etc. Satan comes to steal, kill, and destroy. These are not just strong words, it is his literal game plan.

Every product is created and designed for a specific task, but no matter how perfectly designed, it can still be used for the wrong purposes. This would obviously result in an outcome less than it was created to achieve.

We were created and designed to have a personal relationship with Jesus Christ. That would be the perfect use of our design. Remember, before a product can be used it must be bought and paid for, and we have been bought with the highest price. We were purchased by God and the price was His Son.

Choose to be consumed by God! Do the things you were designed to carry out for the Kingdom. See God move as you are yielded and "Holy Consumed" by Him.

Did I Miss Something   April 25

On three different days in the last month or so, I had made up my mind I was going to go fishing.

On the night before the first attempt I went out to crank my boat motor and it would not stay running. That cost a few dollars and days at the repair shop.

A couple of weeks later, on the morning of the second attempt, I went to buy some non-ethanol gas for the boat (ethanol reeks havoc on marine motors). I drove across town to one known station that sells the prescribed fuel. My card would not work in their scanner and she refused to type the number into the register! Well, she's was out forty bucks! On my way to another non-ethanol fuel station, I stopped at a nearby bait shop only to find it closed! What?! A bait store closed early in the morning! After the thirty minute trip across town, I finally got my gas and headed for the boat ramp. I didn't make it. The truck broke down.

A week later, on the night before the third attempt to go fishing, I spent at least two hours rigging reels and rods, hooking up the trailer to the truck and making sure all is ready to get up the next morning and just pull out. I got up the next morning to see clouds all over the weather radar! In my stubbornness, I traveled to two boat ramps to check out the situation for myself. The skies were dark, so I relented and headed home.

I know this probably seems humorous having happened to me and not you. You're probably thinking that you would have determined something was amiss with the plan after the first attempt, certainly after the second. I did. After the second try I wondered if I was missing something. I wondered if God had a different plan for me that day. I didn't ask, I didn't care. I was a horse with blinders on, running loose. I was being ridden by aggravation and determination to have my way!

On two occasions yesterday, Hannah told me how she had ask God what to do before she took action. Then she proceeded to tell me how perfectly it worked out for her as she obeyed Him. It just doesn't get any wiser than that! Ask God what to do before we take action. It will definitely turn out for the best. Not to mention we won't have to run to Him asking Him to fix what we messed up!

Now I am asking. Now I do care, and I pray God will show me what I missed. Maybe He will let me have a shot at doing those days over according to His plan, not mine.

The Shiny Things April 26

Along about the age of twelve, I started to play a little golf. It was fun and challenging, and for me and some friends it brought about some related adventures. One was seeing who could find the most lost golf balls.

We liked to sneak onto this nearby golf course (a really nice one where we couldn't afford to play), and work our way through the woods along the fairways looking for wayward golf balls. This was good golf ball hunting ground because the rich guys that played here used new golf balls, not the second hand stuff we would have to buy. When they hooked a shot into the woods they rarely looked for the ball. They would just pull another new one out of the bag, hit it and keep moving.

One day while on one of our golf ball hunts, a friend and I spotted a "shiny", brand new-looking ball at the same time. The race was on! I won and lost. As I took my last step while reaching for the ball, I sank up to my armpits in swamp muck! It's like quicksand, but thank God, not very quick. I was not touching bottom and I was in there tight like when you bury yourself in sand at the beach. It felt like I was trapped in a suction lock.

I was determined this ordeal was not going to be in vain! I grabbed the golf ball. It took some serious tugging to get me out of that muck. My shoes were sucked right off my feet as my friends pulled me out of there! It also ruined a perfectly good pack of cigarettes.

The worst part of it all was that the new shiny golf ball, that I had lost my shoes, smokes and dignity over, was only half of a golf ball! That's right, just half of a golf ball had been laying there looking like it was partially buried in mud. Whether someone had left the golf ball there intentionally or not, it was a trap. I resisted the temptation to put the ball back where I found it (I guess that would have been some sick attempt to get even).

We laugh about it now, but it does serve as a reminder not to go running after every shiny thing that catches our eye. There are so many shiny things out there like pretty houses, cars, boats and any number of goodies that catch our eye. But they may require us to go just off the "fairway" where we could fall into a deep trap that will be very hard, and take a long time, to escape from and be free.

I pray I have finally learned my lesson about the "shiny" things that lure me off the fairway.

See The Signs? Are you Ready?   April 27

Matthew 24:1-46 (Come on, read it!)

If you want to have success fishing, you need to know the signs that will tell you when the best opportunity will present itself. For instance, around here on the Gulf Coast, some of the signs of the right time are: when is the tide moving, the water temperature, clear water, what fish are moving and where. Right now the Squid are in, with Bonita chasing them. Pompano are scarce but will be in as the water temperature warms. The Spanish Mackerel will be next, followed by the Kings and the Lings. You can fish in the surf for Pompano, the Bay for Spanish, troll the Gulf for King or sight fish for Ling. That's just a taste of the info to know and when and where to go.

But, all that info is useless unless you are ready when the time is right. Your boat needs to be sea worthy, if not, you could find yourself adrift at sea, or worse. You need to have the right tackle in working order; rods, reels, hooks, line, for the fish you are wanting to catch. The people going fishing with you need to be there when the time is right. If I tell someone to meet me at the boat ramp at 5:30 am, they better be there or get left behind.

With fishing, you have to be ready when the time is right. There are those awesome days when the time is right and you're there, ready and equipped, and it's on! Seafood platter, baby! But if the time is right and you're not ready, it just won't matter and the opportunity for the fish fry is gone.

That's what Jesus was telling His disciples here about the end times. He was saying, "Here are the signs, but don't just sit around waiting for all the signs. Get ready and stay ready! So that when the time is right you can go with Me."

So what about you and me? He tells us here of the signs of His coming. Reading and studying His Word will equip us to discern the false teachings of false prophets. He says that His coming will be unmistakable. He also says not to be alarmed. We are to be aware, ready and about our Father's business. If we are ready, we will not be surprised, adrift or left behind. We will instead be with Him at the "Big Seafood Festival"! Wanna go?

Thrilling Endings...They Can Scare The Hell Out Of Us...I Hope   April 28

What a week in sports! It's hard to remember this many fantastic finishes in such a short stretch of time.

I'm not a big soccer fan, but how about Donovan's overtime goal to get the U.S. into the round of sixteen in the World Cup? I still say they could score a lot more if they would just use their hands!

Then there was Isner's victory at Wimbledon in the longest tennis match ever played!

My favorite this week: South Carolina's comeback win in the bottom of the twelfth after OU had taken the lead in the top half of the inning! Thrilling endings one after another this week.

Although the victors in these events are thrilled at the last minute wins, I would guess that while they are behind during the last minutes of the game, they would rather be ahead by ten. What I'm saying is that the team or player that goes into the final moments of a game behind on the scoreboard, more often than not, ends up losing the game. I certainly would rather go into the bottom of the ninth ahead by ten than down by one, hoping for a miracle, even though they do sometimes occur.

In this life on earth there is only one score that matters: "Do you know Jesus?" If you do, you know it! If you're not sure, then you don't know the "score." Not knowing the score is a very scary place for a player to be when it comes to the end of the game.

I know of people who have (genuinely, I believe) accepted Christ on their death beds. A thrilling finish no doubt, but also a very close game that could have had eternally fatal results! They had the blessing of knowing it was their last at bat. In life, we don't have the advantage of knowing how much time we have left in the game.

Hit the game winning homer right now! If you don't know Jesus, if you're not sure you know Him, ask Him right now to forgive your sins and be your Lord and Savior. No more saying, "When I get myself cleaned up I'll go to Him." He's like any fisherman, He catches His fish, then He cleans them. I'm still on the cleaning board!

If you're still thinking about waiting to the bottom of the ninth, well it might work out. Then again, your game could get rained out at any second!

The Goalie   April 29

My first duty station in my time in the military was right here in the South, on the sandy beaches of the Florida Gulf Coast. It was the last place I thought I would be out-numbered by the boys from "Hockeyland." Everyone was kind enough and we got along, except for when it came to what we were going to watch on the TV in the shared dayroom.

Most of those guys liked hockey better than all other sports put together! Sure I could watch something on my TV in my room, but if there was a weekend cookout or a party of some sort in the barracks, then a hockey game was the TV fare.

Somewhat by osmosis I guess, I absorbed a little of the game. Enough anyway to be able to tell why they were excited enough at times to cheer, and at other times ticked off to the point of rearranging furniture by the "airborne" method! If the hockey was not entertaining enough for me, their fandom sure was fun to watch!

Anyway, the only player I could relate to was the goalie. I guess being a baseball guy, the goalie looked to me kind of like a catcher. He wore a mask and had a glove, (I knew what that was for) and he had a stick, kind of like a bat to swing at the incoming missile called the puck.

The goalie is the last defensive guy the other team has to get the puck past and into the net he is guarding, to score a goal. When an opposing player fires the puck at the net, the goalie tries to catch it in his glove or slap it back out onto the ice (field of play). If the goalie can catch the puck in his glove, the immediate threat is over and the attack has failed for now. If the goalie slaps the puck back out onto the ice, chances are it's coming right back at him.

Like a hockey goalie we have "pucks" flying at us everyday. Often times in the form of hurtful words or insults from adversaries, friends, co-workers and even loved ones. So how do we respond to these "shots on our net"? I suppose it depends on how our net is made up. If our net is made up of self-importance (pride), we're probably going to fire that puck (insult or hurtful words) right back at the shooter! On the other hand, if our net is made up of godly character, we should just catch the puck (insult) in our glove (our knowledge of who we are in Christ). When we catch hurtful words in our glove, they can't "score" against us and are not shot back at others so that they can continue the onslaught. Then they haven't scored against us or the kingdom.

Sure, this is easier said than done. But the Coach can keep us practicing our glove work.

A fool shows his annoyance at once, but a prudent man overlooks an insult. – Proverbs 12:16

A gentle answer turns away wrath, but a harsh word stirs up anger. – Proverbs 15:1

Cruisin' April 30

Tough times. Who wants them? Not me!
Tough times. Who needs them? Probably all of us.

The old saying goes: "Hindsight is 20-20." This morning, for me, is one of those times of reflection. Personally, I know that I can easily fall into a state of spiritual cruise control. This has happened in the past to me when everything in life is going great. No big problems, issues or tragedies. It's all good, just cruisin'.

I think God sees me in this mode and knows that I'm going into a slide in my relationship to Him. He sees me reading the Word less and less. He hears from me less and less. He sees me thinking of Him as my source less and less. He sees me acting as if I need Him less and less. He misses me more and more.

But He doesn't love me less and less. He doesn't leave me or forsake me. Instead as my Father who loves me and my Lord who guides me, He takes appropriate action to draw me back to Him. This can take the form of discipline, trials, or testing in order to teach me and draw me back.

For instance, "Cooking in the Rain" (March 15) was written in a time I was in a severe financial squeeze. When things got bad enough I ran to Him. He was there waiting. I started reading the Bible regularly again, spending time in prayer and obeying His direction. He allowed me to go through some areas that I had to depend on Him. He was my only source of rescue.

I learned a lot during that time. I'll share more of that later. Suffice for now to say that I learned my lesson, because I occasionally feel that temptation to put my life on cruise. However, because of His power and the lessons He has taught me, I have been able to slam on the brakes, pull over at His rest area and spend some time getting the right directions.

Zoom, Zoom, Zoom May 1

When I was in the 7th and 8th grade, I played on the school basketball team. My coach liked to "fast break" when we had the ball and use a "full court press" when we were on defense.

His fast break offense was intended to move the ball up the court as quickly as possible. The idea was to catch the other team by surprise or just outrun them up the court to the basket.

The full court press was intended to keep the other team from moving the ball up the court by playing man-to-man defense from the moment that they inbounded the ball. This was as much an aggravation to the opposing team as anything else and we were able to get a lot of steals while pressing the other teams.

These two ploys, together with our team's overall speed, was usually our game plan and would often payoff as our opponents would tire late in the games.

This all came to my remembrance as I thought about how much my life seems to have sped up from when I was a child. I realize responsible adulthood carries more demands on our time than a child at play, but I don't think that's the sum of what has changed.

I remember as a child just lying in the grass with friends looking up at clouds in the day or stars at night. I was in no hurry at all to do anything else but spend time like that with my buds. We would spend an entire day exploring the woods or walking down some railroad track just to see where it went. I have driven a hundred miles with friends just to get a sandwich. It wasn't the sandwich, it was the unscripted hours spent with people.

I think that's why I like fishing so much; no hurry, no duty, just hanging out with someone. I figure if you catch fish, that's a bonus.

Last night Hannah and I went out to eat. The food was OK. The service was lousy, but the time we just sat there talking was priceless.

I feel as though the speed at which we live out our lives has become like living at fast break speed against a full court press. Computers, cell phones, Facebook and Tweets can certainly be tools. Nevertheless, tools like these and our own desires to get more and get it faster, often put us in the passing lane going right by face-to-face relationships. We were created for relationships; to God and to our fellow man. You just can't replace our need for real relationships. You don't believe me? Tweet God and ask Him yourself.

## The Rescue Worker					May 2

As we watched the tragedy of the tsunami in Japan unfold before our very eyes, I was moved by the tireless work of the "rescue worker." We have seen these people work non-stop for long periods through other seemingly hopeless situations. We have seen them at Ground Zero after 9/11. We see them relentlessly digging at the scene of one mining disaster after another. I believe it's compassion and love for their fellow man that keeps them digging.

For days after these tragedies, people are pulled out of the rubble alive due to the efforts of these rescue workers. Imagine hanging on to your last glimmer of hope for survival as you are immobile, covered by a collapsed building. Perhaps you are trapped in a car covered in ten feet of mud. The air seems to be running out as water slowly fills the car. You may have given up hope when you hear voices above you. You cry out at the top of your lungs, "Help! Save me!"

Issues of life, sin, addictions, stress, and all sorts of "rubble" can pile up on us and we find ourselves buried so far under that there is no way we can get out on our own. We don't have the strength, we realize we cannot lift this rubble off alone, and we may even feel all hope is lost. Hope is not lost!

There is a Rescue Worker who is relentless and will not give up until He finds us and digs us out of the rubble! Even while we are buried under the rubble of our collapsed lives, we can hear Him call out to us. We can hear Him calling our name deep in our being. All we need to do now is scream back to Him, "Save me!"

"For I know the plans I have for you," declares the LORD, "plans to prosper you and not to harm you, plans to give you hope and a future." – Jeremiah 29:11

## Keeping Our Eye On the Ball			May 3

It is said that the hardest thing to do in sports is to hit a round ball (pitched to you) with a round bat. While coaching someone to hit, you teach them to swing level, go to the ball and hit it out in front of the plate and how to shift their weight during their swing (among many other tweaks). But the first thing you teach them is to keep their eye on the ball. Otherwise, all of the other coaching is a waste of time. You can't hit what you can't see.

You teach them to watch the ball early, right out of the pitchers hand. The longer you see the ball, the more time you have to react and hit it successfully. As hitters grow in their ability, so do the pitchers; so you teach the batters to watch the ball even more specifically. You coach them to watch the spin on the ball, so they will be able to tell if it is a breaking ball, a change of speed, or a fast ball.

As a batter masters these skills, he then can begin to be taught what pitches he might expect in certain situations, or what tendencies, strengths and weaknesses a given pitcher might have. This is still only useful if the batter keeps his eye on the ball.

The enemy of our soul likes to throw a fast one at us, sometimes a curve and other times a change of speed. A fast one from the enemy might be a high hard one right at our heads, intended to injure us in some way (physically, mentally, emotionally, spiritually or financially). He may throw us a curve, enticing someone to let us down unexpectedly or dangle some earthly desire that appears to be a good thing, only to be just out of reach and no good at all. He may throw us a change of speed, possibly something that seems easy, too good to be true. Then we swing quickly and we are out in front, missing what God has for us.

When we come up to bat against the enemy, we need to watch the ball. If it's a high hard one, we need to get out of the way, then dust ourselves off and step back in there. Watch the "spin" the enemy puts on his pitches. Don't swing at the trick pitches that look good at first. We know where our weak spots are and we need to guard that part of the plate. Then when we see his pitch coming at our weakness and we are guarding that part of the plate (our lives) we are ready and able to drive his pitches right out of the park.

Spiritual Tragedy   May 4

God has been after me to "think of others more highly than myself" and to "love my neighbor as myself." Another component of what's going on is that I am trying to obey Him step by step, not just be generally obedient. Here is the story of how I missed His will.

I got up this morning (my day off) with the feeling that I was supposed to go to the Mission House (a food bank ministry at my church with a fruitful evangelistic outreach). I said supposed to because I was really having mixed emotions about going. For example, I was thinking of how sometimes people seem to have an attitude of entitlement about getting free food and don't appear to be thankful. On the other hand, some are getting saved or renewing their relationship to Jesus and I shouldn't judge them as I just did in my thought process.

After all those mind games, I submitted and went. So far so good. I went inside the Mission House and asked Jeanette if they needed any help, and somewhat to my surprise she says "I think we got it covered unless you want to pray with people, if that's your cup of tea." She said that because she was not for sure who was coming to pray with folks. No, I thought, I do not want to do that today. Just as soon as I said that to myself, the man who usually prays with people (a mighty man of God that I would want to be praying for me) pulled up and I was off the hook.

Well, I was being spiritual, wondering in my "wisdom" why I was there, so I went to the church office and talked to one of my friends awhile, figuring that for some reason God had wanted me there and then I went home.

Shortly after getting home I went outside and sat down on the deck. I was actually thinking, "OK Lord, what's next today?" Right then Hannah let Louie out and said, "Your buddy wants to come outside with you."

I said, "What's up, Louie?" and he immediately wanted to jump up on me (as he always does when someone gives him their attention). Louie smelled like a dog right then and I did not want him jumping up on my clean body!

Is this how we respond to others when we think they want something from us? Is this what I was saying to the people at the Mission House this morning? Did I not want their "smell" on me because I thought I was cleaner?

I was willing to let them hang out with me (give them some earthly food), but not let them jump up on me (pray with them). In my flesh there was something that tried to tell me that I smell better to God than they, when it really was the "ode de Greg pride" stinking up the place! It was a spiritual tragedy!

You know, they could no doubt go one more day without earthly food. The question really is: Can they go one more day without Jesus?

Do not seek revenge or bear a grudge against anyone among your people, but love your neighbor as yourself. I am the Lord. – Leviticus 19:18

For by the grace given me I say to every one of you: Do not think of yourself more highly than you ought, but rather think of yourself with sober judgment, in accordance with the faith God has distributed to each of you. – Romans 12:3

Be devoted to one another in love. Honor one another above yourselves. – Romans 12:10

The Other Side Of The Storm   May 5

If you stay out at sea long enough, you'll have to go through some storms. The same is true if we live in this life very long.

Years ago, a friend and I went out fishing. It was a beautiful day at the start but we weren't catching anything. Then it clouded up in a hurry! We were in a small boat and quickly saw that the Gulf was not the place to be. We sped back into the bay and then to the boat ramp. By the time we got through the high seas and the deluge of rain, we just tied the boat up and did not try to load it on the trailer during the storm. We took shelter in the store for well over an hour. Many, many boats and fishermen took shelter there during that storm.

When the storm had subsided somewhat, we decided to trailer the boat and call it a day. The boat easily had six inches of water in it. As we went out to trailer the boat, a larger boat pulled in with a nice catch of Chicken Dolphin on board. We had to ask where they caught them. Their answer was: "On the other side of the storm." They had stayed out to the north of the storm (they had radar) and continued to fish.

We couldn't stand it! We got in the boat and headed back out to sea. We caught fish the rest of the day like we knew what we were doing.

There had been a point in that day where it was truly frightening! Storms in life can be truly frightening. I know, "trust in God," but for me anyway, that's often easier said than done. One of the things that storms in life show us is how much we do or do not trust God.

The thing is, if we do ask God and we do trust God (He's got great radar) and we take shelter in Him during the storm, we will find ourselves stronger and more fruitful on the other side of the storm.

And we know that in all things God works for the good of those who love Him, who have been called according to His purpose. – Romans 8:28

Stay In The Boat — May 6

I was thinking about yesterday's story. I told of when a friend and I were in a storm while in a boat in the Gulf. After reading it someone ask, "How did you get all that water out of the boat?" I explained that we cranked the boat, got it moving and then pulled the plug, and that as long as the boat is moving, the water will run out of the boat.

It was a good question. If you've ever been in a boat (probably if you've never been in a boat), you realize the idea is to have the boat in the water, not the water in the boat! Furthermore, if you are any distance at all from land you want (need) to be in the boat, not the sea.

We are told to go into all the world and preach the Good News. We are also told to be in the world, but not of the world. We are also told that there will be troubles (storms) in this world, but that Jesus has overcome the world.

Well there it is: our "boat" is our trust in God. The "water or sea" is the world that we sail into everyday. The "storms" are the troubles we face while in the world (the sea).

We have to go to sea everyday. We better take the boat or we'll surely drown! If we start taking on water (letting the things of the world take God's place in our lives), this will sink our boat (our trust in Him). When we do take on water we should pull the plug (repent) and get moving again out of the storm.

As we trust God more and more, our boat becomes bigger and stronger. It becomes a deep sea fishing boat, a battleship, or even a rescue ship.

While we're out there, especially in a storm, maybe we should be on the lookout for someone who has fallen overboard and needs rescue.

To The Rescue   May 7

I have always liked watching those rescue shows on television; especially the ones with rescues at sea.

Sometimes these programs would show the intense training the rescuers would have to endure and pass, just to be considered for the job. The physical and mental strain the applicants were forced to go through would prepare them for the riggers of actual rescues.

When it comes to the real rescues at sea, the rescue teams could be faced with capsized ships, high seas, storms, deadly frigid waters, panicked survivors and, more often than not, some combination of these dangerous conditions.

After watching many of these rescues at sea on TV (whether reenacted or live), it is obvious that the basic plan is the same. The rescuers only go in the water as a last resort. If they are on another ship, they will try to throw a rope, life preserver or some kind of flotation device to the victim first. If the rescuers happen to be in a helicopter, they will first lower a rope, cable or basket before sending a swimmer into the water.

The reason for these tactics is obvious. Once a rescuer goes into the water, his life is now in peril. He is subject to all of the dangerous conditions that the very people he is trying to rescue have fallen victim to.

This situation is the very reason the rescuer had to be trained, taught and conditioned so highly. Not only is he now faced with horrible weather, water and other dangerous conditions, he may also be faced with a panicked victim who is going to try to climb up on him and potentially taking him down for good!

So here's another reason to "Stay In The Boat" (yesterdays story). If we want to work on a spiritual rescue boat, lets make sure we are well trained, strong and prepared (like a rescue swimmer) before we jump back into "familiar waters of old sin" trying to rescue someone. I'm not saying that we don't try to rescue friends and loved ones who are lost at sea; I'm saying the first options are to stay in the boat and try throwing a rope. I say this because if we were to jump back into the water with them and are not strong enough to resist the conditions (temptations), we may just get pulled under ourselves.

Let me say it this way. I have often seen a new Christian come to the Lord and in their zeal, go right back to the bar, the drugs or some other environment, with the purpose of witnessing to friends, just to get pulled under again.

I used to tell youth to make sure you are established and equipped in the Word and your faith before returning to old haunts. Until then, throw your old friends a rope. Ask them to meet you on your turf. Maybe go shopping, to a ball game or buy them lunch. If they grab the rope, you can still be a wonderful witness to them! Don't take unnecessary risks that could sink you. Stay in the boat!

The New Gate   May 8

For all the years we have lived in this house, the gate in our fence has been a large 12 ft. rolling gate that opens and closes across the width of our driveway. Many of these type gates have electric openers. Ours does not. Although you don't have to roll it open very far, it was difficult for Hannah to open. She asked me to fix the problem and I immediately jumped on the project. Well, maybe not immediately.

I opted for an additional small gate next to the large rolling gate. This would still allow me to use the rolling gate to easily get the boat, vehicles, jet ski's etc., into the yard.

I couldn't help but think of some words Jesus spoke in the Sermon on the Mount.

"Enter through the narrow gate. For wide is the gate and broad is the road that leads to destruction, and many enter through it. But small is the gate and narrow the road that leads to life, and only a few find it." – Matthew 7:13-14

I know that what I'm about to say is not in total context of what Jesus is saying in these verses, but these verses did get me to thinking. That's what Jesus often did. He opened people eyes to new ways of thinking, especially viewing the natural things with spiritual vision.

So, back to the gates. It seems that our earthly vision would be to open the big rolling gate and haul all the big stuff (earthly possessions) out of there and bring them with us. But that gate is hard to open and all that stuff will slow us down. Yet it's amazing the importance and value we place on possessions that are not coming with us when we leave this earth.

The only thing of value we are taking out of this world is us and others. And the narrow gate is the only way. It is also free and easy. The new narrow gate works like a champ. Hannah was so happy when she came home and saw that gate. All she had to do was lift that latch and it opened so easily.

That's all we have to do to "go home," lift that latch (trust Jesus as our Lord and Savior). The narrow gate, that's the way in. Let's show people where the narrow gate is and how easy it is to open and walk through. I know the Christian walk isn't always easy, but salvation is, because it is free to us (already paid for).

The Importance Of Numbers, Especially "One"
May 9

I think we often fall into the trap of believing the success of our service to God is measured in the number of people we serve or influence. We may see pastors of mega-churches on TV preaching awesome messages and think: "That's the right way to do it, that's how you influence people!"

We may see Billy Graham or some other well known evangelist leading thousands to the Lord at one time and say: "That's the right way to do it, that's how you know you're successful." Not necessarily. In all likelihood that's the way they are supposed to minister. We are told to go and make disciples. I haven't seen anywhere in the Bible where it says we are ranked in importance or loved more by God based on how many people we lead or influence. In fact, the Bible says that we show our love for God in our obedience to Him. We are called to love others and minister to them. However, how we serve, and to how many is a decision that should be based on God's direction of the gifts He gives us, not what will "wow" men. He will bring the harvest He desires through our obedience to Him.

Yes, some are called to minister to thousands and some are called to serve one at a time. Don't worry about numbers. If we are obeying Him in our witness, He will bring in exactly the right number. Besides, one may be exactly the number He wants at the time. Someone influenced Billy Graham to serve God. I'd say that was pretty good, to lead a future great evangelist to the Lord.

How about Stephen asking God to forgive those stoning him? Do you think that may have started Paul (a great missionary evangelist) wondering just a little about those Christians and their God? Yeah, it's good to influence thousands, or maybe the "one" you influence may later influence thousands. The goal could be the soul right in front of you.

Smokin' May 10

I guess I was around eleven when I started smoking. It all began as a cool macho thing and that was pretty much the reason I continued to smoke up into my twenties. Looking back to the beginning of my smoking years brings to me a lot of questions and thoughts to ponder.

It actually began at my grandparent's house. My grandfather was a smoker. He would often leave half-smoked cigarettes in his ashtray. It finally came to a point one day that I just had to try one out! When the coast was clear I took one of the half-smoked goodies and headed to the bathroom. I locked the door and fired that puppy up. I smoked it down, flushed the butt and then sprayed the air freshener before leaving the bathroom.

This became my ongoing plan when I was over at my grandparent's house. It seemed to be working well enough. Grandfather always seemed to leave several butts in his ashtray for me to swipe. I don't think he knew what I was up to because he often would light one up away from his chair and end up with several "half smokes" in the ashtray.

My plan was working so well until "the experiment." I had seen a science show on TV demonstrating the basic operation of a flame thrower. One afternoon while I was "burning one" in the bathroom I decided to try this flamethrower theory out. I took the air freshener and sprayed it across the lit end of my cigarette. It worked just like they said. In fact, better than I expected. Flame shot across the bathroom about three feet and caught Grandmother's fuzzy toilet tank cover on fire! Yeah, baby! Now we have a problem! In my panic, my wonderful solution was to cover up the charred remains of the tank cover with the Kleenex box and a couple of bathroom decorations and then make a run for it!

Interestingly and to my amazement and relief, nothing was ever even said about the incident. I know Grandmother had to have been the one who found the evidence, because if Grandfather would have found it, talking would not have been part of the remedy!

Now, for the sake of analogy (not an opinion or condemnation on smoking), lets view smoke as sin. I probably was not getting away with my "boys' room smoking" because of the use of air freshener to cover up the smell. It was probably due to the house smelling like smoke all the time anyway.

Sin around other sin may hardly be detectable to the sinner. But where there is smoke, there is fire and it can get out of control. And it will find us out. If we deliberately continue in sin, it will burn us.

The solution is to repent and go to the Lord for forgiveness. Then, just like Grandmother did for me, He will pour out His mercy, grace and forgiveness and no one else may ever have to know. Unless you write a blog.

The Little Green Jacket (Mother's Day) May 11

My first memory of my mom is her getting me ready to go somewhere. I remember this little blueish-green jacket with a hood. She would put this jacket on me every time before we went out in the cold. She would zip that jacket zipper up to my nose! Then she would pull the hood over my head and pull the drawstring until my eyes were inside the hood! I think it was an infant straight jacket, but I was definitely warm (Slight exaggerations)! Why did she do that?

She would feed me everyday.

She was the den mother for my Cub Scouts.

She is always my encourager.

She would come to my football games.

She would occasionally help me with my homework. She would have helped more, but I only occasionally did my homework.

She took care of me through every one of my illnesses including, but not limited to: mumps, measles, blood poison (no easy chore back in the day), tonsillitis, bronchitis and the dreaded teenage disease, "cranial rectumitis."

This is only a sampling of the things my mom did and does for me. Why did she? Why does she do these things? Because she loves this old boy of her's, no matter what he is or does!

Whenever I look at my mom, I see a reflection of Jesus' unconditional love.

I Love You, Mom! Happy Mother's Day!

No Fear, Really — May 12

In my younger days as a construction worker, I would often find myself many stories above the ground. In the early stages of building tall structures, the first thing to be erected is the iron and steel frame of the building. During this period of the construction I often had to walk across 6- and 8-inch wide beams high in the air, with nothing to stop a fall but the ground.

On one occasion I was removing a floor form about ten stories up, into which the floor above had been poured. It required me to lean out from the floor below (which had no walls at this stage) and pull nails from the form above. I was not tethered in any way for my safety. Trying to balance myself carefully, I pulled the form apart nail by nail reaching out as far as I could stretch.

As I pulled on one nail, a large piece of the wood form came off and fell the ten stories into the supply yard below. It sounded like an explosion as lumber and metal flew into the air below. Thankfully, there was no one in the supply yard at that moment. The falling form or the scattering supplies could have caused severe injury or worse. Not to mention, the falling form could have taken me with it to the ground.

I put my hammer in my tool belt, went to the ground, got in my truck and went home.

Years later, I went on that ride at Six Flags with my seven year old son, that takes you up high in the air in a seat with a parachute. I had been on this ride before and loved it. As we reached the top of the ride and stopped, I realized I wasn't having fun anymore. I didn't say anything out loud for fear of scaring my son, but I was freaking out on the inside. I was thinking, "I want down now!"

On another occasion I went to talk to my dad on his job site. He was high up on the steel structure so I figured I would mosey on up there and speak to him. Mistake! I couldn't get down from there fast enough. I then realized exposed high places were no place for me to be anymore.

The other day I had this thought of Jesus lifting me up by my wrist high into the sky. I knew if I were high in the open sky I would be able to see the ground far below and that fear of falling could trigger itself in me. Having the fear of falling from high in the air would normally cause me to change what I'm thinking about as fast as possible.

However, this thought of Jesus having a grip on me, caused me no fear at all. Why? Because the only thing that could cause me fear in that situation is what He will never do. He will never let go.

Are you in His grip?

Weapons Of Our Warfare — May 13

In a war, what are the best advantages we can have against the enemy? More powerful weapons? More soldiers? While these are good advantages to possess on our side, I believe two of the best advantages we can have are intelligence and the element of surprise.

By intelligence, I mean knowing what the enemy is up to without them knowing what we're up to. By surprise, I mean that the enemy doesn't even know we're coming to attack, much less when or where we are going to attack.

I think it is the same in the spiritual realm. Our spiritual enemy, the Devil, is not omniscient. He does not know everything. I do not believe he can read our minds. He may know our tendencies, weaknesses and temptations that have worked on us in the past, but he doesn't know for sure what we are thinking or planning. He would need to gain "intelligence" to know what we're going to do next.

For instance, what if Joseph had kept his mouth shut about his dreams of his brothers bowing down to him. As soon as he opened his mouth and told them his dream (providing the enemy with intelligence) he was pouring gas on the fire already burning because of Jacob's favoritism of Joseph over his brothers. The enemy gained ten more soldiers to use right then. His brothers pondered killing him, leaving him for dead, but decided to sell him into slavery.

Some may say: "Well how then would God's purposes have been fulfilled?" Well, God is God, and maybe the slave traders could have just captured Joseph out there wondering around looking for his brothers. Or maybe Joseph could have come into Pharoah's service another way. God is ultimately in control. I just believe we don't need to give the enemy any intelligence he can use to wreak havoc in our lives.

Further, if Joseph had not told his brothers about his dream, what God was up to could have been a total surprise to the devil. God will ultimately prevail. But if we consider God's timing by not letting the enemy know what's up, we may avoid a lot of unnecessary difficulties the enemy may try to put in our paths. The best way to emerge from battle is without any wounds at all.

Having said all this, Our God is the most powerful weapon. He is the nuclear bomb in a war with an enemy whose ultimate effect on us as believers is that of a pea shooter. God will have complete and total victory! Praise God!

Jesus And Baking Soda   May 14

The Fishin Hole is my garage turned into a kind of "man cave" I use for get-togethers of all sorts. You can click on it at the top of my home page and check it out if you like. Anyway I have a refrigerator and freezer out there we use to store our goodies.

The other day, I set my broom in-between the fridge and freezer. Unbeknownst to me, it bounced the plugs loose. I returned two days later to the "ode de fish bait" coming from my freezer!

You see, the Fishin Hole guys really do go fishing. We store our bait in the freezer of the refrigerator. Well, we did until now. When I opened that freezer door, that smell was nasty!

So, I dug a hole and buried the foul bait. Then I scrubbed and cleaned and scrubbed and cleaned that nasty refrigerator. I took all the racks and trays out and washed them individually. That fridge looks like brand new inside. But that smell was still there! Not until I put that baking soda in there did the odor really dissipate.

We can try to do the same kind of thing for ourselves when it comes to our sin. We can try to clean ourselves up. We can make ourselves appear clean and shiny, but the "ode de sin" is still all over us. The only way to get truly clean is to let Jesus inside (like the baking soda) where the stink is. He's the only one who can truly clean, refresh and restore us.

Jesus told the religious leaders of the day that their appearance of cleanliness on the outside did not mean they were clean on the inside.

There is no point in trying to clean ourselves or get our act together before we come to Jesus. In this way, Jesus is like those fishermen He hung around with. He catches His fish before He cleans them too.

"*Blind Pharisee! First clean the inside of the cup and dish, and then the outside also will be clean. Woe to you, teachers of the law and Pharisees, you hypocrites! You are like whitewashed tombs, which look beautiful on the outside but on the inside are full of the bones of the dead and everything unclean. In the same way, on the outside you appear to people as righteous but on the inside you are full of hypocrisy and wickedness.*" – Matthew 23: 26-28

Stay Plugged In   May 15

Another take on yesterday's story, "Jesus and Baking Soda," occurs to me. The refrigerator and freezer out in The Fishin' Hole were designed to keep things cold. They have the "authority" to keep things cold. However, if they are not plugged into the power source, they become a storage cabinet and are not being used to their full potential.

I once heard someone give a great analogy for the need of "power" along with ones' position of "authority." Suppose there was an off-duty police officer in a bar and an all out Pier 6 brawl breaks out. I mean the whole place is going at it, furniture flying and it's totally out of control. A full-blown raging riot!

Now, if the officer stands up in the middle of that room and says: "OK you guys, that's enough, please break it up and lets all go home." That'll work, right? Probably not. It's more likely his head will meet the next piece of flying furniture. In this scenario he has no appearance of authority and an obvious lack of power.

If he lived next door, the officer might be able to run home and put on his uniform and come back. Now he is obviously a man in authority. He can try again to calm the crowd with words. But it's likely if anyone paused at the sight of his uniform, they would get clobbered, as the melee continued through the officer's drowned-out pleas to restore order.

However, if the officer ran home, put on his uniform and got his gun, things may go a little differently. He strolls back into the bar like Wyatt Earp, fires a couple of shots into the ceiling and now has everyone's attention. After informing the participants in the brawl that the next move they make should be just below the exit sign, he encourages them to leave with a few waves of his "peacemaker" in their direction. His authority and power get the job done!

Christ has given us authority and power. If we don't use this power and authority given to us for use in the Kingdom, then we become just a storage cabinet of what we know of Him. Just like my refrigerator and freezer, we should keep ourselves plugged into Him as our source of power so that the authority we have been given will be of best use to Him.

Guard Your Joy...Drink In The Little Things
May 16

I feel sure that there are many reading this right now who are facing real life obstacles, troubles, test and trials. We can pretty easily allow ourselves to be overwhelmed and consumed with these obstacles. I'm not saying that our problems are not hard or that they are easy to face. That would just be an unreal lie.

Our friends and godly counselors can give us good advice and insights and we should heed that advice where possible and right. However, they just can't go through it for us. They are not as emotionally attached as those who are going through a tough situation.

We hear, "give it to God," and we should. He is the only one who has gone through stuff in our place; paying the price and taking the punishment for our sin. Going to Him in prayer for help and rescue in a tough time is the way to get through. He will go with us. I realize there is often a lesson and a strengthening God can do in us in these times if we are faithful in these trials. Yet most often we do go through the trial, and honestly, it's not always easy.

Having said all that, I think the enemy will try to use these times to emotionally hurt us so that we are blinded, unaware, or just too focused on the difficulties we are facing to have any joy. The devil "comes to steal, kill and destroy." The enemy is real and that is his literal tactic. Yet he can't take anything from us as believers unless we let him! We need to get that into our heads and hearts, that "we are more than conquerors" because of Christ in us. We don't have to let the enemy win. In fact he cannot defeat us unless we give up!

While we're going through these times, and even in times when we think we're too busy, let's watch for the joy God sends our way: the little granddaughter's hug, talking with a friend, the fresh air after the rain, eating supper with our family, a boat ride, a fish on a kid's line, the smile from your wife for no special reason, the laugh of a child, an answered prayer. You can think of more moments of joy. Don't miss them. Take time to soak 'em in, even in the tough times, and enjoy the little things, that really are the big things!

Pulling Over Right Here   May 17

A while back I made a road trip. It took around two hours each way. On my way there and back I was drawn to the idea of stopping at the rest areas along the highway. I didn't stop at any of them. I was in a hurry going (to get there on time) and returning (I wanted to get home to do the next task at hand). Although the idea of a restful few minutes to relax, stretch, and drink a cup of coffee was appealing, I stayed on the gas as if someone was going to lock the gate to my city two minutes before I arrived.

I don't know about you, but I feel like I spend a lot of my life (especially the last two years) with my foot on the gas! God is the one who has brought me through those last two years. This morning as I was praying, I realized I have been asking God to hurry up and take me to the next "destinations" on my list. These next destinations on my life's "road trip" are the challenges I see before me now. It's like, "Hurry up God, solve this one, fix this one, do this, and everything will be OK. Then I can take my foot off the gas and coast downhill awhile." Sidebar thought: Did you ever notice that when you are coasting, you're always going "downhill"?

Anyway, as I was praying this prayer, the rest areas on the highway the other day came to mind. It was as if God was saying to me, "Do you mind if we pull over here for a few minutes and just hang out?" It also occurred to me that I had not expressed my thankfulness to Him (the way I should have) for bringing me through these last two years. Instead, I had said thanks and stayed on the gas to get to the next destination.

Spiritually, we should slow down, pull over and spend some time with Him at the "Rest Areas" He provides along life's highway. Just chilling, talking and listening to Him. Telling Him thank you for bringing us this far down the road. Then when we're rested and restored, take a look at His map to see what destination He has in mind for us next. Then we should head down the road (at His speed limit) to the next destination on His map.

OUCH! Praise God! — May 18

When you are the Captain of the ship it is your responsibility to make sure the vessel reaches its destination and completes the mission or task it was assigned. More often than not, the Captain is not the owner of the ship. The Captain is given "stewardship" of the vessel. In a sense that's what God has done with families. He is the owner of the ship known as the *The Family* and has given parents stewardship over children to "bring them up in the way they should go." *Go* is the part I am having the problem with right now.

Thanks mainly to my First Mate (Hannah Poo), each member of The Crew was brought up in the way they should go.

Well, a few weeks ago, one of The Crew became the Captain of his own ship. Ben and Brianna were married in a beautiful wedding right here in our harbor. They had moved here in anticipation of staying in these waters. I can't tell you how thrilled I was to have them living right here in town.

Needless to say, the seas are not always smooth. So, Ben went to the Owner of his ship (God) and ask Him how to navigate the situation. (OK, maybe too many nautical terms, but you get the point). He searched the Word, prayed, sought Godly counsel and applied what the Lord showed him to his situation. As a dad who wants nothing more than his sons to grow up into men of God, it just doesn't get any better than that! Praise God!

What did God show them to do? To take jobs far away from here and to serve Him in a church to which He is calling them. Ouch! I know beyond a shadow of a doubt that they are doing what God has called them to do. I know we can't always see or understand the things God is up to, but I do know it is always best to trust and obey Him. Emotionally, this has been very tough for all of us. Spiritually, I could not be more proud of them. So with tears in my eyes as they sail away I say, "Ouch! Praise God!"

P.S. Ben and Brianna, you two will see God move in your lives and in the lives of your Crew. I love you both!

Church Flavors   May 19

Around my house lately we have a little fun bantering back and forth about the virtues of hot coffee vs cold, hot tea or iced, or if we use flavored creamer. It can get pretty funny, especially when I get on my son, Ryan's machismo about cold, flavored coffee as he rags me about a certain "sissy" floating candy bar I like. Nothing serious, we have a good laugh about it. Bottom line is, no matter how you flavor it, it's still coffee, tea or a candy bar.

Unfortunately, a discussion that most often does get serious and there is no laughter anywhere near it, is when we (church people) discuss (argue) over denominational issues. I'll be honest here and say this behavior is destructive to the Body in no small measure. It usually starts out with a question born from misconception anyway. You've heart it. Something along the lines of: "What religion are you?" And the answer comes back: "I am a Methodist or Baptist or Presbyterian or ... " You get the idea. Then the heat is on because everyone thinks they're right!

Arguments like: "so and so started this church" and "so and so founded this church." Nope! The death and resurrection of Jesus started "The Church" and somewhere along the way, man poured chocolate, vanilla, or strawberry syrup on it to suit their own palette!

First of all these are not "religions" (at least they aren't supposed to be). They are groups that have a different take on theology, styles of worship and purposes of their church. They are (hopefully) different flavors of the same coffee.

I confess that I too have my favorite flavor of church, just like I have a favorite barbecue sauce for my meat and favorite kind of spread to go on bread. What we need to be so very careful about is coming against others who are eating the same meat and bread with just a little different sauce. The sauce is not important. What is important is the nourishment we will get from the meat and bread we eat.

I think that the funniest thing yet to happen when we get to heaven will be the look on some people's faces when they see who they are sitting across from at the Marriage Supper of the Lamb! Or maybe it won't be funny. Maybe we'll realize what could have been.

Let's act like people who will share our water with anyone even if they put a little strawberry syrup in it.

Humorous Humility   May 20

Back in the day I used to play a decent game of baseball. I was proud of it too. I hit for average with a decent amount of pop, had a good arm and could scoop with the best of 'em. So, as my career progressed, it was only natural to move up to the big leagues (church softball). I usually played second base and thought I was pretty hot stuff. Until that fateful day at practice.

During this same span in our lives Hannah was playing softball as well. She had her own wooden bat she was using in the ladies league. We men were using the new aluminum bats in our league at the time. It occurred to me that it might be kind of fun to take her wooden bat to our practice and stick it in our bat rack. If anyone picked it up I would harass them unmercifully for using a woman's bat.

Well, my plan was working perfectly. Lee, a good friend of mine, grabbed the bat and stepped up to the plate. Now he, being a good friend, I proceeded to lay it on pretty thick: "I can't believe you are going to hit with a woman's bat." and "Do you guys think he can hit it past the mound?" I went on and on … Then he swings and drives a hard liner right at my feet. I had missed nothing all day until that ball, with a load of top spin, hit me right in the toes, spins upward tearing up my shin, my chest and my face before heading undeterred into the outfield!

I was left there standing on one leg, holding my chest and face, having been "run over" by a softball off a woman's bat. Of course the place I was hit in the face was the beginning spot for the whole episode, my big mouth! It now had a swollen side to it with a hole in it leaking blood down my chin!

You don't have to be a brain surgeon to figure out the moral of the story here. The funny thing is even though I get the lesson here and learn from it, sometimes I'll forget it and I am taught it over and over again. I know some of you guys are going, "Yeah Greg, you're right. Do you remember the time you said so and so and this and that happened?" Don't remind me! Humor is fun, but prideful humor will hit you right in the mouth!

One of my Christian brothers, who is always a good example to me, has a guard on his lips like few others I know and he seems to have a "holy" pause before replying to serious comments or questions. That is what I am going to ask God to give me. "Lord, put a guard on my lips, that what I say will serve to lift You up and draw men to You, Amen."

Biblical references too numerous to mention …

Let's Go Fishing   May 21

Being a fisherman, one of my favorite stories in the Bible is when Jesus had breakfast with the (fishermen) disciples by the Sea of Tiberias. After His resurrection, Jesus shows up on the shore one morning after the guys have been out fishing all night. They had caught nothing (you've been on those trips). Jesus tells them where to throw their net and they are unable to haul in the enormous catch until they get to shore.

When they get to Him, Jesus has a fire going. They eat fish and bread together again. Jesus restores Peter, asking him if he loves Him. Three times He ask Peter this and instructs him to feed His sheep. Peter is repentant, forgiven and restored. Later Jesus tells Peter to not concern himself with what He has for John.

There always seems to be several lessons in each story in the Bible. Maybe that's some of the reason it always seems fresh and new as we read it again and again. We find ourselves in a different circumstance or place in our lives and the Word speaks to us a new teaching, lesson or revelation from God.

For instance, many insights can be gleaned from this story in John 21. 1) The Son of God wants to have breakfast and hang out with His crew, showing His love for them. He loves us and wants to spend time with us. 2) Obeying Him, throwing the net where and when He says, will reap all we need. 3) He teaches, forgives and restores. 4) Serve Me (feed My sheep) 5) Don't be jealous of or compare yourself to others, just follow Me.

One more thing I get from this story (and putting it with many others in the Bible) is that Jesus did much, if not most of His ministry outside the church building. Few are called to actually spend the bulk of their time in the church building. Make no mistake what I'm saying here. We are to gather together as brothers and sisters in unity as believers. The church should be a place we gather to be encouraged, taught and praise God together. Jesus taught in the synagogues and the Temple.

However, from there we are to go out and make disciples. We can throw our net (testimony and faith) into the sea of people out there in the world where God shows us to fish. Spiritually speaking, we can build a warm fire, cook something good to eat and share the love of Christ with others. We can show His power by telling of the things He has done for us and in us. I think we should also be real, letting others see the "warts" in our lives, so that they can see His mercy, grace and forgiveness He offers all of us. Let's go fishing!

Highway To Heaven   May 22

I was a construction worker from time to time as a young adult. Once we were building a school in a small town about two hundred miles from my home. I would stay in the town where we were working during the week and commute back and forth to my hometown on the weekends. I had a routine when traveling home for the weekend of stopping at Mr. Brown's place. Mr. Brown's, located about half way home, was a hole in the wall kind of convenience store where I could get some munchies and gas if needed.

On one of these trips home I was driving my (new to me) 1967 Fastback Volkswagon. It was clean and I had just got a new paint job. It had a flathead engine and dual carbs. No matter. You can have all that on an old VW and call it a fastback. It didn't really burn up the highway.

On the way home one Friday, I stopped as usual at Mr. Brown's. He would come out and pump the gas himself. He had to be the last guy on the planet doing that! Anyway, he pumped the gas as I went inside to the restroom. After getting some munchies and paying for the gas, I was on my way down the road.

When I got this hot rod up to highway speed, several minutes later, my hood flew up smashing my windshield and wrapping over the roof of the car! I was roaring down a two-lane highway at 75 mph and realized I could see nothing but my mangled hood and busted windshield! I stuck my head out the window while slowing down and pulled off the highway. Although it was a scary few seconds, looking back, it was probably a pretty funny sight to see if you had been in an oncoming car in the other lane!

The other funny sight you may have seen, if you had been on the highway that day, would have been me trying to put the hood of the car back down so I could drive the rest of the way home. I got the hood pulled down pretty close, but I ended up having to get on top of the hood and literally jump up and down on it to bend it enough to latch!

Here's how all this came about. In the old VW's, the engines were located in the back, where most cars have a trunk. The trunk was in the front under the hood. Also under the hood was the gas tank port. To put gas in the VW you had to lift the hood to get to the gas cap. Mr. Brown had filled up my tank and then failed to close the hood all the way. When I got the car up to highway speed the air got underneath the hood and lifted it up.

There's more to this VW story but I'll get to that tomorrow. But for today, remember to "close your hood" all the way! Spiritually speaking, this may be a reach as far as an analogy, but it's what comes to my mind. The hood and the latch on your vehicle have a relationship that requires them to be hooked together tightly so as to not become separated causing any range of problems. The tighter (closer) we are hooked to Jesus, the better we are going to be able to face challenges of the "winds" that come against us. The "Mr. Browns" of the world (pastors, teachers and even parents) can't keep our latches (relationship to Jesus) closed for us. We have to do that for ourselves. Lets stay latched to Him!

Highway To Heaven Part 2   May 23

There I was with a freshly painted VW that had a busted windshield and a wrinkled hood. (See Highway To Heaven, May 22) I was a young man at the time and the cars I had owned to this point were old ones and regularly in need of repair. I had learned quite a bit about working on cars as a result. But the old VW's weren't really cars! They were more like some blend of gas golf carts with a go cart suspension, put together by those little guys who live in tree trunks! Air cooled? Great idea for Florida summers, not to mention, just plain ugly!

Anyway, I found a hood to fit (wrong color, of course). It was relatively easy to replace. But that windshield was going to be another story. The windshield was curved both lengthwise, widthwise and on the ends. I figured it would be better to find someone who knew what they were doing to install it rather than risking me breaking that hard to find windshield. Dad had a cousin who worked in a body shop and he helped me out.

It was a trick to install. He did all kinds of neat little tricks to get the old glass out without leaving shattered pieces in the grooves. Then he did this thing where he wrapped a thin rope all the way around the glass. Try getting that rope to stay on the glass while you're installing that crooked windshield! After it was in the grooves, he was somehow able to pull the rope out and leave the windshield tightly in place.

The bottom line here is to seek out those who have more knowledge, experience, wisdom, discernment, sound judgment and diligence than we may possess, before we make decisions about doing things. The Bible is just full of references indicating that we should get godly counsel before making important decisions.

In my flesh, I want to decide things for myself, by myself. That's just stupid pride! It has cost me money, time, and worse it can be detrimental to family and friends. All because I won't seek out wise counsel. In all decisions, we should check our potential decisions and how it aligns with the Word in prayerful consideration and with godly counsel.

Happily Ever After   May 24

Since I was a little boy I have always loved the "cavalry to the rescue" ending to a movie. I don't even remember the titles of some of these old movies. One typical ending scene comes to mind in which the wagon train is surrounded, under attack, with no escape. At the last possible second, the sound of a bugle playing "charge" is heard in the distance. The cavalry has come to the rescue! Relief appears on the faces of those being saved from certain death and they live happily ever after. Of course sometime earlier in the movie, when the people in the wagon train knew they were in danger, they sent someone to tell the cavalry they needed to be rescued.

I have also seen movies in which the cavalry never came and all were lost. That kind of ending stinks!

Death of a loved one just isn't easy for those left behind. Sometimes it is shocking and unexpected. Other times it is after a long battle with disease. Many times we as believers have prayed long and hard for the healing that we believe God will provide (the way we want Him to provide the healing, this side of heaven). Then the healing doesn't come the way we want it. We may feel like God's healing cavalry didn't bother to show up.

In reality, God's cavalry, His rescue, doesn't always come on this side of death to save our earthly life. However, His cavalry is the only rescue that has the power to save us after our earthly death.

So, have you sent for God's cavalry? Have you told Him you are surrounded and even infiltrated by sin and certain death? He will come to the rescue. Oh yeah, and on the other side of death, you will live "happily ever after"!

One Reason God Hates Sin — May 25

I heard a preacher the other day say that one reason God hates sin is because it affects the innocent. That statement was in his sermon but not the topic of his message. That statement was profound to me. I'm not sure I absorbed anything he said after that statement. It began to make me think about my view of sin.

Sure, if some dictator out there is oppressing and killing people, his sin is affecting others. But what about my sins. Have my past sins had negative affects on others? If I commit sins today will it affect others? What about sins in the future?

I can only look back for results. Sins of lies about others (especially when I was a child) to keep me out of trouble, would get them into trouble. Sins of committing to do a job or help someone do a job, then not keeping my word would leave them in a bind and put it on someone else to complete the task. How about sins of encouraging others to do wrong? For instance, skipping school, siphoning gas from someone's car or buying alcohol while we were underage. What about not being a good steward of my family's finances, spending on wants and desires while having to use credit to pay for bills, doctors, food and other needs. This certainly affected my family!

I wasn't thinking of how my sins would affect others. It was as if my sins were mine and only hurt me! This was not and is not the case. It would seem that along with asking the Lord for forgiveness, there are a lot of people out there that I need to ask to forgive for my sins.

...when you are tempted, he will also provide you a way out so that you can stand up under it. – I Corinthians 10:13

In the future the thought of how my sin might affect an innocent person may be my way out of temptation. Thereby, no sin, no negative affect to anyone, only glory to God.

Have You Been Here?　　　　　　　　May 26

I got up this morning feeling like I was rode hard and put away wet. My head hurts and it feels like it has a gallon of snot in it. I'm aching all over and when I cough it feels like my chest is on fire.

I got up early so I could go over to the twenty-four hour drug store and get some medications. When I walked into the kitchen I heard the TV. Hannah is awake and the first thing out of her mouth is, "I don't feel well, will you pray for me?" She detects my irritation, probably from a look on my face and she asks, "What is it?"

I answered, "I'm sorry, I don't feel well either." What I was truly, selfishly thinking was "You can't be sick! I'm sick! I'm the one who needs the TLC! Me, me, me! I don't want to go to work, I just want to go over there on that couch and have you bring me soup and juice all day long!"

I could probably stop writing right here, but when am I going to get it? I feel like I'm getting better and better at the "Greatest Commandment," but that "the second one is like it" is just giving me fits! Sure, when I feel like it and that person is not being a jerk, I can "love my neighbor" and "think of them more highly than myself."

The only people who go to the all night drug store at 4:30 in the morning, are people who need drugs and the people on drugs. When I went over there this morning, there he stood, stoned out of his gourd in the entrance door. Did I have a Jesus-like "love thy neighbor" attitude towards him? Nope! I waited a few seconds for him to stop badgering the clerk and then I moved towards him with the intentions of assisting him out of the doorway, old school style. That would not have been a great witness and demonstration of the second most important commandment! He staggered out of the way just in time.

Bottom line. He calls us to love them all, all the time, not just when we feel like it and not just when they're being nice. This is a hard one to get down in my heart to stay. I guess the lessons will continue until I get it.

Get In   May 27

The "Woman at the Well" (John 4 :1-45) is a beautiful picture of the love of God. It is also a perfect example of being "in the world and not of the world."

Jesus had a need of His own. His earthly body was thirsty and He could not humanly draw water from Jacob's well. How often do we find ourselves in need of something and during that time of our need we give no thought to the needs of others? Not Jesus. He meets the Samaritan woman at the well and shows concern for her need. She is thirsty too, for water she can't get by herself, "spiritual water."

I think there is a good lesson here. That being, when we find ourselves in need of something, look around, we might just have what someone else needs. Are you getting hungry? Someone might need a meal. Are you thirsty? Someone might need a drink. Are you hurting? Someone might need some encouragement. Be sensitive to God's leading. Their need to quench their hunger, thirst and pain may be a spiritual need as well as physical need. God will not let us down in these (or any other) situations as long as we trust Him. Go ahead, try Him. I dare you!

Secondly, this story demonstrates "being in the world and not of it." So many of us use this instruction as some excuse to avoid unbelievers, sinners and others. We may view ourselves as more important. First of all, that viewpoint (that we or God view ourselves as more important and can't risk being "tainted by sinners") is a lie from the pit of hell!

Jesus went right through Samaria. The land of the people the Jews viewed as a lesser, mixed race of traitors! He then talks to a woman of a less-than-stellar reputation and shows this non-deserving woman the love of God. Then God uses her to draw a whole town to the Lord!

Jesus demonstrated being "in the world." We can be in the world anywhere! All the way in. He talked with sinners and He ate with them too. (In that day and place, if you ate with someone, you were considered as family).

Get in the world and show them Jesus, not church, not how good we act or look on the outside, but show them who Jesus is and how He has changed you on the inside.

Free Refills — May 28

"Well done, good and faithful servant! You have been faithful in a few things; I will put you in charge of many things. Come and share your master's happiness!" – Matthew 25:21

We like hearing that one come out of Jesus' mouth, don't we?

Yeah baby, give me more things and more power! OK, OK, I know that He is talking about being a faithful servant. I don't know about you, but if I'm not careful I can get caught up in "what's in it for me." If I find myself in this mindset, I could let the things I expect to get, be my motive for service. We should serve Him out of our love for Him and what He has done and is doing for us. I guess that's a good lesson in itself but that is not where I was really going with this.

Usually when I think about the things I might receive as a blessing as a result of my service and obedience, it is along the lines of material things. This morning however, I am thinking along the lines of spiritual blessings. The Bible is full of the principle of "reaping what we sow" and "getting in return more of what we give."

This morning I have 1 Corinthians 13 on my mind. You know, faith, hope and love. How about if we sow these things into others lives? Yep, we get a dose of them back as a blessing. A bigger dose! There's something money and power can't buy! Without just one of these (faith, hope or love) spiritually speaking, we are severely wounded. Without two of them we are critically wounded. Without all three, we are "dead men walking." One thing is for sure, there is no shortage of people out there that we can pass along the love of God to, show them the hope He gives us and share with them our faith in Him. God can use us to heal "dead men walking!"

I'll bet you're thinking of someone right now with whom you can share your faith, hope and love. Besides, when all else is gone, "these three remain: faith, hope and love." What great gifts to give! What great gifts to get refilled in ourselves!

Don't Pick The Scab, Wear The Bandage May 29

Sometimes people can be pretty hard on us. When we were children, maybe a parent was hard on us. You know, overly harsh with words or other punishment. There could have been a lot of reasons, good or bad. Maybe we were doing something dangerous to ourselves or others. That'll get a mom or dad hot!

Maybe they're just having their own bad day. Maybe they think they're toughening us up. Maybe they're just jerks and don't care.

It doesn't have to be a parent. It could be a boss, a spouse, another family member or a friend. Anyone who has influence on us.

But who is really the hardest on us? Who bashes us the most? Who keeps us down and won't let us up? For most of us, it's ourselves! That's right! Many of our longest running battles with unworthiness are self-inflicted and we don't search for healing. Instead we keep picking at the wound like a kid pulling at a scab.

When I was a kid I crashed many times on my bike. Many times it was while doing some trick I shouldn't try. My knees were a constant scab. If I picked at it, it would bleed again and it would take longer to heal. But if I left the bandage on my knee (not picking at the scab and keeping it covered) the wound would heal.

When we sin or do something we think makes us unworthy, it's like doing that trick we shouldn't have tried. If we pick at it (beat ourselves up about it) the wound is not going to heal.

But there is a "bandage" and it's Jesus and what He did on the cross. He covers our sin (wound) and heals (forgives) us. So why keep picking at it? When we continue to pick at our self-inflicted wound, are we acting as if His death on the cross was not good enough medicine for our sins?

It seems to me that we are often much more inclined to forgive others than we are to forgive ourselves. His forgiveness is for us too. Anything that says different is a lie from the pit of hell!

So go ahead, try it! Forgive yourself! I dare you! It feels great! You don't need to continue beating yourself up to pay for something you did wrong. It's already paid for. It's a gift from God. Don't you want it?

Don't Roll The Stop Sign   May 30

I've got a few friends who are police officers and they tell me not to roll through stop signs. You know what I mean; slow down as you approach the stop sign, but roll on through if the intersection is clear. The fine for these "rolling stops" has increased dramatically and it can hurt your wallet.

Well, I have come to one of these "stop signs" in a spiritual sense. I almost didn't see it and even when I did see it, I almost rolled on through straight ahead. There is something in me that wants to drive me to be *doing* something. "Don't just sit there Greg, get busy, do something!" That's not God, that's Greg talking! There's probably some pride and self importance on my part, thinking I'm missing some ministry assignment and God can't get it done without me. Anyway, there is this feeling and push in me to wonder: "Which way do I go now, God?"

It turns out the answer (for now) seems to be: "STOP, don't go anywhere, right now." The issue seems to be that I think I am supposed to be "doing" something all the time. My pastor once said we are "human beings," not "humans doing." Good stuff!

In other words, don't be running the stop signs of life. God puts them there for a reason. Personally I am sitting at one right now waiting on Him to give me direction on some financial issues. (Not necessarily a lack of funds, but how to apply them rightly.) Then I see another stop sign at the next intersection that has to do with ministry decisions.

It doesn't matter if we have to slam on the brakes! We should not carelessly run the stop signs God places in the roads of our lives. We shouldn't even slowly roll through them thinking we know which way to go. When we see a stop sign in our lives, we should stop completely. Pull off the road if we have to, but don't roll through the sign. Get directions from God. Stop and pray. Read the Word. Get some godly counsel. Then press on knowing we have the right directions.

Sheep In Wolf's Clothing   May 31

We used to live in a community that seemed to always have trouble with the water possibly being contaminated. It seemed as if every month or two, I would come home from work and find a card on the front door from the local water authority advising us to "boil our drinking water until further notice." There would have been some break in a water main or other situation causing possible contamination.

After the repairs were done and the time for concern was over, the water quality had been verified, we could quit boiling the water and return to using it normally. The water looked the same coming out of the faucet when it was possibly contaminated as it did later when the danger for contamination had passed. Looks can be deceiving.

It my teens, I played a lot of golf. One of the guys we often played with was the most foul mouthed, womanizing (among other things) character I have personally ever known. He would say or do anything, just about anywhere. Those of you who play know that bad golf does not typically bring out the best in a man. And he wasn't that good at golf. I think you get it.

Anyway, I had not seen him in years. I would not have been surprised to hear if he was dead or in prison, but the next time I saw him was in a church. A church! Going to church in and of itself does not fix us. God does the repairs on willing, surrendered people. Nevertheless, there he was, and yes, I was suspicious! It was not my job to judge him, but he looked the same to me. I had to know what was up.

It turns out that somewhere between the last time I saw him and that day, his personal and professional life had caved in on him and he had turned to the Lord. He had committed himself to serving God and ran a jail ministry. I was blown away. And even though he looked the same (like the contaminated water does before and after you boil it), the change in him was real. He has a new life and God is purifying him daily.

If God can do this awesome work in that man, I know he can do it in anyone who is willing to turn to Him!

Deeper Waters — June 1

We have always lived down here on the Gulf. If you're going to be around water, you better learn to swim and how to otherwise be safe in and on the water. I remember taking my oldest son to the beach one day to teach him how to swim. It was a beautiful day and the water was calm and clear, perfect. If you're going swimming in the Gulf, you want these kind of conditions so you can see how deep the water is and what's in it, along with no dangerous surf or current.

The swim lessons were going great. He got the hang of it really quick; a natural. Then the first school of stingrays came right by us. Stingrays are not typically the most dangerous things in the sea, especially when they are on the move, so we swam some more. Then another school came by us, lesson over. Many more came by that day but we weren't in the water.

Although my son's confidence grew in his swimming ability, I still required him to wear a life vest when we were out on the boat. The boat can take us out into very deep waters; water that we can't see how deep it is or how strong the current is or what dangers lurk below.

As I wrote the other day, I have come to one of those crossroads in life that we all come to in one form or another. For me it is a ministry crossroad that will require me to go into "deeper, uncharted waters." I don't think of myself as special in any of this. In fact, it will require me to trust God more and to have more faith in Him to come through. He knows what's in these waters.

Some of the things I believe are in the future: A website, a book, ministry to orphans, widows, and the homeless, and a more focused discipleship ministry to men. I believe the Lord needs more godly men.

I cannot see what is in these deeper waters ahead, so I ask sincerely for your prayers. Although Jesus will be my life vest, I believe through our prayers, He will show us how to navigate in uncharted waters, keeping us from the dangers that lurk in deep water.

Eye Of The Storm   June 2

Having lived my life on the coast I have seen and been through my share of hurricanes. Most of the time they have been glancing blows but a few have been direct hits. There is quite a difference in the eye of the storm coming ashore 50 or 100 miles down the coast, and the eye making landfall over your house.

For instance, I remember Hurricane Frederick that made landfall about 50 miles from my home. We had gusts of over 110 miles per hour and some minor tree damage. Years later however, Hurricane Erin came right over the house. Erin was by comparison a much smaller storm, but was a direct hit and the winds were sustained at about 90 mph for hours, causing considerable damage in my area, more than Frederick.

Although hurricanes are no fun, there is something amazing to me about being in the eye of these massive storms. After being hunkered down for hours as winds increase steadily with destructive force, the eye passes over and the sky clears for a period of time. Then, the back side of the storm passes through, causing more destruction and havoc.

I remember the feeling of safety as I went outside when the eye passed over me, all the while knowing and anticipating the rest of the storm's coming wrath. For a while, as the eye passed over, it was safe. The sky was beautiful and the wind was still, yet I knew the storm was raging right there around me as was evident by the surrounding damage.

Even these monsters of destruction run their course, either by dissipating out at sea or being worn down by land fall, but the storm does end. I was struck by the idea that it would be awesome to remain in the eye of the storm until it had run its course. Even with all of our technology being used by the brightest minds in the weather world, man cannot accurately predict where these storms are going to go or what they are going to do next.

As awful and destructive as these storms can be, there is some good that can come from having been through them. We have all seen and read the heroic stories of rescue during and after these storms and the friendships that were formed by neighbors helping each other, having previously done little more than saying hello to one another. These stories are a testimony to the heroism and true character of the common man when faced with adversity after these terrible storms.

Although it is no fun, hurtful in ways, and no one desires to go through them, the storms of our personal lives bear the same fruit. We are strengthened by these storms in our inner man. The storms of life build our character and faith. They show us what we really are made of and give us confidence of who we are in Christ.

The wonderful thing about the hurricanes of our personal lives is that Jesus is the "Eye" of the storm that we can run into in the midst of most intense winds.

Recently, when I found myself in one of the more difficult times in my life, I knew that it was time to trust God. I had been here before and handled things my own way. I had wandered outside the Eye and was beaten brutally by the intense winds just outside the Eye wall.

During this time in my life I can honestly say that I did a better job (with God's guidance and help) of staying safe in Jesus (the Eye of my storm). The storm rages on outside, but I am safe within Him! It is amazing how much the stress and worry has gone away as my faith and trust grows as I get closer to Him.

My encouragement to us is to stay in the Eye of our storms, Jesus, because He knows where the storm is going and what it is going to do to us and in us. One more encouragement, our current storm will dissipate and all we will see is the beautiful clear skies of Jesus, the Eye of our storms.

Consider it pure joy, my brothers and sisters, whenever you face trials of many kinds, because you know that the testing of your faith produces perseverance. Let perseverance finish its work so that you may be mature and complete, not lacking anything. – James 1:2-4

Go To Practice — June 3

Last night some friends and I were talking about the importance of reading the Bible and spending time with God. This is what the Lord seeks from us. It is what we can give Him; ourselves in a personal relationship.

Through reading the Word and spending time in prayer, He gives us knowledge, strength and builds our faith. In obeying His Word, we can see Him work in our lives and we learn to trust Him. More trust brings more faith, brings more obedience, brings more of His blessing into our lives.

The College Baseball World Series is being played this week. These young men did not get this good at baseball overnight! To be sure, each one was born with some gifts and talent, but they had to be told and shown how to use their gifts. They were instructed by their coaches and routinely practiced those instructions daily. That takes a lot of discipline. The payoff comes at game time when they perform at their peak levels because they have invested time and effort in preparation for the game. Each player knows what he is supposed to do. He is strong enough to compete and believes he can do what is required of him to attain the victory.

Baseball is just a game in the flesh that can be played again tomorrow when your team loses. There are no life and death consequences.

The game for souls (ours and others) is most definitely life and death (eternally). Ooooh, dramatic? No, ooooh, the truth. We need to be equipped out there for the "soul" benefit of ourselves and others.

We should go to practice daily (read the Word), talk to the coach (pray), and then get in the game (live our lives as Godly as we can). We won't win anything if we just sit comfortably on the bench. Be ready; the game of souls could be on at any time. Go to practice!

But in your hearts set apart Christ as Lord. Always be prepared to give an answer to everyone who ask you to give the reason for the hope that you have. But do this with gentleness and respect. – 1 Peter 3:15

Style In The Kingdom   June 4

I was reading this devotional the other day and it triggered in me lessons learned long ago having to do with judging others. If you've ever been in or around "revival," you know that all hell can break loose! The more God moves, the more hell hates it! I won't get into what was God and what was the devil. Suffice to say there was a whole lot of both! God moved mightily and Satan hacked away at His work.

The revival profoundly affected the church I was attending at the time. It affected the worship, in that some wanted the new music and some wanted the old hymns. Some services had no time limit, to which some folks were opposed. Some wanted extended personal prayer times and others wanted traditional pastoral prayer.

I am ashamed to say I fell into the camp of we do it all the new way (change). Others (just as shamefully) were in the camp of staying the old way (no change). Others, the wiser of the three camps, wanted separate services for each "style" of worship.

Now go ahead and get upset with me if you want to because I said "style" of worship, but that's what it is, as I was to learn later. Both styles are good and pleasing to the Lord, but it is your style. Potatoes are potatoes, fried, baked, mashed or salad. Eggs are eggs, scrambled, over easy or hard-boiled. Steak is steak, fried, grilled or broiled. These will all fill you up and satisfy you no matter which style you serve them.

Anyway, I was in a service one day when this man of God stood up to speak. You know who the men of God are in your midst. Nobody has to tell you. This man was not outspoken, instead a quiet man, but when he did speak it was profound and wise. He preferred the traditional style of worship himself, but knowing him to be a man of God, he had my attention. He said things like, many styles of worship will please God as long as your heart is after Him. He also said that we knew each others hearts, that we had loved one another and should continue to do so, understanding that we each may prefer a different style of worship.

I was changed (again) in that moment! Unfortunately everyone was not changed. Some stood their "old" ground and some stood their "new" ground, to the detriment of many. To this day, nothing, and I mean nothing, sets me off like brothers in battle (not difference of opinion, but differences without love).

So which is it going to be, the new way or the old way? I believe the Lord would say: "Its the same, only different."

"A new command I give you: Love one another. As I have loved you, so you must love one another. By this everyone will know that you are my disciples, if you love one another." – John 13:34-35

Stupid Pride   June 5

So the other day while delivering my route, I see this elderly man on the next corner sitting on his turned over garbage can. Trash has spilled out and fallen into the ditch a few feet away. He doesn't appear injured, he's just sitting there on his garbage. I should have taken a picture because it made me grin.

I turned up a short street to make a few deliveries and then made the corner right in front of his house. At this point more of his garbage had spilled out and he had spilled himself right into the ditch! He was on all fours and looked like an old crab sliding sideways down into the ditch. I stopped the truck right in front of where he had landed. I popped off my seat belt as I asked him if he needed help getting up. Now get this. He looks up at me and starts to act like he's picking up the trash in the ditch. Then he defiantly refused my offer to assist him out of his predicament! I fastened my seat belt and rolled on down the road. Pride will leave your butt in a ditch every time!

Do you remember that poster from the 70's of the rat giving the finger to the hawk swooping down on him with his talons ready to grab him for supper? It was titled, "Last Act Of Defiance." Pride can also cause us to be eaten alive. Maybe the hawk would think twice if a lion were sitting next to the rat. Especially if it were the "Lion of Judah." Maybe the rat wouldn't even feel the need to give the hawk the finger because he's not afraid of the hawk when the lion is with him. Maybe if the rat really trusted the lion, he wouldn't even notice the hawk was around. Maybe the hawk wouldn't even come around. A prideful rat certainly needs the Lion's protection.

Woe Is Me   June 6

One beautiful summer day we went with some friends to the beach. We went to my favorite place that only locals seemed to know about that was down an old beach road. There was a little place to park and then a pretty good walk to the water. It was worth the walk because even in the middle of the summer there would be very few people around and never a crowd.

On this day my friend and I were jumping off a sand dune about twenty feet high trying to out distance each other. I won on my last jump. It was my last jump because of the pain that shot through my foot on my landing! And as I described, this was a secluded spot a long way from the car. Friends tried to carry me, but it was no use through the soft sand.

As we pondered our options, one of the few other people on that stretch of beach offered to go back, get his Jeep and take us to our car. I obviously could not drive my car. Thankfully, I had just taught Hannah to drive my standard shift. She got plenty of stop and go experience that day because we were in slow heavy traffic several hours before being able to get off the extremely crowded island.

By the time we got to the hospital my foot looked like it had a golf ball in it. I clearly remember, only a few days earlier, bragging about having never broken a bone. I had some "woe is me" going on as the anxiety and apprehension began to build with the thought of a doctor having to reset the bones in my foot. My focus was on my problems.

When we walked into the ER at the base hospital, hours after my winning jump, there were no patients waiting. I thought, "at least this won't take long," still thinking of myself.

Then it happened. They took me back to a ER room that had about six beds with partially closed curtains separating them. I was told there was no bone doctor on duty so they called one and he was on his way. Great, more waiting! As I sat in there waiting, the place became a M.A.S.H. unit!

They brought in a young teenage girl who after being out all night, went up on her roof that morning to take a nap in the sun. She had been there all day. She was nearly purple and dehydrated terribly! My problems seemed a little smaller.

Right when my doctor arrived to examine me, a little boy about eight or nine was brought in by his mom who said: "I think my son broke his arm!" His arm had a "U" shape in it, it was broken in two places. My doctor immediately left me and to tend to the little boy. He held the boys arm and talked soothingly to him right before setting his arm. That little boy's scream was horrifying! My foot seemed a little less important.

It got even worse, as the doctor finished with the little boy, two guys who had been in a head on collision were brought in. The nurses had never stopped to close the curtains during all the chaos. I could hear and see everything that was going on. As they put these guys on the beds across the room from me, I could see how serious it was; they were cut and broken from head to toe!

The doc looked over at me and said: "Sorry, it's going to be awhile."

I nodded; my foot didn't really hurt that bad. In fact, I realized I didn't have any problems in comparison to so many others. Perspective man, perspective.

Been Fishing Lately　　　　　　　　　　　June 7

My first boat was a little, ugly, green, metal jon boat. It was so small two guys could make it sit down in the water literally inches from the water line. It was an adventure every time I took it into water bigger than a mud puddle! The motor was so small (10hp) that you could almost row with oars as fast as that motor would push the boat. Nevertheless, it was a boat and we were no longer fishing from the shore.

On one particular adventure my Dad and I headed out into the pass to catch "the big one." It started out very calm that day and we were looking forward to the fun to come. It soon did. I hooked into something that immediately began ripping line off my reel. Dad reeled in the other lines. I handed him my rod and cranked the motor in an attempt to chase down the fish and get some of my line back.

The fish was headed for the open gulf and that's no place for a little flat bottom Jon boat! I angled the boat for the beach at the mouth of the gulf. I pulled the boat up on the beach and we fought the fish from there for the next 45 minutes. We were hoping for a big red or something else good but it turned out to be a 39 lb jack. It was fun anyway.

After we got squared away and rested up a few minutes, we decided to head back into the bay. However, by this time the water and the current in the pass was fast and pretty rough, especially for a tiny boat. We decided against dragging the little boat across the sand. It was too far and we were way too tired! We got into the boat and headed into the pass. It was a little hairy, but we were unscathed. We made for the smooth water in the bay behind the jetties. We fished there the rest of the day in the calm smooth waters and caught some very nice Redfish.

Funny how grown men will risk rough water for the unknown when there is peace and good fishing in the calm water nearby. Fishing is all about knowing what you're going after, knowing the environment you are going to have to be in, and being equipped with what you need to catch the desired fish.

"Fishers of men" need to do the same. We need to know the person we are going to talk to (usually). I believe there is a much greater likelihood of them believing us if we have befriended them and they see our lives, not just hear us claim to be something. Maybe meeting them on neutral ground will provide "calmer waters." Maybe not their favorite bar or a common workplace or our church, but maybe a restaurant, a ball game or even home. And we need to be equipped as much as possible with the knowledge of the Word of God and our testimonies of His work in our lives.

Got what you need? Then let's go fishing!

I've Got To Get Out Of Here — June 8

Back in the day, when I first started carrying mail, I had a walking route. It was mostly neighborhoods and some of the streets were rather short with four or five houses on each side. On this walking route there were many dogs. Most of them were harmless, but a few had really bad attitudes. It was wise to know where the dogs with the 'tudes liked to hangout.

On one of the short streets on my route lived a Doberman with a real bad disposition. He was inside the house most of the time barking and banging his head against the window as I put the mail in the box on the porch. Occasionally he would be outdoors, inside the fence, chained to a tree. This was a little unnerving as the fence appeared really short when he was standing against it, growling.

One day it finally happened. I routinely parked my jeep at the end of the street and proceeded to deliver the mail on this dog's street. About half way up the street (as I was delivering the mail across the street from the Dobie's house) I turned to see him sitting unrestrained in his front yard. Now it's on! I really felt the "fight or flight" thing.

It was really breezy which made the dog spray less effective, if not useless. I reached in my pocket and pulled out my pocket knife, put my mailbag in front of me and braced for the fight. As I tried to walk slowly back to the jeep, he positioned himself between me and the jeep. I decided to try to walk away in the other direction and surprisingly he just stood there and let me go!

I walked all the way around the block to get back to my jeep. He was back in his own front yard and I made it to the jeep without any further incident. By the way, the school bus was to stop at his driveway in about a half an hour. I went to the convenience store and called the police who came out with the dog catcher and removed the grumpy pooch, who I never saw again.

I can't help but think about I Corinthians 10:13:

No temptation has overtaken you except what is common to mankind. And God is faithful; he will not let you be tempted beyond what you can bear. But when you are tempted, he will also provide a way out so that you can endure it.

This analogy may be a bit of a reach because I wasn't really tempted to fight the dog but I saw no other way out. I'm telling you, I was resigned to the idea that this situation was going to get real messy, real fast. However, just looking to see if there was any other way out paid off. Yes, I had to take the long way around, but I got to where I was going.

That's what this verse tells us God will do for us. When we are tempted (which implies our watching out for temptation to come our way) it will not be more than we can say no to, and He will provide a way out. We must be on the watch for the way out and be willing to take that course. Even when it feels like the long way around.

Who's Driving Your Truck   June 9

I was driving a fully loaded moving van across country last week. I don't know about you, but I like having control of things. One thing on this road trip that I could not control to my satisfaction was the speed of my truck at all times.

Due to the weight of the truck and its cargo, the longer and steeper a hill, the more it would slow down going upgrade. It just didn't have the power to gain or even maintain speed going up long hills. Downhills had the opposite effect. That truck wanted to scream going down hills! This also presented a problem as there was a lot of traffic most of the day. Additionally, there seemed to be a rather sharp turn at the bottom of many of these hills.

One good thing on the truck was a limitation (a governor, we used to call them) to keep the truck from exceeding 75mph. This feature often kept me from having to use the brakes or downshift going downhill.

I think our lives can often be like that truck. We load ourselves completely full of the "cargo of life." Sometimes it can feel as if everything is cruising downhill. We seem to have it under control when we come upon a curve in the road of life. This is when we will either wish for or be thankful we have God in control of our lives. If we are obedient to Him, He can be the "governor" of our lives to keep us from speeding into certain disaster.

And when all the cargo we are carrying is an incredible, unbearable burden, we can turn to Him and He will supply the horsepower we need to climb the biggest hills in life. He often will lighten the load as well!

He knows where every curve and hill in our lives is located and He knows the best way to navigate them. Why wouldn't we let Him drive?

A Fish Story   June 10

Last week Ryan and I were out fishing in the gulf. I had brought a fish into the boat and was taking it off the lure when suddenly I felt the pain of a sharp hook. I have been pricked by a hook many times in my life but this felt considerably more painful. You know what I mean, not just "ouch", but "uh-oh" and your afraid to look at the wound because you know it's NOT good!

When I got my breath back and looked, I could see the hook all the way into my finger! (Breath gone again).

Ryan says: "You OK, Dad?"

Simple reply: "Nope."

You "sea dogs" know whats coming next. When a hook goes all the way in, it's not coming out the same way without doing serious damage while pulling that barb out. The best option is to push the hook the rest of the way through my finger. Then cut the barb of the hook off and pull the rest of the hook out, back through my already bloody, throbbing finger.

Following this "self-performed maritime emergency surgery," we continued to fish until we had our limit.

I really like that Jesus chose fishermen to be some of His disciples and analogizes drawing souls to Him with catching fish.

"Come, follow me," Jesus said, "and I will make you fishers of men." – Matthew 4:19

Just like going fishing for fish, if we go fishing for men we may get wounded some time. We will experience some rejection and hurt. In these cases we should just pull the barb on through, cut it off and throw it into the sea of forgiveness. Then go right back to fishing! We may yet catch the fish that caused the wound.

P.S. The guilty fish is now in my freezer awaiting my consumption!

Pick Me   June 11

Do you remember when you were a kid picking teams? You know, all the kids in the neighborhood would get together for a pick-up game of baseball, football, basketball or something. Two captains would be chosen, then they would take turns picking guys until the teams were decided.

I was always one of the first ones chosen. I had a good skill set for a lot of sports. Not bragging, just making a point. Even though it felt good getting picked first, I always felt a little bad for the last one or two to be picked. It was always the big slow kid or the little smart nerd who was last to be chosen.

Funny how things turn out; the big slow kid turns out to be a huge pro football lineman and the nerdy little kid is a rocket scientist! I became a delivery man!

Anyway, this all came to mind yesterday when I started wondering if Jesus would have chosen me to be on His team. You know, would He pick me to be one of His disciples? Would I be one of the last ones picked?

Well, He does equip those He calls. Look who He did pick! A tax collector, and a bunch of ordinary guys, including some fisherman! He picked a bunch of ordinary dudes to spread the Gospel. No Plan B, it was up to them. Seems like I would have picked the smartest, most dependable, and talented guys I could find to surround myself with if I were Him.

Then again, His ways are not our ways. His way is the best. So whose way should we use when we have to make choices? Pick Jesus.

Spiritual Pet Peeve #1   June 12

I do think God has a sense of humor. Which is my response to the people that say "don't speak that into my life" when someone is clearly kidding around, as if God is too stupid to know the difference between humor and a loose tongue!

Careful you "don't speakers," someone may catch you smiling. What would this world be if the lost started catching the believers smiling? They may wonder what we have and want it!

The lines above are from a comment I posted on a friends blog. She does a great job in explaining the fallacy in the thought process that God wants to hinder or hurt us to teach us and make us stronger. For instance if we pray for patience, He is going to send misery our way. It's a great read! It's entitled, "Is God A Practical Joker"?[1]

Her blog got me to thinking (more like stoked a fire in me) about what I think are some misconceptions we have about God in a lot of areas. This is probably my number one spiritual pet peeve! These are people's perceptions of our good God that are just pure crap!

Here's just one off my "Spiritual Pet Peeve List" (sounds like it should be a series).

The perception that God is a "hanging judge," sitting in His courtroom, gavel in hand, just frothing at the mouth to send the next sinner on a prison jet to hell! He is not a "hanging judge!" He is a loving righteous judge, who sent His own Son, (stop a second here and let that soak in, His own Son) to pay the price for our sin. The sentence was death and His Son paid it! Every time I think about God our Father sending His Son to die in my place, I can see the difference in His love for us and my love for others.

I love a lot of people, family and friends. I believe I would be willing to die to save many of them. The difference between my love and His is that, in truth, I would not be willing to die for all of them. And I would not send any of my sons to die for any of them!

So don't give me this bull about God's out to get me. He's sitting at his judgment seat waiting to pardon us, not convict us, of all our sin because the price has been paid. And He paid it with His Son! Now that's love!

[1] http://treasurecontained.com/2011/02/19/is-god-a-practical-joker-galatians-522/. Accessed on September 7, 2012.

Stay Tuned — June 13

So, I was driving down the road in my delivery truck today listening to my radio. That seemed all good, except my delivery truck does not have a factory installed radio. Therefore, I am relegated to using a stone age transistor radio, with marginal reception at best. "Forty plusers" will remember what I'm talking about; those radios you have to move around every time you change direction or channel! Go ahead and move that antennae (with aluminum foil on it because you broke it off the first day you bought the radio) at your own peril, because you may not find that station again!

I said all that to say that every time I turned a corner I had to tune back in to the station to which I had been listening. This took some effort and concentration but was well worth it because I was listening to a sermon that God was using to speak to me about issues in my life. What the preacher was saying was important and instructive to me. I needed to be tuned into that station to be able to hear him, to be able to receive the instruction and guidance.

Well, the route isn't straight, so you can guess what happened. As I turn the next corner, the reception changes and I seem to be right in the middle of two stations. This seemed to happen right as the sermon was reaching the lesson point that might give me some guidance. The other station was playing an old rock song that I really loved. The flesh was ready to rock!

Decision time.

This is clearly a natural demonstration of a spiritual battle we face as growing Christians. We must make every effort to stay tuned into God. We should "move the antennae around" to get ourselves into a position to hear God:

- by tuning ourselves to where God speaks to us such as His word, that we should read, study and obey
- by tuning ourselves to him in prayer, not only to talk to God, but also to listen to Him, and
- by tuning ourselves to Him in seeking Godly counsel for every circumstance we see God guiding us into or through.

Come near to God and He will come near to you. – James 4:8

This will take effort and concentration, but it is of utmost importance. He will speak to us through these "channels." He will give instruction and guidance as well as loving on us as we dwell in His presence.

However, be sure of this. The enemy will try to interfere with your reception by sending temptations your way. Often these temptations will be in the form of desires of the flesh.

But when you are tempted, He will also provide a way out so that you can stand up under it. – I Corinthians 10:13

When the temptations come, we have to decide where to tune our reception. You know we can't listen to both stations at the same time. Choose to stay tuned to God!

The Old Blue Truck   June 14

What to do with a day off? A road trip of course. It was a holiday, I was off work, and the guys were out of school. We decided where to go (the next state) and we had a little mischief in mind (rolling a friend's house) . The vehicle of choice (we didn't have a choice really) was an old blue pick-up my aunt had given me. There had been signs not to drive this truck further than a few miles away from home. For instance, it had caught fire on a previous road trip, but we were adventurous.

The first destination on this three point road trip was about ninety miles from home. As we crossed the state line we heard a loud noise followed by the sound of things flying around under the hood. We checked it out. The a/c belt had busted and wrapped around everything it could reach. No sweat; we cut it loose and pressed on. The a/c didn't work anyway.

We reached our first destination with no further problems. After having all the fun we could stand there, we pressed on to our second destination. As we were heading back down the highway, a patrolman passed us in the left lane – almost. Then he slowed down and fell in behind us. Next I was thinking, "Why would he want to checkout an old beat-up truck, that doesn't look road worthy, with out-of-state plates, full of guys with mischievous smiles on their faces?"

The lights and siren came on behind us. I pulled over.

I got out of the truck and walked back towards the officer's vehicle. I found out later, officers making a traffic stop prefer you to stay in the vehicle until they instruct you otherwise. We walked to the back of my truck and I answered his questions: "Is this your truck? Where are you going? Why? ..."

My answers: "Yes. To see a friend for a visit."

The officer was not buying it. A couple of squad cars of back-up are now arriving on the scene. He asked for my license and registration. I gave him my license and he had one of the other officers run it. I told him the registration was in the glove box and we walked (he was right behind me) around to the passenger side of my truck to get it. He told the boys to remain in the truck as the other officers took up positions around the truck. I reached into the truck, opened the glove box and there it is. No not the registration. My uncle's pistol!

Things are about to pickup if you know what I mean! As the officer assists me to "assume the position," I explained to him that it is a pellet gun my aunt gave me and I forgot to take it out of the truck. He didn't stop frisking me. They were about to get the boys out of the truck when a call came back over their radio saying I came up clean and my story checked out (my aunt and uncle's names on the title, etc).

Looking back I can see where the officer may have considered the old blue truck and its passengers suspicious. He had a suspicion and investigated the situation before making a decision (a judgment) on how to proceed. All of the officers handled the situation professionally. I have no complaints of their behavior and I appreciate the things people in law enforcement do daily to protect and serve.

Do we do the same when it comes to other people? I know that I have skipped right over suspicion of someone straight to judgment, just because of their appearance! Pathetic! Ask any law enforcement officer and they will tell you appearances can be deceiving. Good and bad.

We are to watch out for and be wary of "wolves in sheep's clothing." But you know what? There are a boatload of sheep out there who can't afford anything but (what may appear to us) as wolves' clothing! Maybe if we have a suspicion of someone being a wolf we should have the nerve, concern, and the love of God to investigate before judging.

Maybe we should be real careful about who and why we judge.

Maybe we should leave all the judgment that we can up to God. I'm thinking He can tell who the real wolves are a little better than we can.

Scripture references: Too numerous to mention …

Boat In The Water, Not Water In The Boat
June 15

When I was in my twenties, I went out fishing with a cousin of mine and an uncle (they are not father and son). This cousin is much older than me. The uncle is my dad's sister's husband. My cousin is a real deal fisherman. I've lived on the Gulf all my life and know quite a bit about fishing. My uncle thinks he knows a lot about fishing.

Anyway, he's down from the north, so my cousin and I take him out fishing in the Gulf. It's not exactly the frozen pond he's used to fishing.

We launch my cousin's boat and tie it off to the dock. We pull the truck up into a parking area and then head back to the boat to see it filling with water! Not good! The boat is made to keep water out, not let it gush in! My cousin had forgotten to put the drain plug in the boat. There was about a foot of water in the boat by now and it could have been worse if we hadn't got back to the boat when we did.

This reminds me that we as believers are supposed to be "in the world but not of it". The boat is like our relationSHIP to God. The water is like the world that we are to "throw a lifeline" (saving knowledge of Jesus) into to rescue the unbelievers and bring them into the boat with us. We shouldn't jump ship to join the world.

However, if we allow the world (sea) to flood into our relationship to God (our boat), we will certainly not be successful fishers of men. Keep the plug in the boat, read the Word, pray, follow the Holy Spirit to a good fishing spot and drop a line.

Boat In The Water, Not Water In The Boat – Part 2
June 16

So, we get in the boat, crank it up and we are on our way. With the plug still out, the water drains from the boat as we are on our way to our fishing spot. In a few minutes we are drifting in the Pass fishing for flounder.

We had been there for an hour or two and we were doing quite well. We had a metal stringer hanging over the side of the boat with 15 or 20 nice flounder on it. My cousin liked using a stringer to keep the fish fresh because a cooler would take up room in the small boat.

As I was reeling up another fish when something appeared at the surface behind it. A 10 foot shark was following my catch up to the surface with intentions of making my fish his lunch! My uncle from the North was staring in amazement. Not me, I wanted my fish in the boat! All of a sudden the shark breaks off from my catch and heads under the boat. My cousin has the presence of mind to get to the other side of the boat and snatch up the stringer of flounder as the shark passed underneath with his mouth wide open. He was intending to hit our stringer of flounder!

With the stringer being metal, the shark may not have been able to break it loose from the boat. If you have ever seen a shark tear at something he is biting, you can see that a large shark may have swamped our small boat and endangered all of us. I would say grabbing that stringer was a heads up move by my cousin! The look on my uncle's face was priceless!

The enemy comes to steal, kill and destroy. That's his literal game plan! Like that shark intending to eat our flounder, Satan will try to devour any of our catch (unbelievers we may have brought to the Lord) that find their way back into the sea (the world and sin). What I'm saying is, we as God's fishermen should not only catch the fish, but also help and encourage them to stay in the boat (being in the world but not swallowed up by it).

Road Rage For a Biscuit   June 17

Do you ever have a setbacks in your life? You might think: "I've got this situation licked" or "I've overcome that difficulty." Maybe you say: "It's great to have the car paid off," right before the transmission goes out. Setbacks come in all varieties. For me, the setback is often a personal character flaw that raises its ugly head. My battle ground, anger and a smart mouth with a brain bypass that results in a quick trigger!

The other morning on my way to work I pulled into a fast food joint to grab a biscuit. I followed this white car into the parking lot. All of a sudden the driver of that car decides she wants a parking spot she has already passed. She stops abruptly and immediately starts backing up, right at me in my new truck. I hit my horn and she stops inches short of my grill! She then wheels into her desired parking space. I pull into a space across from her, thinking no more of the incident.

As I get out of my truck this enraged woman gets out and starts berating my driving! The first thing out of her mouth (at extreme volume) is: "Is there an issue?"

OK, there it is, a stupid question and it includes my new, most hated, politically correct word, "issue"! My temp starts to rise inside as I think but don't say: "The issue is you don't watch where you're going, Bozoette!" Instead, I just said: "You were backing right into me, that's why I blew the horn."

Even that lit her up! Now she's cussing at the top of her lungs. Next, an obviously embarrassed man gets out of the passenger side of her car. His head is down and he never looked up. Back in the day I would have knocked him out, for her mouth! He was hurt enough already by her behavior. Although I thought about asking him, "How great is it to go home to her every night of your life?!" But, I didn't.

I just turned around, got back in my truck and left. I had lost my taste for a biscuit. Or maybe I'm just losing my taste for a fight. I even prayed for this lady later, asking God to bless her and work in her life, no matter what her "issues" might be. Now that had to be God, trust me!

Honestly, the anger was still inside of me a bit as I left. Heart "issues" for me to work on, I see. Anyway, I think we can all look back, if we are believers, and see how far God has brought us even though there is still a ways to go. If and when we are yielded, He will continually work in us.

...being confident of this, that he who began a good work in you will carry it on to completion until the day of Christ Jesus. – Philippians 1:6

Just Asking   June 18

Years ago we would see it on t-shirts, wrist bands, and coffee mugs. WWJD (What Would Jesus Do?) I understand the good intentions of the question, but was there more money made on that question than action taken because of it? What I'm asking is, do we spend more time "looking and acting" like the world's perception of a *religious* person, rather than *being* a follower of Christ?

I confess I've fallen into the religious hole all too often. I can look the part with the best of them, but my stomach truly turns at the thought of it these days. I used to buy the coolest Christian "tees" I could find, and then wear them to church or some youth event, otherwise they didn't come out of the closet. I would wear a suit and tie to church and look like the world's idea of the clean, well to do preacher man. Pure phoniness! I even gave money to ministries with no intention of doing any of the services for others myself.

When Jesus walked this earth He wreaked havoc on the religious leaders. He cleared the temple of the moneychangers. He told the religious leaders they taught one thing and lived another way. There is something terribly wrong with just looking and acting like a follower of Jesus.

What would Jesus do if He were walking the earth today? I don't think He would enjoy sitting through a "dot the i's and cross the t's" church exercise. I think you might find Him hanging out at a homeless shelter or a nursing home. I don't think He would routinely race for the all you can eat buffet restaurant on Sunday at 12 noon sharp. I imagine He might grab a bite to eat at the local soup kitchen.

We are going to *be* something. Are we going to be *religious* people or are we going be His followers? Just asking. Oh, by the way, people can tell the difference from a mile away.

This Changes Everything   June 19

Generally speaking, those living in Old Testament days were looking forward to Jesus, the coming Messiah. Now, after Jesus' life on the earth, we look back and see the Messiah. From this side (after Jesus life on the earth), we see what happened to Him and through Him with some certainty. Hind sight is usually clearer. I suppose those living in Old Testament days thought they had a pretty clear perspective of how the future was going to play out. Most were pretty far off the mark, but I doubt they were worried about what was going to happen.

But what about those who were there with Him? What was going through the mind of Peter and the other disciples? What would it have felt like living right there with Him?

I can picture myself chilling with my buds next to the boat dock as the Son of God comes strolling down the pier! I know they didn't know who He was as He walked up, but they soon knew something special was happening. This Jesus has powerful words of wisdom and He speaks them with amazing authority. I think to myself: "Who is this guy?" and decide to hang out with Him for a while. Soon I'm spending all my time with Him. He teaches about the Kingdom of God and does amazing miracles. I'm starting to figure it out, this is the Son of God and I am living in the most incredible time ever!

Even though we live under the oppression of the mighty Roman Empire, I know we are with He who is mightier, and I expect everything to be made right, when He overthrows Rome and it becomes His Kingdom.

But then it happens. They come to arrest Him. Still confident, I draw my sword to take off one of their heads. I miss the target, but get an ear for my effort. Jesus puts it back on for the guy and I wonder what's happening. As they take Jesus away, I follow at a distance, confused and afraid, claiming to others that I don't know Him.

Things are coming terribly unraveled! They beat Him unmercifully and hang Him on the cross. What is going on here?! This is the guy who wilted the fig tree, fed the thousands, calmed the storm and raised the dead. I saw it happen! "Come down off that cross!" He doesn't. He dies. I run for my life and hide with the others who followed Him.

Three days later we get word that someone has seen Him, ALIVE! We run to the tomb to see for ourselves. His body is not there! This changes everything! Later we see Him. We talk to Him. He forgives me and restores me. We even eat some fish together! He says He's leaving to go prepare a place, a home for us. In the meantime it's up to us to spread His good news. We won't let Him down this time.

I wish everyone could have lived during this time, but maybe you'll be here when He comes back. I imagine that will be a time that changes everything too!

He Said Go, Not Whoa--   June 20

We're going fishing this morning. Yeah, baby! I write quite a bit about lessons learned through past experience. You know, after the fact. Today I'm writing before an event, where we will be trying to apply a principal beforehand.

We often times load the boat with all the gear we can find in hopes of being ready for anything (no specific plan), but not today. Today, we are going to try get a specific outcome by planning to use what we hope will give us our desired outcome. In other words, we are not going with the "scatter gun" approach today. We are specifically targeting a few kinds of fish (but a lot of them) with one method and one bait. A "sharpshooter" approach.

When hunting you don't kill large game with a scatter gun. When fishing you don't catch all the fish with the same bait! It takes correct planning. We need the right gun and the right load to hunt certain game. We need the right bait and conditions to catch the desired fish. This is over simplified, but you get the point. We don't just load up all the stuff, head into the woods and see what walks by!

I realize we are told to be ready "in season and out of season." That's availability.

We are also directed to plan and seek counsel. Hold those plans loosely, seeking God's will and guidance, adjust if directed and proceed. That's a hunt with a specific, targeted outcome!

Just sitting around in our comfort zone claiming we are ready for whatever, that's just lazy!

Proverbs 16:3 - *Commit to the LORD whatever you do, and he will establish your plans.*

Proverbs 21:5 - *The plans of the diligent lead to profit as surely as haste leads to poverty.*

I'll let you know how the fishing goes!

Easy Renovation   **June 21**

With a few days off this week, we decided to replace a glass door at our house. This door had been a pain since we moved into this house. It was not a standard size glass door, so this put me on notice that I was in for a bit of a challenge. I was right. No one carried that size glass door in stock. It could be ordered, for a good bit more than a nominal fee.

We opted for a french door that looked very nice and was the right size. I was soon to relive some of my construction days when I learned that just because a door or window is the right size, even the right one, does not mean everything will go smoothly.

Among many other difficulties I faced installing the doors, here's just a few. The jamb is supposed to fit right into the opening where the glass door came out. It did. Except there was nothing to mount it to right behind the brick. I had to take the brick mold off and recess the door jamb. I had to chisel away brick, make all sorts of adjustments, not to mention half a dozen trips back and forth to the hardware store for the goodies to make the adjustments work.

It looks and works great now, but it took a lot of adjustments to make it function correctly.

Are we like this when God tries to use us? He knows we are the right ones for a certain task or ministry. In fact we are special ordered, a perfect fit for the situation or task. Yet we may resist, not trusting God, thereby making it difficult or impossible for Him to use us.

I know there have been times when God had to chisel away my fears and doubts to get me to move on with Him. We have to trust Him from the start so that He won't have to continually adjust us. I know we grow through all kinds of situations. But I also know the sooner we obey, the sooner everything comes into alignment and things "fit" correctly into God's plan.

Its Only Tuesday   June 22

    Friday night I was talking to a friend who was telling me about his day. A vehicle he was working under fell off the jacks that were holding it up shortly after he had gotten out from underneath it. While eating a fish sandwich from a fast food restaurant, he found a bone a couple of inches long in the fillet. Also, he was putting some medicine on his cat and the cat bit him good! I'm telling you his wrist looked like he had been snake bit! He said other than that his day was fine.

    Last night (Tuesday) we were talking again and he was telling me about his day. Early in the day at work my friend (a supervisor) was giving a man some instructions and the man blew a gasket. The man was loud, belligerent, and uncooperative. My friend stayed calm and resolute. He thanked God for the power to maintain control of his emotions and not blow a gasket himself. This event wasn't all, as there are issues he has to deal with concerning other employees.

    Later last night, after telling me about these experiences, he said the most amazing thing. He said, "God has been answering my prayers this week and it's only Tuesday!"

    Frankly, this would probably not be my mindset if I had experienced the last few days he described to me.

    Here's the difference, I think, between what my mindset would have been versus the mindset my friend expressed. It's all in the lens we look through! My response would have been based on looking at the events through an "earthly lens." Something like, woe is me, I almost died under that vehicle that fell, that fish bone could have choked me to death, I may still die of cat scratch fever, and when I get to work tomorrow, I'm going to bust that clown upside the head!

    My friend's approach was totally different in that he looked at the events through a "Heavenly lens." His response was, look what God has done! He got me out from under that vehicle before it fell, showed me a fish bone before it could choke me, my cat will be OK because I put medicine on it, and tomorrow there will be emotional healing at work!

    It's amazing how clearly we can see when we look through the correct lens. Seek the Lord if you need some corrective "Heavenly lenses." I'm going to go ask Him for some now.

Eyes To See   June 23

As Jesus and his disciples were leaving Jericho, a large crowd followed him. Two blind men were sitting by the roadside, and when they heard that Jesus was going by, they shouted, "Lord, Son of David, have mercy on us!"

The crowd rebuked them and told them to be quiet, but they shouted all the louder, "Lord, Son of David, have mercy on us!"

Jesus stopped and called them. "What do you want me to do for you?" he asked.

"Lord," they answered, "we want our sight."

Jesus had compassion on them and touched their eyes. Immediately they received their sight and followed him. – Matthew 20:29-34

WOW! How would you like Jesus to say to you: "What do you want me to do for you?" Then in one moment He would demonstrate His love, compassion, and power.

But there's even more here. These blind men could already "see" very well. There "spiritual eyes" were 20-20. They knew who they were asking for mercy. They knew the Messiah would come from the line of David. Therefore, they were shouting out: "Lord, Son of David, have mercy on us!" And He healed their physical eyes.

The religious leaders of that day may have had perfect physical eyesight, but most were totally blinded when it came to their spiritual eyes. Unbelievers today may have perfect physical eyesight but are also blind in their spiritual eyes.

So, if Jesus asked us today, "What do you want me to do for you?" Maybe we should ask for Him to give us clear focus with our spiritual eyes, as well as heal the spiritual eyes of our unbelieving family, friends, and others we encounter daily.

The Giver   June 24

I know this music teacher who gives lessons to children each week. She makes a little money at it to help things along. The other day she went to see another music teacher giving children lessons. She was very impressed by the method, energy, originality, love and care the other teacher had for the children she was instructing.

The music teacher I know was so impressed that she is going to encourage her students to take lessons from the other teacher instead of from her. That's Kingdom stuff! Although I am not surprised this person would do this, it is amazing to me! This will be a sacrifice of some income, but there is probably nothing farther from her mind. She knows who her source is. She won't have to choke back any pride because she has always wanted the best for others. She started some of these children on their musical journeys, but she sees who will be the right teacher for them as they take the next step in their learning. She is putting the needs of these children ahead of her own needs.

Yes, I am amazed, but why am I not surprised? I am not surprised because I have seen her seek after God and His will all of her adult life! She has always put the needs (and wants) of others (including me and our sons) ahead of her own!

I know Jesus will say to her: "Well done, good and faithful servant!"

I say: "Well done good and faithful wife, mother, teacher, friend and love of my life!" God Bless you Hannah, I love you!

Today I have been married thirty-three years to this woman. The love of my life! Thank you Jesus!

He who finds a wife finds what is good and receives favor from the LORD. – Proverbs 18:22

Father's Day   June 25

A few years ago (I think it was his anniversary, not Father's Day), in a card, I wrote my heartfelt appreciation of my dad's sacrifices for me and gave it to him as a gift. One of the things I expressed to him was that the extent of his sacrifices did not fully hit home with me until I realized what sacrifices were required of me to be a good father. This is not to say that I was always a good father because I did not always make the sacrifices I should have for my children. However, I have sacrificed for my children as I am sure all of you have who are making the journey through fatherhood.

I must say that there have been times when I have made these sacrifices for my children and they appear to have gone unappreciated, taken for granted, or flat out unnoticed! My heart says, "I truly want to give my kids the best I can provide," but my selfish flesh adds, "I really wish they would notice and throw a whole bunch of adoration and thanks my way."

In reality all of my sons have been very good at expressing their appreciation to me in things I have done for them, especially as they have grown into adulthood. They are each a blessing to me and have a seemingly inexhaustible amount of love and tolerance for me.

Here's the point. I know now that I took my father's sacrifices for granted, especially as a child while not knowing any better and then as a teen and young adult, when I should have known better. So right now in plain view of the whole world I say, "Thanks, Dad. I get it now and I appreciate all you have done for me. In some way I hope you can get a glimpse of the fruit of your labors in this book."

One more thing to all the fathers out there. Let's all check our hearts and see if we have taken our Heavenly Father for granted. We know the sacrifice He made sending Jesus. Let's make sure we are sincerely grateful to Him and express that to Him in prayer personally and in the way we live our lives as living sacrifices. Fathers, your sacrifices are not going unnoticed by Him!

Children, obey your parents in the Lord, for this is right. "Honor your father and mother," which is the first commandment with a promise, "so that it may go well with you and that you may enjoy long life on the earth."

Fathers, do not exasperate your children; instead, bring them up in the training and instruction of the Lord. – Ephesians 6:1-4

Mission Ready — June 26

I spent a long stretch of my time in the Air Force in Hangar 4. It was the place that regular periodic maintenance was done on aircraft. I enjoyed that time very much. I liked the people I worked with and it was fun working on fighter jets. Working in the hangar also kept us out of the weather and we avoided the obstacles of the flight line.

Working on the flight line (where jets stood ready for flight) placed a lot of extra requirements on us mechanics. There was a desire to have the aircraft back in a "ready for flight" status as soon as possible. We also needed to be positively sure to clean our work area when the job was done. We could not leave small parts, tools or even metal shavings in, on or near aircraft. This could cause damage to the aircraft by finding their way into an intake, an engine or in some other way cause damage to the aircraft. The result of FOD (foreign object damage) could be catastrophic by crashing the plane and injuring or killing the pilot.

Working in the hangar was a little more methodical. There was a schedule but not a rush. Cleaning up the plane and the area was a specific part of the regular maintenance. It was usually a routine that everyone knew and had down pat.

As much as I liked to work in the hangar, I realized that the jet fighters I was working on were of no use while they were sitting inside the hangar and unavailable for flight.

In my faith, I was like one of those jet fighters sitting in the hangar for a long time. Sure, I may have been getting repaired in some areas, but I was not out on the flight line available for the mission. What's the mission? To go and make disciples. I was content to stay in the hangar (the church), the controlled, safe environment. I was OK to let others bring them in, then maybe I would work on them.

Church is a necessary, rewarding, building, an uplifting, learning and repairing "hangar" where God can renew and restore us to be able to go out on the next mission. But if we just stay in the hangar we won't complete the mission! The best, most advanced jet fighters in the world can't just fly around in the hangar and complete a mission.

When we have had our maintenance done we should report to the flight line. We're scheduled for takeoff. Don't be afraid. The One in the control tower sees everything flying around out there. He'll give us the perfect flight plan for us to complete our mission. Then we can go back to the hangar and get a tune-up.

Is Your Battery Low   June 27

Yesterday morning I got in my truck headed for work. I turned the key and heard that tell-tale "click click" of a very low battery. With no time to spare at that moment, I went back into the house and ask my wife to take me to work.

After I returned home from work last night, I pulled another vehicle up to my truck, hooked up my jumper cables to both batteries and my truck fired right up.

Sometimes the "battery" in my spirit seems to run low and lose some power. This might be caused by letting it sit around not being used and thereby it doesn't stay charged up. It could be that it's been running and running without being charged up.

A battery in an automobile has to be used and not just sit for long periods of time. It also needs to stay charged up to be useful and have to power to crank the motor. The battery in a car is charged by an alternator or generator while the engine is running.

I think my spirit is like that too. It seems that when I am helping others in need or doing something that is in God's will for me to do, my "spiritual battery" is being charged constantly! Zoom, Zoom, Zoom! Anyway...

What's our "spiritual generator?" It's reading the Word, doing His will and doing for others in need. It's amazing how much these things charge my spiritual battery!

Oh yeah, and if I find myself seemingly out of power with no charge left, I call on a friend to give me a "jump." By hooking my 'spiritual jumper cable" to his battery, I can often crank right up and be moving again down the road in the Kingdom.

When our battery is low, it is great to have a brother or sister that is all charged up" to give us a jump! Don't be afraid to ask for a jump.

As iron sharpens iron, so one man sharpens another. – Proverbs 27:17

Poop On It — June 28

I park my old white truck under a tree at my house. It is shady there and keeps the truck from being so hot when I get in it, especially in the hot summer months. Except there is one drawback, birds live in that tree. Several birds I would guess, based on their deposits on the right side of my truck hood.

I have several choices for a remedy here. I could park the truck somewhere else but there are no other real options available (like a carport or garage), except other occupied trees or open spaces. The result of one of these choices is obvious: continuation of a spotted truck or a hot interior to climb into every time I want to go someplace.

I could cut the tree down. Just let me say, that's not going to happen! That would be a ton of work just to create another hot spot to park.

I could get rid of the birds. One blast from the shotgun... OK, maybe not. Neighbors aren't crazy about shotgun blasts in the front yard. Besides, more birds would probably move in as retaliation and bring some squirrels with them!

As you can see, my options are limited and I don't really like any of them. So I guess I'll just keep washing the poop off until I get another option. The trouble with this idea is it doesn't solve the problem. Washing the truck only masks the problem by temporarily removing a symptom of the problem. Actually solving a problem sometimes includes making a tough choice.

I think we often do this in our spiritual lives as well. I know I have done this. It's like taking cough medicine when we have a cold. It will help the cough temporarily but it doesn't make the cold go away. We allow crap (a particular sin, even a bad habit, laziness, procrastination, any number of poor traits) to continue instead of making a choice that may have a difficult or inconvenient remedy. In reality, this only allows the problem to continue. The birds are only going to birth more little birds that are going to make the mess bigger!

Why do we let crap pile up until we just can't wash it away anymore? Then we are faced with a huge mountain of mess to try to clear away! Why don't we remedy the problem when it's first appears as a small obstacle? Lets make a choice now to remedy our problems as soon as possible instead of masking the symptoms, just to face harder choices later.

When it comes to temptation to sin, lets just say no, rather than trying to hide the sin later. Because we know what happens when we give in to temptation; the crap (lies, deceit, and the things we would do to try to hide our sin) will just pile up on us until it just gets to be too much to wash off. Just like the hood of my old white truck.

When we do find ourselves covered in crap (that's exactly what sin is), Jesus is there to wash it away for good. What a great and wonderful God that is willing to wash this crud of sin off of us time and again. I'm sorry, Jesus. I'll try to not have to come to you in this condition so often, but thank you for always washing me clean!

If we claim to be without sin, we deceive ourselves and the truth is not in us. If we confess our sins, he is faithful and just and will forgive us our sins and purify us from all unrighteousness. If we claim we have not sinned, we make him out to be a liar and his word is not in us. - 1 John 1: 8-10

Thanks   June 29

Before retiring, my dad was a construction superintendent. He would often be sent out of town on big jobs that would last a year or so. He would come home on weekends. However, his living out of town during the week would require him to have a second residence. He would choose some pretty cool places to stay (at least from my perspective as a young adventurous boy).

I remember visiting him on some weekends or even spending most of a summer with him in some of the most fun places. He stayed in a camper on a mountainside and a couple of different trailers by lakes, among other places that were in easy reach of fishing, places to ride motorcycles, shoot guns and just have general young boy fun.

I guess my favorite place was near Lakeland, Florida. I spent a summer there with Dad in a trailer park with a pond on one side and pasture on another. I spent my days shooting snakes and turtles, catching catfish and bream, flying model rockets, and swimming in the motel pool just down the highway.

Many of the other people in this park of about eight trailers were people who worked with my dad. The only ones I remember who lived there that did not work with Dad were two brothers who drove trucks. They went by the names of Long John and Archie (great truck driver names).

I remember one time when we had a fish fry. We cooked the fish my friend and I caught. Long John and Archie even made turtle soup and cooked one of the landlords ducks!

I'm not sure what the spiritual significance of this story is except maybe to say this: I know it was difficult on Mom and Dad being apart during those times but they were doing what was best for the family at the time. So thanks, Mom and Dad, for the sacrifices you made for me; but let me say that along the way I had some wonderful times as a boy, right in the middle of your tough times.

Fishing In a New Spot   June 30

That summer in Lakeland (read "Thanks" from yesterday) I fished that pond almost daily. I could catch a lot of catfish, but only catfish, and they were a pain to clean. I got to the point of thinking the only kind of fish in the pond was catfish!

There was this area of the pond that resembled a channel on one side. It was almost inaccessible because of the overgrowth of grass, bushes and the like. It would take a little work to get very far down the channel because of the overgrowth. There was an old bridge a little way down the channel that was probably the access to what used to be a barn or something on the other side.

One day my friend and I made the effort to clear a path through the brush and get to the little bridge. The idea was to check out the barn. After making it onto the bridge and seeing that we would need land clearing equipment to get any farther, we abandoned our quest to get to the barn. But we did run back to the house and get our fishing gear.

We came straight back to that little bridge, dropped our lines through the lily pads beneath the bridge and immediately caught bream as big as your hand! We did this the rest of the summer! We could plan a fish fry and know we were going to have bream and catfish (if we wanted) every time. We had found an endless supply at our own secret "Fishin Hole"!

I was thinking the pond and the Bible have some similarities. At first it was fun catching and eating the catfish. But every time I went back to the pond I was catching the same fish. Would it always be catfish? No. My friend and I decided to try it from a different place. Our perspective changed and we were looking at it from a different point of reference. It was the same water, producing a new and exciting result just for us!

The Word of God is said to be "living and active." We are creations of God that go through constantly changing emotions, situations, stages of life and any number of daily changes in perspectives and points of reference. Doesn't it make sense that each time we read the Bible we would hear God from a different angle? Doesn't it make sense that God speaks to us through His Word at the place we are in our lives? He is not a God who says, "I will only speak to you here!" He continually says and shows us that He is with us everywhere we go!

The Word of God speaks to us wherever we find ourselves and no matter how many times we read it, it continually gives us new and fresh revelation, every time!

Have you fished any new spots lately?

Getting Stoned — July 1

Today's definition of getting stoned is totally different than back in Biblical times. Today's meaning is temporary artificial happiness in trade for some of our self-control. Getting stoned back then was a form of execution! A person could be stoned to death for adultery and blasphemy, among other things.

Jesus was teaching some people about His Father and His Kingdom at the Temple one morning. In John 8:30, the Bible says: "Even as He spoke, many put their faith in Him."

That's what was happening as a result of Jesus' teaching and sharing His testimony. He was doing this without fear of the powerful religious leaders who wanted to stone Him to death! On the other hand, the people were afraid of the religious leaders and only whispered among themselves what they thought of Jesus and His teaching.

We as believers may never be stoned to death for our witness for Christ, but you can bet and expect "rocks" to be thrown at you for your testimony. Satan wants us to be afraid of man and he will try to shut you up! The verbal rocks thrown our way can hurt. We must remember who we are in Christ and not be affected by who we are in the eyes of the world.

Look at the possible results. Even as we speak, some will put their faith in Him. Further, our witness and testimony in the face of rocks being thrown our way will give courage to others who might otherwise just go around whispering their beliefs secretly.

Jesus said: "Whoever acknowledges me before men, I will also acknowledge him before my Father in Heaven. But whoever disowns me before men, I will disown him before my Father in Heaven." – Matthew 10:32-33

Road Trip With Grandmother　　　　　　July 2

One summer (I think I was 11 and my sister was 7) we spent a couple of weeks with my grandmother and a cousin in the state of Washington. She decided to take us to see some of our relatives in Oregon. I was cool with that and the trip had its times of adventure.

I got lost once on a hillside of sliding gravel and rocks, scary! Another day, while driving down the highway near the coast, we creamed a seagull. We hit that bird so hard I thought it cracked the windshield! Those seagulls have more guts and feathers than you might think!

The coolest thing about the trip was Grandmother's camper trailer that we pulled along behind her little car. This thing was small, a "mini-bago"! It was about the size of a 4 x 8 U-Haul or a little taller maybe. Anyway, through my 11 year old eyes, it was more like a rolling fort, even though all four of us could not stand up in it at one time.

We had been out on our road trip a couple of days when we pulled over for lunch at this cool little rest area. Grandmother ask if I would like a tuna sandwich. I love tuna sandwiches! Grandmother's taste and my taste did not always agree. She made great pies, but everything else had a Northern bias, if you know what I mean. (Sorry, no offense, I'm a Southern boy and I know good eats!) So, after many days of the "Northern bias food," I was practically drooling as she made me a tuna sandwich. I waited outside the camper as she prepared lunch. I couldn't see how she was preparing the meal.

She handed me that sandwich and I bit into that bad boy and starting chewing before I could taste it. Then I tasted it. Oh no, "Northern bias tuna!" She had put little blocks of butter in each corner of my tuna sandwich! Not to mention using some off brand tuna that taught me the meaning of "sand" in the word sandwich!

Listen, I love my grandmother. Would you take three kids on a road trip all by yourself, just for them? Probably. If you loved them, like she loved us.

Is there something to glean from a funny little story from the North?

I've been reading Proverbs lately and Solomon encourages us to gain wisdom, knowledge, discernment and to use sound judgment. A buttery tuna sandwich may not hurt us, but if we "bite" into things before we know whats inside, we may end up with more than a bad taste in our mouths.

If any of you lacks wisdom, he should ask God, who gives generously to all without finding fault, and it will be given to him. – James 1:5

Dreams For Sale — July 3

The Field of Dreams is for sale! I've got to have it! Somebody loan me 5.4 million. OK, I just called them. I think I can get it for 5 even! I know! I'll sell everything I own, even Louie! That will be a puny down payment but I can make big mortgage payments. I'll live in a tent in center field and rent out the house! I'll eat ball park hot dogs, popcorn, sunflower seeds and ice cream cones. This is doable! Yes!

OK, I probably do sound pretty obsessed with this idea. But I do love that movie! A top fiver for me easily.

So, did you see yourself in there with me? Did you ever go off the deep end to get something you thought would make you happy forever, only to find out that hot dogs, popcorn, sunflower seeds and even ice cream gets old fast?

Sometimes buying a new thing will put a smile on our face temporarily. Soon the new wears off and the funds we purchased the goodie with are gone. Then we go out and labor for more money to buy the next short lived new toy that will provide the next temporary smile to our mugs. This cycle can continue for a lifetime, or until we realize the true source of our joy and go shopping elsewhere.

Jesus said not to go after things of this earth, but to seek first His Kingdom and righteousness and all this stuff will be given to you too (Matthew 6:31-33). David said to delight yourself in the Lord and He will give you the desires of your heart (Psalm 37:4). It seems pretty clear that the true source of our joy is God and the currency to obtain that joy is to know Him.

Psalm 34:8 says: "Taste and see that the Lord is good." Yep, way better than ball park food!

## Independence Day, The Perfect Time For Surrender	July 4

We celebrate Independence Day today here in the U.S. It's a big deal, although I believe many have lost the appreciation for the cost our country has paid to win our freedom and keep it. Many lives were lost and changed because of the willingness of soldiers and leaders to pay the ultimate price.

Greater love has no one than this: to lay down one's life for one's friends. – John 15:13

We had to fight wars to gain and keep our freedom. Men and women joined our military, and in one respect, basically gave up the freedom they already had to become "slaves or servants" to their country, so as to gain, protect and preserve freedom for the rest of us. Thank you to all of those past and present!

That is what we can do for the Kingdom of God. When we first come to the Lord I think we might resemble one of those animals that has been in captivity for a long time. You've seen those animal shows where they take an animal out into the wild to be released. They open its cage and the suddenly "free" animal just stands there, or frantically looks around wondering "What do I do now?"

As new believers we may find ourselves in the same situation as we are "suddenly free" from the imprisonment of sin. Where do we go from here?

The Bible says one of the things we should do is to become a servant or slave to Christ. For almost all of us I think our first reaction is something like: That's absurd! It doesn't make any sense. I have just been freed! That's not a fair request!

You know what? You're probably right. It may not be fair. But it's Biblical. And it's the only way others are going to be set free. We have to surrender ourselves to God and serve Him by showing others the way to His freedom.

Independence Day ... the perfect time to surrender!

Reasons Enough   July 5

When I was in the Air Force, one of my main job locations was the flight line. Airplanes ready for flight sat near the runways awaiting the next mission. We were regularly sent out to do repairs right on the flight line if it would not take a lot of time or require putting the aircraft in a hangar. Following any repairs, we would account for our tools and supplies and return to the shop.

When I reported to work one day, my boss called me aside and asked me to go get my drill from my toolbox. Each mechanic had his own toolbox and the only key to that box. I thought this was a weird request but I went to get it as instructed. My drill was not in my toolbox! Not good.

He told me that an aircraft I had repaired went down the night before. The pilot was forced to eject and the aircraft was a total loss. Investigators believed the engine failed due to FOD (foreign object damage). In other words, I had left my drill in the engine bay I had repaired and caused the engine failure. Terrible thoughts ran through my mind as I thought the pilot could be hurt or dead. People could be hurt on the ground. I could be discharged or even jailed!

Then my boss reached in his desk drawer, pulled out my drill and handed it to me. I cannot express how relieved I was to see that drill. I had left my drill in the engine bay, but the crew chief of the aircraft found it during pre-flight inspection.

Instructions for safety procedures, such as accounting for tools and materials are very important. Not following them could lead to catastrophic results for others as well as ourselves, not to mention being costly in terms of valuable assets.

God has given us His commands and teachings to keep us from harm and destruction. He has given us these instructions for our own good and the good of our fellow man.

Yes, it's true that if we break His commands and teachings we can be forgiven if we are repentant and ask Him for His forgiveness.

So why care so much about obeying His instructions? Back to my story. Would God forgive me if leaving my drill in the engine bay was a sin? Yes, but the pilot would be just as dead, people on the ground where the plane crashed would be just as dead or injured and the aircraft and the homes and businesses it crashed into would still have been destroyed.

Not to mention that Jesus tells us if we love Him we will obey His commands and teachings (John 14:15,21,23).

Reasons enough?

Helping The Poor, All Of The Poor — July 6

I ran into a homeless guy down at the boat launch the other day. He held my bow line as I backed the boat into the water. His breath reeked with the smell of booze, but he was pleasant enough. After helping me get the boat in the water, he asked if I had any spare change. I said I didn't, but that if he wanted to jump in the boat I would take him to the Marina's store and get him something to eat. He seemed to think about it for a moment, then declined. I wondered if he just wasn't hungry, afraid of a short boat ride, or maybe he didn't trust me.

For most of my life I have been somewhere between condemning and indifferent towards the poor and homeless. I often thought: "You got yourself into this situation (which may be true enough) so you can get yourself out; it's not my problem." What if God had the same attitude I did? "Hey, you guys got yourselves into this sin that leads to death thing, you can get yourselves out! What do you think I'm going to do, send my Son to die for your sins?"

In Matthew, Jesus says not to judge: "Do not judge, or you too will be judged. For in the same way you judge others, you will be judged, and with the measure you use, it will be measured to you." That's a pretty direct and strong statement. Just as direct, in Proverbs we are told repeatedly to help the poor.

And there are all sorts of "poor" out there. I see and talk to them daily. They are poor in self-esteem, poor in joy, poor in happiness, poor in friendships, poor in hope and on and on...

I hear:

"You know my wife just died ..."

"They're trying to fire me because I got hurt at work ..."

"I can't pay my mortgage; they're taking my house ..."

"I'm getting divorced ..."

"I moved here after my husband committed suicide ..."

"I drink too much; my wife left ..."

"My daughter is back together with that drug addict ..."

"My house burned to the ground last night; we barely got out ..."

It's amazing how their faces light up when I just hang around a minute and really listen to them. Maybe say a word of encouragement or that I'll pray for their situation. I need to help these kind of poor people. Not just the "cash poor", but the "hope poor" too.

OH. You hear them, too?

Letting Go Of The Wheel July 7

I suppose you've heard that semi-sarcastic advice to not pray for patience. Meaning that if you do, God will send or allow all sorts of annoyances into you're life that will require patience. Although that may be somewhat accurate, that advice (to not pray for patience) is often given and/or received by someone not willing to pay the price to attain the results they desire.

If you want to get stronger, you lift weights routinely. If you want to lose weight, you go on a diet. If you want to get better at your job, you work harder.

We can cheat or work into an appearance of victory for awhile. We could take some steroids and workout, but that'll come home to us in a bad way later. We can take some diet pills or have some liposuction, but sooner or later we have to eat less to keep the weight off. We can cook the books at work, but down the line inventory is coming.

We can do drugs or get drunk all the time, but that only puts our troubles on hold (while increasing other troubles). Sooner or later we wake up sober and there the issues are – staring us in the face.

We can fake how much we trust and have faith in God too. We can also be satisfied at some point that we have enough faith and trust in God. I think I was at that place for awhile. "I'm good. This is how much I want and need to trust you God. Faith level 5 out of 10, this works." Thanks, keep it right here, comfortable and controllable.

Well now I've done it! I have been praying to be a more a godly, obedient man. Guess what? He's showing me what that will require. That's right, a higher level of faith and trust in Him. He is answering this prayer. How is He taking me there? By putting me in places and situations where I have trust Him and believe He is going to come through.

O.K., I'm "letting go of the wheel." I'll let you know how it goes.

A Little Thing   July 8

I've got this huge pecan tree in the yard on the side of my house. It has some very long limbs with pecans on them right now in bunches like bananas; tons of 'em! Some of the limbs that are normally way out of reach can be easily grabbed from the ground. What I'm saying is, these limbs are obviously weighed down on the ends with a lot of pecans.

The other day during a rain, one of the limbs about a third of the way up the tree broke off and brought a lower limb down with it into the yard. OK, a couple of limbs broke, I'll clean up the mess.

Then the day before yesterday, again during a rain, a very large limb high in the tree broke but did not come completely off the tree. This one was hanging down over the house and presented a potential for serious damage to the roof. There was no way for me to reach it and I was not about to climb high up in a tree where heavy, wet limbs were breaking and falling!

I called a tree guy but had to leave a message. His advertisement showed some of his prices that I did not want to endure, but I seemingly had no choice. Even though my Father owns the "cattle on a thousand hills", the cows have not "come home" yet. But He has other ways that don't always come to my mind.

The tree guy didn't call back. Yesterday morning we discovered that the limb had fallen some more but was caught on a lower limb that did not break! Go figure. Some of it was barely touching the roof and hanging over the deck, but it had caused no damage. It was now relatively easy for me to free it off of the limb it had landed on and get it down.

I had been spared great expense and suffered no damage. A little thing? Maybe in the big scheme of things. Coincidence? Nope! My God is the God of the little things in my everyday life. I just wanted to tell you so that we can all know that we don't have to wait for some "big thing" to happen to see God. He's there in the little things every day.

This is how God shows His love to us: He has spared us great expense (death, hell and the grave) and through Him, we suffer no damage. We can spend eternity in Heaven with Him. Not to mention joy in Him now.

The Shadow Doesn't Know   July 9

Have you ever been in a dark room at night and there is some light outside that cast shadows on the window curtains or blinds? Maybe there is a little wind blowing, and the shadow of leaves on the trees outside move around on the window shade.

Early in the morning, while it is still dark outside, I often come to my dining table to sit down and pray. I don't usually turn on the light until I am ready to read the Bible. This morning, when I came to the table it seemed as if light was shining through my window, casting shadows of leaves blowing in the breeze on the window shade.

I went to the door to look outside, expecting to see a car parked across the street with it's headlights on or a porch light somewhere that's not usually left on. When I looked through the shades on the door, I saw no lights. At least none were on nearby that would explain the shadows on the curtain. I had to figure this one out!

Oddly enough the light and shadow were originating from inside the room. A small night light that Hannah had left on was shining directly through a chair back, near the door with the window shade. The angle of the light through the chair made the design of the chair's backrest look like a shadow of small limbs on the window shade. The ceiling fan over the table was blowing slightly on the blinds, causing the shadow of the chair to appear to be blowing in a gentle breeze. As soon as I turned on the light over the table, the shadow was gone.

Sometimes when things seem to go wrong in my life or I am faced with some difficulty, I look first for an outside source or cause of my problem. I want to blame something or someone else for my problem or attitude. Most of the time my attitude and response is a result of the inside condition of my own heart.

It is not until I allow God to turn on His light inside of me, that the source of my problem or difficulties can be discovered and seen. I am then able to see clearly, by His light, how to navigate and correct myself.

Simply put; the source of the shadows in our lives are often on our inside, not cast upon us from an outside source. Let's allow God first to turn on His light inside of us and expose the shadow's true source.

Catching Anything   July 10

When I walk up to my aquarium to feed my fish, about 3/4 of them start swimming frantically at the top of the water in anticipation of being fed. A few others start to move around excitedly while remaining deeper in the water. Then there is one fish (the shark) that seems to stay at the far end of the aquarium in deep water. He seems to be acting like he's indifferent to the food (he thinks he's cool) but he does swim around and under the others, eating what food falls through the feeding frenzy.

The same behavior could be seen while we were fishing in the Gulf last week. We were trolling for the most part (lines out as we cruised slowly until we got a bite). Often as we were cruising around, we would see fish just "tearing up" the top of the water while they were feeding on bait fish as if they were starving! These were the easiest to catch. We could just troll through them or even stop and throw a lure into them and almost always catch several before they quite feeding.

The next most successful way of catching the fish was trolling our lines a little deeper. The fish we caught at this depth seemed to be a larger in general than the ones we caught on the surface. Perhaps they were a little more experienced or skeptical of lures and needed a little more convincing to latch on to our offer.

Another way to catch fish is to bottom fish. You just stop somewhere and set the anchor. You use a weight on the line to keep it on the bottom because the swiftness of the water current will often make it difficult to keep the bait in one place. Most of the time more patience will be required to fish this way but the rewards can be just as good or better.

I think people's behavior is like these fish often times when it comes to beginning a relationship to Jesus.

There will be people who are hungry for God and they will practically "jump in the boat" to be with Him, like the fish feeding at the top of the water.

Then there will be those like the fish just below the surface that are hungry for something, but may be a little skeptical and inquisitive before they latch on to Him.

And there are those who are completely leery or unbelieving (in the deep water on bottom) who need to see His offer for a while before trusting and believing He is the real and true God.

Any fisherman (of fish or men) will tell you the most important thing about catching fish is the presentation.

The difference (in fishing for fish or men) is this. When trying to catch fish we want to make the bait presentation look and act as real as possible. When fishing for men the offer is real and must be presented as such. Some will see and trust right away. Some will check it out first and then accept the offer. Then some will have to see the offer for a long time, observing the offer and the fisherman, to see if he really knows himself what he's offering.

Two Whiners July 11

David just blows my mind! Why would God say about this guy: "...I have found David son of Jesse, a man after my own heart; he will do everything I want him to do."? (Acts 13:22)

This guy was a conspirator and accomplice to murder, among other things! Oops, well there was that time when I said right out of my own mouth: "I could do the time if I took that so and so out."

Yeah, but David was the king, the man! He had it made in the shade, world by the tail and never had to fly coach. He had the coolest chariot and best seat at the ball games. He was the "giant killer!" Then he goes messing with someone else's woman and that is a certain train wreck! So he goes whining to God! "Oh God, I'm so sorry, please help me, please forgive me! Rescue and restore me again. Waaaaaa!"

OK, OK. So there was that time, after some of my own whining, God rescued me from big financial debt of my own doing and I promised Him I wouldn't do it again. Yeah, OK, I did it again. So with a broken heart, I cried out and He delivered me again.

I guess it doesn't matter if you're a king with you're own army or a commoner making it day to day. We all need some rescuing because we'll mess something up along the way.

So what was the deal with this "man after my own heart" thing? I think it was because David would praise God for his rescue and genuinely thank Him continually for all good things the Lord sent his way. David praised God with singing, dancing and a whole ton of psalms. In one psalm, David basically says: What good is my demise? "Will the dust praise You?" David praises God for his deliverance and says: "I will give You thanks forever."

God rescues us because He loves us and wants us to love and praise Him. He also wants us to tell others of His love for us and share His love with everyone else. That's what David did and I think that's why God said he was a man after his own heart.

Let's go after the heart of God, by praising and thanking Him in all things and telling others of His love.

When I felt secure, I said, "I will never be shaken."
Lord, when you favored me,
you made my royal mountain stand firm;
but when you hid your face, I was dismayed.
To you, Lord, I called;
to the Lord I cried for mercy:
"What is gained if I am silenced,
if I go down to the pit?
Will the dust praise you?
Will it proclaim your faithfulness?
Hear, Lord, and be merciful to me; Lord, be my help. "
You turned my wailing into dancing;
you removed my sackcloth and clothed me with joy,
that my heart may sing your praises and not be silent.
Lord my God, I will praise you forever. – Psalm 30: 6-12

Good Stuff!

Trusting Dad   July 12

My dad used to be a construction superintendent. His job required him to work out of town for extended periods of time. Somewhere along about age 13 I began to spend some of my summertime with him. We would travel to his job location on Sunday evenings to be there during the week. Then on Friday afternoon we would travel back home for the weekends. When I got older, I worked with him on some of the jobs until I went into the military.

During those years we did a lot of traveling up and down the highway together. As a young teen I would ride in the back of the pickup sometimes for nearly 500 miles. It was an adventure for a kid! There was no fear on my part for my safety. I was mostly oblivious to the traffic and was enjoying the ride.

As I got older and the adventure wore off, I started riding up in the cab. I had my license and was a driver myself by this time but I never drove if Dad was in the truck. Being more aware of traffic now, some of Dad's driving habits unnerved me a bit. My driving habits probably unnerved him a bit too, hence me not driving when he was along!

Anyway, his habit that got to me was how he would run up right behind someone, practically drafting on them until he could pass them. I would be on the passenger side of the truck mashing as hard as I could on the imaginary brake pedal in the floor! He probably thought I always wanted to drive because I was a new driver and it was all fun to me. Nope. I wanted to drive so I could get my foot on the real brake pedal! I wanted to be in control. Being in control is a lot easier than trusting someone else to be in control.

Over the course of time, I did begin to trust his driving. I got used to his ways and I knew (not just hoped) that he would slow down before we drove through the car ahead of us.

It's often this way between us and God. We want to be in control. Certainly at first, we flat out don't trust Him with everything. That's just the truth! Yet as we walk (or ride) with Him, and see that He cares for us, we give Him more and more control until He is driving all of the time. It's better to let Him drive because He knows where to take us and the best way to get there. We trust Him because He has brought us through time and again. We trust Him because He is true. Trusting Him drives out fear and gives Him control.

Having trouble trusting God? Think about the times He has steered you right in the past. If you've never trusted Him before, start by trusting Him with one thing and you will see that He won't let you down. He won't leave you or forsake you, even if you have a "breakdown."

Who's Right   July 13

Discussions have a way of turning into heated arguments or fights when the subject changes from what is right, to who is right. Defensive pride flies out of us like an erupting verbal volcano! It's probably impossible for us to truly remain objective if we are involved in a discussion that turns into an personal confrontation.

So let me say it this way, the next time you observe a discussion or debate that turns ugly, think back. When did the gas get poured on the fire? The answer is, when it got personal. When the discussion turned from the issues to personal attacks. When one person said: "You did this," or "you guys said that," it's on! Watch a debate of political issues on some news show. It will start out as a calm and proper discussion. But as soon as one person accuses another person or his side of doing or saying something wrong, thats the flashpoint, and the fight is on. It's a no-holds-barred fight to the ugly finish! And no issues get resolved.

In our flesh we all want to have our will and way in things. So, we will have disagreements. In the midst of them, we should try to remain civil, kind, polite, understanding, stick to resolving the issue at hand and even have a listening ear to the opposing viewpoint. Why should we have this kind of attitude and approach to handling differences of opinion? One obvious reason is that we are not always right. I confess, that is pretty hard thing for me to come to grips with, maybe you too. More importantly, the only person who is always right is God. So it obviously follows that His will and way is always right.

The application to this in our daily lives should then be to seek out He who is always right and ask Him what His will would be in a disputed matter. Then we should be obedient to Him in striving to resolve the issue according to His will. Often times this will be easier said than done, but doing it God's way will certainly provide the best outcome.

The ways of the Lord are right; the righteous walk in them, but the rebellious stumble in them. – Hosea 14:9

Sphere Of Influence July 14

There is a lot going on in the world today. We can find many things to be concerned about, and they're not hard to find. Is there really more going on than 100 years ago? Maybe it just seems this way because so much information is brought to us instantaneously in this age of Internet and Twitter.

What our President says about world events and situations is of great concern to me. A movie star or sports personality can easily speak out on topics they know little or nothing about and convince their fans to support a cause or vote a certain way. Someone's assumed expertise or even their popularity in some other medium can influence people as to their views and decisions.

People being influenced by others are followers that are being reached within their leader's "sphere of influence". Being a follower and supporter of someone is not in and of itself a bad idea. The Bible (particularly all through Proverbs) tells us to gain, even go after wisdom, knowledge, discernment, use sound judgment, and be prudent. A leader and teacher can be a big part of this learning and growing experience and it can be of the utmost benefit to the follower; as long as the leader knows where they're going.

Our responsibility before becoming a follower or supporter of anyone (putting ourselves in their sphere of influence), be they a politician, movie star, sports personality, and especially a spiritual leader, is to validate their information, teachings, opinions and integrity. This validation in our hearts and minds needs to take place prior to buying in to any of their opinions, instructions, or teachings.

What I mean is that we should do our own homework to find out if a person we consider following and supporting is who they say they are, that they have been true to their word and beliefs and do they know where they're going and how to lead us there.

By following leaders that know where they are going and how to get there, followers can then become good leaders. The perfect example is shown through Jesus as he led His followers and they became great leaders. If we follow leaders that know where they're going, we can become the next ones to lead others rightly.

Who influences you?

How are you influencing others?

Rain...Gloom Of Night...Close Ones   July 15

There have been many "close ones" during my career as a mailman. A few fender benders and a mail box fatality or two. Even a sprinkler once (don't ask). But the accident I fear most would be running over a child. It's been close a few times, but in those cases I was alert and aware at the time and those instances just turned out to be another "close one."

Occasionally, mostly when it cannot be avoided, I find myself delivering at dusk or even in the dark. This poses obvious dangers. In these conditions I try to stay that much more alert and aware of my surroundings. One early evening, as I was delivering in the dark, I was coming up to a box when a kid came barreling down to meet me. I saw him just in time to lock up my brakes and stop my jeep inches from his legs as he slid down into the curb. Had I not been going slower than usual I would have hit him for sure!

On another occasion, I was delivering mail in a driving rainstorm, the kind of rain that you can hardly see the front of the vehicle. In fact I had taken a break in hopes of it letting up some. I pressed on and had delivered mail to one box when a boy on a bicycle came busting through some bushes right in front of me! Had I not been watching and trying to be extra safe, I would have hit him full force. I was inventing cuss words as I let that kid have it for being out there in a thunderstorm riding a bike!

How does this translate to our spiritual lives? Satan will attack us at our weakest point, in our weakest moment. We each know our weak points and God can give us the strength to overcome the enemy's attack. However, it is certainly to our advantage to identify our weaker areas so as to be aware and not caught by surprise when we are tempted in those areas.

Let's be aware of what's happening in our spiritual surroundings. Is it getting dark and rainy around us? Then let's turn on the headlights (pray), check the map (ask God to show us the way out), turn on the wipers to help us be alert to our surroundings (look for the out He shows us) and turn "what was meant for evil into good."

"I am sending you out like sheep among wolves. Therefore be as shrewd as snakes and as innocent as doves." – Matthew 10:16

You Get What He Paid For — July 16

Oreo's are the best cookies bar none, but they cost more than the rest. CoffeeMate is the best creamer, but it cost more too. Brick is better than siding, steel is stronger than aluminum, sharp cheddar cheese is better than blended, beef burgers are better than soy and the Yankees are better than the Orioles. What am I saying? "You get what you pay for."

Generally speaking, the better something is, the more it will cost. The nicest cars are the most expensive. The expensive tools last the longest.

Sometimes we can get by with the generic, a reasonable facsimile, or fake. Who's going to know if that diamond is real? Who's going to really know if you used fresh peas in the pot pie? Sometimes it just doesn't make any difference.

But what about when it does most certainly matter? If you're climbing a mountain, don't you want the best rope and equipment money can buy? If you're going to battle, don't you want the best weapons and armor in the world, along the best trained and equipped troops at your side? Knowing you get what you pay for, we would probably pay a pretty penny for that mountain climbing equipment. On the other hand, we may not be able to afford the best weapons, armor, troops and troop training that money can buy. It would take the investment of others, someone with more resources than us. If the government or some gazillionaire came through for us and it cost us nothing, while it is free for us, it still costs someone greatly.

In the "Kingdom Gift Shop," everything is the best. There are no fakes, facsimiles and nothing is generic. It's the real deal! Yet not one of us can buy a thing in there. The price is way to high. Still, you can have anything in it you need. All you have to do is ask. Why? Because the great price has already been paid by Him. In the Kingdom Gift Shop, you get what He paid for!

Working All Things Together For Good   July 17

I don't mean to whine; well maybe a little, but if traffic lights were situations in my life I would rather not find myself in, well then I'm driving downtown in New York City and none of the lights are green! However, it does seem that the Lord is teaching me many things in His "School of Spiritual Hard Knocks."

Now, having sufficiently whined, I do have perspective and realize that compared to most people, my troubles are minimal. I thank God my crew has good health, shelter, and is confident of their next meal. So, with perspective established, back to the story.

The latest stop light in this life of traffic jams was at the courthouse. Matthew 5:24 says: "Settle matters quickly with your adversary who is taking you to court." I tried! I really tried, but to no avail.

A comic strip I saw one time (*Far Side*, or something like it) had this picture of God creating the earth on His stove. In a pan was the globe, and with a sly looking smile on His face, He was sprinkling out spices on the globe from a shaker labeled "jerks." Several of these "spices" landed way to close to me and came calling on my wallet.

Proverbs 15:22 says: "Plans fail for the lack of counsel, but with many advisers they succeed." I am way too independent and prideful, but I could see that I was out of my league in this situation. So I sought some counsel. On the advice of a friend who is an attorney, I retained another lawyer to represent me in this matter.

These people were coming for me full force. They were suing me and not backing up one inch! I was truly concerned about the outcome. I would have had no idea how to proceed on my own. I was totally out of my element and comfort zone. I was in a fight!

My attorney told me exactly what measures to take to protect my assets. He then explained our strategy for the court room. He further explained that this would turn out for my good.

On the day of my court appearance, we were at first in a courtroom of about fifty people. Each person was being sued for one thing or another. This was the pre-trial hearing stage. Only a handful of these people had an attorney with them. An obvious mistake, not being represented by someone knowledgeable in the law. Sadly, I saw many people fail for lack of counsel.

We tried one more time in that setting to "settle the matter," but they would have none of it. At that point my attorney went into action. It was like having your big brother show up in the room when a bully was about to kick your butt! The outcome was in my favor, even to the point that where I had seemed to be at their mercy, now they were at mine! Just like my attorney said.

God can be to us like an attorney that never loses a case. He will be with us and protect us when the enemy comes to "steal, kill, and destroy." He will show us the way out of our difficult situations. He will work all things together for good. The requirement is to do as He instructs us, to obey Him. Then it will turn out for good, just like He said.

And we know that in all things God works for the good of those who love him, who have been called according to his purpose. – Romans 8:28

The Phone Call I Should Have Made   July 18

"Hey J, how ya' doin'? I wanted to let you know that I have been praying for you and G the last couple of days. I also wanted to tell you what a godly example of commitment and service you and G are to me. Both of you have always been faithful to God, our church and its people.

You and G are always there in the praise band leading worship. You are there cooking every time the men, youth group or the whole church family gets together to cookout and chow down for some event, fundraiser, or fellowship. Not to mention your work with the trustees at the church. And the Christmas and youth parties at your home – what a blast!

More to the personal side, G, I will never forget my first day working at the Mission House. I had gone there with a good bit of apprehension, but I ended up working with you handing out groceries and had a great time serving others with you. We sure laughed a lot that day!

And J, how many times have I called you to come to my rescue in the heat over an A/C malfunction of some sort? In no time you fixed me up and I was chilling again!

One of the best memories of my time as a youth pastor was in large part, thanks to you and your efforts as camp cook, on what I will always remember as "the perfect camping trip." That was an awesome weekend, one that those kids and I will never forget. Man, you know how to camp!

So, I just wanted to tell you both how much I appreciate and admire your commitment and service and thank you for what it means to me. Both of you are an example of these special gifts fleshed out in humility in everyday life. Thank you and God Bless you beyond your wildest dreams!"… end of call …

Every bit of that "call" is true of J and G. They are wonderful, Godly, devoted servants. They are expecting nothing in return. Unfortunately, that is often just what these kind of wonderful servants get from us, nothing in return. Many of us let the faithful work of servants like this go unnoticed and it is taken for granted. Please forgive me, J and G, for not noticing enough, not thanking you or encouraging you. So, everyone take notice and thank servants like these around us.

Be sure of this: God notices these servants!

But many who are first will be last, and many who are last will be first. – Mathew 19:30

P.S. Why was I praying for them? G had surgery today. Lift her up to the Lord for healing and quick recovery. They are used mightily in the Kingdom.

Take Out The Trash　　　　　　　　　　　July 19

Last week, we forgot to take the garbage can out to the street to be picked up. City sanitation only comes once a week. I'll bet you can guess the results.

The can filled up and now it's overflowing. The extra bags are piling up around the can. The smell is growing and the flies are multiplying. Tomorrow is pickup day and you can believe the can will be out by the side of the road in time for pickup!

I can imagine what would happen if I just continued to pile this garbage up. The foul odor would become a funky stench. The visitors to this rotting mess would get bigger and more numerous. Flies, roaches, mice, rats, possums, raccoons, foxes, and bears could arrive to pilfer through the rot! Yes, there have been bears in the area.

Sin is like that can of garbage. We need to be sure to "take out the trash." If we don't, the stench of it grows and it will attract all sorts of pests and even dangers. We may for a time compromise with the smell of it and what it draws. We may even get used to it to some degree, but sooner or later it becomes unbearable, unmanageable, and overwhelming. The result is a whole lot more garbage to take out.

We should take all our stinking sin out to the street (the Cross) to be picked up. He will pick it up and it will be gone for good into the "dump of forgiveness." Sunday is not the only day for sin pickup. We can take it out any day, even today, right now, because Jesus forgives sin anytime we ask!

If we confess our sins, he is faithful and just and will forgive us our sins and purify us from all unrighteousness. – 1 John 1:9

The Gun Guy   July 20

I have a son who is an avid gun enthusiast, to put it mildly. When he first started showing an interest in guns, he really knew nothing about them. Today, after years of study and experience, he can tell you everything you want to know about any gun from a pea shooter to a cruise missile. He loves and enjoys his hobby.

He owns several different kinds of guns, some requiring special knowledge and permits. Each time he wants a weapon that is not so ordinary, he has to fill out a multitude of forms for the ATF and get clearances from government agencies to legally possess some types of weapons. This requires a great deal of knowledge and understanding of these procedures.

The Bible tells us in Proverbs to faithfully go after wisdom, knowledge, discernment, and understanding so as to be equipped for righteous living. These attributes are our some of our most important tools for life as believers.

We won't just come by these traits by osmosis. Like my son with his interest in guns, we will have to learn what it takes to possess and use wisdom, knowledge, discernment, and understanding correctly. It will take effort and desire to attain and apply these things to our lives.

This will take a true desire in us. It will require time in prayer asking God for these attributes in our lives and character. It will require our continued effort reading and studying the Word to understand how to rightly apply our wisdom, knowledge, discernment and understanding. A good dose of godly counsel will help too.

Like my son, we have to learn what it takes to succeed in attaining the good things we desire.

Check out Proverbs to read all the good things the Lord will bring us as we go after wisdom, knowledge, discernment and understanding.

The Road King   July 21

Last night I was late for a get together with some folks. I finally got in my truck five minutes after I was supposed to be there. It's a 20-25 minute ride. I was looking at being 30 minutes late! I can't stand being late for anything, so you know I was in a hurry!

I zipped out into traffic and fell in behind a guy who thinks he's driving a horse and buggy in his own private parade. Knowing (by obvious comparison) that I am a much better driver than he, I am now calling this guy "granny" and suggesting what he might do to move it along a bit so that I would not be an hour late! Of course, this is a two lane road and cars were constantly coming in the other lane, so there was no getting around this guy.

I tailgated this snail for miles! Finally, he slowly pulls off into a church parking lot. Oops, now a little (very little) guilt entered me as I recalled the verbal abuse I was putting on this crawler. I pondered: "I'm sorry, I should have a least been more tolerant of someone headed to church." As if a church goer is somehow given a pass compared to a "non-churcher." How does such bull travel around in this brain?

Then I realized this guy was cutting through the church parking lot as a shortcut to avoid the traffic light at the upcoming intersection! Now I was back to: "You sorry, egg sucking dog! How could you cut through there with a clear conscience? I would never do that (a lie). And why do you need to use a short cut when you've only been going 10 miles an hour for the last hundred miles?"

The short version: "You are a sorry driver dude, and I am 'The Road King' compared to you!"

I suppose many of us are guilty of comparing ourselves to others where they may fall short, at least in our view. They become our yardstick to feel better about ourselves because we may perceive ourselves at some higher level or rank. Just as damaging could be us viewing our own short comings against others successes.

As followers of Jesus we should not use others as a yardstick to measure ourselves as successes or failure. The rewards for success on this earth are a fleeting vapor. We should instead measure ourselves in our own obedience to God. And even as we fall short in that, He has provided the way to success over this world. Success over crappy drivers. Success in spite of ourselves. Success over death to life everlasting. We can't fail if we trust in Him!

P.S. I used to work across the street from where we met last night. I had never made it in less than twenty-something minutes. I made it in seventeen minutes last night after following "gramps" half way there. Go figure that one.

Ponder This   July 22

I ponder stuff! Not really doubting, but wondering, how can that be? For instance, how does God remember all of our names, much less every hair on our head? How about remembering where He placed every star in the sky? I know I would forget where I put some of them!

As a little boy I really liked playing with little plastic army men. I remember getting my parents to buy me bags full of these guys. I would set up a battlefield and go at it for hours. I would even give many of them names, and I could remember each of them. But God has a lot more people in His army. Doesn't it have to be hard to remember all of our names? And what about the hairs on my head? They keep changing color. Is that gray hair the same as the brown one it replaced or is it a new one? Confused yet?

I've been a mailman for over twenty-six years. I have had many routes consisting of somewhere between 500 and 1000 stops each, depending on their length and volume of mail. After a little while on every route I ever had, I knew every last name at any given address. Pretty good huh? But God knows every first, last and middle name at every address. And every hair on their heads too! Amazing!

I suppose if I had a hundred children (Hannah says that's not going to happen!) I would remember all of their names.

Something I do know and don't have to ponder is that it is great to be an individually loved child of our God who has so many kids. We are all God's children and He does know every one of our names.

Just Wondering   July 23

For a long time God has been having me look through the eyes of the unchurched (believers and non-believers). "Church people" are not the only ones with discernment. Most people in the world can smell a fake or someone faking it a mile away. In fact, I think most people searching for something or someone to fill a void in their lives would rather listen and learn from a "real" person struggling than a phony with all the answers. At least when a *real* person messes up they will get to see the love, mercy, and grace of God in action.

When we're struggling we want answers with action behind them. If someone comes into the church while they're cold, wet, hungry and thirsty, then praying for them, wishing them well and sending them on their way doesn't impress them too much with God's love! What we should be doing is getting them a towel and a warm place to eat the food and coffee we give them. Yep, even before we pray with them.

I had gone to church as a child, but as a teen people "playing church" had turned me off and for that matter, kept me away. The first time I went back to a church as an adult it was a very rainy day. I sat down in the middle of the sanctuary (near a side door in case of the need for a quick exit). While the service was underway a homeless guy came in out of the rain and sat down right next to me. He was ragged looking, soaked and smelled like Louie. He flipped through the bulletin for most of the service. He probably just wanted a dry place out of the rain.

When the service concluded, several "coat and tie" guys came up and greeted me warmly. I saw one guy go up to the homeless dude and ask him how he liked the service. I imagine the homeless guy was the only one who regretted the service was over as he was escorted back out into the rain.

I wonder if that guy ever got saved. I wonder if I'll see him in heaven and be able to say I'm sorry for how he was treated. I wonder if he was Jesus sitting there just waiting to bless just one true servant. Just wondering.

What Can Possibly Hurt Jesus   July 24

The last four days have been different to say the least. For someone who claims to prefer spontaneity to routine, I sure missed my routine for a few days! I was confronted with computer malfunctions, weird sleeping hours and not so good memories. Something happened to trigger a memory of being severely rejected and the emotional pain came rushing back like it happened yesterday.

I truly have forgiven all involved in this incident in the past. I have no anger, hatred, or desire to get even with anyone. So I went to God with it and ask what was going on? Why this emotional blow again? I'm over it, right? This morning God did give me peace that I am indeed over it. So what's up? Well, it's not about you, Greg. If I could keep that truth in my heart, I would do a lot better in my obedience to His first two commandments! But that's another story.

We deal with rejection from a very young age. Mom says "no no" in a loud voice when we want to stick the clothes hanger in the wall socket. Good for Mom, but even with a loving explanation, we may feel a little rejected. We don't make the first basketball team we tryout for (it would've helped to make at least one shot). The first girl we ask out smirks and laughs loud enough for everyone in the school hallway to hear, and struts away.

The truth is that rejection hurts and can take a lot longer than a physical beating to heal up. Rejection can be an emotional train wreck! It can be a ticking bomb of revenge waiting to go off. It can be cancer to our spirit. It hurts!

So what did I do with this emotional pain that had returned. I ask God to take it away. He did, and that's when I realized that this hurt I was experiencing was not about me, but to make me realize in a new way, what He has gone through for me.

I started thinking about Jesus being crucified and the events leading up to it in light of the massive rejection He must have been feeling. He was beaten and tortured unmercifully! Yet I believe that the rejection of all those He loved hurt Him far worse. Yeah, His love for us kept Him on the cross, but our rejection of Him hurt Him far worse than the nails did.

I also believe it hurts Him every time a soul goes to hell. You see, when someone goes to hell, it is not Him rejecting them, but them rejecting Him. And that's what hurts Jesus, the loss of those He loves.

Is Your Love Being Held Hostage   July 25

When I was growing up, I had an uncle who was really great to me. He would play his guitar through a little amplifier and let me sing through the microphone. I sang the same song over and over, to the chagrin of the rest of the family, but it was a blast for a little boy.

I spent two summers of my teen years at his house in Tennessee. I worked at his ice cream store and he let me drive his old Ford. We were buds. In my view, very good buds! He even let me make the work schedule for the store each week. I would always somehow end up on the schedule with the cheerleaders. Life was great!

However, like all of us, he had issues. I didn't see him for many years after I was on my own. He didn't come to my wedding. Anger turned to long term rage in me when he didn't come when my first son was born, or the second, or the third. He didn't even call. I vowed that if he ever showed his face in my town again there would be serious consequences for him and I meant it!

As the years went by I wouldn't think about him much, but when his name did come up, rage would build in me instantly. That fire of hurt was still there.

I really don't remember why I agreed years later to go visit him. I think it was because of my son's interest in music. But I was on my guard, believe me.

When I walked into his house and saw him my anger, rage and resentment left me. He was old, but looked even older. One leg was gone and his kidneys were shot.

He hit it off great with my son. Watching those two together helped heal me, and I started remembering the good times that my uncle and I had together.

He had been to a rehab and even ended up working there a while. I think that's where he opened up to God. We talked about old times and when we left, he offered up a prayer.

I believe I'll see him again. Maybe we'll sing that same old song again together in Heaven.

Where had all that love for this man gone during those years of my anger towards him? It was being held hostage behind my unforgiveness towards him.

Got somebody you need to love again? It's still there, right behind the forgiveness.

He heals the brokenhearted and binds up their wounds. – Psalm 147:3

Old, New, What To Do...Love One Another
July 26

I was reading this devotional the other day and it triggered in me lessons learned long ago having to do with judging others. If you've ever been in or around "revival," you know that all hell can break loose! The more God moves, the more hell hates it! I won't get into what was God and what was the devil. Suffice to say, there was a whole lot of both! God moved mightily and Satan hacked away at His work.

The revival profoundly affected the church I was attending at the time. It affected the worship, in that some wanted the new music and some wanted the old hymns. Some services had no time limit, to which some folks were opposed. Some wanted extended personal prayer times and others wanted "traditional" pastoral prayer.

I am ashamed to say I fell into the camp of we do it all the new way (change). Others (just as shamefully) were in the camp of staying the old way (no change). Others, the wiser of the three camps wanted separate services for each style of worship.

Now go ahead and get upset with me if you want to because I said style of worship, but that's what it is, as I was to learn later. Both styles are good and pleasing to the Lord, but it is your style. Potatoes are potatoes, fried, baked, mashed or salad. Eggs are eggs, scrambled, over easy or hard-boiled. Steak is steak, fried, grilled or broiled. These will all fill you up and satisfy you no matter which style you serve them.

Anyway, I was in a service one day when this man of God stood up to speak. You know who the men of God are in your midst. Nobody has to tell you. This man was not outspoken; instead he was a quiet man. When he did speak, it was profound and wise. He preferred the traditional style of worship himself, but knowing him to be a man of God he had my attention. He said things like many styles of worship will please God as long as your heart is after Him. He also said that we knew each others' hearts, that we had loved one another and should continue to do so, understanding that we each may prefer a different style of worship.

I was changed (again) in that moment! Unfortunately, everyone was not changed. Some stood their old ground and some stood their new ground, to the detriment of many. To this day, nothing, and I mean nothing, sets me off like brothers in battle, not difference of opinion, but differences without love.

So which is it going to be, the new way or the old way? I believe the Lord would say: "It's the same, only different."

"A new command I give you: Love one another. As I have loved you, so you must love one another. By this everyone will know that you are my disciples, if you love one another." – John 13:34-35

Miracles, For What — July 27

So I'm reading about Jesus feeding the 5000 and I'm thinking: What would be going on in my mind if I was one of the disciples with a basket in my hands, passing out this ever multiplying fish and bread? This had to be a most amazing event! "Seconds? Sure mister, I think we have enough." This had be an unforgettable experience for all attendees at this uncovered dish dinner!

So why is it that a short time later the disciples wonder how they are supposed to feed 4000? I would hope that if I were there, I would be standing over to the side of this exchange between Jesus and the disciples with a big grin on my face, knowing what is about to happen. However, the truth is we don't always get it the first time, do we?

Have you ever seen a miracle? Think about it, a true to life real deal miracle right before your very eyes. I remember a time in my life when I was after God to let me see a physical healing. Sounds scarily like some people in the Bible saying, "What sign will you show us to prove..." Well, it happened. I witnessed a real life instantaneous physical healing, and after I did I felt ashamed for having ask for the wrong reasons.

I had not asked so that God would get the glory. I had not asked so that someone would receive healing. I had not ask so that testimony would come from it, so to further the Kingdom. I had asked so that I could see it happen and that God prove Himself to me.

John the Baptist even had doubt. He sent messengers to Jesus to ask, "Are you the One who was to come?" (Luke 7:20). Jesus sent word back to John telling him that the blind see, the lame walk, those who have leprosy are cured, the deaf hear, the dead are raised, and the Good News is preached to the poor (Luke 7:22).

So why did Jesus do all these miracles (many of the same kinds over and over again)? To show not only His love by feeding and healing our flesh, but to also show His love for us by feeding and healing our spirits.

Jesus told Peter once that he did not have in mind the things of God, but the things of men. We are told in Romans to transform our minds. We need to have in mind the things of God. We should want to see healing take place for the right reasons. Sure, it is wonderful and good for us to receive healing in our physical bodies. But the healing of the soul is the greatest miracle. That is what He wants us to get deep down in our being, and in our mind!

So, having in mind the things of God, let's look again at the word Jesus sent back to John the Baptist. The blind see (with their spiritual eyes), the lame walk (in my ways), those with leprosy are cured (hopeless are given hope), the deaf hear (me), the dead (in sin) are raised (saved), and the Good News is preached (they tell others about me).

These are the miracles He wants us to desire most of all. Miracles, for what? For the things of God. For His Kingdom. For His Glory.

He Won't Bite   July 28

Dogs and Mailmen, adversaries since the Pony Express. You've seen the pictures, and heard the jokes. You've seen the cartoons in the funny papers of the dog latched to the mailman's leg, or the mailman stuffing a dog into a mailbox.

Here's the line I hear all the time, as the hair goes up on his back and he shows his teeth: "He won't bite," or "He doesn't bite!" Let me tell you something. I have been bitten. The bites may hurt in different degrees. A snip, a clamp down, chew on you or even a death lock. But he will bite!

I have come across all kinds. Spot is the one that is stealthy and tries to sneak up on you. Not a sound, and then pain. I knew he was around. I just didn't take care to watch out for him. Then whamo! My heel is bleeding and he's running away grinning!

Then there's Rover. You know he's there, but he's not life-threatening. He's almost a challenge. You think, I can get in and out of there before he knows I'm around. It'll even be fun trying to sneak by. Then he comes from the other side of the house that you've never seen him coming from. He locks down on you like the best-tasting bone he's ever chomped!

Then there's Duke's pack that looks so friendly. Tails wagging. It almost appears there's a smile on their faces. "C'mon in and pet us," they seem to be saying through their whimper. And then you're suckered into attempting to make them your friend. As you reach down, one of the Duke's pals latches onto your arm. Another locks onto your leg, and as you go to the ground, the others join in, and you're the dog-dish special of the day.

Lastly, there's Spike. Spike makes no bones about it. "You come in my yard, and I'm gonna bite your face off, and then chew you into little bite-size morsels for my next mailman stew."

In contrast, there are men of God and demons, adversaries since Adam. It shouldn't even be a battle, knowing who we are in Christ. "Greater is He that is in me, than he that is in the world" (1 John 4:4). It's when we let our guard down or when we think we can handle the enemy in our own power that we get in trouble. Satan and his horde come at us every way they can, looking for a weakness or a doorway left open, just like dogs after the mailman.

For instance, the demon of Spot slips up on us and snips at us with a temptation that seems so insignificant and takes so little compromise on our part to sin that we're not even believing he needs to be guarded against. Isn't that where a lot of big sins begins, with a little compromise?

How about the demon of Rover. This one serves up temptation to sin in a way that seems fun and almost a challenge. It may manifest in sin when we put others down with hurtful words in an attempt to get others to sin with us, calling it fun or a dare. This may hurt a third party or even damage their property in the name of fun or a practical joke.

Then the demon of Duke wants us to gang up on others. This manifests in sin as gossip about someone or in a conspiracy to bring someone down a notch or two, causing harm to someone's reputation and integrity, thinking this will build us up in the eyes of men.

Then there's the demon of Spike. He's pure ol' hell cutting lose, and wide open out-of-control sin and abuse. This demon wants us to flat-out lose it, saying things that are directly abusive, mean and ugly, destructive, violent and out-and-out visible hatred.

You see, just like the mailman, we have a message to deliver. That message is a letter of the love of God to everyone that has not received His love and salvation.

Just like the dogs after the mailman, these imps of the enemy come after us, seeking to stop the message from getting through. They will steal, kill and destroy whomever and whatever they can to stop the mail (John 10:10).

But, if we have in us the Super Dog Spray, this dog spray is the power and the name of our Lord Jesus. We can use that power to fend off the dogs and God's letter of life will get through.

Using the power of His name in faith, we will see the completion of our appointed rounds.

Road Trip Anyone — July 29

Nick just got back from a "road trip." It was the real deal! He went to Mississippi, Missouri, Colorado, Nevada, California and Arizona just to name a few. Let me tell you, your son's first road trip will increase your prayer life! At church, when Hannah asked for prayer for him while he was out on his trip, our pastor replied: "All the moms want to prayer for him and all the men wish they were him!" I'm sure it was a bit of a dream come true for Nick. It is a cool, adventurous thing many of us would like to do.

Nick had taken a road atlas to help him navigate his journey. He did however take a few wrong turns and adjustments had to be made. He had to choose either to not go where he started out for, or readjust his route to get to his original destination. He commented that he wished he had a GPS to help guide him.

Spiritually speaking, there are a lot of ways I could go with analogies here. For instance, a road map, being man's plan and a GPS being "God's Planning System." In this analogy, man's plan is laid out according to what he knows at his level versus God's plan that sees more clearly from above. That works.

Another analogy is the road map and the GPS both guide us like the Bible and His spirit. The road map like the Word, shows us the best way to get there (a plan). A GPS, like His Spirit, confirming the plan, guides us through detours and obstructions along the way. I like this analogy personally. When we depend on God for guidance by reading His Word, being guided by His Spirit, along with prayer and some godly counsel, we will surely reach the destination He has in mind for us.

Remember how God guided the children of Israel in the desert.

By day the Lord went ahead of them in a pillar of cloud to guide them on their way and by night in a pillar of fire to give them light, so that they could travel by day or night. Neither the pillar of cloud by day nor the pillar of fire by night left its place in front of the people. – Exodus 13:21-22

If He would go to these lengths to guide them, He will certainly guide us who ask Him.

Encourage   July 30

The hardest I ever worked on sermons was one of the first times I went on the road to speak at a youth week. I worked on these messages for weeks prior to the event. I wrote out each sermon, no outline or notes. I wanted to be prepared and I wanted to see God move in these young people's lives.

Although the testimonies from the young people who came with me were awesome, I felt like my messages bombed! I truly had tried to be faithful in preparation. As I preached that week my messages seemed dull and boring and nothing seemed to be getting across to those listening. I came away from that event very discouraged.

To me, youth ministry often seems to be spiritual feast or famine. You seem to be scratching at a brick wall with a crayon or blowing the wall to pieces with dynamite. You're either filling an empty glass full or the lid's on it.

Anyway, several years later, some young people from that youth week (one who was a family friend) came to visit us at our home. During the course of that visit one of the other young ladies, just as calm and serious as could be, says to me "what you said that week changed my life." There is no way how I can express what her encouraging words did for me! My "ministry tank" was refueled and I was good to go!

As much as words can hurt, they can also heal. Words of encouragement are the best medicine we can prescribe to others. It's like giving them free gasoline. We can feel like our tank is empty, but our encouragement can fill someone up again to continue the journey in the Kingdom.

Paul knew the importance and value of encouragement. After being thrown out of Antioch, nearly stoned in Iconium, and then literally stoned and left for dead outside Lystra, he and Barnabas "returned to Lystra, Iconium, and Antioch, strengthening the disciples and encouraging them to remain true to the faith" (Acts 14:21-22). At the risk of their lives, they went back to encourage others.

I doubt any of us will have to risk our lives to encourage anyone, but encouragement to others is a blessing that we can give that fuels the fire within.

Encourage someone today. Tell them what they mean to you. Thank them for what they have done for you. Tell them that you see their hard work and devotion. Tell them what they do matters. Let's be a gas station of encouragement to those around us and those who bless us.

P.S. I receive encouragement almost daily from family and friends. I would tell you how great it feels and what it does to help me press on but I'll bet you already know by receiving encouragement yourselves. I wrote this almost a year ago after someone encouraged me right when I needed it. This morning, I woke up to encouragement from another friend, right when I needed it.

I Hear You Knocking   July 31

"Knock, knock."
"Who's there?"
"Orange."
"Orange who?"
"Orange you going to let me in?"

I can hear all you Believers out there saying: "I know where he's going with this one. He's going to write about letting Jesus into our lives". AANNNNTTTT! (buzzer sound) Nope, but thank you for playing! I'm writing this one to us believers about letting others into our lives.

Just so there is no misunderstanding, letting Jesus into our lives is the most important thing we need to do, period. Having said that, I think we often throw up a roadblock or a detour to people who are seeking to fill that void in their lives when we don't let them into our lives.

Last night a friend and I were talking and we wondered why people don't come to church when we invite them. We meet someone and they start sharing some concerns or problems in their life and we think: "I know what will help" and we invite them to church like it's some kind of "spiritual emergency room." They kindly reply: "Sure, I'll be there" and they never show up. What is that?

Church should be and often is a good place. I'm not at all down on church. It's just not where we believers are to "pass the buck"! It is not a "spiritual emergency room." It is more an "after care" facility. Church is a place to meet with other believers, to be encouraged and worship. To hear the Word of the Lord.

We, as believers, should most often take the hurting to the Physician (Jesus) ourselves. When we meet someone, or even if it's a friend we already know who is sharing difficult things in their life with us, they are not doing it so we can pass them on somewhere else. They are opening themselves to us because they trust us or see something in us that gives them some glimmer of hope. They want into us, not into our church that might appear to be a room full of strangers to them.

So, what's it to be? I hear you knocking, but you can't come in. Or do we open "our door" and offer them Who we have?

Fill The Cooler — August 1

Saturday morning Ryan and I headed out fishing for awhile. We had no intention of staying out too long and had no certain plan of action. We were able to net some live bait quickly but it wasn't working too well. We found ourselves going through the pass into the Gulf and trolling down the beach. Still nothing happening. We had gone a few miles down the beach before we turned around to head back in. We really had not expected to catch much as we had left late and it was getting hot and still. Not to mention an unfavorable tide.

On the way back in I saw an area I wanted to try, so we trolled through. It was only about fifty yards offshore in fairly shallow water. Ryan caught a small Blue. We made another pass through the spot. This time he caught a big Blue. We continued to make passes through this area for near an hour I suppose. We caught nice fish on almost every pass!

Even the local "tourist helicopter" came over us at one point and circled above us a couple of times at low altitude. Naw, we weren't feeling puffed up and proud as we caught fish after fish! It's funny though, because a fisherman never really seems like he has enough. Even after a good day and a full stomach, he wants to go back for more.

Part of this dissatisfaction for fishermen is "the one that got away." And yes, it happened yesterday. On one pass through that spot, Ryan hooked up with the big one of the day. I've been fishing more than a few years and have never seen a bigger Spanish Mackerel than the one he got to the side of the boat. As he got it up to the boat, the fish was able to shake off and disappear into the gulf.

When that happens, your heart sinks, your mouth opens and all you think about is the "one" that got away. Your not thinking about the cooler full of nice fish you've already caught, but the one that got away. "How'd that happen?" "If only ..." and you play it over and over, but the fish is gone.

Sadly, as "Fishers of Men", this happens too. We may have led a "cooler" full of souls to the Lord. Or discipled many in their walk. That is wonderful, exciting and life changing. But what about the one that got away?

Let's pray and ask God to guide us in all we can do to see that the cooler is full and that none get away. So that we aren't muttering to ourselves: "If only", or "I should've". Lets also pray for the heart of a fisherman, that there is never enough in the cooler!

Then Jesus told them this parable: "Suppose one of you has a hundred sheep and loses one of them. Doesn't he leave the ninety-nine in the open country and go after the lost sheep until he finds it? And when he finds it, he joyfully puts it on his shoulders and goes home. Then he calls his friends and neighbors together and says, 'Rejoice with me; I have found my lost sheep.' I tell you that in the same way there will be more rejoicing in heaven over one sinner who repents than over ninety-nine righteous persons who do not need to repent". – Luke 15: 3-7

It Is Who You Know — August 2

I know you've heard someone start a sentence with: "It's not who you know ..." We may want that phrase to be true if we are the one on the outside trying, for instance, to get a new job. However, we might welcome the thought of, "it is who you know," if we are already fishing buddies with our potential new boss.

Many times in our lives someone else will get to make a decision that will greatly affect our lives. Frankly, I pray that it is someone I know and that I have found favor in their eyes!

Truthfully, it is often the case that who you know is the deciding factor in turning points in our lives. While there are times this may be unfair and even result in the wrong decision and outcome (unqualified person in a job, a figurehead, etc...), in many other cases it is a blessing.

I have gained employment and favor solely because of who I knew, and it benefited me and my family greatly. It was an answer to prayer and out of the goodness of someone's heart. Not necessarily that I beat someone out of a position, but that even a position was created or developed and then it was offered to me by someone I knew.

How do we get to know someone? Sometimes we just meet them one on one. However, most of the time we are introduced to people. I know people who know Major League Baseball players, movie actors, rich people and others of influence. Yet, I don't know a single one of those people myself. I probably never will know any of them unless a person I know, that knows one of them, introduces me to them.

It's the same in the Kingdom. Jesus said, "I am the way and the truth and the life. No one comes to the Father except through Me" (John 14:6). That about says it, doesn't it? Eternally, it is "Who you know." You want to meet Him? I can introduce you.

P.S. Already know Him? Introduced Him to anybody lately?

Hard Ground   August 3

One of the Crew comes home the other night telling me about his day at work. He tells of swinging a sledge hammer all afternoon, breaking up concrete to do some renovation work.

My mind went back to the days I worked construction as a young man. After the land was cleared on a new construction site, dirt would be brought in to fill the sight. We would then tamp down the dirt until it was very hard and packed, achieving a certain density. We would then drive 2x4 stakes into the hard packed dirt. Then we would mount boards on the stakes to mark the height or "grade" at which we wanted the ground to be leveled. This is where my mind went, back to the days of driving those 2x4 stakes into that hard concrete-like ground.

The stakes had to be driven deep into that hard ground. You can trust me, swinging that sledge hammer over and over was hard, back breaking work. It seemed as if that stake was only going down fractions of an inch with each swing. If I missed hitting the stake square on the top it would split to pieces and I would have to start all over with a new stake.

Does our "ground" get that hard? Does it get "packed down" so hard by offense, unforgiveness, fear of being hurt or rejected, selfishness, and only each of us knows what else in our own individual lives? Does it seem that the Holy Spirit couldn't drive an arrow of love or forgiveness into our hearts with a sledge hammer?!

This is exactly the place God can work if we let Him. It may not be easy and probably not painless. Hard ground isn't easy to break up, but it can break up in big chunks. There is good that comes after the breaking up of hard ground. God can turn us into good soil. Maybe we will let Him throw in some fertilizer (something like obedience or forgiveness) that seems to stink at first, but in using it our soil will become richer and more productive, yielding fruit for the Kingdom.

Bottom line: Hard ground is selfish, self-serving, unproductive soil. Broken, yielded, fertile ground is Kingdom soil.

The Boat Races — August 4

My friends and I used to love to play in the rain. I grew up in the warm humid climate of Florida, which afforded us many afternoon showers in the summer to play some muddy football. Outside of football in the rain, we liked to race "boats" down the street.

When it rained enough to fill the curbs in the neighborhood with water running down the street, the boat races were on. We would select leaves, small twigs, broken little pieces of plastic, anything that would float (the faster the better). Then after choosing a course down the curb of the street with the best "rapids," the races were on for as long as the rainwater was draining. We would do this until the river ran dry. We just couldn't get enough of boat racing!

The racing itself was fun for us and we would have different outcomes in almost every race. We would change leaves and twigs in hopes of having a faster boat to win the race. We could change the course or distance of the race for a different outcome. Often it would rain harder or slack up while we were racing and change things up. But we always had to have the rain water coming down to keep racing. No water, the curb dries up and the boats don't move anymore. The water is what made the boats move along. The more water there was, the better the boats ran the race.

I'm thinking our lives are like our little racing boats. We will continually try to tweak the boats of our lives (for better or worse) in our own strength, but we need fresh running water (the Word of God) to move us along. Without the water running we are boats that have run aground. We need the rain of the Word to move us along in the "river of life."

Unlike the rain from the sky, we don't have to wait for a random shower to seek God. We can open the heavens by opening the Bible and have our boats moving downstream again. Lets not get stuck in the mud of life and run aground because we won't take time to seek Him or suffer from a drought of our own indifference.

Lets open up the skies of His Word and let it rain. It's still fun to play in the rain!

Is It All Facebook — August 5

Who am I really? Who are you? Really. Outside of God, does anybody know us? Or is it all "Facebook" where we can control and manipulate the appearance we want to portray of ourselves to everyone else.

I just got to thinking what does it take for us to be real? I mean to really live out our lives for what truly matters to us deep down inside.

This kind of questioning came to me as I was thinking about how I might live my last day on this earth if I knew it was my last. As I thought about this my priorities became much clearer to me. We need to set priorities, but honestly I most often do not set priorities, I'm just cruisin' through life. However, when I think about my last day, heartfelt things that need to be said and done come rushing to my mind.

For instance I would want to make sure that everyone I should have shared the love of God with, now hears about Him. I would want that loved one or friend that I was angry at to forgive me. I would want to share a time of healing with them. I would want to make sure my family knew how much I truly love each one of them.

In short, if it was my last day, I would want everyone to know how I truly felt and what is truly important, that being my Lord, my family, and others that He puts in my life.

"Teacher, which is the greatest commandment in the Law?" Jesus replied: " 'Love the Lord your God with all your heart and with all your soul and with all your mind.' This is the first and greatest commandment. And the second

is like it: 'Love your neighbor as yourself.' All the Law and the Prophets hang on these two commandments." – Matthew 36-40

Because what is really important is not the things we have or who we appear to be, but who we love and how we show we care about them in a real way.

Maybe, I should try living every day as if it were my last on earth. How would you live yours?

Jesus For Sale   August 6

The other day I heard several people making fun of some religious leaders of our day. Basically they were saying, this guy preaches such and such and then does this (which appears to be and often is hypocritical). They were also saying that these leaders scream, "Send me your money! I know what to do with it" and then they return to their mansions of comfort.

I know what the Bible says about sowing and reaping and giving and then receiving a return. But I also know what it says about appearances and causing your brother to sin. One's motive shouldn't even appear to be for selfish gain (power, money, prestige...). That's the kind of behavior that made Jesus clear the Temple!

Unbelievers may not know God, but they are not stupid and they do have a spirit in them (placed there by God) that can be hurt! One of guys in this conversation (one of the most generous, giving men I know) was telling how he had been hurt deeply by a religious leader. It was like he had a sucking chest wound! His soul was bleeding out right there before my very ears! Others in the conversation seemed to have souls scarred to the point of total distrust of God (even though the hurt was caused by man).

If we were a riding lawnmower salesmen, we wouldn't mow through the flowerbed to show that the blades are sharp. We represent the maker of this product. We would demonstrate the proper use of the best mower in the world. We could show how it cuts evenly, how powerful it is and how well it gets us through tough, thick grass.

As believers, do we really believe in our Maker and His Product (what Jesus has done and can do for us)? Do we really believe that He has the to power and capability to do what He offers? If we do, we should demonstrate who He is and what He does for us in how we live our daily lives. The wonderful thing here is that what God offers (salvation through Jesus) is a free gift. He's not for sale! They don't have to buy Him. The sad thing is, as the church, if we appear to be selling Jesus for our own personal gain, we won't even be able to give Him away.

## Out Of Our Hands								August 7

Every good parent wants to protect his children. However, we may sometimes get careless.

When my oldest son was about eleven we (my dad, brother-in-law, and I) took him with us golfing. I like playing golf and a big part of the fun to me is zipping around the course in the golf cart. When I go, I put some mileage on the cart I drive because for some unexplained reason my golf shots vary in accuracy. Anyway, Ben and I were in the cart headed to the next tee. As I made the hairpin turn in the cart path and pulled up to the tee box, Ben was no longer in the cart. I had slung him out at the hairpin turn! A total lapse of parental protection. He was none the worse for wear and we laugh about it now, but it could have been a lot worse.

Other times things happen through no fault of our own. It's a helpless feeling looking at your child unconscious in a hospital bed and you can do nothing to fix the problem.

That helpless feeling isn't just parental. We have all lost loved ones and there was nothing we could do about the situation.

I know prayer is in order in these times as the proper and effective thing to do, but ultimately the outcome is out of our hands. The question then becomes, do we trust whose hands the situation is in? The answer to that question in each of our hearts will result in us having or not having peace.

The Bible tells us often that we are God's children. We are His creation and He loves each one of His children. He is the perfect parent and will not have a lapse of parental protection. Therefore, we can trust and believe that when things and even the fate of our loved ones and friends are out of our control, they are not out of His control.

When situations are totally out of our hands is the only time they will be totally in His hands, which is the best place they can possibly be!

Forgiveness, The Key To Healing   August 8

Colossians 3:13 – *"Forgive as the Lord forgave you ..."*

Last night I saw an awesome movie about the healing of forgiveness. It is based on a true story. The movie is entitled *Amish Grace*. It is a must see, especially if you are holding back forgiveness from someone who has done you wrong.

Without giving away the movie, I'll just say that if we hold unforgiveness in our hearts against someone, it eats away at our hearts. It sucks the love right out of us. Unforgiveness is probably Satan's best weapon of divisiveness between men. Paul says to forgive "in order that Satan might not outwit us." The longer we harbor this unforgiving spirit, the more we become cold, angry, cynical, mean, and possibly contemplate revenge. I have plotted in my mind some pretty evil revenge, but I realize now I might have gotten even, but I would not have been healed inside.

When we forgive others it often heals a relationship and for sure heals us, freeing us from bitterness, anger and the whole range of the devil's devices and chains.

I know what some are thinking because I have said it myself: "But you don't understand what they did to me, to my children, to my bank account."

I personally know someone who has forgiven the person who murdered her daughter. I don't know if I could do that! I don't want to know if I could do that.

Here's the love of our Father in Heaven. He watched as Jesus hung on the cross and died for us. He watched that so He could forgive us for doing Him wrong. Seems to me we ought to be able to forgive others for doing us wrong. I'm not saying it's easy, I'm saying it's godly. I'm saying it heals.

Got unforgiveness?

Get free.

Forgive.

Forgiveness, The Key To Healing Part 2
August 9

Part 1 of "Forgiveness, The Key To Healing," was about us forgiving others and that process freeing us from our own anger, bitterness, and resentment towards those who wronged us.

Further healing comes when we forgive ourselves. Yep, many of us (maybe most of us) don't forgive ourselves for things we have done. So, do it! Why carry around guilt and remorse that probably leads to a continuing decline in our own self esteem. Tearing us down emotionally and mentally is a device of the devil to make us useless in the kingdom, and if we are not believers, a tactic to drag us into hell.

What is your forgiveness worth to the Father? The life of His Son. "For God so loved the world (you and me) that He gave His one and only Son, that whoever believes in Him shall not perish but have eternal life" (John 3:16). "If we confess our sins, He is faithful and just and will forgive us our sins and purify us from all unrighteousness" (1 John 1:9).

If you have trusted Jesus (believing in Him as your Lord and Savior) then your chains of guilt have been unlocked. Your sin has been forgiven. Throw off the chains of guilt by receiving your forgiveness. Don't let the price God paid be wasted. He wants us to be free of any and all guilt, shame and sin. Just trust Him, confess and live in the joy of the freedom He offers.

Eat Right, Exercise, Get Plenty Of Rest And See Your Doctor Regularly
August 10

"Eat right, exercise, get plenty of rest and see your doctor regularly." Have you heard that one before, or some variation of that advice? Well, it works. I am no self-help health guru. I also realize that people have health issues, medical conditions, addictions and other issues that complicate and hinder physical fitness. But for the sake of illustration and analogy please understand that I am speaking in general terms of seeking fitness.

A couple of years ago I lost seventy pounds. I ate healthy and in correct amounts, exercised regularly, rested sufficiently and kept up my checkups. It worked. The results were: knowledge of the most beneficial foods for me, much increased energy and endurance, and I was not tired and drowsy continually. I even stopped snoring and my doctor took me off half of my blood pressure meds.

Well, life goes on and as with many things, a fight often has many rounds. Slowly, I eased up on eating right, didn't exercise, rest sometimes turns into laziness and, what was my doctors name again? The results are as anticipated. I am lugging around about thirty-five of those pounds I lost previously.

The same principle applies to our relationship to God. We must eat right (read and digest the Word), exercise (obey and put what He shows us into regular daily use), get plenty of rest (yep, that Sabbath thing is for a reason) and see our Doctor (spend time in prayer to Him) regularly. It works, it's His prescription for life.

The results of "eating the Word" will be knowledge of Him and His ways and His desire for our lives. His work in our lives as we exercise our obedience and trust in Him will make our "spiritual muscles" (our faith) stronger, increasing our ability to do greater things. The rest (Sabbath) will give us time specifically dedicated to Him, as well as recharging our body and spirit. Seeing the Doctor (prayer appointments with Him) will keep us in good relationship to Him as He prescribes the "meds" for a godly life.

As I said earlier, life goes on and the Christian life is not "happily ever after" on this side of Heaven. So in the midst of the fight (this life) we will most likely suffer some knock downs, injuries, and lost rounds.

My advice; eat right, exercise, get plenty of rest and see your Doctor regularly.

Going Nuts August 11

What's the hungriest you've ever been? Seriously, think on that one and see if you remember ever starving. I'll bet most of us reading this have never been completely out of food for any lengthy period of time. When I think about starving, those "feed the children" programs come to my mind, not my own experiences of lack.

We have a pecan tree on the side of our house. A few weeks ago the pecans were all over that tree, and so were the squirrels! I swear, they must come from the six closest states. There are tons of them running, barking and eating like they haven't had a meal in months! It seemed like the more they ate the hungrier they got! Trying to finish one pecan so as to hurry to the next one. One squirrel would grab a pecan and run off somewhere. Another would eat one while sitting in the tree. Still others would sit on a post on the deck enjoying their meal.

There were pecan shells all over our deck, driveway and yard. The deck and driveway required daily sweeping so that we could walk on a flat surface! The yard under the tree crunches under my feet.

Those pecans either taste like steak off the grill or those squirrels are really starving! Some people say they will store the pecans up for the winter.

All this got me to thinking: Why aren't we that way about the Word of God? It is our "spiritual food," is it not? If it is, why don't we scamper like starving squirrels to a Bible study? Why don't we read it until our "spiritual bellies" are about to pop? Why don't we store it up for the winters of our lives?

Maybe it's because the result of us digging into the meat of the pecan (seeing where our lives need adjusting) will leave shells (changes needed in us) all over the place for everyone to see. That would then require a decision; whether to sweep the shells off the deck and driveway (our outward lives everyone sees) or to actually clean up the whole yard (our inward secret lives).

I think I'll go climb into the tree (the Word), find me a pecan (a teaching in the Bible) and chew on it awhile. It's always good and I know I'll find myself hungry for more.

Fishing In Comfortable Waters   August 12

Have you ever been out bottom fishing in a boat? That's when you go out, find a spot (maybe with your fish finder), throw the anchor (keeping the boat in one place), and fish in that spot.

When you're on the fish, this is a blast! Of course, if you stay in that one great spot long enough, issues will arise. For instance, the fish may move on or quit biting. The weather may change and the wind may come up so strong that waves come over the boat, making it difficult and even dangerous to stay anchored. (Don't give me "the Anchor holds", I know He does, but that's a different analogy. Stay with me.)

In this analogy, He brings the winds to move us on to a new spot to fish. "But God, I don't want to go! I like it here! I caught a lot of fish here! I know this spot, it's safe, and I'm comfortable here!"

Yeah, there's that word, "comfort," as in "comfort zone".

We were talking the other day about different ministries and how we get to a certain place and feel like we have a grip on what to do and how to carry out a plan. We get the mentality that just maybe, we've arrived. We relax and get comfortable. Then He brings the winds to encourage us to do more (or even something else) in the Kingdom.

The more time we spend seeking and learning, the more He teaches and grows us. He doesn't teach us and grow us so that we will sit in one place (spiritually) because it's comfortable. We like comfortable. But maybe He wants us to fish a little deeper, or go trolling, or maybe just throw our nets on the other side of the boat.

We should check our fish finder (His Word and Spirit), loosen our grip, and maybe pull up anchor and sail to the coordinates He shows us.

Jesus, No Additives Needed   August 13

I just got my boat back from the shop yesterday. The repairs were very costly. It seems that "ethanol" in the gas was the culprit of my motor's problems. Ethanol acts as a solvent and can break down parts that will eventually clog the small carburetor jets in the engine. Ethanol is particularly damaging to small engines and marine motors that may sit unused for extended periods of time.

I am told that the best way to resolve this situation is to use pure (non ethanol) gasoline and to run the motor often.

I removed all of the old gas that had been sitting in my fuel tank and will replace it with pure, non ethanol gas. I will also run the motor more frequently. My outboard will run better and more efficiently with pure, fresh gasoline.

I think there is a spiritual lesson to be had here as well. We as believers are told to live lives that are "pure and holy." We too can pour additives into our lives that can clog us up and cause us to breakdown spiritually.

There are so many additives that can clog us up and cause us to breakdown. We may think alcohol, drugs, or sexual immoralities are good additives for us, that will make our lives run smoother. Maybe we think that the additive of isolation is the answer to our lives running well. We may even think that religion, in and of itself, will be the additive we need for us to be a smooth running person.

But what truly happens when we pour these additives to our lives is that we begin to corrode. We run less and less efficiently and eventually we will have a breakdown. We are then in need of cleaning and repairs.

There is a Master Mechanic who can and will perform this cleaning and repair in our lives, and He has already paid for the work. All we have to do is go to His shop. The work is free. So lets don't just sit there. Lets go to His shop and fill 'er up! Then we can crank up and run effectively and with the most power, as long as we are running on pure Jesus!

We're Not Lost   August 14

Some stereotypes are true whether we would like to avoid them or not. The best and often most true stereotypes are the funny ones. For instance, while traveling, men do not like to admit they are lost and then be reduced to asking some stranger for directions. Especially asking another man who is obviously thinking: "This Bozo can't follow a simple map!" Unfortunately, having to ask directions usually is the culmination of the lost man's lovely wife's inquiring question: "Are we lost?" Only guys know how much that question burns! A little gas for the fire comes if she adds: "I told you we should have bought that GPS!"

Thank God that when we wander off His path for our lives we don't have to walk around lost and embarrassed, hunting someone to give us directions. He is right there behind us, following us, waiting for us to turn around and say that we messed up and strayed off His path. He then will not only give us directions, but if need be, pick us up and carry us back to His path!

Petra had a song entitled *One Step Back* which said even though we walked a million miles away, it was only one step back to Him. Powerful stuff! It's a wonderful sense of relief to turn around (maybe thinking it's going to be a long walk back to Him), and see Him standing there with open, forgiving arms.

"What do you think? If a man owns a hundred sheep, and one of them wanders away, will he not leave the ninety-nine on the hills and go to look for the one that wandered off? And if he finds it, I tell you the truth, he is happier about that one sheep than about the ninety-nine that did not wander off." – Matthew 18:12-13

Boat Pride — August 15

When I got my second boat I was fired up! It was nothing special, a beat up off brand bow rider. It had been worked over and worked on so many times you couldn't tell what brand it had been when it was originally built. But it had a steering wheel!

That's right, no more sitting in the back with the motor handle in my hand inhaling that gas/oil mix as I steered a tiny boat along. I had moved up! I had a "wheelhouse." Well, I had a steering wheel.

The boat trailer was worse. It was a home made contraption with regular size car tires on it that made it difficult to launch at shallower boat ramps. In fact, I broke the axle off in a shallow ramp on an attempted fishing trip at a later date (but that's another stoty).

Anyway, I think you're getting the picture. That fishing outfit (boat and trailer) was nothing special, even though I thought it was at the time.

On my way to the boat ramp (for my first steering wheel boat fishing trip) I stopped by the local bait and tackle shop to pick up some gear and bait. I no sooner got inside when a short Oriental man walked up to me and started talking to me in broken English. I was trying to talk to the shop owner to get my stuff and be on my way, but the little man persisted!

"You … me … fish today?"

"No dude. I'm just getting some bait and I'll be on my way" I said.

"NO! You … me … fish together! Yes?" he replies.

Now I'm getting irritated. "Listen man, my friend is meeting me at the boat ramp in a few minutes (a lie). I'm going fishing with him, OK?!"

The little man finally gives up, and walks out with a dejected look on his face.

I turn to the shop owner and say: " Man, do you believe that guy, coming in here to ask people he sees pull up with a boat if he can go fishing with them?"

The shop owner looks at me with this grin on his face.

"What?" I ask.

He answers: "That man wasn't asking if he could go fishing with you. He was asking if you wanted to go fishing with him. He comes in here all the time. He catches a ton of fish too!" He pointed to the pictures on his bait shop wall of the little Oriental man's trophy fish!

Now I'm the one walking out with the dejected look on my face! As I go out the door I see the little man across the street get in his giant dually pickup, that is hooked to a 29-foot Renken dream fishing boat, and pull away!

The thought that comes to mind is: Who's really the "little man" here?

Proverbs 16:18 – *Pride goes before destruction, a haughty spirit before a fall.*

I was so proud (and selfish) about my little boat, I didn't even see the big boat I could have fished in right across the street. Some times I am so blinded by the things of this world that I don't see the bigger things I could have with God! I guess the question is: "Am I going fishing with God instead of not letting Him go with me?"

Don't Blink, You Might Learn Something
August 16

I have written before about the importance of gaining knowledge. Check out "Easier Said Than Done" (March 16). The benefit of gaining knowledge is in being able to put that knowledge to good use. I saw this play out in my life just a few days ago. God also threw in a little lesson on being patient in frustration, as well as a good dose of pride-removing-humility.

I was outside replacing a turn signal bulb on my truck when Nick pulled up and told me the blinkers weren't working on his car. I told him that I could fix that problem. I informed him that it was probably a faulty flasher.

Thinking I had an easy fix, I zipped down to the local auto parts store. After telling the parts clerk the make and model of the car, he looked on his computer. He then told me, this model car doesn't appear to have a flasher. I'm thinking, "OK, then how do the blinkers blink?"

I went back home and checked underneath the dash (where flashers are located in some cars), no flasher. There was no flasher in the fuse boxes either. My frustration was growing. There was no manual to be found in the car that might identify where the flasher would be located.

I had another idea, the Internet. My search only revealed how and where I could buy a repair manual for the vehicle, no free diagrams. My frustration level continued to rise. I headed for "You tube," you can see how to fix everything on there, right?

My search continued as I typed in the make, model and the part I needed. No exact matches. My patience was gone and I was about to blow my own fuse! As I scrolled down the related topics, I saw a video of a blinker/emergency flasher problem. What's this?

In Nick's car the flasher is built into the emergency flasher. If it malfunctions, the turn signals won't work either. That's why the parts guy couldn't find the flasher. He didn't know it was incorporated into the emergency flasher. I pulled the faulty flasher and headed to a different auto parts store.

I handed the clerk the defective part and ask him for a new one. He said: "What's this?" Seriously! With my new found knowledge, I proudly explained what it was and had to help him find it on his computer. It felt good (prideful) to know more than the parts guy! To his surprise he had the part, which cost about three times as much as a typical flasher.

I went home and replaced the part. After acquiring the knowledge of how to do the job, it was a simple fix. I felt proud of my victory over the broken blinkers! I felt proud that I knew more than two parts guys! I was feeling smart and capable!

As I picked up my tools and walked away from a job well done, I looked back to see that I had left my truck's headlights on. Had I not looked back, I would have had a dead battery the next morning! A voice inside me says: "Both parts guys know that, they would have turned off the headlights. They would probably be able to look up the right battery for you too, smart guy."

Once again, pride smashed by the "humility bomb!"

Scriptural references too numerous to mention ...

The Deep End　　　　　　　　　　　August 17

    I remember one summer, in my pre-teen years, learning to swim. I loved swimming and took to it like a fish. In one summer I took beginner, intermediate and advanced swimming lessons. I even took rescue lessons and could have been a lifeguard if I had only been old enough. I went from tiptoeing around in four feet of water in the shallow end of the pool, to going off the high dives anywhere I could find them.

    With good instruction I was able to go from fear of the "deep end" to having confidence that I could go off the high dives and stay in the deep end as much as I wanted. This confidence came from reading books about swimming and life saving techniques as well as good instuction and demonstration by knowledgeable teachers and then put what I had learned and been shown into practice.

    Later, after becoming confident with not only the knowledge of how to swim, but with the ability to do it, and to be able to demonstrate and teach others how to swim, I became the teacher.

    That's how it's supposed to work in the Kingdom too. The best way to become a well rounded believer is to gain enough knowledge, ability and confidence to be able to pass it on to others who need to "learn to swim." Jesus did it that way with His disciples. He passed on His knowledge of God, showed them how to walk in that knowledge and built their confidence (faith) by showing that God would not let them down, but build them up.

    What part of the pool are you hanging out in? Are you just sitting beside it, catching a few rays and listening to God from nearby? Are you bobbing around in the shallow end, content with cooling off (saved and content to chill there)? Or maybe you are desiring more as you look toward the "deep end", looking for someone to show you how to swim (disciple you)?

    Maybe you know how to swim in the deep end. Are you looking for someone in the shallow end, to show them how to swim in the deep end?

    Just asking.

Stoke The Fire   August 18

I was watching a movie last night about a teenage boy who became lost in the wilderness. Prior to him being lost, his father had taught him many skills for camping and some survival techniques. Lost, the boy found himself faced with cold, rain, rough terrain and on one occasion, wolves.

During one night, he was sitting in a shelter he had made. It was raining and cold. The shelter wasn't waterproof or warm. He had a fire, but obviously, all the wood around him was wet. He had no way to stoke his fire. Any camper knows that a good size fire will help keep dangerous animals away.

His small fire was almost out as two wolves approached him with intentions of making the boy and his dog their next meal. Had his fire been larger, the wolves probably would not have been so bold. Had the boy been able to collect more dry wood earlier, he could have kept a much larger fire burning.

As believers, we can keep our enemy at bay much more effectively by keeping our "fire stoked." We can stoke our fire by reading, studying and obeying the Word of God.

When Jesus was tempted by Satan, He used the Word of God and His knowledge of it to "run the wolf off." We can do the same thing. When we study His Word, we become equipped with the knowledge of how to send Satan running. We have stoked our fire. When we have stoked our fire, all that is left to do is stick a log from the fire in the wolf's face and he is off and running away.

Then Jesus was led by the Spirit into the wilderness to be tempted by the devil. After fasting forty days and forty nights, he was hungry. The tempter came to him and said, "If you are the Son of God, tell these stones to become bread."

Jesus answered, "It is written: 'Man shall not live on bread alone, but on every word that comes from the mouth of God.'"

Then the devil took him to the holy city and had him stand on the highest point of the temple. "If you are the Son of God," he said, "throw yourself down. For it is written:

'He will command his angels concerning you, and they will lift you up in their hands, so that you will not strike your foot against a stone.'"

Jesus answered him, "It is also written: 'Do not put the Lord your God to the test.'"

Again, the devil took him to a very high mountain and showed him all the kingdoms of the world and their splendor. "All this I will give you," he said, "if you will bow down and worship me."

Jesus said to him, "Away from me, Satan! For it is written: 'Worship the Lord your God, and serve him only.'"

Then the devil left him, and angels came and attended him. – Matthew 4:1-11

Stoke your fire! Get the Word in you. Send the wolf running!

Sick — August 19

Recently, in a seven day stretch, I have experienced four of the sickest days of my life. Without exaggeration I can say that I have never felt so physically ill. This included two stretches of about thirty-six hours of being in bed, with little sleep. One case of vertigo in which any movement caused dizziness and made me sick to my stomach. The other a flu virus that continually caused painful stomach cramps.

All of this was miserable physically, but what I also hated about this was the helplessness of my condition. I like to take care of myself and not have to depend on others. I want to be self reliant! Maybe that's a good thing, maybe it's pride, maybe it's some macho man thing or some combination of the three. I know this though, I needed help this week.

In steps my hero, Hannah Pooh. She prayed for me, she was my nurse, she waited on me hand and foot and she did everything else that needed doing, household and family-wise. She did it all when I could do nothing and she did it with a loving, caring, servant heart.

We all should have someone like this in our life. Not because we deserve it, but because that's the way it should be in the Kingdom. This is an attribute that God wants us all to have: to love our neighbor as our self and to think more highly of others than ourselves.

I had plenty of time to think while trying to lie still in the bed. I wondered, is this dizziness I feel the same feeling that the hopeless feel? Are these horrible stomach cramps an example of how the hungry feel all the time? Why is it that there are so many in nursing homes and elderly care facilities and so few visitors? Why is it there are so many homeless?

Why is it so many orphans live in group homes and state run facilities, instead of an adoptive home? Why is it there are so many helpless widows just existing in their last days?

Could it be that we are so self-reliant that we don't realize there are those who are not capable of taking care of themselves! I was not able to take care of myself this week. Thank God for Hannah! We all need someone sometime. I think I know how we can all have someone to get us through when we can't get through on our own. We should be that person (servant, rescuer, provider, friend) to someone in need. You reap what you sow. Love will return to you.

Thrill Ride   August 20

When I was a boy, one of the things my friends and I liked to do was pretend to be driving a car. We would get into our parent's cars in the driveway and become race car drivers or the police chasing some bad guys. We didn't have any keys, so we weren't going to get in any trouble, except for that one time.

A few of my buds and I got into my dad's old Rambler one afternoon. Again, no keys, no harm, no foul and safe to play. Many of you may remember some of the old Rambler's with the push button transmission. As we were "racing" along, I was pushing the buttons pretending to speed up. Our driveway was on a slight hill and as I was shifting gears the car started to roll backwards.

We were all able to bail out and watch the car (seemingly in slow motion) roll down my driveway, across the street (no oncoming traffic) and back up into the neighbor's driveway across the street from us. I watched in horror waiting to see the ensuing crash of the getaway Rambler into my neighbor's house.

The transmission must have gone into gear because the car stopped literally inches before hitting that house! The "thrill ride" wasn't over yet. I still had to tell my dad we had moved his car! It was not one of my best days.

Sometimes I feel as if I live my life like my dad's old Rambler, just rolling downhill in neutral at the mercy of the world, with the distinct possibility of a terrible "crash" as a result. Just like when we were kids and needed a responsible adult to drive us from place to place safely, we need our loving Heavenly Father to steer our lives through the traffic of this world.

When we find ourselves just cruising through life with no particular destination, maybe it's time to slide over and hand the wheel to the King of the road.

Time And Money — August 21

Jesus said the most important commandments were to love God with all our heart, mind, soul and strength and, to love our neighbor as yourself. So, how are we doing with those two instructions? The desire to be obedient to these commands is the beginning place.

In our Christian walk, we want to return the love God has for us to Him. The problem is we battle our own fleshly desires screaming at us to try our own way of loving and living. We succumb to busyness and fending for ourselves. Instead of spending time with Him, we use it up being our own source, not trusting Him to provide what we need.

We also want to love our neighbors with God's love. However, we face obstacles here as well. Frankly, some of them are jerks and seem unlovable. Maybe they're jerks because no one has tried loving them. Maybe the unloving are the jerks and not the unlovable. Anyway, if we are unloving towards others, it could also be us selfishly placing our needs ahead of others. We are told this commandment in other words too. The Bible says to think of others more highly than ourselves.

These are just a few of the traps and turmoil that are thrown at us by the enemy, the world and ourselves, that try to block us from the will of God for our lives and the blessings He has for us.

One way to check ourselves for fulfillment of these commandments is to ask ourselves questions like: Where do I spend my time and money? Yes, work and family and home can take a lot of time and money. And we are supposed to take seriously those responsibilities. But when it gets right down to it, the answer to that question will go a long way in showing where our priorities lie. No, it's not about money, but these are two of our most desired fleshly possessions (time and money). If they are surrendered to God, it is a pretty good indication that the things of God are more important to us and that our trust in Him is genuine.

Let's ask God to show us how to love Him more. Let's ask God how to love our neighbors (jerks or not) with the love of Christ, even if it costs us some time and money. Besides, God can give us more of both; He's got plenty.

"Love the Lord your God with all your heart and with all your soul and with all your mind and with all your strength.' The second is this: 'Love your neighbor as yourself.' There is no commandment greater than these." – Mark 12: 30-31

The 54 Year Trip To Freedom   August 22

There is an old saying: "We've lost the battle, but not the war." That's how our spiritual enemy thinks. His game plan continues after a lost battle for a soul. When we become believers, he has lost us, but he continues to try to wreak havoc in our lives to keep us from being useful in the Kingdom.

He wants to bind us up in chains in an attempt to keep us from bringing others into the Kingdom. These chains may be his reminding us of where we feel inadequate or unworthy. But the word says that "the Lord equips those He calls." It also says that "He separates our sin from us as far as the east is from the west."

One of the chains he used to bind me up was my fear of man. I was always concerned about what people thought of me. I wanted man's approval of me. Sure, everyone would prefer to be liked and loved by everyone. But I'll tell you this, seeking man's approval over God's plan for your life is a detour into Kingdom uselessness!

A secret sin that I would not confess, kept me bound up. My concern was for me and not for others. My usefulness to God was severely hindered as a result. The enemy had a hold on me. My freedom came at my confession of that sin. When I have nothing to hide, when the enemy cannot threaten me with "everyone is going to find out," he then has no hold on me! I confessed it (now everyone knew), repented of it, and now I am forgiven and free! God had taken the bullets from the enemy's gun aimed at me.

Still the fear of man was there in the sense of wondering "what will people think of me now that they have heard my confession. What will my friends that are not believers think when finding out that I'm a Christian?"

Well, even with all my faults, for the most part friendships haven't been broken and I feel accepted as long as I am real and am not pious, uppity and religious for the sake of religion. Although there will be those who "throw me overboard," for the most part it's not the belief and trust in Jesus that drives men away. It is the religious "I am better, and more important to God than you" attitude that some believers portray. And that portrayal is a lie from the pit of hell!

Having said this, I just want to thank God that a 54 year trip to freedom from the fear of what man thinks of me, is over! It just doesn't matter in the Kingdom what man thinks of me. It only matters what God thinks!

Look who's out of bullets again!

The Masters   August 23

Every year when the Masters Golf Tournament comes around, I remember a moment in history. In my high school years I was playing a lot of golf. When the tour came to our town, I would skip school and go caddy at the Pro-Am Tournament the day before the Monsanto Open would begin. It was a blast!

Local players, sponsors, businessmen and the like would pay big bucks to play a round with a pro. These guys needed caddies and they paid pretty good at this event. It was pretty cool walking up the fairways (inside the ropes) and seeing the pros up close just crush golf balls up the fairway.

I would also go back and watch the pros play the next four days in their tournament. In 1974, the Monsanto Open ended in a tie between Lee Elder and Peter Oosterhuis. There was a sudden death playoff for the championship. I was standing at the edge of that green when Lee Elder sank his putt to become the first black man to qualify for the Masters tournament. An amazing moment, an amazing breakthrough and a mountain of goosebumps as I realized what had just happened.

In this time which we live of instantaneous gratification, we need to savor the extraordinary moments in life. When a baby is born I think about each of my son's birth. At a wedding, I think about my wedding.

When I see or talk to old friends, memories flood back into my mind. Let's purposely slow down and savor our times with friends and family because when we look back, these will be the shining moments we remember, our times and relationships to others.

Let's be that way with God too. Spending time with the Lord shouldn't just be an appointment we make for a few minutes. It should be time with our Father and Friend. What really good times do you remember with God? I'll bet you weren't in a hurry that time. Spend some time at the real Masters.

Fishermen, Skipjacks And Dolphins   August 24

I have been fishing several times this week. However, the seas have been less than calm. The fishing has also been less than great. We have caught some fish each time, but no banner days.

This Sunday, a day I had not planned to go fishing, I attended a church service right on the beach. Of course the water was as slick as glass and it was a beautiful day! I could just feel God grinning at me.

So we decide to try it again yesterday (Monday), hoping the weather and seas would continue on from Sunday. We were in the water before 6 am and the bay was already choppy. We persevered through the pass into the Gulf only to turn around. The seas were way too much for my small boat. We returned to the bay and fished along an island that was blocking the wind. It was slow but we managed to catch a few keepers.

Dolphins are common in the bay and around our beaches here. At one point we trolled near a pod of them. We were not trying to catch them but they will not necessarily avoid fishermen. In fact, they will often follow fishermen and try to eat the fish we are reeling up.

That's what happened yesterday. I had hooked a skipjack and was reeling it in when a dolphin started chasing it. The dolphin chasing my catch looked like a torpedo. He was hauling, and he could change directions on a dime. It's unbelievable how fast and quick they are in the water! It was a rush of excitement to me, trying to get my fish in and keep the dolphin from getting it. I also did not want to hook the dolphin.

However, for the skipjack, it was life and death. I'll bet you've never had this said to you: "Let's look at this from the skipjacks' perspective." (Skipjack speaking): "There is a hook in my face and it's pulling fast in one direction. There is a hungry dolphin coming at me even faster with breakfast on his mind! I am doomed! Do I pull against the hook or swim as hard as I can away from the hungry torpedo fish?"

After a short fight and an exciting chase, I swung my catch into the boat. I would assume the skipjack was tired, and I'll bet his mouth hurt, but he was alive. I took the hook out, released him and he swam away none the worse for wear.

I can relate to the skipjack. There have been times when I thought no matter which way I turned, my bad situation was not going to end well. If the skipjack had used his energy to swim towards me, he would have been out of danger sooner. But he was trying to have it his way. That was not to be. It was going to be my way or the dolphin's way.

That's the question we have to answer. Are we going to (follow) swim towards God's will or pull against Him when He is trying to rescue us? Or are we going to be eaten by whatever "dolphin" is chasing us (hard times, the world, sin, or the devil)? The choice is our own. What'll it be? Don't wait to decide until the hungry "dolphins" are chasing you!

Trash Fish August 25

Hannah had me cracking up yesterday after she read this part of the "Fishermen, Skipjacks and Dolphins."

"After a short fight and an exciting chase, I swing my catch into the boat. I would assume the skipjack was tired, and I'll bet his mouth hurt, but he was alive. I took the hook out, released him and he swam away none the worse for wear."

She said something like: "That was nice of you to let that fish go. What made you do that?"

I cracked up and told her that skipjacks were bony, bloody and just no good to eat. I wasn't being "Mr. Nice Guy." I was just throwing away a "trash fish." I was just trying to keep the dolphin from getting it so it would not get hooked.

Years ago as a teenager fishing on a gulf pier, we were catching a bunch of skipjacks. We didn't want them, but some island guys that were running a grill at the end of the pier wanted them. They were making some kind of fish balls right there at the grill and eating them. I didn't try them because I had always heard they were no good to eat. They were trash, just because someone had said so, I never checked for myself.

This got me to thinking. Do we think of people as if they are trash just because someone has told us so all our lives. The homeless guy on the street is trash just because he's homeless? That guy of a different race is trash just because his skin is a different color than the people we hang around with most of the time? Is she trash because her culture is different? How about the drug addict, alcoholic or even an out-and-out sinner? Does God want us to throw them away as trash?

Just wondering.

Rufus   August 26

This one may be hard for some of my animal lover friends to take. However, I am supposed to tell this story. I believe animals are pets, food sources and beast of burden according to their lot in life. We can love them, we should care for them, but to raise them to the status of humans or a little higher is a bit much. For example the bumper sticker: "Don't Tailgate, Show Dogs On Board." As if they are more valuable than the kids in any other backseat! Having said all that, I was just plain wrong in the following story.

Our first dog after we got married was a German Sheppard mix (probably Dobie). He was a fun dog as a puppy and as he grew he loved to chase the Frisbee. He was a good watch dog too. The one thing he did that just ticked me off was digging. And the bigger he got, the bigger the holes became. Our backyard would have these huge holes in it with these mounds next to the holes as big a circus elephant deposit. Rufus was smart, and as soon as he figured out that if he dug under the fence he could be loose, he was off to the races.

It became a constant battle to contain him. He would dig out and take off. I would go find him and bring him back. Sometimes I would have to bail him out of the pound. He was genuinely happy to see me and we would go home. I would fill the hole under the fence back up (often even barricading the area), but it was to no avail. He would find a new place to dig out and runaway. This went on for months.

Then one day he took off again after digging under the fence. I had had enough. I didn't go out to find him because I didn't care anymore. He never came back and that was OK with me.

I am so glad that God is not like me when Rufus ran off. If I am committing some sin (digging a hole) and then I run from Him (not repenting), that must seem to Him like Rufus running off was to me. But He never seems to get tired of coming after me and bringing me home to Him again. He always forgives me (fills up the hole as if it was never there) and loves me as if I had never left.

Our God is relentless in His pursuit of us and He never tires of caring for us. What a wonderful Master. He loves me so much that I want to stay near Him more and more. Thanks for coming after me, Lord.

P.S. I saw Rufus a year or two later in a back yard of our neighborhood not too far from our house. He was chilling with another dog behind the fence. There were no holes in the yard. He had been found by a better master. Hopefully I have learned how to be a better pet owner too.

Nail In My Finger   August 27

As a young man I worked quite a bit in construction. Working on construction sites offers plenty of possibilities for getting hurt even when you are working as safely as possible.

For instance, on one occasion I was nailing strips of wood onto concrete walls with the old concrete nails. I had to hammer the snot out of these nails to get them into that old, hard wall. During this process, I noticed blood running down my fingers. My blood! A sliver of one of the concrete nails had gone into my finger. I never felt it and the little sliver was all the way in, not partly sticking out like a splinter.

On another occasion, I was driving small wooden grade stakes into some hard packed ground with a 3-lb sledge hammer. As I was driving in a stake it splintered, sending a sliver of wood into the joint of my thumb. I thought I got it all out and went back to driving stakes.

Both of these wounds seemingly healed. The skin grew over and everything looked OK. However the wood in my thumb festered and became a pretty gross sore. I eventually had to open the "wound" up again and squeeze out the rest (about 1/4 inch) of the splinter.

The sliver of nail in my finger is still there. It doesn't hurt or hinder me in any way. It's like it's not even there. It's like it never happened.

Our response to others wounding us (verbally or otherwise) is going to be a lot like these physical wounds I had. We can let what they have said or done fester to the point of the wound being as bad or worse than it originally was or we can forgive them and let the wound heal completely over. And if we truly forgive them it will be like the nail in my finger. It will no longer hinder or hurt us in any way. It will be like it never happened!

After all, who is the one "festering" with bitterness if we don't forgive?

Looking Good   August 28

As a young boy I remember growing tomatoes with my grandfather in his backyard. We would plant the seeds in old egg cartons. When they grew several inches high, we would transplant them into a garden. Next would come some TLC, fertilizer and water as these little plants grew into maturity, bloomed and produced tomatoes. Sometimes this was a daily routine effort repeated over and over, but the resulting BLT's were awesome! That's in the natural.

In the spiritual, like our plant growing and producing, we as believers are to grow and produce in our lives. A seed is planted in us. We should be "transplanted" from our worldly path into a "garden" of believers where we can be spiritually protected, fed, and trained into spiritual maturity. Then, going out and planting seeds ourselves, we begin the process of producing "fruit" in our lives.

Early in the morning, as Jesus was on his way back to the city, he was hungry. Seeing a fig tree by the road, he went up to it but found nothing on it except leaves. Then he said to it, "May you never bear fruit again!" Immediately the tree withered.

When the disciples saw this, they were amazed. "How did the fig tree wither so quickly?" they asked. – Matthew 21:18-20

In this Scripture, the disciples asked how the fig tree withered so quickly. Another question might be, "Why did Jesus wither it?" He withered it because, even though it looked good and healthy, it was producing no fruit. Which brings the next question to mind. Are we "looking good" in our spiritual lives without producing any fruit? Have we got our salvation and are now on some spiritual cruise control? If so, maybe it's time to go tend the Kingdom's garden.

The Devil's Store   August 29

"Can I help you find something sir?" Salesman asked.

Flesh replied: "Yes, I am looking for some stature and importance in the eyes of others."

"Certainly sir, here's three jobs you can have and make a pile of money. Then people will follow you everywhere!"

"OK, great! I can probably still squeeze in some time with the family," Flesh replied.

"What else can I help you find," asked Salesman?

"Well, I need a friend who will tell me how good I'm doing."

"Right over here," said Salesman, "Here's two friends you can have cheap. Their names are Liar and Fool. They'll tell you anything you want to hear!"

"Umm, OK" said Flesh. "Have you got anything that can give me some quick comfort?"

"Are you kidding! How about this beautiful woman? You can rent her by the hour. I also have a couple of bottles of booze that can make all your problems disappear – for awhile anyway."

"Good" said Flesh. "Now, one more thing. I need something to make me feel invincible."

"I've got that too" said Salesman; "Right over here in my special pharmacy. You can snort this or shoot some of this other stuff right into your veins, and whamo, you're Superman!"

"I'll take it all!" Flesh said excitedly. "How much do I owe you?"

"Oh, not much, just a little bit at a time. We'll put you on the Life Time Payment Plan, said Salesman.

"Great, thank you very much" exclaimed Flesh. "Now how do I get out of here?"

How Do I Get Out Of Here: The Devil's Store Part 2　　　　　　　　　　　August 30

The truth is that many people are content to frequent the "Devils' Store." We are happy to continue this lifestyle until it drains us in some way. Whether that be a financial, mental, physical, emotional or spiritual drain, it does happen. Then we go seeking some kind of remedy.

However, if we don't know our way "out of the store," we'll just keep searching the shelves of the Devil's Store for the remedy. Rarely does anyone in this predicament just decide: " Oh, I know, I need to go to church! Problem solved!"

Not exactly. The remedy is not just going to church; it is going to Jesus. Don't misunderstand. The Bible tells us to gather with the believers for plenty of good reasons. However, we could sit on our butts in church our whole lives and never know Jesus! The remedy, the way out of the Devils' Store, is not where we go, it's to whom do we go!

So, how does someone find there way out of the Devils' Store? It seems to me, more often than not, it goes a little something like this: When someone living a lifestyle of sin finds themselves drained by that lifestyle, they start seeking a way out of it. But having been tricked before by many of the devil's schemes, they are weary to trust others. They can spot a "wolf in sheep's clothing" a mile off! So they search, hoping to find the "real thing." What's the real thing? Someone who walks their talk. Better yet, someone who's walk does their talking! Then slowly, the trust comes and they follow the real thing right out of the Devils' Store to Jesus' Kingdom.

The sad truth is that many never ever leave the Devils' Store. I wonder if that's because they're just fooled into thinking they're happy there, or is it that there just aren't enough of the "real things" to go around?

There's No Whining In The Kingdom August 31

Do everything without complaining or arguing, so that you may become blameless and pure, children of God without fault in a crooked and depraved generation, in which you will shine like stars in the universe... – Philippians 2:14-15

Out on my route there are many free standing multi-resident mailboxes. These come in handy as a central location to deliver many addresses to apartment complexes, office buildings and the like. However, during delivery, I may not meet or get to know the residents.

A few weeks ago, a sanitation truck demolished one of the small multi-boxes in front of a little office complex on my route. For several days I had to walk into each office affected and deliver their mail to them personally. It took a little longer but I was able to meet the people in each office. Almost everyone I met was pleasant and cordial. One man in particular, who's office is in the back, off the main street, was very well mannered, attentive, and focused on my subject of conversation. He didn't complain about the inconvenience of the destroyed mailbox, instead all of his responses were "yes sir" and "thank you." That is to say he is a very nice guy that was being more than pleasant. He seemed genuinely interested in what I had to say. He is a "shining star."

Now the flip side of the coin. Further down the same street, right on the main throughfare, is a much larger, franchised version of the same type business. When I deliver here each day the wisecracking, smart-aleck manager always has some derogatory comment or whiny complaint to share about the Post Office or one of his dissatisfied customers. You know the type; something is always wrong and it's somebody else's fault that his life is not perfect. A "Whiner."

Now, you tell me who you would pick to do business with! I bet you can guess which one I will recommend! Who do you think will have the better influence in the Kingdom? Without question we all have influence. The question is: What kind of influence are we?

Poor Grandma   September 1

Last night I heard a guy talking about fond memories of his grandmother. His story reminded me of my great grandmother.

As far back as I can remember Grandma Justiss was a widow. She lived in the country in a one room house, by herself, well into her nineties. In the eyes of the world she would have appeared to be very poor. She had no money to speak of and her one room house was the kitchen, bedroom, and living room. In the latter years of her life, I helped my dad and grandfather build another room onto her little house. I don't think it changed things much to her.

She had a sink in the kitchen, but no running water. The water came from the well out back. We kids always loved to pump water from the well. She didn't have the amenities we enjoy today; no A/C, and I don't even remember a fan or TV.

My grandfather used to say of poor people: "She doesn't have a pot to piss in or a window to throw it out of." Well, she did have that, literally! Her bathroom was a pot and she had an old coffee can to spit her snuff in. She was a good shot too! I can still can hear the sound of snuff spit hitting that can!

So why is it that five generations of family would show up out there at her house on the weekends to have cookouts and eat watermelon? Could it be that Grandma Justiss was just the real deal, no pretense, no fake, no put on self importance? Could it be she was willing, even wanted to share what little she had when all she had was herself and her time? Could it be that she had instilled the really important things like the importance of love and relationships with family and friends? Could an impoverished, little four-foot, gray haired, 90+year old widow woman with a sneaky little giggle actually be a person of such influence to others to the point everyone wants to hangout at her place?

You bet she could! She was the richest woman in the world!

Until The Leaves Quit Falling   September 2

Many years ago we went to spend Thanksgiving with some of our relatives in Kentucky. When I woke up there on Thanksgiving morning the wind was howling outside. I looked out the window to see an uncle and his son trying to rake the leaves up in the yard. It seemed a silly waste of time to me as the leaves were obviously falling faster than they could possibly rake them up.

When they finally stopped raking and came inside, I thought to myself: What a waste of time! The ground is still covered with leaves!

However, as I think back now, their thinking could have been: "We stemmed the tide. We will have an easier time raking up the rest of the leaves. Besides, soon all of the leaves will have fallen off the trees and we will have succeeded in cleaning the yard."

When I first raked the leaves as a small boy, the rake was bigger than me. It seemed as if it was going to be an impossible task to complete. I would get blisters in the fold of my thumbs and hand every time!

As I grew each year, this chore became easier. I was tougher and the blisters became calloused. I was stronger and more confident each year that I would successfully overcome the mess in the yard. My confidence, growing strength and faith in my ability to overcome the fallen leaves, made raking the yard little more than a speed bump between me and getting back to playing with my friends.

I also became wiser, using that wisdom along with my growing confidence and strength as a man and bought a blower to clean the driveway and sidewalk.

I think this is a good example of how God builds our faith and strength. We face many challenges in our lives. Some only once, some a few times and some seemingly daily. But more and more as we place our faith in God and He shows Himself faithful over and over, we will become stronger, more confident, wiser, less stressed and more trusting that He will bring us through until "the leaves quit falling."

Running On All Cylinders September 3

Hannah Poo and I took a little road trip a few weeks ago on a day off. We shopped a little (Bass Pro, not Walmart), ate a little and had a good time. On the way back, just a few miles from home, the truck began to spit, sputter and carry on as if it had "jumped time." We barely got it home. It conked out several times the rest of the way. I thought we were going to be walking for sure!

For an engine to run at peak performance, all the plugs and cylinders have to fire correctly and in the right sequence or it won't hardly run, if at all! If for any reason (distributor gets lose and turns, or wires aren't replaced correctly) the engine does not "fire" in order, it could be "out of time" or could have "jumped timing."

Timing is something that has come home to me in my spiritual life. I may know or think I know God's will for something in my life. Well if I know His will, then it must be time to go do it, right? AANNNTTTT! (buzzer sound), thank you for playing! It is not necessarily time to do something even if we know God's will because the timing is part of God's will. If we do not include God's timing as part of His will in something, we could spiritually "jump time" and be barely moving down the road in the Kingdom. We could even break down right in the middle of the road!

It can be really hard to wait on God's timing. Look at David. He knew for a long time he was to be king. He had several opportunities to kill Saul (who was king at the time and was trying to kill David). Yet David viewed Him as God's anointed one and he knew it was not God's timing.

One of the hardest things God tells us to do is to wait. Do you know God's will for something in your life? Is it time? Just ask Him first.

One of the times the truck conked out that day, I thought that was it. I thought we might be walking the rest of the way. As we sat there in the intersection under a green light, with cars zipping past us in our stalled-out truck, I told Hannah to pray. She began to pray as I tried to crank the truck. As I frantically pushed the gas pedal and turned the key, the engine started making that all too familiar sound, indicating a dying battery. Then it cranked! It spit and sputtered the whole way, but we got home.

It was Saturday evening when we got home and I was too frustrated to fool with trying to fix the truck that night. Sunday after church I went out to the truck to see if I could figure out the problem. I got in, turned the key, and it fired right up. No miss fire, spitting or sputtering. That's been weeks ago. It has not missed a beat since. It runs like a top!

I believe God can heal (fix) anything. But doubt does try to creep in and explain away any miracle. Fuel pump malfunction? Maybe a clogged fuel filter? But then how would you explain when Hannah prayed for the washing machine that time? I'm just asking.

It's MY Day Off   September 4

I have been working a ton of overtime lately! My schedule is supposed to be: Sundays off and a day off during the week. Well that day off during the week hasn't happened in at least two months, until today. I'm on an overtime list that is basically a request by me for available overtime. I'm not whining (much) about working the days I'm supposed to be off. It's more like I'm whining about God invading my day off!

Honestly, it is my day off! I got up this morning with no real solid plan in mind. I might just loaf around, I might go fishing, I might watch TV, maybe even work in the yard, maybe not!

I know that God wants us to be happy, have times of rest, relaxation, recreation, and spending time with family and friends. There is absolutely nothing wrong with these things in and of themselves.

So, here's the rub. I slept in a little this morning, until six. That's really OK. I have a routine for a workday that begins like this: Get up and hangout with God, talk to Him, read a little of the Word, but I can snooze a little on my day off!

Then it happens. That voice in my spirit, you know the one: "Hey Greg, wanna hangout together awhile?" Truthfully the thought occurred to me that I could get on the computer and check the marine forecast instead (fishing on the brain).

I wouldn't say I was all fired up this morning to pray and read, but I guess you could say I yielded or gave in and went in a room and started praying, even though it is my day off. Then things get a little more pointed. I'm trying to pray (my kind of routine prayer) and God keeps interrupting me. I'm trying to press on with my prayer but He's having none of it. Seriously, it's as if He's saying: "I've heard this before and I know your heart, but I'm trying to tell you something!"

As I write this I wonder if God feels like a parent who's child has ask seventeen times for a bicycle for Christmas. All the while the parent is trying to tell the child to go clean the garage. The kid keeps beefing about the bike, but the reason the parent wants the garage clean is so the child will have a place to put his new bike on Christmas night, after he is pooped out from riding his new gift all day long.

Back to God interrupting my prayer. He was saying to me: "You often treat Me as routine on your workdays and as a necessary inconvenience on your day off." Ouch, truth wounds!

God has provided me with a good job through which He provides much more than I can ask or imagine (or need). He also (through this job) provides my days off. But I see now that these days off are not days off from God. They are days off because of God!

Hey Lord, what do you want to do today?

God To The Rescue   September 5

If you are anything like me (or a lot of people I know), when a friend or relative goes through something hurtful and tragic, we want to come to their rescue and fix everything. With all good intentions we give our best efforts and advice to help bring them through to a place of healing, restoration and a new start. Often times, we might feel a little better for our efforts (pride), but soon frustration sets in because the person we are trying to minister to shows no signs of healing.

My grandfather taught me a good bit about growing plants (vegetables particularly). Basically, he said, you give them the water they need, the fertilizer they need and the right amount of sunlight to get the best results. He explained further, if you give the plants too much water, the seed or small plant may wash away. If we give it too much fertilizer they may burn up. Give them too much sunlight and they could dry up and die. When I ask how do I know what is the right amount of water, fertilizer and sun, he said: "You just ask me." Easy enough.

We Christians need to have this approach when it comes to rescuing someone we know or love. Grandfather wasn't God, but he knew how to grow plants. But God is God, and he knows how to heal his children. So, when someone we know is hurting, we shouldn't jump in without our "floaties" on! We should just ask Him if He wants us to do something, and if the answer is yes, then we should ask what it is we should do. We don't want to drown them, burn them up or let them dry up and blow away. We do want God to heal them, and He knows the best way.

Here's what God showed me in just the past two days. Are you ready? His plan for their healing may not involve me any further than my prayers for them. And if I tell the truth here, that pricks my pride a little. You want to use someone else, God? I'm right here, I want to be the hero!

I have heard two testimonies in the past two days of God healing hurt and broken people. One person I was directly trying to help myself and another situation with someone trying to help a loved one. In both cases, Christians had the right intentions for ministering and helping someone overcome a tough situation. But in both cases God used someone else to bring healing.

God will use the right rescuers for the job. It's not about us as the rescuers anyway. It's about the one that gets rescued by the Real Rescuer.

It's Not a Game   September 6

Last night Hannah and I attended a Valentine's Day Banquet. It was a lot of fun. We ate great food, spent time with friends and played games like *Name That Love Song* and *Heart Bingo*.

Then it was on to *The Truly Wed Game,* in which Hannah and I were contestants. It was based on the old TV game show, *The Newlywed Game*.

At the start of the game we were fast out of the gate, getting the first three questions right. We were in the lead and on our way to winning that brand new car! Then we bombed the next three questions and fell back in the pack. It was tooth and nail the rest of the way!

You would think after 32 plus years of marriage we would know most everything about each other. Not truly the case. Well, we made a come back right at the end, getting the last question right, and we won! Except we didn't get a new car. We won a couple of really cute stuffed Valentine Monkeys that are smooching each other. I was only kidding around about the new car as a grand prize.

But what if I wasn't kidding? What if it was as big a deal as winning a new car? What if it was even a bigger prize or decision than a car. What if in the Kingdom, your miracle is on the line? What if the health of a child or the fate of someone's soul hung in the balance of you and your spouse's decision?

Funny how we think we know the answers to so many questions and just decide an outcome on what we think we already know. As I ponder these questions this morning it seems prudent and wise to not decide answers to questions just on what I think I know.

I believe I (we) should seek the guidance of our God who does have all the answers. He is willing and able to guide us perfectly through all situations. He is surprised by nothing and knows everything. He knows our spouses and us better than we know our spouses or ourselves.

If we match our answer to God's, we will come out victorious every time and win the Grand Prize.

Hardball At Home   September 7

There may be a better sport in heaven but baseball is the best sport on this planet, bar none. No, we're not debating it. I'm writing this story and I say baseball is #1. It has everything a sport should have: Athletes with speed and hand-eye coordination. They can catch, throw and run at the same time. Baseball takes individual prowess and team play. It has more fans (that actually understand the game) than any other sport. Above all, it takes brains not just brawn, to play baseball because of the constantly changing strategy in every inning.

Now that I have ticked off the football fans with an introduction that has little to do with the story here, except that there is going to be a baseball analogy, I'll get on with it.

One thing that can happen in a baseball game is that you can get taken apart on your home field. Losing at home is tough in any sport. Sometimes we can (spiritually) get our hat handed to us in our home. Too often, in spite of my best efforts, I'll end up saying something stupid, thoughtless, and even mean that hurts the very people I love the most. There are times (like a few hours ago) when I will even stop and think before I act. Then thinking that I know what to say or do next, I proceed with my words and it's on!

In baseball terms it would be like I'm the pitcher on the mound and it's the 9th inning. The game had been going great up until the last batter drove my best fastball into the gap. Now I'm angry. The game is tied, and now I'm going to continue to stare in at the catcher until I get the sign I want. The manager (the Holy Spirit) is giving the catcher (my spirit) the signs from the dugout. The catcher keeps flashing 3, a change-up (soft, loving, affirming words). I don't acknowledge the 3. I want the 1! I want the fastball high and tight (slicing, cutting words of condemnation). I'm not paying attention to the catcher and I'm definitely not looking over at the manager. I set and fire with all the anger I have in me. When my pitch hits the batter in the ear, their dugout empties at full speed right towards me. My team isn't going to get to me in time. I think I'm going to learn something before rescue arrives.

If we want win in the game of life, we need to pay attention to the signs the Manager is sending in to us.

When the catcher gets the sign, we need to proceed with the Manager's plan so that we can experience the best outcome. Go ahead, trust God, throw the change-up.

With the tongue we praise our Lord and Father, and with it we curse human beings, who have been made in God's likeness. Out of the same mouth come praise and cursing. My brothers and sisters, this should not be. – James 3:9-10

P.S. Sorry about that "1," Hannah-Pooh. I Love You.

Sabbath vs Drugs   September 8

It just cracks me up sometimes when man figures out that what God said has been the truth all along! For instance, how scientist are always coming up with some human idea of the age of the earth and how everything was created.

Yet, they can't ever seem to change God's order in which things were created. My favorite came out several years ago, when the "great minds of the world" told us that our bodies not only require a nightly rest, but should also be rested one day a week! Where have I heard that one before?!

God was serious about "a Sabbath of rest, Holy to the Lord." Do you want to see how serious? Read Exodus 31:12-18; I dare you! Anyone who worked on the Sabbath was to be put to death! That's serious! OK, so one of our first thoughts might be, well, nobody's dying nowadays skipping a Sabbath rest. Oh really?

Physically speaking, (whether we believe God or the scientist) if we go and go and go, draining our bodies and not renewing our strength by resting, our body will wear out. It will not recover until it rests.

Spiritually it is the same for our souls. It must be refueled by resting in God.

My soul finds rest in God alone ... – Psalm 62:1

In observing the Sabbath we will find our "...joy in the Lord." (Isaiah 58:13-14)

But I'm just too busy. Ah, there it is, the slow killing drug of the devil. The devil's best weapon for keeping us from being effective in the Kingdom is busyness. Then we can't stop, rest and refuel our body or spirit.

We should "just say no" to the devil's drug of busyness as we would a drug that could kill our body! In short, the devil will try to kill the usefulness of our spirit by offering us the drug of busyness. Do you still think no one is dying by not observing the Sabbath?

Looking Past Opportunity   September 9

I woke up this morning and realized it was only Wednesday in a six day work week. Bummer. I guess I was hoping it was already my day off, or at least a little closer to it. I do that often, look forward to time off from work so I can have some time to do what I want to do. There's nothing inherently wrong with looking forward to good times but often in looking forward I end up looking past some opportunity right in front of me! This was brought to mind last night as I listened to my friend tell about meeting a couple of interesting famous people in unexpected places.

I was with a small group of people once outside an airport waiting for our rental cars when a famous prizefighter (with his ear reattached) walked right up to us and we had a short conversation. Opportunities happen, and not just to meet famous folks, but to meet everyday folks.

One thing I have learned is that almost everyone wants to be heard. Maybe some want to get to know you a little bit first, but I think one of the greatest things we can give people is our listening ear without our judging advice. There's truth in the saying, "that's why God gave us two ears and only one mouth."

I have written in the past about "characters" out on my route. Frankly, some of them are down right annoying. One guy, who is almost always drunk, tells me daily to "keep the bills" (so original). Another guy is always complaining about his neighbors. Still another is just lonely and says "I know you have to go but...". Another always complains about the government.

Are these opportunities placed in front of me so that I can love my neighbor just by being "two ears" to them? On the occasions I have taken a moment to just listen to them, a drunk told me a tearjerker about almost loosing his wife in surgery and another time about his battles with drinking. The "neighbor complainer" one day spilled his guts about his troubles at work. Was he talking so fast because no one else listens or because I pulled away so quickly in the past? The government basher is always kind to me and thanks me for bringing his packages. I don't think he has many friends.

I have two ears. I am going to try not to look so far down the road to the next good thing that's going to happen for me that I overlook the opportunity to be a "good thing" that happens for someone else.

Just Along For The Rides   September 10

When we were growing up, my sister loved to ride horses. When Ryan was growing up, he loved riding horses. My first experiences riding horses were not so good. The first few times I rode a horse, I was a small boy and was made to ride double with a grown up. This did not work for me! Just hanging on to someone's waist, having no control over a beast that is ten times my size, was no fun! Not to mention that every one of the horses I rode as a youngster (riding double) was fresh off the rodeo circuit and wanted to run in circles and throw me off! This was a terribly frustrating development for a little wanna-be cowboy.

I did not totally give up. Eventually, as I got older, I would have a chance to go horseback riding a few times. It became my experience that riding solo and having the reins in my hands (some control) worked a lot better for me.

O.K., God is not a horse, but for the sake of my analogy, stay with me.

Two things, First, my relationship with that horse or my God is not functional through some other person. If I am riding double on a horse (holding onto the person holding the reins) then I am not personally in communication (through the reins) with that horse. Screaming "let me off " is not communication to the horse!

It's like that with God. Jesus said you must be born again. He didn't say you can be the son or daughter of a born again person. God doesn't have grandchildren. Jesus said, "Come unto me." He didn't say, "Come to a friend who knows me and send me a message." Jesus is all about a personal relationship to Him, not just being along for the ride.

Secondly, when it comes to our lives, it may often seem that we are in control. We go where we want because we have the reins in our hands and we may even think we have more control than God. But let's remember this, if it gets right down to it, a horse many times larger than us is able to throw us right on our butts and stomp a mud hole in us! Ultimately, we are not in total control.

Trusting God may seem as difficult as dropping the reins of a spirited horse, but like the horse, God will eventually take us home and maybe to a good "watering hole" along the way.

Go ahead, drop the reins.

Handicapped Jesus — September 11

New Year's Day night I had this dream. I came up to a country road intersection. On the corner to my right sat Jesus in a chair, a wheel chair I think. I walked over to Him. He looked very ordinary. He had a blanket over Him up to His chest. I reached out my hand to shake His as He slowly lifted it towards mine. It obviously took more effort than it should for Him to lift His hand. I placed my hand in His and shook hands.

I had a short personal conversation with Him and then I woke up.

When I woke up I thought: What an amazing experience! Wait a minute. What's up with that wheelchair and His slow moving arm and hand? And what's He doing sitting out there at an intersection?

The night after this dream I spent more than two hours, in the middle of the night, talking and listening to God. He showed me the direction He wants me to go next.

For me, the dream comes across like this: I am at another crossroad in my life. He wants we to go in the direction He chooses and He will go with me. However, He wants me to be sure to not "handicap" Him.

I can hear it now. "You can't handicap God!" Yes I can, yes you can, yes we can! Every time we are disobedient we handicap Him. Sure, He can overcome it. He can get someone else to be obedient and do His work. But is that the way He wants it? Is that the way we want it?

God anointed Saul king. Saul disobeyed so God got David to do His work. I get that. But what if Saul had obeyed God? Certainly God could have worked through him. And what blessings would have come to Saul and his house?

We believers, are to a great extent, His arms and legs, His feet and hands, and if we don't obey Him (go and do) what He says, then we handicap Him.

I'm going to take the road He wants me to take. I sure don't want to handicap Jesus! I don't want to be replaced and I don't want to miss out on anything He has in store for me and my house.

Freeing Up Hard Drive Space   September 12

What I don't know about computers would certainly be a bigger story to write than what I do know about them.

One of the things I do know is that you can fill up a computer's hard drive with information. It will clog up like a sink full of hair, getting slower and slower. The options we have to clear this "clog" include getting more space (an external hard drive) or clean out the junk we don't want on our existing hard drive. This would free up space for more things that we do want to keep.

Our hearts are the "hard drives" of our being. The place where we store up our feelings towards others. We can store up feelings of love, caring and good will, or we can store up hate, discontent, rage, desires for revenge and all kinds of ill will. These negative feelings towards someone often occur when a person has done something to us that has offended us.

Anger and resentment towards others will fill up and clog our hard drives quickly and completely. These feelings can consume our thoughts and time, turning us toward a bitter, cynical, and even hopeless existence. Even if we can suppress these feelings for a while, the offense is still on there in a file somewhere. When that file is opened again, those feelings come straight back to our screen.

So, what's the remedy when our hard drive fills up with anger towards someone? Two things, I think.

First, let God be our external hard drive. Give the situation to Him. When someone has done wrong to us, allow God to do the needed work in them. Our revenge will not make them or us better people. His care can heal a situation.

Secondly, have mercy on them by not giving them what we think they deserve. Forgive them. Forgiveness is the drain cleaner for the clog. Forgiveness is the ultimate eraser for freeing up all that space on our hard drives, giving us back all that space for the good things God has for us.

Let's look inside our hard drives and see if we need to free up some space.

Out Of Hope September 13

Are you hopeless and helpless to overcome a difficult situation or condition in your life? Have you been fighting against it for what seems like a lifetime? John 5 describes someone like this who has an encounter with Jesus.

A lame man (for thirty eight years) is hanging out at the Pool of Bethesda. It is a location where people hope to receive healing if they can get into the pool when the waters are stirring. The lame man's hope has disappeared because he can't beat others into the pool when the water stirs.

Then one day Jesus comes strolling by and ask him if he wants to be healed. I can almost hear the hopelessness in his voice as he explains his predicament. Unphased by the man's response, Jesus tells him to "pick up your mat and walk," and a hopeless man is whole again! I imagine this guy was dancing, whooping and hollering like nobody's business for a long time! He may have been the "Daddy of Disco!" Anyway...

Later Jesus runs into this guy again, at the Temple and says to him, "See, you are well again. Stop sinning or something worse may happen to you." His body had been healed. Had his soul been saved?

Here's my take on all this. This guy who had given up hope for his healing was given back his hope and his ability walk. This says to me, "never loose hope!" Watch for Jesus to come strolling by in your life in some form of person, prayer, or guidance. Expect Him to use every situation in your life for His glory and your benefit. That's what He does!

Also, lets keep a spiritual perspective. He performs miracles that we may not rank as high with these physical eyes, but are indeed much greater than any physical healing and those are: the forgiveness of sin and salvation. These miracles snatch us from the hopelessness of death into His Kingdom of eternal life. Now those are miracles! "And now these three remain: faith, hope, and love" (1 Corinthians 13:13).

Who's Eyes Are We Trusting September 14

Sometimes I wander off with the crowd. Other times I wade into dangerous waters.

Last night, I watched some of the Jimmy Buffett concert from Gulf Shores. The first camera shots I saw were of individuals dancing and singing, then shots of the crowd from ground level. There were obviously a lot of people in attendance. Then they showed a shot from the air. It was this shot from the air that gave a clear picture of how big the crowd was and the layout of the concert grounds there on the beach.

You could see everything from the air, the size of the crowd, their location in relation to the shoreline, the entrances and exits to the concert area, the roads in and out, the boats in the water, where people were and what direction they may have been going. You could see things from the air that you could not have seen if you were on the ground, in the middle of that crowd.

If you were in that airplane with a two-way radio above the concert and I was on the ground with a radio in that crowd trying to get somewhere, you could tell me the easiest, quickest way to get out of there, avoiding the crowds, obstacles and blockages that I could not see from the ground.

Have you ever been to the beach and gone out into the water, say waist deep? I know a few guys who fly helicopters. One in particular who flew over the beaches quite frequently. He's told me of flying down the shoreline, seeing people swimming in the water and all the while he could see sharks between the folks in the water and the shore. You just can't see everything from ground level.

Ground level is our vantage point spiritually speaking. We may see a situation we find ourselves in as daunting or maybe even something impossible to escape. However, the Lord has a birds eye view of our predicament. All we have to do is "radio in" to Him and He will give us instruction and direction for the way out.

Who's Your Hero　　　　　　　　September 15

Who's your Hero? For some it's a ball player or a movie star. You know what I mean, the guy your friend just can't shut up about! I suggest that some of these people (movie stars, ball players and other celebrities) may be good role models, but not heroes. I mean "Hero" in the sense of the word being defined as someone who has saved your life.

Hero defined this way has just left a lot of people out of the conversation. Yet I have heard of and read about real life, genuine heroes. Meaning a person who has literally snatched someone from the jaws of certain death! Heroes who have yanked a child from a raging river. The Coast Guard swimmer who pulls men out of stormy seas as their ship sinks. Just the other day men heroically rescued passengers from a disabled cruise ship.

Then there are the Heroes who literally gave their own lives to save others: the police and firemen of 9/11, the guy who dives into the street to push a child out of the path of an oncoming truck and then is hit and killed himself, the soldier who jumps on the grenade to save his friends, the mom who decides to go through a high risk birth for the sake of her unborn child and then doesn't survive the delivery.

Do you know how I heard about these stories of heroism? The same way you have heard of the acts of heroes. Somebody told you. Often the stories are told to us by the person(s) whose lives were saved by their Heroes. People whose lives were saved by an act of heroism will gladly tell their story at any opportunity!

So why is it that many of us as Christians walk around with our mouths shut when we have a Hero who has saved our immortal souls? Don't we have a wonderful story of salvation to tell? A Hero who died for us so that we could live. Forever!

Lets take our opportunities and tell others about our Hero. He's still in the Hero business. He can save them too!

The Roller Coaster Of Life   September 16

Roller Coasters. I like the ones that go fast, but relatively straight. The ones that do a lot of sharp turns in a row or go upside down a lot, that's lunch containment endangerment. They'll make me puke! My favorites are the old wooden ones that make that clickty-clack sound and then when it goes over a hill the sound stops for just a second, like you have come off the track and you are flying.

Prior to my first roller coaster ride, I saw how fast it went and wondered how it stayed on the track in those tight, fast turns. I observed people coming off the ride who's faces were flushed, pale, relieved or just plain scared. Then again, some came off and ran back to the end of the ticket line to ride again! With apprehension (not knowing what to expect), and wondering what excitement I might experience, I followed the ones running back to the line.

Life is like a roller coaster track. It's full of ups and downs, twist and turns and sometimes it will just make you want to puke! The question is, do you want to live life or not? Secondly, do you want to live life by your own devices? Do you want to maneuver yourself around this track (life) by climbing around on it yourself, as if the track was a giant set of monkey bars on a playground? That would be hard, lonely and dangerous.

Jesus is like the roller coaster on the track. He presents our option to riding out life alone. We can ride in Him on the track of life. The track (life) still has it's ups and downs, twist and turns, but the Coaster (Jesus) knows every twist, turn, hill, and bump. There are no surprises for the Coaster. He knows everything coming up the track! The ride of life will still seem dangerous and scary, but we are eternally safe as long as we are buckled into the Coaster!

I just thought of how people often ride roller coasters with their hands in the air. That picture kind of has new meaning to me now. Surrendered in Jesus! Cool!

Shade Tree Christian   September 17

My first car was a '63 Falcon. It was clean and it ran just fine. The only thing I didn't like about it (other than it wasn't a '64 Mustang) was the engine had a knocking lifter. Although I had little knowledge of engines and even less experience working on them, I proceeded to fix it. I fixed it alright.

After I got it back from my mom (I wrecked her car a few days after I got the Falcon, so she drove it while her car was in the shop), I proceeded to tear that Falcon engine apart. I mean I tore it to pieces! I suppose it was weeks later when I got it back together. Well it looked OK. I was proud too, real proud, until I drove it almost all the way to work before I slung a rod and blew the engine! Dead it was, in a puddle of oil in the middle of 9th Avenue.

Why did I think I could fix that car when I really didn't have a clue what was wrong. Maybe that engine could have run ten more years if I had left it alone or taken it to a real mechanic. Especially since I really had no idea what was wrong or how to fix it! It just appeared and sounded like something was wrong.

The real problem was my pride. That's what was wrong. "I know what's wrong. I can fix it." Doofus!

Well then, at least I learned something about pride from this experience. Or maybe not. Lately, I have been able to see what's wrong with everyone else. I could see and hear what was wrong with everyone I came across and I could fix it, I thought. So, I'd judge them and offer my "insightful correction." Yeah, that's been working out great!

Why would I think I could fix anyone else when no one can save me from myself except Jesus? PRIDE!

I can't tell you how much I have been coming across in the Bible lately that has really spoken to me about pride. "Think of others more highly than yourself...love your neighbor as yourself...remove the plank from your own eye..." OK, stop it already!

So, I have been asking God to change me, fix me, because I can see that my engine is the one with the lifter knocking, causing all the noise. What's not easy is that as He answers this prayer the rebuilding hurts a little as I see what's been causing me to run so rough. The motor needs repairs now and then. I suggest getting it fixed before too many parts break.

The Guide   September 18

I remember as a small boy seeing a few bear skin rugs. I would walk into someone's house or lodge and the living area rug would be a bear skin with the bears mouth wide open showing these huge teeth! I thought that was the coolest rug ever, and a little scary too! I don't see bear rugs much anymore. I see a whole lot more huge sharks than big bears down here around the beach.

I used to say that I wanted to go up to Alaska or somewhere like that and hunt a bear just one time. I have enough sense to know that I would have to employ a guide to make this trip successful. I would define a successful bear hunting trip as one in which I get the bear, not one in which the bear gets me! So I would want to get the best guide I could find. The successful guide will be someone that I would trust, that has hunted bear many times before, knows where to find them again and can instruct me along the way so that the hunt will be successful.

I would thoroughly check out guides in every way I could think to do it. I'm not going squirrel hunting here! I would search advertisements in hunting magazines, check the success records of the guides, and so forth. I would even seek out the people who have followed these successful guides and listen to their stories, their testimonies.

Going through this life we need a guide to navigate the terrain and find the bears along the way. The way to do that is to find the best guide. My suggestion is to read the "Spiritual Hunting Magazine," the Bible. You will see that God has a perfect record as a guide in any terrain from deserts to oceans, from gardens to cities, from pastures to mountains, from life through death and back to life again. But you don't have to believe me, ask anyone who follows Him, they'll tell you.

Smashed Foot   September 19

When I got home yesterday, I walked right through my door into a battlefield, a spiritual battlefield. Thankfully, I was prepared for this fight. That's what this story is, a story of God preparing me, not a prideful display of my own strength.

Lately I have been reading stories of how men have faced adversity and the attacks of the enemy. They have persevered in the strength of the Lord and their love for others. I really had no idea or expectation of an attack coming my way.

Adversity and all sorts of challenges will come our way. Our Lord is ready, willing and able to guide us through these difficulties if we will submit to His will and way of getting through these times. Yet we will have to go through difficult situations. What we do not have to do is allow the enemy any kind of foothold whatsoever in these times of difficulty.

The devil will try to enter into these times, if he didn't cause them in the first place, to use them to advance his agenda to steal, kill and destroy. This is his plan: To steal, kill and destroy our lives, ministries, relationships, bodies and souls. We had better take his motives seriously so as not to be taken out!

When I walked in yesterday, God immediately showed me what the devil was up to! A health issue has come up and the enemy wanted to send us spiraling down into a pit of depression and despair. It's not happening! After short discussion and then prayer, we came into agreement that we are going to trust God to take us through this and we are not going to agree with the enemy for our demise. In the name of Jesus we slammed the door on the devil's foot!

More tomorrow.

Amazing God — September 20

Amazing God! I often say that I am amazed but not surprised at God and what He does in our lives. What I mean is that He is capable of any miracle and His ability to perform these miracles should come as no surprise to us. Yet when He acts in miraculous and loving ways, intervening in our lives on our behalf, "amazing" only begins to describe Him!

What we came face-to-face with yesterday (see "Smashed Foot") could at the very least become a life long hassle and at worst life-threatening. The choice at the time was whose report to believe and what response to apply. We went to God.

We could have agreed with the enemy and responded with an "I give up" attitude, succumbing to the situation. That's easy to do sometime. Woe is me and I have to live with what has come upon me. God does sometime have us walk through difficulties in our lives. Yet shouldn't we check with Him to see if this circumstance is something He wants us endure? It could be He wants to show Himself powerful, loving and sovereign by delivering us from the grip of adversity.

That's what He did yesterday! After our prayer and agreement, there was another follow-up visit to a doctor on an unrelated matter. The "issue" no longer existed! Just so you know, I can prove the issue existed the day before yesterday. I can also prove that it doesn't exist now! Thank you, Lord! You are Amazing!

Submit yourselves, then, to God. Resist the devil, and he will flee from you. – James 4:7

Taking Back The Land — September 21

The other afternoon when I came home and we prayed together against the enemy's attack on our health, I felt the joy of victory in a "taking back the land" sort of way. (see "Smashed Foot" and "Amazing God" on previous two days) We agreed together and believed God for healing as we prayed against this attack. The proof of that healing came the next day.

"Again, truly I tell you that if two of you on earth agree about anything they ask for, it will be done for them by my Father in heaven. For where two or three gather in my name, there am I with them." – Matthew 18:19-20

That afternoon I went out and mowed the lawn. As I was cutting the grass, I felt I was prophetically taking back the land again. With each time I mowed up and down the yard, it began to look more like an inhabited piece of property. *My* property that God had given me, and I was not going to give it back to the enemy. Weeds, grass, shrubbery and trees will continue to grow and become more and more out of control.

That's what the enemy wants to do in our lives. He wants to wreak havoc on our lives in every way we do not take time for God and others. He wants to steal, kill and destroy us!

Yet there is One who has defeated all of the enemy's devices. Jesus died for us in defeat of the enemy's most feared weapons, including sin and death. We can use the power of His name to take back the land the enemy has taken from us, and keep it! We can even take land we may have never had like peace, joy and love.

Just gather with a few "soldiers in His army." Agree together and take the land!

That Second Commandment   September 22

I think we all have a driving force or forces. Sometimes it can be as basic as survival. Other times it can be money, sex or power. It can be our faith or maybe concern for others. It could be addictions, revenge or low self-esteem. Whatever it is, it drives us on to action and that action not only affects us but others as well.

And like it or not, we are our brother's keeper or our brother's hindrance.

Jesus said: "'Love the Lord your God with all your heart and with all your soul and with all your mind.' This is the first and greatest commandment. And the second is like it: 'Love your neighbor as yourself.' All the Law and the Prophets hang on these two commandments." – Matthew 22: 37-40

It seems to me that as believers we often make some effort at obeying the first of these commandments while not making an especially good effort at the second. I believe the lack of obedience in this area is the biggest single failure of the Christian church and the individual believer. If we are falling short in this area, is it any wonder people don't come to Christ? No, because they are not seeing His love in us as we live out our daily lives.

The essence of God is His love for us. All of us. We should be giving away His love, not keeping it for ourselves! He has plenty to go around. What is our driving force? Shouldn't it be our love for God being manifest in our love for others? Their acceptance of His love is what it will take to change an unbeliever's driving force.

Easier said than done? Yeah, in our flesh it's easier to hate, dislike or ignore than to be our brother's keeper. But He drew us because He first loved us. He will draw others the same way and we can be used to do this. If we will just obey that "second commandment." Besides, we can't really be obeying the first commandment if we are not obeying the second one, can we?

Rocket Man   September 23

Right along the time I was about thirteen, I was into model rockets. I would spend my summer days building, painting and flying these rockets. They would fly surprisingly high. When the engine fuel ran out, they would fall to the ground. However, after the parachute popped out, the rocket was at the mercy of the prevailing breeze as to where it would drift to the earth.

When I set up my launch pad, I would set the trajectory of the takeoff into the wind based on the direction and speed of that wind. I did this in hopes of sending my rocket down range far enough to bring it to it's landing close to me. That way I would not have to chase it long distances to retrieve it.

Some times I made a pretty good estimation and the rocket would come down close to me. Other times my guess of trajectory was wrong and I had to chase my rocket a great distance to get it back. My rocket had no choice where to go; it was at the mercy of the wind.

Often God will put us on a launch pad to go on some mission in His behalf. Being that He is the Master of the wind, He knows exactly what trajectory on which to launch us so that we will arrive at the exact landing zone He wants us to hit.

The difference in the rocket and us is *we're* flying the rocket (our lives). By our own free will, we can change our trajectory, pull the parachute when we want and manipulate the parachute to our own desired landing zone. My unmanned hobby rocket had no such free will in flight.

So, to fly our rocket (life) around according to God's will, we will need to fly on His trajectory, using His landing coordinates. Flying by the "seat of our pants" will only bring us crashing down in a landing zone far off target. He will come get us but we will have allowed ourselves to get downrange from His perfect will. Let's stick to His flight plan.

Pasture Of Sin   September 24

One of the best places to launch my rockets (see Rocket Man, September 23), was a nearby cow pasture. It had acres and acres of open land with no obstructions for rocket flight. I would go to a part of the pasture the cattle weren't using at the time and fly my toys. Nevertheless, anywhere I went in that pasture to set up my launch pad, there was always evidence the cows had been there.

Cows eat a lot. Cows poop a lot. And a lot of cows poop a whole lot! Piles of it were everywhere. There were steamy fresh piles, piles that were sun baking, piles already fried and some piles petrified! You get the picture.

Anyway, I was surrounded by cow chips. At first I didn't like dealing with them at all. Then the chips became just an aggravation and annoyance to deal with them. Soon the piles became little more than something to avoid for convenience sake. Later, I got used to the sight and smell. Finally, I would just pick up the dry ones and throw them out of my way. It was even fun to throw them at friends who came along to watch the rockets fly.

I have found that sin can be like those cow chips were to me. At first sin can be offensive, but if it offers something we want (a pasture to play in), then we may tolerate it. Slowly, as we are in the pasture of sin more and more, we may begin to put up with the sin around us while trying to avoid it ourselves. As we are around sin more and more we can become used to its sight and smell. Then possibly, we are drawn into sin ourselves because it is fun, for a season anyway. We may even become so comfortable with sin that we even throw it at our friends.

If it looks like crap, smells like crap and feels like crap between our toes, well then guess what?

Maybe after a good "washing of our feet," we should look for another place to "fly our rockets."

Unprepared   September 25

Following basic training in the Texas summer heat, I went to Tech School in Illinois for the winter. A terrible turn of events for a Southern boy! I hate the cold! This base was out in the middle of nowhere, surrounded by cornfields and a tiny town (with nothing to do) just outside the gate. Without vehicles, we couldn't really go anywhere in the few hours of free time we had. We were i-so-lated!

After several weeks there came a three day holiday. The thought of staring at the four walls of the barracks or spending three days in the club was too much for me to bear. Home was too far for a three day trip. So, I hurriedly talked a buddy of mine into going camping.

It was afternoon by the time we rented two bikes, a tent, and figured out where to go (the campground looked closer on the map). When we got to where we were going it was dark. As we began to try to put up the tent in the pitch dark, it began to rain. In minutes we were in the midst of a monsoon! We were soaked, with no hope of erecting our tent in this cold, dark, wet night.

We decided to run for cover. There was a small country store way back at the entrance to the campground. We remembered a porch on the front of it and we headed that way. When we were almost there, some folks in a camper spotted us and told us to come get under the awning of their camper. We did!

They gave us something to eat (we had planned to make a fire and cook) and lets us stay out of the rain for a while. As it got later we could see there was obviously not enough room for strange wet G.I.'s in their little camper. Not to mention that the ground was soaked under the awning and the rain was blowing underneath it anyway. We thanked them and headed for the store's porch.

When we got there (soaked to the bone again), the rain was blowing up under the porch too! As a last resort, we went around to the back of the store where we found bathrooms and shower stalls. At least it was dry in there. In the shower stalls there were some very narrow benches. I climbed up on one and went to sleep.

Not exactly how I envisioned this camping trip playing out! It gets better...tomorrow.

Unprepared Part 2   September 26

The shower bench was hard but it didn't seem to matter. It was narrow too, but I didn't fall off. I was also narrower back then! Finally I was asleep and drying.

In the wee hours of the morning I was rocked awake by a noise like a gun going off! The toilet stalls in this bathroom were made of wood. An old man had come in to use the bathroom and his stall door had slammed shut as he took a seat. You know the sound, like your grandmother's old screen door slamming shut on the porch. It scared the crap out of us. We screamed as we jumped up and crashed through the shower room door, which scared the crap out of the old guy. He came barreling out of his toilet stall trying to pull up his drawers, as he crashed through the bathroom door heading out into the dark stormy night!

Going from something that sounded like a gunshot to seeing an 80 'ish year old man running for his life while trying to keep his drawers on was quite a relief. Not to mention one of the funniest things I have ever seen!

Although I crack up every time I think about the naked 80 year old track star running off into the dark of the night, this whole camping trip could have gone a lot better with a little planning and preparation.

For instance we could have checked the weather. We should've checked the distance in order to leave early enough to arrive in the daytime to set up our camp. We could have taken some food that didn't need cooking. We should've planned better and been prepared.

In contrast, some 20 plus years later, we took our youth group on a camping trip that was well planned, including food, equipment, planned events at a great site and a few guys who really knew what they were doing when it came to camping. It was the perfect camping trip!

Kingdom work takes planning and preparation too. Sure, there are times for spontaneous obedience to God, but the Bible tells us over and over to seek counsel in planning and to "Commit to the Lord whatever you do, and your plans will succeed" (Proverbs 16:3). As we make a plan we should also prepare according to that plan.

Even God had a plan for the forgiveness of man's sins. The plan was Jesus. What was the preparation, according to the plan? The witness of the Old Testament and God's people right through John the Baptist.

God Almighty has a plan and He prepared for it. Should we just wing it (our lives) or should we commit our way to the Lord and then plan, prepare and act according to His direction and will?

The Chalkboard — September 27

When I was in middle school, many of the students had chores of some sort to do at the school. My friend and I liked cleaning the chalkboard erasers and wiping the chalkboard down with a wet cloth.

We would take the four chalkboard erasers outside and bang them together (and on each other) until there was little or no chalk dust left on them. It was fun to see how big of a cloud we could make and watch it drift away in the breeze. Then we would go back inside and wipe down the chalkboard with wet cloths, leaving the chalkboard looking like brand new.

There was some amount of fascination to me about a chalkboard and erasers. If no one was in the classroom we could write anything we wanted on the chalkboard. When we were done, we could erase it all and no one would know the difference, or so we thought. What I remember about this (and you can try this at home), is that often after writing on the chalkboard and erasing what we wrote, you could often see shadowy looking remnants of what we had previously written. This was painfully obvious if the light through the window hit the chalkboard just right. We soon learned that the only way to completely remove what we wrote on the chalkboard was to wipe it with the wet cloths, which left the chalkboard clean.

As I was thinking about this the other day it reminded me how I forgive others sometimes. I'm not necessarily talking about telling them

I forgive them (although that is appropriate, if possible), but really forgiving them completely in my heart.

For instance, I was once successfully cheated out of several thousand dollars by someone simply because they knew it would cost me more to sue them than the amount they owed me. I say I have forgiven them, but each time I think about that incident I become upset or think of some way I could get even.

I don't think I have completely forgiven them. I think it's more like I have "dry erased" the chalkboard and not really washed the chalkboard clean. There are "shadows of contempt" that still are in my heart over this incident.

The sad part to this is that the only person holding resentment and anger is me! Forgiveness doesn't just free the forgiven. Forgiveness also frees the forgiver. I think it's about time I get a wet cloth, wipe the chalkboard clean and get my freedom!

Things Seem A Little Shaky   September 28

Last night (someone who will remain nameless) was driving home from a nearby city a little more than a hundred miles away. A few miles into the trip, I received a call from her telling me that the truck was shaking badly. Her description of the problem seemed to be that of a tire separating.

She was crossing a long bridge at the time and pulled over into a parking area at the end of the bridge. Upon inspection of the tires she could not see any problem but she did detect a burning smell. Still on the phone with her and trying to remain calm was a little tough, knowing that I was over a hundred miles away and of little help to her in this situation.

We decide to call her nephew who lives nearby. I had hoped he would come out and check the truck for her. When I called her back a few minutes later, she was driving the truck around the lot slowly to see if it was still shaking. If tires are separating, you may not feel it a slow speeds. I told her I thought it would shake again, damaging the tire more and possibly coming apart at a higher speed. I did not think that driving the truck was a good idea until we knew what was wrong.

Right about then she said: "Oh! I have been driving with the emergency brake on."

I thought (sarcastically but relieved), "Let's see – hot brakes, burning smell and shaking vehicle. Yep, that could be it!"

She had set the emergency brake on an inclined drive earlier, but probably not all the way down, so that she may not have felt the brake on as she began to drive the truck. After the brake got hot, the problem began.

I know there are times I am like that truck. I sometimes have my "brakes" on just a little. What I mean is that I know there is something I am supposed to do. This could be anything from mowing my lawn to helping someone, but any little excuse (brake on) can keep me from doing anything from a chore to the obvious will of God!

Signs of my "Brakes being on" listed here:

1. "Well, I can't cut the grass, no gas in the gas can." – When there's a gas station across the street.

2. "I can't help my elderly neighbor move his freezer, the game's on right now." – DVR

3. "Can't read my Bible right now, gotta get something to eat." – Wrong choice of food!

4. "I can't go help at the homeless shelter, I have to cut the grass." – see # 1

Is your brake on? If things seem a little shaky, pull over and take a look.

Release the brake; your life will run a lot smoother!

P.S. I'm still not going to name the driver, but her initials are H.P.

Well Blue   September 29

I really enjoy baseball. I have spent quite a bit of my time in and around the game. I think the most fun and success I had in the game was in managing teams, mostly my sons' Little League teams. However, I did get to the point of being offered a job as Athletic Director and Manager of the baseball team at a local high school. I really enjoyed the strategy of the game as well as teaching players how to play the game and improve their skills.

Later, at another point in my life, I had aspirations of being an umpire. I thought it would be so cool to one day be out there on a big league ball field calling balls and strikes. I went as far as sending off for registration papers to a Major League umpire's school with the intention of going down to south Florida in the off season to attend this umpiring academy.

Meanwhile, I took an opportunity to umpire a pre-season Little League game. At least I could get a taste of calling a game. I got behind home plate and was doing OK calling balls and strikes. The other umpire was stationed between second and third because the team at bat had a man on second.

Then it happened. The batter hit the ball to the right side toward the second baseman. I guess I am programmed to watch the game with a managers mindset, not as a impartial judge. As the ball was hit I was watching the runner at second, expecting him to take off for third, as he should when a ball is hit behind him on the ground. He didn't and I was thinking he should have been taught that by now at his age.

Meanwhile, the second baseman has fielded the ball and thrown to first, as he should, to get the batter out. As the plate umpire this would have been my call, if only I had been watching the batter run down the line, but I wasn't. I was watching in frustration the runner at second just stand there! I had not even looked towards the play at first!

The crowd on the first base side bleachers hollered at me: "Well, blue?"

"Well, what?" I reply as I snap out of it.

"Is he safe or out?"

I honestly said this: "I don't know, what do you all think?"

Umpiring career over!

Umpiring is often a thankless job done very well for the most part. Yet even when the good umpires are looking right at the play their judgment can sometimes be wrong.

In life we often make judgments about people and things based on hearsay. We don't even have the true facts and we make a judgment. A wrong judgment that can set off a whole string of untruths, gossip and even unfortunate events. We should never make judgments without all the information. Sometimes we may even have all the available info and still make the wrong call. Check with the Lord before making a judgment call in life. He's the only perfect Umpire. Let Him make the call. Otherwise we may adversely affect the outcome of a very important game, someones life!

Safe At Home   September 30

I was watching the Braves game this week and they were showing the clips of Sid Bream's slide into home in 1992. It was the bottom of the ninth in the seventh and final game of the National League Championship Series. Bream is the winning run on second base. The ball is hit into the outfield and Bream is off and running with no intention of stopping at third. It's all or nothing. He's going to try to score to win the game.

Now watching Sid run is like watching paint dry. When I played ball, we used to say someone running this slow looked like they were dragging an anchor! As a Braves fan I was on my feet hollering "GO, GO" at the top of my lungs! I went and made a sandwich and came back as "lightning" was rounding third. OK, that's a slight exaggeration.

Anyway, after what seemed to be too long, Bream slides into home safe. Braves fans everywhere go berserk! Sid's safe! We win and you can see the video that has immortalized that moment. Bream is "forever safe."

Someone wins the championship every year. The World Series, the Super Bowl, NBA championship, right on down to T-ball at your local ballpark. When our team wins the championship, we go nuts! When that guy sinks the last putt, kicks the winning field goal or is safe at home, the party starts!

Did you know there is a party in Heaven when one sinner repents? Is that cool or what?! To think that when I ask Jesus to be my Lord and Savior, it was as if the angels in Heaven were watching me slowly round third, and then jumping up screaming their approval as the Lord called me "safe at home," forever!

"In the same way, I tell you, there is rejoicing in the presence of the angels of God over one sinner who repents." – Luke 15:10

Let's party when people come to Jesus! Seriously!

Taking Care Of Our (His) Stuff   October 1

At my job, I have had the same route for many years now. After such a long time on the same route I have gotten to know many people and see their homes, automobiles, boats and yards daily. You can learn a lot about someone by how they take care of their possessions. Chances are (except for a hot rod guy and a car or a single-minded fisherman and his boat) if a fellow takes care of some of his stuff he is someone who pretty much takes good care of all his stuff.

For instance, I daily go by residences with nice lawns and a home in good repair. Out front maybe the guy has his ten year old truck sitting there for sale. The truck is clean and I feel confident by looking at how he cares for his house and lawn, that the truck he is selling has been maintained over the years. I am likely to be much more interested in purchasing his truck rather than the newer one down the street at the house with the window broken and a tree limb has been in the yard for two weeks.

I think you know what I mean. I'm not down on people who are going through tough times or who have less things or resources than others. I'm just saying (to myself especially) that we should be good caretakers of what we have.

Being a good steward of what God has given us (all good things come from above) is not only right, obedient and smart, but is a good witness to others that will draw them to us. I know that as a guy I am drawn to a nice boat, a good-looking truck or a sharp-looking yard. I might even go ask the owner why he bothers taking such good care of his place. He might reply: "Oh, I'm not the Owner. He's just letting me use it. I'm just taking care of it until He comes back. Then He's going to give this place to someone else and give me some place even better."

Now that preaches! I'll see you tomorrow. I gotta go wash my truck and cut the grass.

What Did You Say   October 2

Just before I woke up this morning I was dreaming that I had bought a new car. After parking it, I noticed it had a sticker on it. I instinctively pulled it off and some paint came off my new car with the sticker. Seemingly on automatic, foul curses came out of my mouth. Upon hearing my outburst, the parking attendant informed me that the Lord would not be pleased with my language. I knew that.

I've been a believer for a long time and one would think that I would have a good handle on my language by now. Yet there are times, as in my dream, when those kind of outbursts seem to happen by automatic instinct.

When does our true character really come out and show itself to us? How about when we are alone? What do we say and how do we behave when no one else is around and others will probably never know what we are doing, saying or thinking?

For example, how about when we are driving the car alone and someone pulls right out in front of us? That's when it happens the most for me. Cuss words, sign language, name calling of their family members, questioning of their sanity and description of their lack of driving skills are among my loud verbal insults.

James 3:8-10 says:

... but no human being can tame the tongue. It is a restless evil, full of deadly poison. With the tongue we praise our Lord and Father, and with it we curse human beings, who have been made in God's likeness. Out of the same mouth come praise and cursing. My brothers and sisters, this should not be.

So why does it seem so automatic? I've tried to tame my tongue in my own strength. The answer lies in Matthew 12:34 and Luke 6:45 that says: "For the mouth speaks what the heart is full of." Ouch!

Sounds to me like if I want really change the things coming out of my mouth I'll need a change of heart. I'll ask God about that one because I do want real change and I can't change my heart by myself.

Motives — October 3

I spent many years of my life on a baseball field. I played baseball, coached baseball and even umpired a little. When you are a coach, you give signs throughout the game from the dugout and the coach's box at first and third base. You would rub your arm, touch your hat, pull on your nose, pat your leg or any number of things to direct the players. These signs would tell the base runners, a batter or pitcher what to do next. All the while, trying to conceal the plan from the opposing team.

Occasionally, because of a mixed signal or a problem with reception, the wrong message would be sent resulting in poor and often humorous outcomes. Such as, telling a pitcher to throw an inside fastball to a pull hitter that results in a three run homer, when all I was doing was picking my nose! Or sending two base runners stealing when there is no one out, a big hitter is up and you need a big inning. The runners were safe but they intentionally walked my big hitter, struck out the next guy and ended the inning with a ground ball double play. I didn't mean to give the steal sign, I was only scratching because my leg itched!

I was momentarily motivated by my desire to comfort my flesh rather than winning the game.

I must confess, that in my spiritual life, my motivation has often been to live comfortably in my flesh rather than win the game. More to the point, I wanted it both ways. I knew the Bible said "if you do this then you get this" and "if you do that He will do that." You know what? For awhile it seemed to be working just fine. I had more money, I was important to myself and others, I was loved, liked, admired and affirmed by men. I was looked up to, had tons of toys, big house on a little lake, a boat, cars and other goodies along the way and oh yeah, God too. It was like a package deal and I was OK with that at the time. I believed I just wanted it both ways.

For instance, at work I would join in the bantering that would go back and forth daily. I have humor and a wit that I can put others down with and I used it. I gained approval of man by putting people down as others laughed at their pain and embarrassment. I was giving a poor witness to people who know I go to church! Many knew I was the Youth Pastor! It's doubtful, given my behavior at work, that any of them would want to come to my church, but if some did, I would certainly appear hypocritical to them as I led prayer, preached or taught something out of the Word.

The Lord said through Isaiah 29:13: "These people honor me with their lips, but their hearts are far from me."

Certainly nice things and admiration of others are not inherently evil desires, but these should not be the motives that drive us. "Seek first His kingdom and His righteousness, and all these things will be given to you as well." God has to be first. Love for Him has to be our motivation. Our love for Him is shown through our obedience. John 14:15-24. (Yes, I know I use this one a lot, but it's that good!)

1 Samuel 16:7 says, "The Lord looks at the heart." What's our motive for the things we do? Psalm 37:4: Is our motive "the desires of our heart" or "delighting ourselves in the Lord?" Malachi 3:8-12: Is our motive in tithing "to be blessed" or "to give to the Lord?" Is our motive to comfort our flesh or to win the game? Is our motive in life to be someone who serves God, or someone God serves?

She's Not Poor Anymore   October 4

As Jesus looked up, he saw the rich putting their gifts into the temple treasury. He also saw a poor widow put in two very small copper coins. "Truly I tell you," he said, "this poor widow has put in more than all the others. All these people gave their gifts out of their wealth; but she out of her poverty put in all she had to live on." – Luke 21:1-4

God has worked mightily in the area of my finances. He has brought me from deep debt to living within my means. He has taught me a great deal about good stewardship of money and other things He has entrusted to me. Yet there seems to be so much to still learn.

I have been feeling like I should give more in a financial way to His work. When I say give, I mean over and above a tithe. So, I have been figuring out some percentage of my extra or left over money to give into His Kingdom work. This verse stops me cold! Don't misunderstand me, giving to His work is good. But giving out of my "extra" doesn't really show much trust, now does it?

If that's the way I decide how much to give, it sounds eerily like the rich in Luke who gave out of their wealth. For them, there was no real hit to their wallet, no pain, no sacrifice and no trust in God! I am not saying we should give our last pennies, unless He tells us to give it all. What I am saying is that we should give all He ask us to give and then trust Him to take care of our needs.

One things for sure, we will put our money where our trust is, won't we?

P.S. Where do you think that poor widow's seat is at the table of the marriage supper of the Lamb?!

Trusted Friend   October 5

I once wrote about the effectiveness of witnesses. We believe something happened because others who were there and saw it, tell us about it.

When a car dealer advertises a car for sale he may use satisfied customers to witness to the value and satisfaction they received from the dealer and the car they purchased from him. There may be flashier commercials and fancier cars out there but the dealer is using "testimonials" of satisfied customers. Testimony out of a witness' mouth is far more believable than a flashy commercial.

How much more then is a testimony from a trusted friend? What if I see a commercial for a fancy auto repair shop on TV? It looks clean, has fancy equipment and they say all the right words. Yet a trusted friend comes to me and tells me about a mechanic who does great work for a fair price in a little garage across town. Which one of the repair shops do you think I am going to have fix my car?

Jesus' most used tool for evangelism has always been word of mouth. Someone with a heart for the Lord and a heart for the lost, telling the lost of the love of God. Who better to hear the Good News from than a trusted friend?

Believers, we have all witnessed God at work in our lives and the lives of others. We are trusted friends to people who may not listen to a stranger tell them about Jesus. But they would listen to you. Don't wait until you become a better Christian and think you have all the answers. Being a witness is not about knowing everything. A witness in a court room testifies to what they saw and heard. The witness doesn't have all the answers to a court case. He just tells as much as he knows. Yet his information may be key in finding the truth.

When the opportunity arises (and you'll know when that is), share with others what you do know and what you have seen God do in you and other believers. Then they can put your testimony together with where they are in their life and the Holy Spirit will guide them to the Truth. And we know the Truth will set them free!

There is no better witness than a set of lips connected to a heart for God.

Integrity Or Ill-Gotten Booty   October 6

The other day I walked into a restroom in a store on my route. Up on the soap dispenser was a ladies wallet. No, I wasn't in the ladies restroom, this store has only one potty. I took the wallet to the store manager who opened it looking for some form of identification. The lady who had left the wallet worked just down the street, so I took the wallet to her. She had not even missed it yet and was surprised and thankful.

Her wallet had $250 cash inside, not to mention credit cards. There was a day this would have been a severe temptation for me. That's not bragging on me, but God has obviously done some work in me. Selfishly, I did have some hope of a little financial reward, but there was none.

It seems to me that our society today looks at lying, cheating and stealing in degrees of severity. We may wink at a little lie or think that cheating on our taxes is OK and stealing some tool or supplies from work is just not that big of a deal. We may even think it's funny and try to justify getting over on the government or some big cooperation by saying "no one is getting hurt" or "they'll never miss it."

I have been guilty of this sort of thing in my life. Years ago, I had made a deal to buy a car. I was literally on my way to trade in the car when radiator pieces started going through the fan in front of the radiator. I pulled over, yanked the pieces out of the fan and proceeded to the car dealer. I traded the car without telling them of the new damage to the vehicle.

On another occasion, we were about to sell our house and my wife wanted me to tell the buyer about the septic system needing repair. I was furious. This would cost us more money or we could lose the sale completely! I wanted to go through with the sale telling the buyer nothing.

However, I have never cheated on my taxes and I'll tell you why. Several years ago I ended up owing a considerable amount in income taxes. I couldn't pay them, so they took what I owed them right out of my paycheck. They didn't ask. They didn't have to. They had the power to take what they were owed. I now have a "fear" of the IRS, along with a conscience, that would prevent me from cheating on my taxes.

If we lie, cheat or steal, (for our own selfish ends) no matter to what degree or justification, we are demonstrating we have no "fear of God" in the matter. Not to mention showing disobedience and lack of integrity. By the way, He has the power to take away our "ill-gotten booty" we think we have pirated.

Integrity is not just doing the right thing, like returning a full wallet and people know about it. Integrity is doing the right thing when no one but God will know about it.

I respect no man more than a Godly man of integrity.

For a man's ways are in full view of the Lord, and He examines all his paths. – Proverbs 5:21

Position Yourself For A Blessing   October 7

Shalom! Hannah here. I want to tell a story that Greg is responsible for. It's at least half his story.

This morning, before Greg left for work, he let Louie (our basset hound) out of his kennel. Normally, I don't let him out till later because I don't want to be bothered for a while. Greg insisted that he normally lets him out before he leaves for work. I said, "OK. Whatever." He said, "The boy needs to pee!" Then he said to me, "You wait, God's going to start speaking to you through Louie like He does me!" We laughed and he went on to work.

Well, just now, I was making a hot dog (interesting choice of food for this story) and Louie began to "bother" me, like he does, when I am in the kitchen making anything. He bothers me by getting right up under my feet!!! He was waiting for the food to fall from the sky.

The Lord said, "Louie is positioning himself for a blessing." That's what Louie does. It's his instinct. He wants something from me, so he positions himself to receive. God said, "That's what I want my children to do." To receive His blessings, we must position ourselves, or if you want to call it what I called it, "bother Him!" To bother Him is to position ourselves for the blessing. We don't want to miss anything!! The thing is, when Louie does this, I, as his "provider" have to respond! I can't help myself! I see his dog-like trust in me, and I don't want to let him down. So, a piece of cheese or a crumb of something always manages to hit his head. I enjoy blessing him. God feels the same!! When we position ourselves, I believe He loves to respond to us.

Position yourself for a blessing!!
Hannah

Real Eyesight...From A Blind Man's Perspective   October 8

Perspective: The place or condition we are in from which we view and formulate our beliefs, opinions and actions. (Greg's definition). Unless we are willing to look at any given situation from another perspective, our personal view may be selfish, wrong and even harmful.

For instance, what if one town near a river wants to dam up the river to produce needed electricity? Their perspective is, we need more electricity. Yet another town down river says no! We need that water to irrigate our farms. Their perspective is based on their livelihood from farming. These two towns may end up in court because their views, based on their perspectives, are opposed to one another. A good judge would then listen to all of the evidence from both perspectives before making a determination or verdict.

In Matthew, more than once, the story is told of Jesus healing blind men. They scream out at Jesus while he passes: "Jesus, Son of David, have mercy on us!"

Meanwhile, the Pharisees are accusing Jesus of blasphemy, hanging out with sinners (He did, but that's not wrong because they say so), ungodliness, and they called Him "the prince of demons."

Two different "perspectives," one might say.

The blind men were screaming "Jesus, Son of David, have mercy on us!" Although these men were physically blind, their "spiritual eyes" were seeing just fine. These blind men saw Jesus for who He was. By calling Jesus the "Son of David" they were recognizing Jesus as the Messiah because they knew the Messiah would be a descendant of David.

On the other hand, although they had physical eyesight (even to see the miracles Jesus was doing), the Pharisees chose to not believe. Instead they chose to be spiritually blind and not accept Him as Messiah. From their (spiritually blind) perspective they saw Jesus undermining their authority and control as well as exposing their true selfish motives.

Trusting our spiritual eyesight will show us His way in the Kingdom and to Heaven. Trusting our physical eyesight can send us into a tailspin to hell.

Just two different perspectives, one might say. Take a good look with both sets of eyes before you choose!

My Tough Day   October 9

Yesterday, while I was at work, I got a message from my son that my wife was feeling very bad. When I called, I found that Hannah was in severe pain and could not get up out of the chair. The pain was so bad she considered calling an ambulance. I left work and headed home. I suppose my first thought at hearing of severe back pain while in a chair was kidney stone. You're right, I'm no doctor!

Anyway, when I got home, Nick and I pushed the foot rest part of the recliner down and we were able to get her up and to my truck. As we were in this process of getting her into the truck and on the way to the hospital, I thought to myself: "This is going to be a tough day for me."

Woe, wait a minute, I can hear you now! "Tough day for you! What about Hannah?" And you would be right, except I think God is showing me something here.

You see, I love the woman. This may seem like an obvious statement, but you don't just spend thirty plus years with someone just to have some permanent company. My love for her has grown, it hasn't waned. If there were times I have taken her for granted, that has truly changed into admiration and appreciation of her (for lack of a better term) "worth." I know that doesn't sound like the most romantic term, yet I think it fits here.

In an admiration sense, I admire her worth to God and His Kingdom. I admire her worth to my sons as their mother. I admire her worth to the rest of our family. I admire her "worth" to me as a wife and partner in this life. She is the love of my life and my gift from God. She is easily "worth" my life, no question, no doubt! So, now do you see why I had a bad day yesterday?

In the emergency room, they checked her heart, they took x-rays, and they checked for blood clots, among other things. All through this she was calmly praying and claiming the Word of God in victory.

My reaction through this was a little different. I was screaming on the inside; "No God! No! Heal her!" I would rather have the pain that see her hurting. And if it's worse than just pain, take me! She's just worth too much to all of us!

I kind of get it now, in a new, too close to home kind of way, this love that God has for us. What I don't get is how He loves us more than I love Hannah, but He does. So, if He does and He is willing to give His life for us, then we can and should trust Him. How could that much love have anything less than our best in store for us?

P.S. Hannah's going to be fine. I'm still pretty rattled!

Another Room In My House — October 10

"My Tough Day" is turning into a week of lessons and things to ponder about myself. I often ask God to speak to me, show me things and work in my life. How He does this is amazing to me! I'll be going along, seemingly just fine, when it happens. I'll be thinking I am growing and doing good in some area and that's when He opens this door to "another room in my house" that requires some (usually a lot) of adjustment.

Sometimes it even appears that He is coming across in a sarcastic tone! Wonder why that is? Anyway, while Hannah has been recovering, I have assumed a few extra duties including cooking supper and some cleaning. Yes, this is the "room in my house" God is opening up right now for me to work in.

My issue isn't necessarily I need to clean or cook more often. My issue is an attitude of the heart. My issue is I've taken Hannah for granted in this area. She doesn't complain one bit about cooking or cleaning. In fact, she does it gladly. She has a servants heart and does these things in stride as the wonderful wife and mom that she is.

The deal is, as I have come home after work and almost immediately gone into the kitchen to prepare a meal and then clean it all up afterward, I realize all that is required to do this task. Instead of coming home and hitting the recliner with my computer and remote in my hands, my workday is not over, just like Hannah's day is hardly ever over as soon as I get home!

I really have not sat down to chill for the evening the last few days until about 8pm. I'll bet there are others out there who wish their day only lasted until 8pm.

Even though she doesn't complain, I have been reminded through this time that cooking and cleaning is a lot of work for her and I should be more considerate of that, and help Hannah out more in this area.

Or the short, sarcastic direction from God to Greg: "Quit loafing and being a bum, get off your butt and help the woman. Besides, I didn't just give her to you, I gave you to her."

Once again, Scripture references too numerous to mention!

Spiritual Autopilot   October 11

Why do we often not ask God for His direction, guidance and will for the circumstances, situations and troubles that we may find ourselves navigating? Because we know what He's going to say! Right?

I know that if I ask God what to do about my annoying neighbor down the street (that thinks I'm his buddy), He's not going to say: "Just put up with him." God is going to say, "Greg, love your neighbor." Worse yet, He may say, "...and take him fishing!"

"No, God! Please!" Then there are these thoughts rolling through my head of not only spending hours stuck in the boat with this guy, but fear of being stuck forever on an island with this "Gilligan!"

So, I just don't ask. That's not disobeying. Is it?

Another reason I don't want to ask God for guidance is because it's just easier to live in the flesh. Spiritual autopilot I call it. I just live, handle stuff as it comes, no thinking, no planning, no wisdom, no use of knowledge or understanding, no discernment or use of sound judgment. Easy, thoughtless, and stupid!

We're supposed to be steering our lives according to His will and direction. If we are not following His guidance, we are like the pilots sleeping while the plane is on autopilot. Sometimes they miss their destination because they sleep through the instructions from the control tower. I certainly don't want to be on an airplane that the pilot is taking a nap!

We may have kids, friends, employees and others who count on us to know where we're going and how to get there. We need to stay in touch with the "control tower" who will direct us around. or guide us successfully through, the turbulence in this life, to our heavenly destination.

Keep Your Ears On   October 12

When I was about eighteen (just a few years ago) CB radios were the rage. It seemed as if everyone had an antennae on their car and the semi-trucks had two each. It was fun to go down the road and talk to everyone. It was not like cell phones today. This was a rolling party line made up of some blend of police code numbers, road and traffic information, and Smokie reports (where the Highway patrol was last seen) laced with redneck country voices. Generally polite, often humorous (at the expense of the old lady going forty down the interstate) and everyone wanted to talk.

The conversations usually began with a person asking someone if they "had their ears on." The obvious meaning on the CB was: "Are you listening?"

There is the question of the day for us: Are we listening? Not, do we have our ears on? Of course we have our ears on. You can't just pull 'em off! But we can "turn 'em off," can't we? Don't we? Do we do just like the guy who has hearing aids and turns the volume down, nodding intermittently, as his wife berates him?

As I write this now, I realize in some ways my CB days prepared me for what I do today. I spend at least 75% of my work day driving and doing deliveries. I talk and listen to a lot of people. But do I have my ears on? For some reason a lot of people will come up to me, as I deliver their mail, and spill their guts. Some are annoying. Some are heart broken. Some are gossips. Some are searching. Some are just lonely.

A couple of comments I've heard lately with my ears on:

A little boy ask: "Mr. Mailman, did you have friends to play with when you were little?"

A middle-aged woman says: "Every since my husband committed suicide ..."

I must admit that I often only had my ears on when it was someone happy and friendly talking to me. When the others talked I would often nod, smile and move on down the road. God's working on me about this attitude. He wants me to keep my ears on.

So lately when someone wants to talk a minute when I pull up, I turn off the radio and listen a bit (even if it cost me some of my break time). If I have my ears on, I can truly hear their heart and maybe offer some encouragement. Who knows what God might do from there!

P.S. That old lady going down the interstate at 40 mph ... she's still out there! I passed her yesterday! She was texting. She shouldn't do that if she wants to get much older. **Everyone stop it!**

Outside The Walls　　　　　　　　October 13

There were castles in the Middle Ages, forts in early America, and now electronic defense walls around our homes. We are creatures that seek a safe place. We fence prisoners in and strangers out. Safety and defense is good and necessary in many situations. But they gain nothing, and at best keep only what we possess now.

To gain ground (as in a battle or war) or to produce food (farm and ranch) or earn income (work), one would have to leave the safety of the castle, fort or home. You couldn't farm inside a fort and to defeat enemies, warriors had to leave the castle and go on offense. Most of us have to leave the house to work.

Often our churches can become a castle, fort, or a locked up house with us inside. We seem to think that we are safe, we've got our salvation, and intentionally or not, we can become selfishly indifferent to those outside the fort. Occasionally a stray traveler comes along and beats on the castle door until it annoys us enough to let them in, but for the most part, the outsiders are not "compelled" to come in.

Simply put, to gain ground for the Kingdom we must go outside the walls. Hanging out at the fort (worship and fellowship at church) should be an occasion to resupply our spirit to go back outside the walls. We should not be afraid outside the walls because He is with us. We should not think since we are imperfect we are of no use. We should go as He grows us. Training can be gained inside the church, but experience is gained only outside the walls. Besides, even when we mess up, those outside the wall need to see the grace and mercy God gives us.

Jesus said: "Go and make disciples of all nations" (Matthew 28:19). He didn't say, hang out here and grab one that comes strolling by!

Luke 10:1-3 says: "After this the Lord appointed seventy-two others and sent them two by two ahead of him to every town and place where He was about to go. He told them, "The harvest is plentiful, but the workers are few. Ask the Lord of the harvest, therefore, to send out workers into His harvest field. Go! I am sending you out like lambs among wolves."

He told them to Go! He sent them! The harvest is out there in the everyday world. Sitting around in church hoping for a harvest to walk in is like tending a potted plant in a farm house surrounded by a million acres of ripe fruit trees!

Lets go outside and work the harvest everyday. Not pious and full of pride, but with love and respect.

But in your hearts, set apart Christ as Lord. Always be prepared to give an answer to everyone who asks you to give the reason for the hope that you have. But do this with gentleness and respect – 1Peter 3:15

Listen   October 14

Greg: "Sometimes I just don't know what to say."
God: "Good."
Greg: "What? You heard that lady yesterday when she said that she lost her dad the day before. What do I say to that? I've maybe seen her once in all the years I've carried this route!"
God: "She's hurting. She needs some healing words. She needs to know someone cares about her loss."
Greg: "OK, but I don't know her. Doesn't she have family and friends for times like this?"
God: "Sure, but if it was you, wouldn't you want all the comfort and healing you could get?"
Greg: "Yeah, but doesn't she have a pastor, a favorite bartender or somebody to talk to? I'm practically a stranger to her! I feel like I have a sign on me that says 'tell me your troubles.'"
God: "Imagine that. You said you wanted to be my servant. Do you think I put you out on that route just to carry mail?"
Greg: "Yeah, but this kind of thing happens all the time. People out on the route just spill their guts to me. I get 'my wife does this,' 'my husband does that,' 'I lost my job,' 'my boss sucks'... on and on. Sometimes I feel like I have a 'People's Problems Magnet' in me!"
God: "Now you're getting it. You do have that magnet in you; it's Me. I want them to bring their troubles to you, then you can show them me. I will bring them healing, love, mercy, grace, salvation, whatever they may need."
Greg: "OK, I get it, but would you please tell me what to say to them when they start telling me all this stuff?"
God: "Sure, but just start with listening, that will go a long way in showing them you really care. You do really care, don't you?"

Helpless Is Not Hopeless   October 15

There are few things in life that make me feel helpless, and I hate that feeling! Maybe it's a man thing, a parental thing or just an "I can fix it" attitude inside me, but being helpless in a situation I can't fix, just plain sucks!

Last night it was emergency care again. My son text us to say he had taken his wife to the ER. Hannah and I are concerned but calm. A different feeling than I had on "My Tough Day" (October 9) and maybe it is a result of God building faith in me through the previous event. I love my daughter-in-law and would do anything for her and be sure of this, there was no less concern for her than for Hannah on her trip to the ER.

The difference in my feelings in the two events was a difference in the level of my faith and trust in God. In Hannah's visit there was not only the feeling of helplessness, but there were flashes of fear and doubt. Yes, last night I did have feelings of helplessness but not fear and doubt.

Helplessness in ourselves is not hopelessness for the believer! There may be helplessness in us but there is hope in God. Who do we believe, trust and have our hope in? Last night in the calm helplessness on the way to the hospital, Hannah and I prayed. Once we got there I paced and prayed some more.

When we are weak, He is strong. When we are helpless, He is help! The outcome could not have been better if I had not been helpless. Helpless isn't so bad if we have our hope in Him. In fact, the more we need and depend on Him, the better off we will be.

Should've Just Gone To School   October 16

I remember as a teenager how much I loved to water ski. My friends and I liked it a lot better than high school. We liked a lot of things better than high school!

Anyway, one of my friends had access to his dad's boat. What we didn't have was money for gas. To remedy this situation we decided to relieve our neighborhood's "Mr. Wilson" of a few gallons of gasoline from his old pickup truck.

One of the guys had a 15 gallon jug, but back in the day, we had no fancy siphon like there is available to juvenile fuel thieves today. However, this obstacle was easily overcome by cutting off a 4-foot piece of Mr. Wilson's garden hose, which we would use to empty his truck's gas tank.

The process was easy enough. In the early hours on the morning of our scheduled ski trip, we met at Mr. Wilson's truck. First, placing the gas jug on the ground next to the truck, then putting one end of the hose into the truck tank, I began sucking on the other end of the hose. Soon gas was flowing into the jug. Once we had filled the jug with gas, we left the hose there by his truck just to add insult to injury. In no time, we were fueling the boat and on our way to a great day of water skiing, instead of a boring day at school.

And we lived happily ever after. Well ... not exactly.

In the early hours of the next morning, I woke up burping the nastiest smelling aroma you ever smelled! I guarantee a skunk would run for his life smelling this garbage! Have you ever burped up eggs? It was like that in a nuclear version! It lasted for weeks! Yes, weeks! I didn't know what to do except endure it! What else? "Hey Mom, what do you do about gasoline breath you get when you're stealing fuel to go water skiing?!"

There are consequences for everything we do in life. You reap what you sow. You burp what you swallow! We should consider the consequences of our actions before we act.

Thou shall not steal? I get that one!

Thou should've gone to school? I get that one too (after a couple of extra semesters)!

Seeing Clearly   October 17

My job requires me to read continually. When I was 39, my arms were no longer long enough for me to hold things out away from me far enough to see them clearly and read them. It was way past time for glasses. Upon getting corrective lenses, I was amazed at how clear and focused everything became.

This is what happens when we come to Jesus. Things become more clearly defined. Obstacles still appear in our lives, but viewing them through "spiritual eyes" we can see how to avoid them or navigate through them. Priorities become clear to us and we can focus in on things in the order of their Kingdom importance.

That's how I want to order my life. That's how I want to set my priorities. Is this God's will for me, in the order He would have me do it? Are my priorities ranked according to their importance to the Kingdom?

This is the battle line with the enemy for a serving believer of God. If Satan can't keep us from coming to Jesus, his second strategy is to keep us from being an effective witness for the Lord. In a nutshell, the devil will try to keep us busy doing anything but truly serving and living for God. This busyness thrown at us could be anything from worry, housework, and cutting the grass to including even "church work" (you know how I mean by that). Many of these things need to be done, not worried about, in their order of importance to the Kingdom.

Housework doesn't come before reading the Word or time spent in prayer. Cutting the grass doesn't come before a brother in need. I think a good place to start to arrange our priorities would be to base their importance according to the commands of God. Love God with all your heart, mind, soul and strength and love your neighbor as yourself. In short I want my priorities to be: 1) God, 2) other people and 3) everything else.

Keep Putting The Food Out   October 18

Do you ever get discouraged in your ministry or in your witness to others? You know to keep on keeping on, but you really want to see fruit manifested faster. Nothing is happening, or it just seems that way sometime. I'm not whining now, this is encouragement to someone, I hope and pray. (It would have been whining on my part last week.)

I can get a little irritated when things don't go the way I envision they should play out. I'm pretty straight with God about this kind of stuff. My irritation and impatience is easy for Him to "discern" as I openly complain to Him or to someone in who I may confide. These open displays of impatience are often met with a necessary swift kick in the butt (spiritually speaking), not a gentle nudge!

Sometimes, in ministry or witness to people, we may make our best effort to draw them to God. We may even be right on the mark as far as moving in His will towards someone, but it doesn't play out as we think it should. Result: Frustration. We may think we missed God and His direction. Probably not!

If we have been seeking His will and way in a matter, and have been obeying His direction, the problem is probably one of expecting a different or quicker outcome, not missing God's plan. We are called to obey, not to ensure the outcome. That's His department.

I've got this Mom and Pop business on my route that feeds all these stray cats that live in the woods next to their shop. These cats seem to be acting a lot like people searching for something to "fill them." Mom and Pop put out some food and when they go inside the cats come up and eat. At first, any attempt to approach the cats sends them running. As time goes on, and Mom and Pop continue to put the food out, the cats become more trusting because they see Mom and Pop taking care of them. After awhile, Mom and Pop are petting the cats as they eat the food.

If you are in ministry or trying show Jesus to someone, don't be discouraged the first few times you put the food out. Just keep feeding them until they know you love them and that they can trust you. In God's time they will see Him and come to know Him themselves.

Keep putting the food out!

Routine Busters   October 19

I get comfortable in my routine. Each day I go to work I expect a certain consistency. I case up mail in order of delivery. Then I load it in the truck in a particular way and deliver along the same route everyday. I'm OK with that, in fact there is a certain peace and comfort to the routine of it all, knowing what to expect, with no surprises.

Except, there is often something that breaks my routine. Sometimes it's a little thing like leaving late with more mail than usual. This throws my timing off for breaks, lunch and potty stops. These are small inconveniences.

Other days it's someone parking in front of their mailbox, so that I can't just pull up in my vehicle and drop their mail in and pull away. This causes me to have to stop, turn the truck off, get out and walk to their mailbox to make the delivery. This is a moderate aggravation.

There are other small and moderate routine busters such as parents letting their small children run out in front of the mailbox to meet the postman and bring the mail back to them. And of the course those who let their "he won't bite" dogs out.

Then there's the big obstacles, like road construction. These guys may block mailboxes for blocks or even pull them up to do their work. This is a major "routine buster!" Depending on how big of a project this is, I could have to get out and walk through their work area to deliver to people. It can cause time consuming detours. I may even have to readjust the route's line of travel temporarily. Major aggravation!

I feel like God does this to my routine quite often. I'm just cruising along with everything clicking smoothly as I go through life. Then an inconvenience, aggravation or obstacle pops up and I have to come out of my "comfort coma" and decide how to proceed.

In the Kingdom, routine busters may inconvenience us and be aggravating. They may even be large obstacles to overcome, but they will most certainly grow us.

For me, these road blocks in life continue to teach me to trust God more and more. I admit to wanting to take control of these kinds of situations in life and just fix things myself. But it's the times that I ask God and trust His answer that things work out for the best. When I just charge ahead through the road block, I'll usually drive right into a hole!

Some times the detour is the best choice. Other times, we may have to push through the road block. And then there will be times when we need to just stop our truck (life, agenda) and help fix the road. Stop. Ask Him. Trust Him. Obey Him.

First Round Pick   October 20

For You created my inmost being; You knit me together in my mother's womb. I praise You because I am fearfully and wonderfully made; Your works are wonderful, I know that full well. My frame was not hidden from You when I was made in the secret place, when I was woven together in the depths of the earth. Your eyes saw my unformed body; all the days ordained for me were written in Your book before one of them came to be. – Psalm 139: 13-16

I remember watching the first round of the NFL Draft in 2010. The talking heads were trying to figure out who would be picked next. Team representatives would decide who their team should pick based on the teams needs and the availability of an athlete to fill that slot. The athleticism, character, work ethic, past performance and an ever growing list of traits of an athlete desired by a team played into the selection.

The selection of the player doesn't automatically put him on the team. He must agree to play for the team, sign a contract and then go to work. After all of this, it still may not work out because man isn't perfect, even with all the knowledge he has, man cannot see the future clearly.

God is perfect. God does know all your talents. God can see your future clearly.

Many people say, "I don't have much talent," "I can't speak in front of people," " I'm a behind-the-scenes sort of person, kind of shy, you know." These kind of statements reflect the value we place on ourselves based on what man thinks, not what God says about us. All sorts of talents are needed and can be used in the Kingdom, behind the scenes, not just out front where man places the value.

That night was the first round of the draft. This is when the teams try to get the best players they can to fill their team's deepest needs. In football, quarterbacks, running backs, receivers, and to some degree defensive backs get most of the press. These are the guys that are in the "limelight," the so called "skilled players." This night however, out of the first 32 players picked to fill team's most desperate needs, only 2 quarterbacks and a few other "skilled players" were chosen. The majority of players chosen to fill the deepest needs of these teams were linemen! The guys in the trenches. The guys that make it possible for the "skilled players" to move the ball!

God has drafted you to be on His team. He knows you have the talent to be on His team, He put it there.

Whether you are a "quarterback" or a "lineman," you are His first round pick! So, agree to play on the team (receive Jesus), sign the contract (give your life to Him), and get in the game (serve Him). You've already got the talent. He will show you how to use it. He's the best coach in the game. He's undefeated!

Yeah Baby!   October 21

There is often a lot of buzz around this household and right now is no exception. Currently it's baby time! No, not Hannah, my son's beautiful wife, Brianna, is pregnant with grandchild number two. We are fired up!

Yesterday they went to the doctor. Brianna is healthy, the baby is healthy and all is well. They also found out what sex the baby is and they have pictures. You can actually see the baby nowadays in these pics, unlike when my wife was pregnant and you couldn't see squat! During my wife's pregnancy, I remember the nurse saying, "See, there's the foot." I was thinking, "You don't see diddly!"

Looking at those pictures has me thinking my grandbaby feels all safe and warm inside it's little world right now and has no idea what awaits it on the outside. I'm not talking about troubles. I just mean the change from one world to another.

Those of us on the outside are so excited we can hardly wait! We know some of what awaits this baby. The fun of seeing it grow up into a child, adolescent and then adult. Who will it grow up to be? What will it like to do? Fish with Papa no doubt! We get to help, watch and enjoy this journey firsthand as we love this child the whole way! There will be a lot of times in this child's life that we will see glimpses of Heaven in action!

I'm thinking the angels feel the same excitement in Heaven as each believer is born into the Kingdom family. The prebirth excitement builds until the birth of another Kingdom's Child! Then there's a party!

All of us were spiritual babies in the womb at one time. We were probably warm, happy and content with our lives, not knowing what awaited us before we were birthed into the Kingdom. It has taken, or will take, the love, encouragement and instruction of those who love us, to guide us into being the mature believers we need to be.

Oh yeah, I called the baby: "Baby," "child" and "it," in this story. So do you want to know if it's going to be a boy or a girl? Well of course it is!

In God We Trust...Really   October 22

I guess I have been putting this blog off for a while because I truly hesitate to talk politics.

To be fair, I will say that I am very conservative in my views. For instance, I believe abortion is a taking of a life. Watch one on an ultrasound and tell me something is not dying. To die, it must have been a life. Another sore spot for me is "money for nothing." The lazy should not benefit from the hard work of their fellow man. Don't try to tell me it doesn't happen. I see where the checks go!

Now, to be fair again, I also see where the checks don't go. It is no secret that the truly poor, underprivileged, and downtrodden in our country have not been given a fair shake. This should be remedied in some way.

You would have had to have your head in the sand to not know that our country is becoming more and more divided on many issues. People on both sides of these many issues are becoming more vocal and active.

I know this will sound simplistic, but I see the situation, as it stands right now, like this: One side thinks the government should have a hands on approach in solving the issues at hand, while having a more liberal slant. The other side thinks we should vote out those people now in the government and replace them with those who would have a more hands off approach, while having a more conservative slant.

The problem, with both sides, is that there seems to be the mentality of: "We can fix it, trust us." Well, I don't! I do think that we should do what we think is right. So vote and respectfully speak your mind.

I know there are believers and non-believers on both sides of the issues. I also know that believers should have as their source for decision making, the wisdom of God. Man is not going to fix this independent of the hand of God!

Going after a man or a party, to blame or fix this situation, is not going to heal our land. Going after God is! Believers on both sides need to seek God's will and way in these times. Have we become insensitive to God as a country? Do we still trust Him or have we turned our trust to man? Have we turned away from God as children of Israel did in the Old Testament? Is it time for 2 Chronicles 7:14?

... if my people, who are called by my name, will humble themselves and pray and seek my face and turn from their wicked ways, then I will hear from heaven and will forgive their sin and will heal their land.

Well, is it time?

Relief Now   October 23

Cardinals! In the World Series! Are you kidding me! God is messing with the "Baseball Fan."

For those who are not fans, I'll give you a quick summary. For those who are baseball fans, go back with me a few weeks.

With roughly a month left in the season, the Cards are ten games out of playoff contention. History as well as every sports analyst and unbiased observer have written the Cards off for this year. Even most Cards fans I know are more concerned if Albert will be back next year than the possibility of a playoff berth. (Don't write in the comments here that you knew the Cards were going to make it all along. You know lying is a sin!)

Anyway, several of the Card's players had been injured over the course of the year and seemed to all get well at once. Secondly, the manager (LaRussa) who is a few miles short of a class act, made all the right moves at the right times. He does know his baseball and is particularly adept and innovative in the strategies of the game. As it turns out, everything that had to happen for the Cards to get into the playoffs did happen. The Braves collapsed and the Cards kept winning. The Cards were in the playoffs.

Once into the playoffs, LaRussa again changes the game. He starts using front line bullpen guys in nontraditional roles and uncommon situations. Generally a manager saves the best relief pitchers for the later innings, to preserve a lead. However, for the most part (outside of Carpenter), the Cards starters don't match up well with the other teams starting pitching (particularly the Phillies). Larussa does know that his bullpen is better than most, so he brings his better relief pitchers in at the first sign of trouble because if he leaves in a struggling starter there may be no lead to preserve.

Larussa's brilliant strategy works and the Cards are in the World Series!

There are several things I think we can take away from this unbelievable run by the Cards.

1) Lets not be so proud that we can't learn from others, that we may not be a fan of, like Larussa.

2) Correct bad situations at the soon as possible, so that they don't get worse or even become seemingly insurmountable.

3) Lets not be afraid of change just because it's something new and "we have always done it this way."

Real Or Fantasy   October 24

    This is my second season of playing Fantasy Football. Your season begins as you join a league. This can be a group of guys you know or you can randomly join a league on the Internet. Then, at a predetermined time, you meet with the other league members and draft players in turn. Once the games begin you get points according to how your players perform. The person who gets the most points wins that game. The people who win the most games get into the playoffs. If your team wins the playoffs you are the champ. It's easy, fun and nobody gets hurt.

    As a boy I played "real football." There was no "fantasy" to it! I ran till I puked. I banged bodies violently, getting injured, cut, bloody and dirty. I played in heat, rain, and one game in rain so cold that when I tackled someone we landed in ice! Real football is hard, not always fun and sometimes you get hurt.

    The difference is, in real football I took a risk and it cost me something, sometimes a lot, but "real victory" can be the reward.

    Sometimes we believers live our lives like a fantasy football player. We might be going through the motions of living a godly life but we let the real players do all the work and then we expect the points to go on our scoreboard.

    We all need to be in the real game to gain real victory. Contrary to what some say, living a godly life is not always easy, fun and no one gets hurt. Instead, it takes true commitment and effort. It is often hard, not always fun and sometimes you do get hurt, but the rewards can be victories with eternal value.

    Don't ever tell anyone the Christian walk (following Jesus) is easy. But never forget to tell them of His love and the rewards that await the real players. Put on your pads (armor) and get in the game!

Finally, be strong in the Lord and in his mighty power. Put on the full armor of God, so that you can take your stand against the devil's schemes. For our struggle is not against flesh and blood, but against the rulers, against the authorities, against the powers of this dark world and against the spiritual forces of evil in the heavenly realms. – Ephesians 6:10-12

The View From Above, Childlike Faith
October 25

Don't you wish you could see clearly what is happening all around you in the spirit realm? I remember hearing analogies of God's ability to direct us because He sees all things that we cannot see with our own eyes. For instance, God is like a guy in a helicopter flying above us as we travel down a road with curves and hills. We can't see far enough ahead to tell if it is safe to pass the slow truck in front of us. However, if we are in communication with the guy in the helicopter, he could tell us if it is safe to pass the truck.

I know there is the matter of faith involved with the guy in the helicopter, but if he truly loves us he will not mislead us.

Another analogy is of the little boy looking through a knothole in a privacy fence to see if the coast is clear to retrieve his ball he tossed into the neighbors back yard. It looks all clear through the knothole, until Dad comes out and looks over the fence to see cactus plants next to the fence on the other side and the neighbors bulldog asleep on the back porch.

Again, childlike faith is needed to trust that Dad knows what is best here, even if we can't see things clearly from where we stand.

This truth of God's perspective and childlike faith was driven home in my life again by my three year old granddaughter Ella, as we visited Ben and Brianna this past weekend. Ben and I were out on his balcony that overlooks a very large field of high, thick grass. It was nearly dark, as he was cooking on the grill at sunset. Just then three deer came into the field across from us. We called Ella out to see them. They were getting hard to see as it got darker, but we could make them out as they moved about.

From the perspective of the upstairs balcony we could see the deer in the field, but if we would have been on the ground within a few feet of those deer in that field of thick grass, there is no way we would have even known they were there.

This is the way it is with our God. He can see clearly what surrounds us and He can tell and show us how to navigate our lives. He sees the danger and troubles we may encounter and how to avoid or best go through them. He also sees the treasures and blessings we may walk right by because we are unaware they are within our reach, if we will just obey His direction.

Now for the childlike faith part of the lesson God showed me through Ella. The next evening I purposely went out on the balcony at sunset to watch the colors in the sky, a beautiful sight and work of God. Shortly after I went out on the balcony and sat down, Ella came out and sat down with me.

"What are you doing, Papa?" she said.

"I'm watching the sunset, Ella. Isn't it pretty? But it will be dark soon."

Immediately her reply was: "Then the deer will come out."

My immediate unspoken response in my mind was, "Yeah, I doubt that … "

Before I can complete the thought, three deer started across that field! I was shocked, surprised, blown away by God and Ella's (maybe not even realizing the concept of it) childlike faith! Ella was maybe amazed at seeing the deer again, but I could see it on her face, she wasn't surprised. Those deer were going to come across that field. She didn't just think it, she expected it, she knew it! Thank You, Lord! Thank you, Ella! You're an anointed teacher!

Trust in the Lord with all your heart and lean not on your own understanding; in all your ways submit to him, and he will make your paths straight. – Proverbs 3:5-6

Waiting For The Fog To Lift   October 26

We are all ready to go fishing this morning.

The boat is ready to go. The motor is in good working order. I went and filled it with gas last night. The trailer is hooked to the truck.

The fishing gear is ready to go too. I rigged all of the rods and reels last night for the fish we will be trying to catch. I got trolling rigs ready for mackerel, lures ready for trout, surf rigs ready for pompano and bottom rigs ready for the rest.

I've got ice in the ice chest, drinks in the ice, bait on the boat, a net, a gaff and a tackle box on board. We are good to go!

Yet, here we sit. What are we waiting for? The right timing.

The best results in fishing are obtained when we can be out there at the right time. No matter how sophisticated your equipment, no matter how fancy your boat, if the timing (weather conditions, tides, etc) are not right, you will get skunked!

The problem this morning; fog, thick soupy fog. When it's foggy, the worst fog will be on the water. It sometimes get so thick your visibility is zero. You could hit anything before you see it and sink or be injured. When you're moving in fog in a boat, you can't hear other boats with your motor running, much less see other moving vessels.

So here we sit, waiting for the fog to burn off or blow away. Waiting for the right timing.

It's this way in the spiritual Kingdom too. We may know what God wants us to do or be in our lives. We may feel we are equipped and ready. We may feel the time is now, and it may well be time. But lets be sure, so as not to get ahead of God. His timing is part of His will, not just knowing what to do, but also when to do it.

In the Bible, David knew for a long time he would become King of Israel. It was definitely God's will. He had several opportunities to kill Saul himself and become King. However, he knew it wasn't time for him to be King yet. So, he waited on God.

We should be diligent and patient when carrying out His will in our lives. We should be equipped and ready to move when He says to move. His timing is crucial!

The Regular Guy, Who's Not So Regular
October 27

Last night I was listening to an acquaintance of mine talk to one of my friends as we ate supper. He was telling my friend about where he worked. He is employed at a place that houses and ministers to young people who find themselves in difficult circumstances. They may be unemployed, without shelter or find themselves in a combination of difficult situations.

As I heard him tell about where he works, I became more attentive to the conversation because God has been putting the homeless and people in difficult circumstances on my heart. I have even recently begun to investigate educational opportunities in social work, so that I might be able to help and minister to those in need. So, I ask him specifically what his job was at this place. I was expecting him to tell me about counseling sessions and rehabilitation strategies.

Instead, he tells me he is the maintenance man. I hope he didn't notice the look on my face, as I was expecting him to tell me about his hands on ministry at this place.

Then he did tell me just that. He said; "Sometimes I teach them how to do essential daily task such as checking oil in their car and little fixes around the home." Then it hit me, this guy is probably discipling these young people as much, if not more, than some counselor in a group meeting. I was thinking; if I am someone who is in a bind, do I feel more comfortable sharing my problems in a group meeting or with the guy who will take his time to show me even the little things about every day life?"

I don't think I'm going to seek out educational opportunities in social work anymore. I'm pretty handy! Maybe I will just call some of the shelters and see if they need a maintenance man.

The Back Burner   October 28

I like to cook some real breakfast for myself any morning that I have the time. I have a new griddle that is just the thing. I can flop some bacon down on that bad boy and by the time I flip the bacon the first time I can put some eggs or pancakes on there and I am eating in no time.

Well, yesterday morning that was my plan. That is until I got up and found a pot of spaghetti sauce simmering on the stove where I usually place my griddle when I cook. (Hannah Pooh is selling spaghetti dinners for a fund raiser. Great stuff too!) There is really no other good place to place the griddle when I use it to cook my breakfast.

Grudgingly, Plan B goes into action. I grabbed a pan out of the cabinet and went to the stove. I realized then that the spaghetti sauce was on the big burner in the front. Almost without a thought, I started to move her sauce to the back burner so that I could have the convenience of the front burner. It's as if my breakfast is more important than her sauce. It was right about then God goes, "Oh, you're going to put her stuff on the back burner again?"

Sadly, that is the way it is a lot of the time. I don't think it's just Hannah and me, is it? We think the stuff we need to do is more important. We often want to put other people's needs, or even other people themselves, on the "back burner" until we get around to them or their needs. I mean, how does it feel to us when someone puts our needs on their back burner?

I don't know about you, but the hardest thing for me to give isn't money or possessions, it's my time. Instead of God saying: "Love your neighbor as yourself," what if He said give your neighbor, family member and everybody else all of your time that they truly need? What if He said to put your own stuff on the back burner! As far as I can tell, that's what "love your neighbor" means.

Do not withhold good from those who deserve it, when it is in your power to act. Do not say to your neighbor, "Come back later; I'll give it tomorrow"—when you now have it with you. – Proverbs 3:27-28

God loves us, and He wants us to love others like He loves us. One of the greatest gifts we can give is our time. Which will undoubtedly require us to put our own stuff on the "back burner."

Use It, Cause You Don't Lose It   October 29

One of the most fun things I personally enjoyed while my sons were growing up was coaching little league baseball. Honestly, I probably liked it more than them. However, they enjoyed it enough to play for years.

During this time I saw kids with hardly any raw talent become pretty good players. I saw those gifted with raw talent, who with disciplined practice and use of that talent, moved on to play high school, college, and even professional baseball. Many of these are godly men, most of them are not playing ball anymore themselves, instead they are using their gifts to further the Kingdom and help their fellow man.

I know several who now coach baseball from little league to high school. They are a godly witness to young people and have a permanent impact on young lives. One young man uses his talents and friends with like talents, to put on a golf tournament to raise funds for children hospitalized with serious illnesses.

The other thing I saw while coaching baseball were the kids who tragically squandered the best gifts of raw talent I ever saw! The best pitcher (talent wise) I ever saw was a thirteen year old, who when he got to high school, was rebellious and subsequently thrown off the team. He never played ball again. The hardest playing kid (talent wise) I ever saw made a few trips to jail resulting from vandalism and fighting. The best all around player I ever saw just faded away, I'm not sure why.

God gives us all gifts and talents; the ability to do something well. I think most of us know what gifts we've been given. I also believe these gifts were given to us to glorify God. In glorifying Him we will see God move in our lives and the lives of others, not to mention the joy we experience seeing God use our gifts for Him.

So, without fear or pride, but with confidence that: "He who began a good work in you will carry it on to completion..."(Philippians 1:6) let's step into the ministry God has called us to and equipped us for. "For God's gifts and His call are irrevocable" (Romans 11:29). The gifts and His call are still there. Are we using our God-given gifts for the Kingdom or keeping them for ourselves?

Your Master's Degree　　　　　　　October 30

Last night I commented on a friend's remarks about going back to school at "her age." Those were her words, not mine. She's not that old in the first place. Anyway, if she hasn't changed a whole lot since I've seen her, her apprehension will not affect her resolve. This is not her first trip back to school. She's going for her Masters Degree this time.

Years ago there was a man who lived on my route that I used to talk to often. He would meet me at his mailbox several times a week. He was eighty-ish. He would tell jokes and great stories from his life. As a teenager, he had lied about his age to go to battle in World War II. He left high school, enlisted in the military and went to serve his country.

While I was serving as a youth pastor, I attended many high school graduations. On one such occasion, as they were calling out the names of the graduates receiving their diplomas, an unusual roar came up from the students. This applause was not from the crowd of the proud parents, but the graduates themselves. The name they called out was that of the old man from my route! I had no idea he had gone back to his old high school after sixty years. He had taken classes alongside the young students of the day and graduated with them on that night!

We all grow wiser and gain knowledge through different avenues. Some of us go to the school of hard knocks, some through technical training, some through OJT, and some through formal education.

So what am I saying? First, as in the case of my old friend from my route, God will give us all the time we need to fulfill what He has for us to do in the Kingdom. Time is no sweat. Second, He will train us, so we can train others. The question then becomes will we be obedient to take our training seriously, so as to be good teachers, as we pass what we have learned on to others.

You have all the time you need, "old" friend! God has uniquely equipped you to not only get your Masters Degree, but to pass that knowledge on to others you will lead. Yeah, I believe you are already a long way down the road to getting "Your Master's Degree!" Go get 'em, Nancy!

What Do You Do If — October 31

A friend asked me last night: "How would you react if someone was taking God's name in vain right in front of you?" Good question! It's an obvious sin and is understandably an offense to His Spirit.

Before I tell you my response to his question, let me say that it is wisdom on his behalf to ponder such situations before they present themselves (or before it presents itself again). I used to tell youth to decide, before they are actually put into compromising or difficult situations, how they should respond to that situation. Deciding beforehand gives us time to pray and think something through. The thoughtful, wise decision made prior to a difficult temptation or situation is then easier to act upon and avoids a spontaneous mistake that often results in serious consequences.

For example, I would ask the girls to think and pray beforehand about: What should you do if you are out on a date and the boy you're so crazy about asks you to jump in the back seat of a car with him? Like it or not, this is a real scenario that plays itself out nightly. If decided beforehand in prayer and godly thought, the spiritual and intellectual decision can be made instead of the spontaneous emotional mistake.

So, if possible, it is wise and pays off to decide our response to situations before they present themselves.

What was my answer to my friends question? Get in their face, cast that spirit out of them, tell 'em it's a sin and they're going to burn? No. Actually my first thought was Jesus saying:

"Do not judge, or you too will be judged. For in the same way you judge others, you will be judged, and with the measure you use, it will be measured to you." – Matthew 7:1-2

Then I said to my friend: "I have committed so much sin (including this one) that had it not been for the tons of the grace and mercy God has shown me, where would I be? I'd surely be dead, burning in hell right now!"

I think my friend can take it from there.

Talking Like I Write   November 1

I think I have written more in the last three or four years than the entirety of my life prior to today. Although I desire every word to be inspired of God, I'm sure there are many places where whatever comes to my mind immediately hits the page, without a filter.

This came to mind this weekend as I spent more time than I ever have conversing with (writing back and forth to) individuals over the Internet. Some conversations were long and some short. Yet it seemed as though the things we were discussing were of importance. They were discussions about the purpose of life and things of God.

I paused and considered how I wanted to reply to the other people's questions and comments each and every time, so that I would not only write the right thing but also be clearly understood. Yet as I talked to some folks face to face this weekend about issues of the same importance, I later realized that I had again responded spontaneously, without a filter.

My son and my wife have written books and I have seen the time they have taken to painstakingly go over their words to be sure they are conveying the message they want to get across clearly. I am going through the same type of effort now in my writing. I slowly "proof" what I have written so that nothing is written carelessly. I want to think about what I'm going to write so that I write exactly what I want my words to convey.

So why doesn't my mouth work the same way? My mouth can go off like a rifle stuck on automatic. I can carelessly shoot out "bullets" (words) without a thought to where they are going or the wounds they will inflict on others. And careless words can wound severely. Why is it then that I give pause to my written words more than my spoken words?

The answer lies in James 3:1-12 which includes: "It (the tongue) is a restless evil, full of deadly poison."

I'm going to ask God to give me a pause before I speak to or answer someone, so that I would consider my words and their effect before I spew them out. I want Him to be my filter.

Real Grass Or Artificial Turf   November 2

Have you ever been to a Major League Baseball stadium? Before the game starts, the field is manicured to perfection. It's picturesque and ready for play. I am a purist when it comes to baseball. My favorite way to play and see the game played is outside, in the daytime, on real grass, with wooden bats and without a designated hitter.

I can't stand what artificial grass does to the game. And it's not just baseball when it comes to fake turf, it's football too! Players get hurt on it more often, not to mention it changes the original intent of the game. Have you ever been tackled on artificial turf? It feels like concrete! How about trying to lay down a bunt on fake turf? It rolls like its on glass!

Real grass on a ball field takes a lot of care and effort to maintain at a level that is ready for use. It needs fertilizer, water, constant tending and meticulous care. Even with all this effort, it's worth it because real is best.

It also takes effort to be real in life. So often it would be easier to just put down some artificial turf over our lives and just fake it. But when we do lay down the "fake turf" on our lives it changes the original intent of our lives. Then maybe things get moving too fast for us to control and we get hurt. The artificial turf fades and wears out and we have to resort to laying down more fake grass so we can look more like the real thing for a while.

I believe God wants us to be like the real grass. Sure we are going to have a little wear and tear but He is the ultimate grounds keeper. Healing us when we are torn and restoring us when we are worn. Trimming us when we need it and watering us to make us grow. And when those weeds of sin pop up, we won't have to lay some fake turf over them, we just ask the grounds keeper to pull them out.

Jesus Christ: Tough Guy, Man's Man November 3

I think Jesus is and has often been viewed wrongly as a man (especially by men). When we see old movies, some music videos, Easter plays at church with the appearance of Jesus as a victim and at Christmas as a helpless baby, it contributes to a world view of Jesus "the man" as soft and even wimpy. We continue to hear of His love and mercy as we read the Bible or listen to a preacher and some (men especially) scoff at the notion of outward expressions of love and caring for others. What a load of crap!

First let me say that His birth, death, resurrection, His compassion, love and mercy are all central to our faith in Him as believers. However, in this case, I am addressing the not so uncommon view by some (mostly men) of Jesus (the man) as a soft, wimpy pushover.

Jesus was a carpenter. I have been a carpenter, a fisherman and a soldier and nothing is soft or wimpy in those occupations! I have worked on construction sights where carpenters endured extremes in weather and continual hard labor, and we had power tools. My grandfather was a carpenter and he thought he had it made when he got a circular saw! Do you think it was easier in Jesus' day?

Have you seen the various fishing shows on television where men fish for a living? Does that look like easy money? That was even harder back in Jesus' days on this earth! That's the kind of guys Jesus was around. He chose "real men" to be His disciples!

Not enough. How about Simon the Zealot? A rebel with a cause and I'll bet he would have fought the Romans to his death. He was one of Jesus' buds too!

Do you think it wimpy to go around the country openly preaching against the very people wanting to kill you? How about willingly dying for those you care about? I don't think so, I think that's at the top of the courage scale!

Do you fancy yourself a real man? Then how about following in the footsteps of a genuine "Tough Guy?"

Jesus Christ! Tough guy! Carpenter! Friend of fishermen and righteous rebels! Son of God! Loving and merciful Savior, too!

Waiting On Revival — November 4

Revival #1 - A move of God, by God, to refresh, renew, restore, revive and empower believers as well as powerfully drawing unbelievers to Himself.

Revival #2 - A scheduled event by a church or religious organization in expectation of God doing the same things as in Revival #1.

I am not knocking revival. I have been a participant in both types; some of the most exciting and wonderful times in my life!

But I do have questions. For instance; if God has moved in our individual lives, especially through some awesome and powerful revival or miracle, why do we sit around waiting for HIM to do it again? We pray: Do it again God! Do it again! I mean, is HE supposed to do it for us or are we supposed to do it for Him? Who works for whom?

My point is this: Sure pray for revival. Sure have special services inviting God to move in a mighty way. However, if God has worked in our hearts, then He and all His power is still in us every day, wherever we go, whatever we do, whoever we see.

So why hold Him in like a worm in a cocoon waiting for the next revival #1, if you get to see another one in this lifetime. Or wait on Revival #2 and see what happens Sunday through Wednesday night, when we are going to be there anyway and would probably not have to serve at all!

We should live revived everyday. If we truly want to see revival in our land we are going to have to live as a "revived people" in our lives daily for others to see Him.

What are we waiting for? Revival is right there inside of us. Open the cocoon and see what comes out.

The Dirty Boat — November 5

I spent about half the day yesterday cleaning my boat. I have been diligent about keeping the motor in good operating condition. I washed the boat and trailer down after each use. For most of the time I have owned this boat it has been garage kept so that the elements of nature and weather didn't affect it too much. However, for the last couple of years I have stored it outside in shaded areas of my yard. This helped keep the heat of the sun from damaging the boat seats and such, but the trees leaves, sticks and dirt just made the inside of the boat filthy. A lot of mold and mildew built up on the inside of the boat over time.

I was determined to clean the inside of the boat. I began by vacuuming out the leaves, sticks and pecan shells. Quite a bit of difficulty in this task because of all the nooks and crannies in the stern of the boat. Then I would spray an area down with cleaner, scrub like mad for awhile and was getting pretty good results. About a third of the way back in the boat I had sprayed an area on one side and forgot about it as I worked my way down the other side. I looked back a few minutes later and saw that the area I had forgotten about was clean and shiny. I had not scrubbed it a bit! The cleaner had done the job all on it's own.

It's a whole lot harder to keep the inside of a boat as clean as the outside appears to be. When I get back from fishing, a quick rinse of the smooth outer surface is all it takes for the whole boat to appear clean from the outside. But if you climb up inside the boat you can see the grime and filth that can build up on the inside.

Jesus said:

"Woe to you, teachers of the law and Pharisees, you hypocrites! You clean the outside of the cup and dish, but inside they are full of greed and self-indulgence. Blind Pharisee! First clean the inside of the cup and dish, and then the outside also will be clean.

Woe to you, teachers of the law and Pharisees, you hypocrites! You are like whitewashed tombs, which look beautiful on the outside but on the inside are full of the bones of the dead and everything unclean. In the same way, on the outside you appear to people as righteous but on the inside you are full of hypocrisy and wickedness." – Matthew 23: 25-28

The boat is not completely clean until the inside and the outside are clean, and neither are we. We can do the quick "outside rinse" on our appearance and put on a false face trying to appear as if everything is alright. Some may notice or suspect something is wrong on the inside of us, but only two persons know for sure, ourselves and God.

The Good News is that it's a whole lot easier to clean the inside of ourselves than you might think. You don't have to do one bit of "scrubbing." You just spray on the right Cleaner, Jesus. He'll wash us and make our inside clean as new! For free!

Potatoes And Gravy   November 6

I've have always been blessed to have outstanding "Southern Cooks" in my family, including Hannah Pooh, who learned from some of the best. My mom, who grew up in the North, must have caught on really quickly because I honestly don't remember a bad meal she cooked. And as for my grandmother, you just don't get food any more "Southern" than from her kitchen.

From the time I can remember having to use a fork or spoon, my favorite has been mashed potatoes and gravy (with Oreos as a close second and a great follow-up). To this Southern boy, they go together like cake and icing, syrup and biscuits, peanut butter and jelly, cookies and milk … you get the idea.

Mom or Grandmother would make mashed potatoes and put them on the table while they were still steaming! Next would come the bowl of homemade gravy. Let me say the blessing please, 'cause we need to get to these taters before they cool off. Yeah, baby!

We all have physical needs. Such as food, clothing and shelter. That's the potatoes. Everything else is "gravy" (cars, furniture, jewels, boats, etc). Spiritually speaking, the good news of Christ, the love of the Father, the working of the Holy Spirit in our lives, those kinds of things of God … that's the potatoes. That's the sustaining food of our soul. That's all we really need. The thing is, God likes gravy too! He likes to put it on our "spiritual table." God's gravy is blessings from Him to us. We just have to be sure that we're not at the table just for the gravy. Put the potatoes on your plate first.

My "gravy?" My family together. Thanks, Lord. The gravy just doesn't get any better than this!

Real Eyesight   November 7

How about this grown man in John 9 who was blind from birth? Jesus came along and healed him of his blindness. I would say he was having a pretty good day!

Try to imagine being in his shoes! Blind since birth and all you know is darkness. Even though people try to explain to you what vision is, you don't get it. You've never experienced it. How can you understand what they are talking about?

Then this guy comes along who can show you what it is to see. He's not all talk. This guy takes miraculous action! He touches your eyes with some cool wet dirt and tells you to go wash it off. Something stirs inside you and though you don't understand what's going on, you do what He says.

As you wash off the dirt, the light in your eyes is so bright you still don't see objects. Then things start to come into focus. You see all the beautiful colors of the sounds you've heard all you're life! The water you washed your eyes with is clear blue. The bird singing is bright red. The dog barking at you as you jump for joy is golden brown. And the faces of people that are witnessing this change in you are turning pale. Their mouths are a gaping hole as they see an act of God before their very eyes.

Spiritual blindness manifest itself in the same way. We can tell people about Jesus all day long. But can we show them Jesus? Can they see Jesus in us? Has He really changed us so that others can see Him clearly in us? Does our "walking" testimony match our "talking" testimony so well that they would be stirred to the point of trusting Jesus?

If they are stirred to an act of faith and trust in God, then they will see spiritually. They will receive new vision that they have never had before because they are no longer blind to the things of God. How will they know where to go if they can't see?

Weren't we all blind until we were healed?

Running To And Fro   November 8

Have you ever had to deal with a bully? When I was around five years old I lived in a neighborhood with a bully. We'll call him Ken. He was larger than me and my friends and would chase us and try to beat us up.

There was one other boy in the neighborhood that was about the bully's size and could handle the bully with relative ease. He was the neighborhood hero. We'll call him Andy.

Whenever Ken would come around, my friends and I were off and running from him, unless Andy was around. Then he would take care of business. If we were out and about in the neighborhood when Andy wasn't around and Ken showed up, we would be running from Ken (looking back as we ran to see him gaining on us) with little or no hope of getting away safely. However, if Andy was around, or we knew where he was, we could run to him with the hope and even expectancy of being rescued.

Sometimes it would end as we wanted it to, with Andy beating the crap out of Ken. Other times Ken would know who we were running to or see Andy coming to our rescue and that would be enough to send Ken running back in the other direction.

I think we may at times fall into this way of responding to crisis or to a sin we committed. We may take off running from the devil without our destination being Jesus. We have some difficult situation come up in our lives and we take off running out of fear of the enemy. We look back at him chasing us and see him gaining on us!

The right response, however, would be to run to Jesus. A good thing in this scenario is that while we have our eyes on Jesus as we run toward Him, He is running toward us and He's the fastest runner in this race!

There is no hope of rescue just running from the enemy. But there is assurance of being saved by running to Jesus!

We can look back at our problems and who we were, or we can focus on Jesus and become who He wants us to be.

Where are your eyes focused?

Stick To The Plan   November 9

Yesterday, I had a ton of mail to case (put in route order) before leaving the office for the day's deliveries. So much so that I required assistance to deliver it all by the prescribed return time.

The boss said to give my helper however much mail I needed to give Him for me to able to return to the office on time. When the help arrived, I gave him less than I should have because I knew he had to go help someone else too. If I gave him more, it would have made him and the other person much later.

Upon returning to the office, my boss was less than pleased. None of us had made it back by the requested time. I pleaded my case. The other two carriers would have been later. Nevertheless, had I given my helper a little more mail (which is what he had directed me to do), at least I would have been back on time. Apparently, this would have been a better result according to the boss' plan.

Ephesians 6:5-6:8:

Slaves, obey your earthly masters with respect and fear, and with sincerity of heart, just as you would obey Christ. Obey them not only to win their favor when their eye is on you, but as slaves of Christ, doing the will of God from your heart. Serve wholeheartedly, as if you were serving the Lord, not people, because you know that the Lord will reward each one for whatever good they do, whether they are slave or free.

I know most everyone reading this is probably not a slave, but this passage does give us encouragement to be responsible and have integrity on the job. Yesterday, even though I was trying to be helpful to the other two carriers, I did not follow the boss' plan. He is the one with the overall picture of what he is trying to accomplish. It is not my job to change his plan.

What happens if we as believers decide we are not going to follow God's plan at this point or that point? What happens if we go around screwing up His "big picture" because we don't like the plan or don't know plan, or worse, think we have a better plan? God knows the big picture. Stick to His plan!

Louie Mode   November 10

When I get home everyday, who's there at the gate to greet me? Hannah? One of the crew? Nope. Louie! That's right, my dog. As I pull up and get out of my truck, he starts barking and whining. He's announcing to the world that I am home.

It's as if he were saying: "Yes, you're home, come on in here! Let me jump up on ya' and lick ya' some!" Then he thinks: "OK, I know where we're going, follow me." Then he struts proudly (yes, he does the "Louie strut") towards the door with an unquestionable assurance that the house is our next destination. That's the way it has always been before.

A couple of weeks ago I began to screw up Louie's routine. I would come in the gate and walk right past the steps up to the door and instead go into the "Fishin Hole" to feed the fish before walking back to go in the house. Louie stopped at the top of the steps and looked at me as if to say: "What do you think you are doing? You're screwing up my routine.

How do you expect me to know what to do next? How do you expect me to lead you anywhere if I don't know where you're going?!"

Unfortunately, I spend way too much time in "Louie mode" in my relationship to God. Without asking God for guidance in an area of what to do or where to go I just take off in front of Him. I suppose I assume: "Well, we did it this way before or I know exactly where were going next. I know where to go, follow me, Lord!" Then I strut away without looking back, expecting Him to be on my heels following me.

It's not hard to see what's wrong with this picture. "Louie mode" is living our lives as if we are the Master; not just the master of our lives, but the master over God. Assuming, without asking Him, what His will is and then taking it from there ourselves.

All it takes to realize who the Master is, is to look back in our lives and see all the wonderful things He has done for us. Not just that, but how He has done many of these things in ways we least expected.

Why should I expect God to follow me? Who's the Master anyway? That's got to be the height of pride! I'm going to try not to live in "Louie mode" anymore. I'm going to try to walk with the Master so that I'll be right there when He does something good in my life.

Overboard   November 11

"These seas have to be twenty feet or better today, Mate!"

"Yes, Captain! What is that in the water off the starboard side?"

"Men in the water! Coming about! Drop the life raft and bring 'em aboard, Mate!"

"Thank you, thank you for rescuing us in this terrible storm!"

"It's OK now, we'll give you these life vests. You'll be alright now. OK Captain, they've got their life vests on. You can come about now and I'll throw them back in off the port side."

"NO, NO, AAAAAAHHHHHH!"

Is this the way it is in the Church today? Is this the way of the Christian world today? Do we lead people to the Lord and leave them as unequipped babes at the altar? Salvation is certainly the most important thing that can happen in a persons life. In John 3, Jesus told Nicodemus "you must be born again." Is this where our commitment to the Lord for these newborns ends? It should not be, but I'm afraid it is where many, if not most, are left to fend for themselves.

All of the words of Jesus are of utmost importance to us. And how important, valuable, and timelessly implanted in our minds are the last words of our loved ones when they leave us for an extended time or leave this life? So how important are the departing words of Jesus? In Matthew 28:19-20 Jesus says: "Go and make disciples of all nations...teaching them to obey everything I have commanded you."

Why don't we disciple new believers like we should? Someone might say: "I wouldn't know how." If that is true, it is certainly evidence that they were not discipled, so that person should seek out someone to disciple them. However, I believe most would say I don't have the time. Do they mean they have better, more important things to do with their time than the "Great Commission?" Again, if Satan cannot keep us from salvation, his next choice is to keep us from being effective for the Kingdom. If we don't make disciples, we are not being as effective as possible for the Kingdom of God.

Becoming a Christian does not make everything in this life easy; in fact, it is often quite the contrary. Just throwing them back in the water won't make the high seas subside. Jesus didn't say to the twelve: "OK, you met Me, now you know Me, see you in Heaven, have a nice day." Nope, He painstakingly poured years of His life into these twelve men after they became followers! Jesus could've snapped His fingers and the "twelve" would have known all they needed to know about everything in and of the Kingdom. Instead, by discipling these men the way He did, He was showing us how to disciple other believers!

Leading someone to the Lord and expecting them to be immediately fruitful is naive, foolish and dangerous!

It's the same as throwing them right back into the high seas they have been rescued from, with a life vest on. The "seas" of this world are extreme, dangerous, and literally life and death! Sure, Jesus could protect them, but wouldn't you rather be in the boat with the life vest on than in the sea? We are to make disciples, showing them how to build a dependable, seaworthy ship. Then we are to teach them how to navigate rough seas, how to catch fish and how to clean them. In other words, it isn't just hearing and knowing the Word, but also showing others how to apply and live out the Word of God in their daily lives. We do this by letting them see us living God's commands and teachings in our daily lives.

Got Disciples?

Now It's The Boat Motor   November 12

A few evenings ago (when I was going to be off from work the next day) I went out to get the boat and some gear ready to go fishing. I hooked the hose up to the motor and cranked it up. It barely ran at all, spitting and sputtering. Sounds familiar doesn't it? It was like an aggravating demon from my truck engine found a new home! Great, no fishing trip!

I know what you're thinking (if you've read "Running on All Cylinders", September 3), just get Hannah to go outside and pray over that boat motor and you'll be reeling in the fish in no time! I knew better this time, and I think you know what I mean. There are those times that I just know that I'm the one that messed up. I hadn't "Maintained The Motor." I had not cranked the motor regularly (each week or so). I had allowed old fuel to go stale in the gas tank. The carburetor jets had clogged up, choking the motor as it tried to run. If I had done what I was supposed to do, I wouldn't be out $300.

Unfortunately, we can let this happen to our relationship to God. Simply put, if we don't maintain the relationship (reading the Word, regular prayer, etc), things may go stale and not run so smoothly. As with any relationship we want keep close, it takes time and effort.

It will be a couple of weeks before I get my boat back from the shop. It seems that a lot of people have repairs to make because of lack of maintenance. Thankfully, it doesn't take weeks to restore our closeness to God.

How's your motor running?

Hold Me Back   November 13

Last night a good friend of mine came over and right off the bat he was telling me about a really good movie. It sounded good and I'm going to watch it soon. The conversation also reminded me that *Blindside* was now available on DVD. I asked him if he would like to watch it and he nodded. I bounced out of The Fishin Hole and went to the store nearby to get a copy. It was right by the checkout. Twenty-three bucks, but I really wanted to see this one. "This will only take a second," I thought to myself. I was only fifth in line.

Then it happened. The first lady in line was having some sort of disagreement with the checkout lady, who seemed to have no sense of urgency. She paged the manager, who never showed up. I began to feel a slight aggravation beginning to build in me. But I felt prompted to hold my tongue and say nothing. After a few minutes the lady customer gave up and went looking for assistance elsewhere.

The line behind me continued to grow, but I was fourth now and figured we would get moving. Not so fast, the checkout lady was beefing at the next lady in line about the woman who had just left as she moved the customers merchandise across the counter in a painfully slow pace. A picture of Hannah looking at me with those eyes that say: "Please don't say anything," came to mind and again, I held my tongue successfully. OK, we were moving again.

Then the phone began ringing as the next customer stepped to the counter. True to form, the checkout lady leisurely answered the phone and had a minute long conversation. Then the slight aggravation in me was growing into a pain, but I was again prompted to just be quiet. As the checkout line grew to about twelve, she finally called for someone to open another register. *Already!* I sarcastically thought to myself, but I didn't say it out loud.

Like a mountain climber reaching the summit, I finally arrived at my long desired destination! This had been a trip through some kind of slow motion nightmare, but I was now at the checkout! Then she picked up one of their sale papers and started slowly flipping through it as if to see what she would like to buy for herself. That's it! I couldn't take it anymore! I'm was about to verbally assault this tortoise-woman! Then, once again, I was prompted to just maintain my fragile composure and be quiet.

Then she said: "Oh, here it is sir, the coupon for six dollars off this DVD." She scanned it and I got the movie for seventeen dollars, not twenty-three.

Was this a reward for holding my tongue? Well do you think that she would have bothered to look for the coupon for me if I had blown up at her at any of my several opportunities?

I know this, I have always battled my tongue. It just loves to be sarcastic, smart aleck and sometimes downright mean. And even though holding my tongue last night was a victory of sorts, I'm asking God to change my heart and mind so that the thought of speaking unkind to someone isn't in me. Then it won't take all that effort to hold my tongue.

"The good man brings good things out of the good stored up in his heart, and the evil man brings evil things out of the evil stored up in his heart. For out of the overflow of his heart his mouth speaks." – Luke 6:45

P.S. The First Hall of Famer at The Fishin Hole just sent me this great piece of counsel as a reply to this story. It is so good I had to share it: "I have learned the only way to not being ticked at slowness in others is to never be in hurry myself. Last minute chores, items to purchase ... last minute anything makes us raging rude!"

Street Wise   November 14

One of the hardest times for me to show and live with a Christ-like attitude is while driving. I don't mean to sound as if I have a godly attitude everywhere else I go, far from it! Anywhere fleshly frustrations happen (work, home or even church) I am apt to mess up. It just seems that the possibility for frustration is amped up while in traffic with folks who got their drivers licenses out of a Cracker Jack box!

Maybe it's the anonymity of it all. I live in a big enough city that I rarely pass someone I know on the road. Maybe it's that feeling of being anonymous that causes me to care a little less about my witness and behavior while driving. You know what I mean? People don't know me out here, so I can beat that guy in the other lane by stomping on the gas and cutting him off to "merge" into his lane ahead of him.

Another street peeve of mine is sitting in a line at a red light and when it turns green, Mr. Nice Guy (in the car in front of me) decides to let several cars from the side street go in front of him. Guess who is the last guy to get through the light? That's right, Mr. Nice Guy! I get to wait through another red light. By the time the light turns green again I am in a great frame of mind to be driving!

The funniest and maybe saddest thing we do is shout and scream at the guy who just pulled out in front of us, and he can't even hear us.

We scream at him how to drive, call him colorful names and curse his ancestry as he continues down the road oblivious to our tirade.

So, outside of safety, why should I be concerned about how I behave behind the wheel? I mean, who's going to know I'm throwing a fit at the guy who cut me off or got my parking spot? I can cuss him, maybe a little sign language when he's not looking or even wish another bad driver on him!

The thought that came to me today was not who would see me or find out about how I acted in my truck on the way to work today. My thought is that my behavior is still a testimony. It is a testimony to me of the true condition of my heart. Yeah, Ouch! The true condition of my heart is how I think and act when nobody else will ever see or know.

Servant Leader (I'm Just Sayin)   November 15

The other night I attended a retirement party for a friend of mine. I really don't get to spend much time with this man but it is always good to be around him. You know the kind of person I mean. The one you see only occasionally but when you do see him there is like this extra little boost of joy. He smiles when he sees you and you know it's real because he is genuinely glad to see you. The friend you have that you haven't seen in awhile but it seems like you could pick up with a conversation you may have had with him yesterday. That kind of a friend.

This night he is the man of the hour. This whole ceremony is to honor him for his life-long service to his country. I don't know about you but on a few occasions in my life when I was the special guy (on a much smaller scale, like my birthday) I was pretty full of myself. My friend was not that way on this night. Instead, on his special night he came over and greeted me. He asked how I was doing. He inquired (with genuine interest) about my family and me.

Later in the ceremony my friend told of how God had a plan for him to meet and marry his wife. He gave credit to her for what he had been able to accomplish. His son spoke of how he had always "left the uniform at the door" and was a great dad at home. All of those who worked with him and for him praised his leadership and care he shared with others.

However, the most memorable moment of the evening for me was when the MC ask if their was anyone (unscheduled speakers) who wanted to say anything about my friend. A young man went up to the microphone and said that CMSGT Paul was the most humble man he has ever known. Now that's high praise! What a wonderful mark Paul has left on those who have lived and worked with him. The love of and for God has obviously shown through him to others as he lived and worked in his everyday life.

I'm sure one day Paul will also hear: "Well done good and faithful servant ..." from someone else who was really good at being a servant-leader. I'm just sayin'!

## Service Men And Women	November 16

I was in the military for four years. I have to say for a great majority of the time, I enjoyed it very much. I remember believing that what I was doing mattered in the big scheme of things.

Thank you to those who have served, who are serving, and those who gave it all. What you are doing or have done makes a difference in all our lives. A heart that serves originates from the heart of God. Jesus is the Master, but He served. When Jesus was asked which commandment was most important He included, "loving your neighbor as yourself." This would include service to and for others.

Having been in the military and now living in a military town, I know a lot of veterans and people on active duty. There is this devotion to duty that overrides fear of the difficult task they may be called to carry out. It is not a pride in self, but a confidence in being equipped for their calling.

Military life cost the men and women in uniform a personal price. Their sacrifice also cost their loved ones. They are shipped off for long periods of time. They will be separated from their spouses and children and yet carry out their duties. You can thank them for every freedom you have, including the right to free speech. Which, by the way, is the one right we use before we think about how much it cost or where it came from or who it may cost for us to keep it!

These thoughts were brought to mind after running into some friends yesterday in a restaurant. I had not seen them in a long time. They are a married couple who are both in the military. I would proudly put their names here but I didn't ask them, and that's not why they serve anyway. They serve because it's their calling, not so they get any notoriety. I think I'll be in prayer for them whenever they or our service men and women come to mind. I'm going to pray that they are blessed beyond their wildest dreams by the God that can do "more than we can ask or imagine." I believe if there are "special" places in a special place like Heaven, that there is one for servants. In that section my two friends I saw yesterday and all the other veterans have a seat waiting for them.

Do you have some service men and women to pray for?

Shootout   November 17

A couple of years ago, as I was delivering my route on a narrow street, I came upon a gunfight in progress. These two (two-and-a-half foot tall) cowboys were going at it, pistols blazing!

The closest gunfighter had his back toward me and I slowly pulled right up behind him. He was oblivious to my presence. I resisted the temptation to blow my horn for fear of seeing Mr. Eastwood Jr. wet his pants and run off into the sunset!

Most pedestrians walking or standing in the street are frightened and immediately move off the road upon realizing a vehicle is bearing down on them. Not this hombre. He stood his ground in the middle of the street. He turned towards me and continued to blast away as spit flew out of his mouth while he was screaming, "pow, pow, pow!" He was going out in a blaze of cap gun glory.

It was time for me to pull out the big guns. Trying not to laugh at this pint size outlaw, I shouted at him to get out of the street. He reluctantly lowered his weapons and began to mosey out of the middle of the road. The siege had ended with no casualties except the gunfighter's pride.

Incidentally, I returned to the office that afternoon to find out there was a warrant for my arrest because "shorty" (his cowboy name) had told the "local sheriff" (his dad) that I had called him a "dork!"

What I came away with from this shootout was the question of, "What was this little bandito thinking as he stood there while my stagecoach was bearing down on him?" Did he really think he was in Dodge City and he had to stand his ground? Or, even though in reality the prospect of a large truck mushing him like a grape was a possibility, he trusted that I would stop and not run him down.

If the latter was what he was thinking, Proverbs 3: 5-6 comes to mind.

Trust in the Lord with all your heart and lean not on your own understanding; in all your ways acknowledge Him, and He will make your paths straight.

What I'm getting at is that we should trust God completely. Then when we find ourselves in a "shootout," He will be there to clear the streets. We will certainly have our shootouts with sin and the devil, but God is the perfect sheriff and will run these bandits out of our town!

God, That's Not Fair   November 18

"But that's just not fair!" How many times have you heard that one? How many times have you said that one? We hear it all the time from children who don't get to do what the older siblings get to do. Then as adults, we may hear it when someone feels they weren't treated equally. We may even scream it out in our own minds if we feel we have been wronged. Then we want the situation remedied to our satisfaction. Truthfully, that satisfaction may be to just get even, not for the sake of justice.

"For the Kingdom of heaven is like a landowner who went out early in the morning to hire workers for his vineyard. He agreed to pay them a denarius for the day and sent them into his vineyard.

About nine in the morning he went out and saw others standing in the marketplace doing nothing. He told them, 'You also go and work in my vineyard, and I will pay you whatever is right.' So they went.

He went out again about noon and about three in the afternoon and did the same thing. About five in the afternoon he went out and found still others standing around. He asked them, 'Why have you been standing here all day long doing nothing?"

Because no one has hired us,' they answered.

He said to them, 'You also go and work in my vineyard.

When evening came, the owner of the vineyard said to his foreman, 'Call the workers and pay them their wages, beginning with the last ones hired and going on to the first.'

The workers who were hired about five in the afternoon came and each received a denarius. So when those came who were hired first, they expected to receive more. But each one of them also received a denarius. When they received it, they began to grumble against the landowner. 'These who were hired last worked only one hour,' they said, 'and you have made them equal to us who have borne the burden of the work and the heat of the day.'

But he answered one of them, 'I am not being unfair to you, friend. Didn't you agree to work for a denarius? Take your pay and go. I want to give the one who was hired last the same as I gave you. Don't I have the right to do what I want with my own money? Or are you envious because I am generous?'

So the last will be first, and the first will be last." – Matthew 20:1-16

Some of the workers in Matthew 20:1-16 felt they were treated unfairly. The guys that worked an hour got paid the same as the guys that worked all day. The owner was fair to the guys who worked all day in paying them what he said he would pay them. But was it fair to pay the ones working only an hour the same wage? Not when viewing the story as a whole in the natural. The late comers got more than they deserved, especially in the view of the all-day workers.

Now we come to the question. What if God was fair when it comes to sin? What if He just allowed those who worked hard and long enough, to get into Heaven? Heaven would be empty! Thank God for His grace and mercy. Thank God for His sacrifice for our salvation. Thank God we don't get what we truly deserve! Thank God He doesn't treat us "fairly!"

Would Jesus Go To My Church   November 19

I sat down to write this morning and a strange question came to mind. Would Jesus go to my church? Would Jesus go to your church? The question in my mind is not one of "my church is better than your church," or some sort of holy ranking system. The question is more: "Is Jesus pleased with the Church in our country today?" I know, way too big of a question to be answered in less than 15 or 20 volumes of analysis and debate, but here's one angle.

Truthfully, as I ask myself this question, the first picture that came to mind was the church building I attend. Was that your first thought, the Sunday morning building you go to for worship? Just to clarify, the building is not the Church. The people that go there make up that church. The building is not the gateway to the Father in heaven, Jesus is. But would Jesus come there and worship or be the guest speaker?

In the Bible, Jesus went into the synagogues and taught and debated people (religious leaders) who had a lot of knowledge. However, these religious leaders did not lead as God desired. They led the way it served them best. They didn't obey God and use the knowledge He gave them to serve and lead others into the Kingdom.

So many people, often rightly so, see church as a dry, boring social club. I have felt this way about some churches I have attended. It seemed like trying to break into Fort Knox, just to find small, cold, uninviting groups called Sunday School classes waiting for me to join them, instead of being warmly invited. It's no wonder people quit hunting for a church, the love of Jesus is just not always evident!

One of the things that kept me from giving up on God was watching people who said they were Christians. Do these people really believe what they say? Do they really live out what they profess a couple of hours on Sunday morning. I know that sounds hard and judgmental, but that's where I was and I believe that's where a lot of people are today. They are hurt, skeptical and want to see the love of Christ in a real way, in their everyday lives.

I was in high school at the time and I was a bona-fide hellraiser. But secretly I watched all these Christians. I would see one after another do something that I would perceive as phony or sinful. I had no concept of applying the love of Jesus or His forgiveness to these peoples actions, so one by one I crossed them off my "Real Christian List." But there were these two guys who I never really saw screw up. I watched them a long time, and thanks to their daily life, I concluded that there were some real Christians out there.

So yeah, I think Jesus would come to my church. I think one of the messages He would bring would be to go and make disciples. I imagine He would say to us that most of those He would like us to reach aren't just going to walk into church. We need to go out into their world and show them His love.

I believe God has already brought this message to my church and many other churches. Prayerful and intentional efforts are being made individually and corporately to reach outside the building to those who are hesitant to enter. This is "Kingdom thinking," not "my church thinking!" Something is going on out there!

Things Are Not What They Appear
November 20

One of the things God has shown me from time to time in my life is that things are not what they appear to be to my earthly eyes. My grandmother told me of an event in her life that is a great example of "how things appear."

Grandmother is in her nineties now and getting younger every day! She has pretty much made up her mind about her likes and dislikes and is glad to inform others of her views. One of the dislikes in her world is roaches, upon which she will have no mercy.

Late one night she got out of bed and walked into the kitchen. It was dark and she had not turned on a light before she spotted a roach on the move just beneath her coffee table. Hurriedly, for ninety-plus, she returned to the kitchen for her fly swatter and commenced to putting the roach out of its misery. I can only imagine her shock, after turning on the light, to realize that she had committed fly swatter homicide on her goldfish, which had jumped from his bowl on the coffee table.

Another example was shown to me while we were having a youth event at the church. Many young people came in off the street to have fun and refreshments. One particular young fellow, maybe eleven or twelve, came into the youth room. He was wearing an old shirt and baggy britches that were obviously too big for him. You know the look. He headed straight for the treats and piled his plate with at least a dozen cookies! OK, fill in the blank here with your first thought _____. Alright, I'll tell you mine. "Did you want to leave a few of those for someone else?" As I headed over to straighten him out I noticed he did not go over and join in the games that were set up, but instead sat right down and devoured every one of those cookies first!

He was not trying to be cool in baggy clothes, instead he was seriously hungry! Be alert, you never know who may be in your midst (Matthew 25:31-46)!

Things are NOT what they appear to be!

We Have Louie Syndrome   November 21

    Yesterday I had to take Louie to the vet. You might say Louie doesn't get out much. We have a yard plenty big enough for him to run around in, so we don't take him out for walks too often. He rules his yard with an iron bark and a short legged strut of the king dog! He is the comfortable ruler of his own domain.

    As we prepared to go to the vet I put a collar and leash on him. He has been outside the gate enough to know the collar and leash means we're going somewhere. He wasn't making it difficult, he trusted me so far. It was when I put him in the truck that he seemed to start feeling some angst, some uncomfortable apprehension of leaving his comfort zone.

    It was funny to me seeing him march up and down the truck seat looking out the windows while trying to keep his balance as I stopped and started at the traffic lights. He was whimpering a little but he was seemingly still trusting me as I talked to him and scratched his back.

    Once we got into the vets office he began to unravel a little more. He never got out of control but he was definitely now in what was a totally foreign, uncomfortable situation. He would bark at everyone who came in and he even howled at a few. He would try to go check them out, but when he really tugged on the leash, the collar would choke him a little and stop him in his tracks. He was yielding to my control, but he didn't like it and he didn't like not knowing what was going on or going to happen next.

    Although he was nervous and unsure of what was going on or what was going to happen next, he figured trusting me was his best option. I did constantly try to calm him because I needed him to be obedient so we could achieve the best outcome for him. He may never understand it, but we did achieve the best result for him. A shot and some meds and Louie is going to be fine now. Yet had he rebelled (for instance bit me and ran off), his result could have been very unpleasant in more ways than one!

    I know I often behave like Louie towards God. There are things in which He calls me to be obedient to His leading. Often times I over analyze the situation and start whining and trying to talk Him out of it, even though I know I am supposed to obey His direction.

    There are times when obedience is easy. We see what's going on and can foresee the good outcome. Then other times we may obey, then see and understand the outcome later. But there are also going to be those times where we will not understand the Kingdom reasons for God's call to obedience this side of heaven.

I believe that God understands our apprehension and hesitation when we don't see what's happening or going to happen, so he will try to comfort us as we go. He will certainly go with us through what He calls us to and we will grow in our trust of Him as we follow His lead. It is OK to wonder. It is OK to question. It is not OK to disobey.

There's No Leash Law In The Kingdom
November 22

When I was a little boy we had and dog named "Muggie." He was part Dachshund, and looked just like one, except he was skinny.

Back then there were no leash laws, so sometimes he would run off for a while and come trucking back home in a few hours or even a day or so later.

One weekend, we went camping on a nearby beach. We thought it would be cool to take Muggie along with us. We set up camp, fished, cooked and did all that camping out fun. We looked up to find that the skinny mutt had run off. We went searching, but to no avail.

I was worried. There was no comfort for me in the fact that he had found his way home in the past. We were miles from home! Was he going to try to find his way back home? Did he go for a swim and a shark ate him? Were we going to have to go home the next day without Muggie?

Hours later he found his way back to the campsite. I was upset and disappointed in him, but I loved him anyway and accepted him right back into the family.

I was reading Proverbs this morning and read 22:6; "Train a child in the way he should go and when he is old he will not turn from it."

We had in some ways trained Muggie to come home. We had fed, cared for and loved him. He took note of where home was and would return to the place he knew was safe.

In my past as a youth worker I have seen many a "prodigal son." The Word doesn't say that none will ever stray. It says if we bring them up in the way they should go, when they are old they will not turn from it. If you have a child who has "left the camp," hold on to that Scripture and pray it over them.

If you are one who has left the camp, be sure of this: God is out looking for you. In fact, in His case, He is right there with you just waiting with open arms for you to turn around. He will welcome you home. Go ahead, turn around and see.

Paid In Full   November 23

Money and finances have been a source of anguish for me most of my adult life. Although I have made a decent amount of money for most of my life, I lived beyond my means. It was my own fault because I stayed stretched out through use of credit and lack of planning for the future. Plain and simple, I was a lousy steward of money! As I have written before, God has brought me a long way towards being debt free. I said all that to give perspective to what follows.

I had finally been able to save a little money and we needed to replace a glass door (See "Easy Renovation," June 21). Well, the price seemed to be creeping up. It wasn't a standard size door. I needed a few extras to make it work correctly. The little things added up. However we needed the replacement and we had the money. I bought and installed the door.

There was a different feeling this time from when I had made rather large purchases in the past. Prior to this, my decisions to make big purchases were mainly dependent on my available credit line. In other words, a not-so-sound financial strategy. This time it felt a lot different! I'm not sure you'll get this if you have been a good steward of money and not had credit crutches. The idea that this entire amount was going to come straight out of my bank account in one big chunk gave me pause to think and evaluate this decision from a different angle.

My thoughts: Is it worth it? It will cost a lot. But it will be paid for in full. Will I take it?

My response: It is. It did. It is. Yes, I did.

The Father's thought about sending Jesus to die for us: Is it worth it? It will cost a lot. But it will be paid for in full. Will they take it?

Your response here: _____

Waiting — November 24

Waiting stinks! We've all had to do it. I suppose our fast food, microwave society hasn't helped improve our patience when it comes to waiting. However, there is risk when we decide not to wait.

"The traffic light just turned yellow and I could stop, but if I stomp the gas I think I can make it before the other side turns green."

"Those lines are long at the theme park. Let's get a wheel chair for me to push you around in so we can cut to the front of every line."

"I'll just use this handicap parking in the front here. I haven't gotten a ticket so far."

Have you ever seen one of those movies with a high speed car chase that goes over a draw bridge? The bridge's horn starts to blow and the first car ignores it as the bridge starts to raise. He goes flying across as the bridge splits and goes up. The chase car, not too far behind, busts through the barricade and flies across the open bridge tearing the car to smithereens and injuring those inside.

Waiting can be aggravating, but it can be beneficial in many ways.

God's timing can seem the same to us: Aggravating, time wasting and useless!

UNBELIEVEABLE! As I am writing this story, the power goes out! It was just for a second, but guess what! I had to wait while everything rebooted so I could finish writing. The picture in my head is of Jesus just cracking up laughing! To continue …

I have written about how David knew he was to be king, yet he didn't take God's timing into his own hands.

Joseph continued to trust and serve God in all his circumstances as he waited to be delivered from his slavery and imprisonment.

Well, I know I'm not David or Joseph. However, I do perceive God is up to something and I don't want to wait! But I will, because jumping ahead of God would be a huge mistake! In the meantime I'll try to trust and obey Him where He has me right now.

I'll be waiting … on His timing.

The Dead Letter November 25

A "Dead Letter" is a letter that is undeliverable for some reason and cannot be returned for some reason. It cannot get to the addressee and it cannot go back from whence it came. This could be as a result of an incorrect address (bad number, wrong street, wrong town, wrong state or some omission of one of these parts of the address) and the same being true for the return address. The person has already paid the postage, so it either needs to be returned or delivered to its intended destination.

So, what is done with a "Dead Letter"? It is sent to the Dead Letter Office. Duh! There the letter is opened up and an attempt is made to determine the origin or the addressee.

Have you ever felt that way? Like a Dead Letter. I have. There I was, a Christian for whom the price had been paid (the postage). I didn't want to go back to where I came from but I also didn't have clear directions (assurance in my spirit) as to my destination. I found myself in an all too familiar place, the "Where do I go now?" place.

Where did I go to get out of that place you may ask? OK, maybe you wouldn't ask, but I'll tell you anyway. The spiritual Dead Letter Office! The situation was out of my hands. I came to the place where I said: "Open me up if you have to, Lord, but please show me where to go next!"

The analogy may come apart a little here because the Lord always knows our intended destination (our calling, mission field, true needs, etc.). However, if we surrender, He may choose to open us up a little (exposing some things in our lives that need to be cleaned out or dealt with) for us to see His will for our lives (the correct address).

God has and still is doing this in me. Every time I surrender and He opens me up, I grow. I am thankful and amazed at His mercy and forgiveness. Then I am humbled because I thought I was so much further along than this in my walk with Him.

Therefore, I urge you, brothers and sisters, in view of God's mercy, to offer your bodies as a living sacrifice, holy and pleasing to God—this is your true and proper worship. Do not conform to the pattern of this world, but be transformed by the renewing of your mind. Then you will be able to test and approve what God's will is — his good, pleasing and perfect will. – Romans 12:1-2

Recharge   November 26

One of the great inventions of my generation (second only to disposable diapers) is the remote control. I often tell people that my dad says he would not have had kids if there had been remote control, but someone had to change the channels. He didn't really say that, I just think it's a funny line.

Often when I go to bed, I will grab the remote and click it to a sports or weather station and nod off as I watch the weather forecast or catch up on the fade of the Braves out of the playoffs.

However, last night the remote didn't work. The batteries were dead. Great! Now I have to get up and go over to the TV and manually click through the channels to select what I want to watch. I have to choose well unless I want to get up again to change the channel. Of course I will have to get up anyway (at least one more time) in the middle of the night to turn the TV off because I will have fallen asleep.

Just for the sake of analogy, lets say that these are rechargeable batteries. I will have to make the effort to recharge them by putting them in the battery charger. However, it will be worth the effort so that tonight when I go to bed I don't have to manually click the channel or get up to turn the TV off. Sweet!

We also need to keep our spiritual batteries charged. This includes: studying the Word, time with God in prayer, times of encouragement with other believers and being taught by godly teachers. Truthfully, if we don't charge our spiritual batteries, we can run down too!

I'm afraid too many Christians run around with their "screen" on one channel. Maybe they're stuck on the "You Sin Channel," "The Gossip Network," or maybe "The I'll Be The Judge Of You Movie." When all the while what someone needs is a quick channel change to a believer's "Love, Mercy and Forgiveness Channel!"

Are we charged up enough to tune in quickly to the needs of others? If not, lets seek out the "Charger."

Choose The Outcome First — November 27

It had been a long day. I had gotten up at five in the morning. I'd been to my job and then I came home and worked some more. It was after nine at night when I stopped working. I was just about to turn on some music and chill a bit before going to bed. That's when it came – the request!

Right when I was about to start some "me time," Hannah ask me to do her a favor. All of that thinking of others more highly than myself, serving others and humility, went up in an explosion of pride, anger and selfishness. If you could have heard all that whining I was doing, you probably would have thrown up!

The result of a short and not so friendly exchange was Hannah being hurt and I went to bed angry. As is always the case after I show my butt like this, God seems to take me through a thought process that results in me seeing more clearly what a jerk I have been.

If I had stopped and thought of the possible outcomes I had to choose from, instead of just having a selfish emotional reaction, things could have been turned out much better. If I had just paused and ask: "How do I want this to turn out for good?"

Obviously, had I done her the favor, she would have appreciated it and been much happier. I could have listened to a little music later easily enough. I also could have gone to bed happier, with a clear conscience and woke up the next day not feeling like a spoiled brat!

The choice is a no brainer, if I will just stop and use my brain before my mouth! Next time I'm going to try to choose the outcome before I answer.

Man In the Mirror — November 28

So last night it seemed that I kept thinking about mirrors versus windows. I'm thinking what is that? Are you trying to tell me something, God? When I think of mirrors, the thoughts of:

For now we see only a reflection as in a mirror; then we shall see face to face. Now I know in part; then I shall know fully, even as I am fully known.
– I Corinthians 13:12

Do not merely listen to the word, and so deceive yourselves. Do what it says. Anyone who listens to the word but does not do what it says is like someone who looks at his face in a mirror and, after looking at himself, goes away and immediately forgets what he looks like. – James 1:22-24

I guess I'm thinking more along the lines of the James passage as it relates to:

Do nothing out of selfish ambition or vain conceit. Rather, in humility value others above yourselves, not looking to your own interests but each of you to the interests of the others. – Philippians 2:2-4

The saying of "take a look at yourself in the mirror" when we may be gossiping or judging someone else also comes to mind, but that wasn't it either.

It was more like: "Get out of the mirror of my own selfish concern and have a look out the window to others' concerns." This was not a scathing rebuke or a correction with a boatload of conviction (which is sometimes needed), but a gentle reminder or nudge to the right path. That is not to say that I have "thinking of others more highly than myself" down pat. It says more to the fact that God is a good Father and knows what degree of correction we need and gives it out lovingly. That can be a lesson unto itself for us as parents.

Anyway, what brought clarity and a reminder to "think of others first" was having a few days off with the attitude of what do *I* want to do? "Me time!" I was looking in the "mirror of my flesh" thinking "looking good, free time for me, yeah baby! I'm out of here! I'm gone fishing!"

But God says: "Quit looking in the (me) mirror, take a look out the window to the lives of others. What about what I want you to do? What about the needs, concerns and yes, even just the desires of others?"

You know, in the times I do get it right and put God and others first, it feels better than anything I may have done for myself. One thing is for sure, obeying Him is always the best thing I can do for myself too. I think I'll go make my family some breakfast. Maybe they'll like a boat ride later.

Are We Getting Carved Up — November 29

There seems to be a whole lot of pumpkin carving going on this time of year. Whatever we believe or to what extent we do or do not participate in Halloween or Fall Festival is another story. What came to my mind is specifically the pumpkin carving.

The first thing to do in pumpkin carving is to cut out the top (or some other access point). Then clean and scrape out all of the inside meat and seeds. The insides are usually discarded, even though they could be used to make an awesome holiday treat like pumpkin pie! Yeah baby! The seeds can be roasted as well to alleviate those night time munchies. After all, the pumpkin's original design was to be a food source, not a decoration.

Anyway, after the insides are removed, the carving begins so as to make an appealing decoration for the season. We may even paint the pumpkin shell or put a candle inside to make it even more appealing and attractive to whoever may see it.

This is how the world operates. It is also how way too many Christians live. We are rated on our outer appearance far more often than our inner worth. The world says forget what's on the inside, just work on that outward appearance and be pleasing to the eyes of man. Then you can be popular, accepted and approved by man.

God says: Don't get all caught up in that "outward adornment." Take care of your inner worth.

Greg says: Sooner or later this outer shell is going to wrinkle up. Then the world will toss us aside like last year's jack-o-lantern!

Let's not give the world an access point to carve out our inner worth. Instead, let's continue on to who we were originally designed to be. We were created for a loving relationship to God and to serve Him and others, not ourselves.

It all comes down to what we want to be in the Kingdom, a food source or a temporary decoration.

Who's Going To Know   November 30

Yesterday, one of my supervisors rode with me out on my route. This is done periodically to check job performance, adherence to safety rules and possible need for adjustments to the route. Everything went fine, no complaints. I honestly try to do (almost) everything according to the rules and instructions laid out for me to carry out my appointed rounds.

Although I try to follow them most of the time, there are some rules and regulations that seem to be more of an aggravation than a necessity. For instance, closing the door before going through any intersection. To me, this is the height of dufus! First of all, it is necessary for me to have my door open to do my job. To close it at every little neighborhood intersection would be an aggravation a hundred times a day! Not to mention that the door panel is paper thin. In the event of an accident, the door would be wrapped around me like tin foil around my tuna sandwich!

Having said that, it is the rule and I should follow it. The door would, I grudgingly admit, provide some minimal protection in the event of a collision. Which begs the question, did I close my door more often going through the intersections yesterday with my supervisor watching me than I would have normally? Yep.

I imagine many of us would do some things differently with someone watching us versus doing something unobserved. Besides, it won't hurt anyone. Who's going to know? Until the wreck.

The Bible tells us to do our work as if we were doing it for the Lord. As if He were the one sitting there with us doing the evaluation of our job. But then again, we don't have to. Who's going to know?

Renovation   December 1

As I said before, I worked a lot of construction as a young man. It was cool to see a project from beginning to end. What once was an empty lot, became a school, hospital or a large office building in the span of 12 to 18 months. I would later find out that new construction was by far and away easier and more enjoyable than renovation.

When I was in my twenties, I was hired onto a job that was a renovation of an old multi-floored furniture store. It had been vacated and had sat empty for awhile. The job was to turn it into an office building. From the first day I hated this one. Up the elevator I went with a 90 lb jack hammer. My first mission was to break through two layers of brick wall at prescribed locations so that windows could be installed (where there had been none) in the second floor warehouse area.

There was no ventilation to speak of so there was dust and rubble everywhere. We had to wear hard hats, mask and goggles on the second floor all day long. There was destruction going on everywhere in the building. It was an old brick structure, so it felt like I was working in a cave or a mine that was about to cave in!

Yeah, I was in my twenties and in good shape physically, but have you ever ran a 90 lb jack hammer (3 ft upside a wall) for eight hours a day?! That was manual labor as hard as I have ever done it!

The outside of the building appeared to be in good shape. Only cosmetic work was done on the outside. Clean the walls, paint the trim, put in some new doors and some nice landscaping on the grounds.

I look back now and see this building's renovation as a comparison of how God has worked in me. Not much was needed on the outside, I could always appear to be OK on the outside. But the inside was an absolute mess. My real condition could only be "renovated" by extensive reconstruction on the inside.

It was not always easy, because sin had absolutely caused me to cave in. God was the one on the jackhammer. Jesus opened me up from the inside and now the fresh air of forgiveness, mercy and grace can come in because I have "opened the windows" He offered and installed in me for free!

Sometimes this old building still needs some cleaning out, but He is always there to renovate!

Resist The Isolator — December 2

As a child, when I would come home from school, I couldn't wait to go outside and play with my friends. The same was true for the weekend. Out the door as soon as possible to Doug's back yard for some baseball or Danny's front yard for some football. Maybe onto the bikes to who knows where, but we were together, having a ball. As we got older, it would be the pool hall or the beach and sometimes a road trip together.

My past is getting longer and longer. When I look back at it those days, I learn more and more. One of the things I have been learning (finally) is an answer to a question I have long ask: "God, what am I here for?" The answer is relationships. I have always had the most joy, feeling of completeness, and downright sense of "this is what it's all about" when spending time with people. It almost doesn't matter what the occasion is, just being there with people brings on the sense of being right where I'm supposed to be at that time. Thank God He has brought me back around to this desire for relationships. Whether it be loved ones, friends, or those in need.

But where did that desire for relationships go in some adult periods of my life? The big answer: I let myself get too busy. If the enemy can't keep you from coming to God, then he will try to keep you busy so that you are of no use to God. I also let myself be distracted and isolated. For instance: Worry about finances made me think I had to work more. Computer time, iPods, video games among other things, can close us off from others and draw us into isolation. Granted, concerns about money may require some action on our part and computers can be useful tools. However, these are some examples of tools the enemy can use to distract us from relationships and isolate us from others.

So, now, I intentionally try to stop what I'm doing when people want to talk or spend time together. I spend less free time on the computer. I have only one "money job" now and I'm putting this in writing so you can hold me accountable. TV, you're next!

Short version of the story: God put us here for relationships. First to Him, then to others.

Hearing that Jesus had silenced the Sadducees, the Pharisees got together. One of them, an expert in the law, tested him with this question: "Teacher, which is the greatest commandment in the Law?"

Jesus replied: "'Love the Lord your God with all your heart and with all your soul and with all your mind.' This is the first and greatest commandment. And the second is like it: 'Love your neighbor as yourself.' All the Law and the Prophets hang on these two commandments." – Matthew 22:34-40

Sharpening Iron — December 3

"Greg, while noticing the many and prolific weeds in our yard, I reflected on how different my life would be if it had as many weeds in it. Then, it hit me – well, wow, gotta go, check you later."

The friend that sent me the above e-mail thinks the same way as I do. You know what I mean, you can be listening to someone and look at each other and go "uh-huh" to yourself, because you know what the other one is thinking. He says he can see a title to one of my blogs and he knows where I'm going. I don't think he means a good guess. He knows because we ponder things the same way. I suppose we all have friends like this. It's amazing and somewhat comforting to know there are others like us, in the same boat.

It even validates us to know there are others that go through the same trials and life experiences. It gives glory to our Lord for one friend to encourage another. Especially when one has been through something that God has delivered him from and he can share that victory with a friend.

I sent this back: "Are you going to be mowing or pulling?"

His reply: "I think the weeds in our yard are just going to be mowed. From a distance, nicely mowed weeds look almost as good as grass. The weeds in our life however, we're going to have to pull. It will be painful and expose a few bare spots, but at close inspection, anyone can tell weeds from grass."

There must be ten good blogs in that reply!

Told ya'. We ponder just alike! Thanks for the assist on the devo, my friend! Man I hope he starts writing! He's good!

As iron sharpens iron, so one person sharpens another. – Proverbs 27:17

Safe And Secure — December 4

When I first got married I remember having the realization that I was in charge of the safety and security of my family and my home. I had never given that a second thought while I was growing up. It had never crossed my mind. My safety and well being was a non-issue while I was living in my father's house. This realization was somewhat of a shock to me. It is a serious role to be the front line of defense for those you love. It had become my duty to protect my loved ones. I could be faced with intruders to my home. I have been faced with people who have come against my family. Living here on the coast, I have had to deal with hurricanes, and of course, the everyday bumps and bruises of life.

I remember one night (we had been married less than a year) we were awakened by a very loud noise, as if someone had crashed through the door. My first thought was, "Dad's not here, I'll have to go see what made the noise." My second thought was: "Just great, Hannah didn't want any guns in the house." It turned out that a big roll of wallpaper had rolled off a shelf in a hall closet and bounced off the hollow door. Hannah relented, and I brought my gun into the house after that incident.

In this life, to function efficiently, we need a sound mind, physical ability, food, clothing, shelter and security. Everything else is pretty much gravy. If one of these is absent, it becomes the driving force of life to achieve that need. Meanwhile, all other things outside these needs are the farthest from our minds.

However, spiritually speaking, all we have to have for the security of our souls is the salvation offered to us by our Heavenly Father through Jesus Christ. Then we can be sure that we will forever live in the safety and security of our Father's house. With our eternity secure we can be about His business showing others how to get to His house, where they can be welcomed in forever.

The Fog Of Stubborn Disobedience December 5

When we headed out fishing yesterday we were facing several unfavorable conditions. It was dead low tide and extremely foggy. Although it was in less than favorable fishing conditions, we had the day off, we had not been fishing in weeks, and we were equipped with just enough stubbornness to carry out our plan anyway.

We hooked up, loaded up and headed for the launch. Obviously others had delayed or canceled their plans due to the poor conditions. It was already after 8 a.m. and there was only one other person who had launched their boat into that soupy looking fog.

We figured we would go ahead and launch and wait for the fog to burn off. The dangers of running a boat in the fog are many. Your visibility can be down to nothing. Another boat can appear out of the fog and slam into you before you see it. You also can't hear another boat coming if your own motor is running. There is always the possibility of running into something yourself, like a boat dock, bridges, buoys or even running aground. We stayed close to the ramp and a nearby bridge for more than an hour.

Finally, the fog began to burn off and we headed out. Trouble is, on the water fog can be thick one place and almost nonexistent in other spots. We had run several miles when we ran into a light fog bank that turned into nearly zero visibility really quick. Now we're in the real soup! This is a dangerous situation.

Thankfully Ryan had his cell that has satellite GPS. We still had to watch very carefully for boats and other dangers but we knew where we were going. His GPS had that entire bay mapped out! It showed bridges, land points, boat docks and other structures. It showed us where to go even though we couldn't see anything but fog!

Funny how grown men can get themselves into "soupy" situations because of stubbornness or chasing after some "thing" that doesn't ultimately matter in the big scheme of things.

My not-so-good choices this day: launching out in fog, and going into a light fog bank, knowing full well that it can be zero visibility instantly! Risking life and limb for a few fish I could go catch, or even buy later.

I've done this to my Lord too! I've taken control of things in my life when I knew I should trust Him. One of my answers was: "I can't cut back, I'll just borrow the money, or put it on my credit card." For years I did that one! Then for years I was in the "fog" of debt. Thankfully He led me out of that fog too (slowly, with many lessons along the way).

Our God can see our situations better than any GPS! He knows the situation and the way to the best outcome for us. And even though He will lead us out of the fog we find ourselves in after not trusting Him, if we choose to obey His directions to begin with, we can avoid the fog banks of stubborn disobedience.

Manual Or Automatic — December 6

It has always been more fun to me to drive cars with a standard transmission. You know, push the clutch in and shift the gears yourself, real driving. Automatic transmissions do all the shifting for the driver and it seems as if having one less thing to consider takes away a responsibility, as well as some of the fun of driving.

It seems at times my life (my mouth in particular) can be on automatic. These are automatic responses (usually emotional, without thought) to questions about things that I have my mind made up about and don't want to hear other views. Sometimes I respond strictly out of emotion (with cutting or hurtful remarks) because I'm angry or hurt. And of course there are times when I'm just not interested or paying attention and I give the automatic response: "uh-huh."

Last night Hannah came to me needing to discuss something she knew was a touchy subject for me. I have been on automatic so long she knew what was coming. When she started talking about this subject I reacted like a fire having gasoline poured on it! Excellent communication strategy, Greg! Now she's rightfully upset and I'm just on fire!

I'm going to ask God to change my "transmission" to a manual transmission. I want Him to give me a "clutch" to push in and knock my emotions and mouth out of gear and into neutral, while listening to others and making decisions. Then when He has shown me the correct response or decision I can let the clutch out and move smoothly down the road. This could make the road through life smoother, with a little more joy and understanding.

Let Me In   December 7

Jesus answered, "I am the way and the truth and the life. No one comes to the Father except through me." – John 14:6

Upon returning from a very busy two days out of town, my sons and I had a few more chores to do before calling it a day. We needed to load some tools out of our storage unit and into a trailer for a cross country trip. I was already tired from the past two days.

It was early evening when we arrived at the "24 hour access" storage facility. As we pulled towards the gate we could see there was no code access panel available to punch in the access number I had been given to open the gate. The office was already closed. I called the phone number on the door at least a half dozen times, leaving a more "intense" message with each call. We could also see (through the window) a sign on the counter that read: "Ask Me About The Gate." This sign was leading us to believe there was some kind of a trick to opening the gate. However, no one bothered to return my call. So, after seriously considering but deciding against "breaking and entering," we returned home thinking we would have to wait until they opened, two days later! This would obviously cost two more days trailer rent and cause us to cut the long trip by a day!

After an hour or so at home I decided to drive back down to the storage unit to see if I could figure out a way to get into the gate. B&E was reoccurring as a possible option! I remember thinking on my way back to the storage buildings: "Lord, it would be so cool if someone would just pull up right in front of me and I could see how to get in the gate."

Well, well, as I approached the turn lane into the storage buildings, the car in front of me turned in and pulled right up to the gate. True story! I zipped in and pulled up beside the other car as the gate opened. I ask the lady in the car how she opened the gate. I think she had mercy on me (seeing the frustration on my face). She explained the simple (but unknown to me) procedure and I was in!

I called my sons and told them how to get in the gate. We were able to load the trailer and be on our way.

In the spiritual, this is not unlike trying to get into Heaven. People really want to get into Heaven but they don't know how. It can be confusing and frustrating to those who think it is difficult to get into Heaven. Many think we need to be good and follow a set of rules without failure to get into Heaven. However, the procedure is a simple one, if someone will just tell them.

When we see those in need of knowing how to "get in the gate," let's be like the lady at the gate was to me. Let's show them the way through the gate so that they can enter in!

Taking The Land   December 8

Football is a game of real estate. It's about defending your land when necessary and taking the other guy's land when you have a chance. Football is an intense, grueling and physical game. But it is a game, because after you take the other team's land and score points against them, you then give them their land (and the ball) back so they can try to take your land. After a few hours, one team wins, one team loses and we'll see you next year for a rematch – a peace treaty of sorts (containing bragging rights for the winner).

Warfare is also about taking land. But it's no game. Land is taken with no intention of giving it back. In battle, like football, there is offense and defense. You take land during an offensive. If you're on defense in a battle, you're trying to protect and keep your land. Being on defense in battle is a grave situation and often precedes the defender's demise. To win you must be on the offensive.

I can't think of any lasting, permanent peace that has ever come through a peace treaty. They are continually broken and the hostilities then continue. North Korea and South Korea have been at it for decades, and how many peace treaties have have been signed in the Middle East? I am not advocating war. I am just pointing out that peace has only come after a total victory by one side or the other and full surrender by the defeated.

For our struggle is not against flesh and blood, but against the rulers, against the authorities, against the powers of this dark world and against the spiritual forces of evil in the heavenly realms. – Ephesians 6:12

Spiritual warfare is no different than physical battle when it comes to the need for complete victory over the enemy! When it comes to battle with Satan, we should make no deals, give back no land, and sign no peace treaties! In the verses that follow Ephesians 6:12 we are told to put on the armor of God, defensive equipment to stand against Satan's weapons. We can stand up under his assaults with these defensive weapons on, but to run him off we need to take up the "sword of the spirit," the Word of God, our offensive weapon.

If we do want to cut Satan to shreds then we must "sharpen our swords" by putting God's word in our hearts and then be willing to use it on Satan in battle. Speaking God's word will enable us to continually take back land from the enemy until his final demise at the hands of God.

Read the Word. Learn the Word. Speak the Word. Take back the land. No deals, no peace treaties – complete victory!

Show And Tell — December 9

I remember "Show and Tell" in grade school. There was this one boy who would tell of his weekend fishing trips every Monday. I could see the other kids roll their eyes at him with that "oh no, not again." I kind of enjoyed his stories. That's a lot of what school is, isn't it, show and tell? The good teachers don't just tell you how to do something, they show you too.

I had this instructor in college (yes I went to college ... some) who was trying to teach a finance class. This was a disaster from the get-go! He could read the text book to us. He could even work mathematical problems out himself. He would even make an effort to tell us how to solve a problem. But he could not show the students how to work these difficult problems. I don't know if he had stage fright or some sort of inability to demonstrate to others. You probably had to see it to believe it. Students dropped that class like rats leaving a sinking ship.

Then Jesus came to them and said, "All authority in heaven and on earth has been given to me. Therefore go and make disciples of all nations, baptizing them in the name of the Father and of the Son and of the Holy Spirit, and teaching them to obey everything I have commanded you. And surely I am with you always, to the very end of the age." – Matthew 28:18-20

This Scripture is called "The Great Commission." Jesus is telling His Disciples to go into the world and make disciples. To "show and tell" others about Him. To tell them and to show (demonstrate to) them how to live the Christ-like life. Jesus didn't just tell them about the Kingdom, He showed them the Kingdom and how to walk in it. He poured His life into them for years.

Sorry, we are not going to make disciples in an hour a week of Sunday School. Bible study and Sunday School can play a big part in discipleship, as a source for information. It is the "tell" part of discipleship. But someone is going to have to "show" people how to walk out their lives in the kingdom.

God, please help us all remember: It's not just what we know, it's also what we show.

Super Tracker — December 10

I like Westerns. These movies often have some tracking going on in them. I have always thought it was cool to be able to follow or find someone by the trail and signs they leave. In the really old westerns, some tracker would put his ear on the ground. By this he could tell how many horses and riders were coming or going, where to and how fast. Sure! Anyway, when I was a little cowboy, all I ever got when I put my ear on the ground was a dirty ear and my mom asking, "How do your ears get so dirty?"

The other night I was reading a couple of these stories at a gathering of writers. I introduced myself as a Jesus follower who loses His trail a little too often. Truth is, Jesus doesn't make it hard to stay close so we can see where He's going; it's more that I wander off down some trail of self direction.

It's like when I was a little boy and I had to go shopping with my mom. She would go towards the ladies' clothes, or maybe even towards the children's clothes to buy me some jeans or shirts. Oblivious to a blessing coming my way, I would instead find the trail to the toy department.

Like sin, hanging out in the toy department was fun for awhile. That's until I realized that I was lost and separated from Mom. The situation had then gone from fun to a serious problem. Suddenly, there was a huge empty spot in me filling up with fear and the dread of what to do now. All I wanted was Mom because she was the only one who could fix this now!

There was one thing I knew for sure. Mom loved me and she wasn't leaving that store without me. She came and found me, every single time!

Because He loves us, Jesus will do the same thing, every time! When we wander away from Him, heading down some pig trail, He will track us down. He will find us and show us the way back to the right path, His path for each of us.

Are you lost or separated from God? Have you wandered down the wrong trail? Well if you have, He's been tracking you. Turn around, He's standing right behind you waiting for you to return to Him. He'll take you back to the right path, every time!

Pain In a Heart Disguised As A Pain In The Butt
December 11

There never seems to be a shortage of people on my route that want to stop me just to talk a minute. When I look at them through my eyes, I view them as an annoyance. They have nothing better to do than to stop me from my appointed rounds and "yack" at me. Often times it's a complaint about nothing in particular or the latest gossip about a neighbor. What is the deal with these people?

That question is often answered if I will look at them through the eyes of Jesus. His answer will often be: "They're lonely". My answer is too often: "Yeah God, but I don't have time to deal with them." Then the reply comes: "Well, why do you think I put them right there in front of you?"

The other day as I was leaving a convenience store I saw one of the clerks talking to a younger lady who seemed upset. I know this clerk pretty well and as I was getting into my truck the young lady walked away. Then the clerk came over to me and said: "Some people are just dumber than dirt!" What came out of my mouth next didn't feel like it came from me. I said: "Well, maybe that's why we're here – to help people like that."

My own comment convicted me because I often have the mindset of the clerk's comment. There are so many people out there who are lonely and hurting and I go right by them every day. If I take time to notice them at all, I'll blow them off saying I don't have time. When in reality, I am deciding I won't take the time! One thing we do have control over is how we spend our time.

Standing in a group of people the other day at church someone asked: "How does Mrs. Smith (not her real name) get here, since she can't drive anymore?" Someone answered: "She rides with Mrs. Jones" (right, not her real name either).

Not exactly. You see, Mrs. Jones gets up and gets ready early, drives out of her way, picks up Mrs. Smith and spends time talking to her all the way back across town to church. After church Mrs. Jones takes Mrs. Smith out to eat lunch and pays for it. Then she drives Mrs. Smith home (after a stop at the grocery store) and hangs out with her half the afternoon. Then she does it all over again Wednesday night and the next Sunday and then again ...

I think maybe the little unknown heroes like Mrs. Jones are really some of the biggest in the Kingdom. She's a caretaker of the lonely.

Loneliness is a knife that can inflict the wound of depression. That kind of wound easily becomes infected and fatal to the heart. There's no pill for that! Only companionship can heal this wound.

Preparing The Way   **December 12**

There is a TV series playing now that is centered around the building of the cross country railroad. For this railroad to be built there had to be men go ahead of the actual construction and to "prepare the way." There had to be maps made, decisions about the route to be taken, land to be cleared, supplies and men brought in to build the railroad, not to mention the perils to be faced that are common to the wilderness.

However, upon completion of this railroad, it was much easier and safer to travel cross country in a minimal amount of time. Men had prepared the way and made going from one coast to the other easier and more accessible to everyone.

That's what John The Baptist did in preparing the way for the coming of Jesus. He dressed differently and lived out in the wilderness, living off the land. I believe one of the reasons he lived differently than his contemporaries was the Kingdom of God that was coming would be different from the one the religious leaders were presenting to the people at the time. The religious leaders knew all the law and had added a lot of their own rules, but had lost the intent of the law which was based on the love of God.

John challenged these religious leaders (as Jesus soon would) and showed that God desired men to come unto Him, not religion. John preached repentance and coming to God. He prepared the way for people to come to God because God loves us and not because we are the best at keeping the rules.

John did say: "Produce fruit in keeping with repentance;" meaning that our lives should reflect God's work in us and our surrender to Him. That we should now be the ones who prepare the way for others to come out of the wilderness of life, into life with Jesus. Work in the wilderness can be tough, but it will make it easier for others to get through.

Are we living out the change that He has made in us so others can see the real Jesus? Or since we have made it through "the wilderness," are we sitting quietly in our own safe zone just trying to obey the rules?

Who Really Needs To Be Changed December 13

Did you ever pray this one: "O.K. God, I can't take this guy any more! You're going to have to change him or shut him up or I'm going to have to knock him out!"

I'm not going to knock anyone out, but I've been a lot closer to cussing people out than I've been in a long time! My patience, temper and annoyance tolerance meter has been on a short fuse for days now and it seems to be burning shorter.

I think I know how all this got started, or at least seemed to intensify. I prayed this and I meant it: "God, change me into the man You would have me to be."

There I go, now I've done it! I guess I was hoping for an instantaneous miracle that would make me into Mr. Perfect. I should have known better. I've heard it many times: "Don't pray for patience or you'll have to go through something that will require you to be patient." Often, that's the way it is, if we want to get physically stronger, we have to exercise our bodies. If we want to see how were coming along in some subject in school, we need to take a test.

That's often how God works in us. He exercises us in the areas we need strength and then tests us in that area so we know if we are stronger.

"Change me," the words that can throw flesh into battle with the spirit. That prayer was a request to God, not a declaration of resolve to change myself in my own power. I can't make any real, permanent change to be true servant of God outside of His power. Thanks for that revelation, Lord. That takes the pressure off me to try to change using my own insufficient strength.

All the power to overcome is from Him. My part is to choose to obey and then in His strength, carry out that obedience. That's how I'll overcome and that's when the change in me will be real. And that's ultimately what I want, real change.

What Will It Matter A Hundred Years From Now   December 14

What will it matter a hundred years from now? Have you heard that one before?

Every morning when I arrive at work there is another stack of stuff waiting there to be delivered. It doesn't matter that I delivered every single thing I had the day before. There will be another stack waiting for me the next morning. What I delivered yesterday, mattered yesterday. The stuff I am going to deliver today, matters today. But little or none of what I deliver today will matter tomorrow. Surely none of what I deliver today will matter a hundred years from now. The result of what I do as a job has its value in the present. It does not inherently build anything that has value in the future.

My first jobs as an adult were in the construction industry. My grandfather was a carpenter and a builder. My father was a construction superintendent. Maybe it's in my DNA but there's something satisfying about starting from the ground where there was nothing, then when you're done, leaving a mark behind that will matter a hundred years from now. I have worked on the construction of a high school, a hospital, college buildings and assorted other structures (all over thirty years ago) that are still in use today.

In the Kingdom, the same principal is at work. As believers we can build into the future by discipling others, pouring the foundations of a godly life into them by the example of our daily lives. When the foundation is good, we soon see the building rise up, often many stories high, to become useful for decades to come.

Constructing a building (disciple) is often a painstaking, time consuming, laborious task taking many hours a day and sometimes several years to see it (them) become fully functional. But when built correctly, on a good foundation, it will matter a hundred years from now.

It's Not My Fault — December 15

Did you ever get blamed for something that wasn't your fault? Has you little brother ever told your mom that you did it? What about your older sister letting you take the blame for something she did wrong? Maybe a coworker didn't get a job done and you took the heat for it.

I don't like having to take the heat for other people's crap, but it happened again yesterday. As I pulled up to one of the first stops of my delivery day, I riffled through the mail for the address and realized I don't have the elderly lady's monthly check. Occasionally this kind of thing happens and is no fault of mine. I have always carried out and delivered everything I have been given for that day. However, everything expected by patrons doesn't always make it to me for that day's delivery.

Anyway, I put what mail I did have for her in the mailbox and moved on. As expected, when I came back down the other side of the street, her son waved me down. OK, here it comes. The guy was not obnoxious, but was understandably upset and it took a few minutes of calm apology on my part (for someone else's gaff) to at least allow him to calm down and let me move on.

I found out later the lady's son had called my supervisor and filled his ear as well. Although he was justified in his anger, neither I nor my boss was at fault here, but we paid the price for someone else's mistake.

This has happened in the Kingdom too. We have all screwed up (sinned) and someone else has had to pay the price. Jesus died (paid the price) for every single one of our screw ups. It wasn't His fault we sinned, but He still paid for it. The big difference is while I hate paying for someone else's screw ups, He paid the ultimate price willingly, because He loves us that much. He loves you and me to death!

The Rebel   December 16

Just over two thousand years ago a Rebel showed up. He flew in the face of the established "religious leaders" of the day. He flat out told them that they had left the heart of God for the rules of man. Their rules, camouflaged to look like God's rules.

God gave Ten Commandments, but to this day, He has only two rules:

"Love the Lord your God with all your heart and with all your soul and with all your mind. This is the first and greatest commandment. And the second is like it: 'Love your neighbor as yourself.' All the Law and the Prophets hang on these two commandments." (The Rebel)

Needless to say, the religious leaders of the day didn't go for this Rebel stirring everybody up and accusing them of piling all these rules on people that they couldn't keep themselves. The Rebel taught with authority and first hand knowledge of the Kingdom of God. This Rebel even went around healing people and raising the dead! As if that weren't enough, He told the people they were forgiven for breaking the rules, even God's rules! He said that is why He was here in the first place.

The religious leaders pious pride couldn't take Him any more. In their mind, the Rebel had to go. They plotted to seize Him and put Him to death. By the way, isn't killing an innocent man against the rules? You know what? They succeeded in their plot.

In the cover of night they seized Him. He was put through a staged trial and with the approval of the government, murdered. After beating Him unmercifully, they nailed Him to a cross until he died. Game over. Religious leaders are back in charge and hope is lost for the Rebellion. Or so it would appear.

But three days later the Rebel is back. He has paid the price to say to His followers: "Your sins are forgiven." The Rebel has defeated Death, Satan and not to mention "religion's rules."

Things are not what they appear. Even, and maybe I should say especially in death, things are not what they appear. He is able and willing to bring us through the toughest of times, just because He loves us.

It appeared that Satan and his boys had the Rebel defeated. They killed Him and left Him for dead. But He's alive and well. Word is … Satan is going to try it again. Just remember Believers, that it may appear that all is lost, but things are not what they appear!

Ringside December 17

I grew up a fan of Pro Wrestling. I remember going to this outdoor arena in my home town with my dad to watch the good guys go at it with the bad guys. As I grew older I reluctantly resigned myself to the fact that it all had a story line with previously decided outcomes. It was rigged! So, as a grown man, I relabeled it in my own mind as fictional entertainment. I put it in the category of a movie or a cartoon with live people. This allowed me to still enjoy the "characters" and pull for the good guys. However, I have watched it less and less over the years for certain reasons unrelated to what I have said here.

Anyway, I was watching it on and off the other night. They say it is some of most watched two hours of TV every week. Millions of viewers tune in and watch. You can have a ringside seat right in your living room.

More and more we see that there are real people behind these characters. We see evidence of this often on the TV or in the papers. So and so died from this or that. So and so got arrested. It seems so many of them have had personal battles. Because of their fame, their real lives and personal issues are out there for everyone to see. It seems that evil and misfortune are intertwined in their personal lives. But this is not always the case. Many are now believers.

You've probably seen some of them on a Christian TV station or at a large Christian Conference of some sort. This is a good thing. But what about people who don't watch Christian TV or go to big Christian events where they might see and hear some of these testimonies.

This is where the other night comes in. This is where you and I come in. The other night, as millions of people were watching ringside in their living rooms, one of the most famous wrestlers ever, gave a farewell speech as he retired. After thanking many people for the part they played in his life (several who helped him through tough personal times) he publicly thanked his Lord and Savior Jesus Christ and said to Him, "… thank You for saving me."

So where do you and I come in? We all live our lives in a ring that is not inside a church, Sunday School or Bible study. We live in other rings in our everyday life. Including our workplace, schools and our leisure time. Life is lived in a "spiritual wrestling ring" with all the fake story on the outside and the true story of our lives on the inside. But when we have the ring all to ourselves and we have a chance to sincerely share our hearts. What do we say to the people at the ringside of our lives?

Well Done   December 18

"Well done good and faithful servant." Those words out of Matthew 25 have been on my mind lately as I ponder some things I may undertake. What believer doesn't want to hear those words come out of Jesus' mouth when they stand before Him?

My decisions on whether or not to be of service to someone has often been based on how it would affect me. Try these scenarios of my possible service for example.

I could send twenty bucks to the local soup kitchen. Twenty dollars won't impoverish me and it would provide some needed meals for some folks. No strain, no time lost and it's a good thing to do for others.

Maybe some family in the church has fallen on hard times and a plea is put out for some money to help them out. OK, I could give maybe a hundred to help out. That may cause a short term strain on me, but not much, and still no personal time lost.

Or it could be the elderly widow with the leaky roof. Some of the guys are going over and spend the entire day repairing it. Now that will cost me my day off!

Then there's the mission trip that cost $2,500 just to go! Never mind that two weeks of my vacation time will be burned up building basic housing, in the monsoon season, for people who have lived outdoors all their lives!

And then the kicker! The first day off after the mission trip, I'm pulling the boat out to go fishing and see the grumpy old guy next door staring at a flat on his car. He sees me and ask me if I could help him.

I scream "NO!" silently in my mind. I told him last night that tire was low! I know he didn't fix the spare the last time because he didn't have the money. This will require removing the tire, taking it to get fixed, replacing it onto the car and then he's going to ask me if he can go fishing with me!

What would you do in these cases ... really? We should make our decisions of whether or not to be a servant based on how it will positively affect others and the Kingdom, rather than how we might perceive that decision affecting us negatively.

It is true that God will bless us for our service in His name. But our motive should be to serve rather than receiving the reward. And what better reward than: "Well done good and faithful servant ..."

The Fix Is In   December 19

You've heard the statement: "The only sure things are death and taxes." When I hear that line it says to me these are the two things we can't stop. We (mankind) cannot fix them. I know we could cut back on taxes (maybe not a bad idea). We could conceivably cut out taxes (probably not a good idea). But we cannot stop or "fix" death. Every one of us is going to pass from this life (Hebrews 9:27).

There are many things we (mankind) can fix, even these are by the grace of God. For example something simple like spilt milk on the kitchen floor, a busted water pipe, a fallen tree, a broken down car, a broken leg, a giant oil spill (yes, eventually we'll clean it up), destruction from storms and earthquakes, threats from wars, and so on.

It is always easier for us to get something fixed if we know someone with expertise in fixing what is broke. For instance, we may need a plumber to fix a busted pipe, a mechanic to fix our car, or a doctor to fix a broken leg. I personally know several plumbers and a couple of mechanics. I don't personally know any doctors. The point is, if my car breaks down I can immediately call on one of my mechanic friends that I know personally. I am sure to get a trusted diagnosis and a correct fix for my vehicle. If, however, I am in need of a doctor, I may have to go to the emergency room and wait. I may have to make an appointment and wait for days. I may even want a second opinion on diagnosis and treatment because I don't personally know or trust the physician.

There is another thing we can't fix. That's sin. Although we may and should strive not to sin, we have, we do and we will sin. Sin leads to death. That's why we (mankind) cannot stop death.

Ah, but there is a fix for sin and death. We just need to know the Physician personally. The Physician's name is Jesus and His treatment for sin and death was His own sinless, perfect life, sacrificed on the cross for the forgiveness our sins. With our sins forgiven through Him, death cannot hold us! All we have to do (as we recognize He is the only way to the Father) is to confess out sins, ask Him to forgive us and live in us and through us as our Lord and Savior. No second opinion needed!

For the wages of sin is death, but the gift of God is eternal life in Christ Jesus our Lord. – Romans 6:23

Running The Race   December 20

I grew up watching car races at a short track in my home town. I have friends who have raced on the local short tracks and drag strips. I know a little about racing and the adrenaline rush of driving a car at high speeds. There is an element of danger to racing and I am aware of that too. I have been in my fair share of car wrecks.

I still enjoy the races. They are extremely fast and intense. This year's Daytona 500 was no exception. I remember going to the Daytona 500 as a teenager and being amazed at the speed of these cars as they raced around the track bumper to bumper at 200 mph. Inevitably there are going to be some messy wrecks. All it takes is for someone to touch their brakes a tiny bit or one car barely touching another at those speeds for this rocketing bumper to bumper parade to become a heap of burning metal. The result being a loss of all that the crews have worked for and probably some injured drivers.

The best way to combat the possibility of a bad result in car racing is preparation, tuning the cars for the best results, adjusting the car during the race (pit stops) and having a rested, skillful, knowledgeable driver.

Our daily lives can sometimes feel like a very long, exhausting, high speed race. As believers, when we look at God as the car owner (of our lives) we know He has everything we need to stay in the race. We just need to go to Him to get it.

To be knowledgeable about the "car and the track," we should read His Word (the manual and race plan). To be skillful and know when and where to make our move in the race, we need to follow the Holy Spirit's leading. Also, to be rested we need to take advantage of our race pit (our resting and adjustment place with Him). Sometimes there is an obvious time (a caution flag) that we can pull into our pit. At other times we may need to make adjustments while the race is going full speed.

One thing is for sure; there is a lot more preparation for the race than there is actual race time when it comes to car racing. The smallest thing can cause a car to not finish a race, a broken valve, a faulty gauge, a tiny leak of oil or water or maybe it just runs out of gas when no one is paying attention.

We can break down too! We should always make time to stop, go to the garage and see the Owner about making some adjustments. Rest in Him. There's another race next week!

The Flip Side   December 21

The sayings of the day. The popular slang lines we speak currently and as they age they become corny and dumb sounding but everyone uses them or used them back in the day. There are millions of them!

Out of the sixties: "groovy," "solid," "man," and "cool." All were used totally out of their definition. "Groovy" and "solid" were always dumb to me but I still say "man" and "cool" as slang in conversation.

Now there's "sweet," "an issue," and "it's not all about you." My prediction is that "sweet" will stand the test of time like "man" or "cool" but "an issue" sounds stupid now and will fall by the wayside of the dumb things we used to say as did "groovy and "solid."

But this saying, "it's not all about you" has come up in interesting places to me and has me thinking. For certain it says to us that we are not to be selfish, thinking of ourselves first and foremost and calls us to care about others. These would be excellent traits for us to demonstrate and live by because these are the same traits Jesus and many others in the Bible call us to. I have heard it used in Christian circles and sermons, calling us to have this attitude as a lifestyle, as we should. Serving Him and others for His glory and the good of those we put ahead of ourselves.

So where am I going with this? To the flip side. The "flip side" on old 45's (small vinyl records) was the side with the usually crappy song opposite the hit song (the reason you bought the record).

But every once in a while you would hear a flip side song you liked. You may not tell anybody so as to not be made fun of and soon would place it in the back of your mind to forget later.

Well here's the flip side of "It's not all about you." It's called "It is all about you." From our side we are to live as if it is not all about us, but the flip side (from God's eyes and heart) it is all about you!

He created you in your mother's womb for the specific purpose of a love relationship with Him. And that love flows from Him to us (even if we do not return it, He loves us all). Ah! but if we turn to Him, we can experience His love for us. Real love, true love, forever love, because from His viewpoint to each of us individually, when it comes to His love, "It is all about you!" He died proving it.

Close The Door Behind You   December 22

Have you seen these storm closets that you can have built into a house. Modern day storm cellars. I guess their more prominent in the Midwest (Tornado Alley). Anyway, they are built to withstand tremendous winds. I have seen pictures of these safe closets still standing after a tornado on a concrete slab that previously had a house on it.

These closets came to mind as I was reading about Joseph of Arimathia and Nicodemus (prominent members of the Jewish Council) asking Pilate for the body of Jesus after He was crucified. We see in John 3 that Nicodemus met secretly (at risk to his position and reputation) with Jesus and heard about being born again. Then in John 7, Nicodemus defends Jesus (more risk). Then in John 19, Nicodemus and Joseph come all the way out of the closet when they ask for and got Jesus' body and put Him in the tomb. These two had been secret believers, who had for a time, stayed in the closet out of "the fear of man." But their faith had grown and they just couldn't hide it anymore.

Not hearing anymore about these two, who had previously been "closet Christians," has me wondering what it cost them to come out. Loss of position, power, wealth, friends, and even more? There is a price. Are we willing to pay it? In the closet time of Nicodemus' life, can we see ourselves? Safe in our beliefs, not willing to risk living out what we believe in front of others?

We saw Nicodemus sneak outside the closet one night, then perhaps stand outside the closet another time. But when these two ask for the body of Jesus, they shut the door behind themselves, never to return to the safe closet of the fear of man.

As a secret believer in the closet of the fear of man, we can stay sheltered from persecution by men. But, if we allow our faith and trust in God to grow, we can walk out of the closet and shut the door behind ourselves for good. This closet can no more hold you than the tomb could hold Jesus. Come on out and walk in the freedom from being cooped up in the closet. Oh yeah, close that door behind you.

Later, Joseph of Arimathea asked Pilate for the body of Jesus. Now Joseph was a disciple of Jesus, but secretly because he feared the Jewish leaders. With Pilate's permission, he came and took the body away. He was accompanied by Nicodemus, the man who earlier had visited Jesus at night. Nicodemus brought a mixture of myrrh and aloes, about seventy-five pounds. Taking Jesus' body, the two of them wrapped it, with the spices, in strips of linen. This was in accordance with Jewish burial customs. At the place where Jesus was crucified, there was a garden, and in the garden a new tomb, in which no one had ever been laid. Because it was the Jewish day of Preparation and since the tomb was nearby, they laid Jesus there. – John 19:38-42

Got What You Need — December 23

Last night the whole crew was over at our house for supper. There are nine of us now, the newest being Nolan, our new grandson. I haven't seen him with his eyes open much. He is a sleeping picture of peace. As he gets older I'm sure that things will come along to concern him, but right now he has all he needs. In fact, I think he already has all any of us need.

When you think about it, all we really need is food, clothes, shelter and love. Everything else is gravy. I'm telling you that when Nolan is fed, bundled up warm and given some TLC from his mom and dad, he can snooze with the best of them. He is at peace and doesn't have a care in the world.

As young children, we trusted our parents and didn't worry about stuff. Most of us had all we needed. Somewhere along the way we started wanting more than we needed. I'm not saying that desires are inherently wrong, but that when they become more important than needs, even more important than the needs of others and not just ourselves, it can become obsession. Wants and desires can become a driving force that blinds us to our needs and the needs of others.

God, our Father, is able to give us all we could ask or imagine. He wants to bless us and give us things even more than any good earthly father. He wants us to learn to give too. I'll bet some people are reading this and thinking, "I see and hear about kids starving and naked all over the world!" Perfect! As a believer and follower of Jesus (the biggest Giver), what are you going to do about it?

The Kingdom is not about getting, it's about giving. It's not about me and mine, it's about them and Him!

How about giving some food, clothes, shelter, and love to those in need. Being in need has got to be hell. Getting what you need when you haven't had it, priceless! Be careful. When you give someone something they need, you may just get something you want in return!

Christmas Joy...Not For Everybody December 24

Many years ago I had the opportunity to do something really neat for impoverished kids. At Christmas time, a volunteer organization would take donations to buy gifts for kids who would otherwise not get anything for Christmas. This was not just some little goodie gift but really cool stuff!

Their teachers were the "info-getters." They would identify the kids in need and find out their wants and needs for Christmas. Each child would receive a "big" gift (bike, tricycle, skateboard etc). They would receive other gifts as well (small toys and new clothing).

Once the donations were in and the gifts purchased, volunteers would wrap the gifts and prepare them for delivery to the childrens' homes. This is where I came in. Mail carriers, power company workers, phone company workers and other delivery and home service types who knew their way around the city, were recruited for the delivery portion of the process. Everything was delivered on Christmas Eve if possible.

I remember getting off work Christmas Eve around 4 p.m. and hurrying over to an address I knew to be a vacant store front in a strip mall. All the windows had been covered. When I walked in, I was amazed to see all of these gifts wrapped and stacked to the ceiling, organized by addresses. Some homes had several kids each! I loaded my pickup with brand new bicycles and boxes of new clothes, then I headed out eagerly anticipating the happy, stunned looks on little faces. I did get a lot of that, happiness and joy from serving and being part of giving to others, but there was heartache too.

I backed my truck up to one house and got just what you might expect. The kids were screaming, hollering and staring in disbelief as I unloaded bikes, toys and clothes with their names on them. It just doesn't get any better than that!

But then there were a few unexpected results and responses. One house I pulled up to was a vacant home. I had delivered mail here before and I knew they could not have moved more than a few days ago. I know what I'll do, I thought to myself. I went back to the Post Office and looked for their change of address. They had not left one.

I pulled up to another house and headed towards the door when a little voice came through the window screen and saying: "Don't knock on the door!" I said that I had Christmas gifts for them. Two kids were now looking at me through the screen. They could easily see the bikes and boxes in the back of my truck for them. They informed me that their mom was asleep. I told them it would probably be OK this once to wake her so we could put the gifts inside. We had been told to not leave them at the door or outside anywhere. I could see the fear in them and hear it in their voices as they told me there was no way they were waking mom up. She was drunk and would beat them if they did wake her.

I was stunned as I drove away with the undelivered gifts. Not just that they weren't going to have the gifts Christmas Day, but that Christmas Day would likely be just another bad day for them.

I prayed this morning for those kids. I wonder what their lives are like now. They must be in their 20's. There is a severe lack of Christmas joy and knowledge of the true Gift we received on that night a long time ago in a manger in Bethlehem. For those of us who know about Him, we should share that gift, Christmas Day and every other day.

Wise Guys   December 25

I just finished reading the story about some "Wise Guys" who came a long, long way to give expensive gifts to and worship a baby they knew was going to be a King. Until then, all we know for sure is that a few shepherds had been by to honor the new baby King. I suppose these shepherds told some friends what had happened a year or two before, but there doesn't seem to have been a media circus around this baby at the time.

Then these Wise Guys (Magi) come rolling into town where this guy Herod is the ruler of Israel, appointed by the Roman Empire. Herod is a murderous ruler bent on maintaining his grip on his kingdom. The Wise Guys, obviously men of some stature and importance, get an audience with Herod and ask him where this child is that is born King of the Jews.

Herod inquires of the religious scholars and sends the Wise Guys off toward Bethlehem. Herod also tells them to stop by on the way back and tell him where they found this baby King. Herod says he wants to worship the baby King as they do, but instead he desires to kill this child who would be King.

The Wise Guys found the baby King, worshiped Him and gave Him gifts. Gold for a King, incense for His deity and myrrh, a spice for someone who is going to die. The Wise Guys knew what was up, while most of the people around Him (who had been expecting Him) didn't even see Him right under their noses!

What's more? Even a Wise Guy's wisdom is enhanced and multiplied by the directions of God. They were warned in a dream to not go back by Herod's place, so they returned home by another route.

Some Bible notes I read on this pointed out that when we come to Jesus, we are put on another path or route in life like the Wise Guys were, after they met Jesus. They were still Wise Guys, they just had a new, wiser Leader.

When we come to Jesus, He erases our sins, not who we are. Yet He molds our character into who He designed us to be, as long as we allow Him. We're still who we are, we're just His.

Yeah, I wanna be a Wise Guy with God's wisdom too! Gimme a lot of that!

Off Your Ass And On Your Feet   December 26

Several days ago, I wrote about the time I helped deliver Christmas presents to poor and needy kids. It was a time of up and down emotions. The best parts were seeing the faces of excited kids and the feeling of knowing I was smack in the middle of God's will. The hard part was seeing how poor, hopeless and fearful so many people are while living out their lives. The Bible is filled with instruction to love, care for and help the poor and needy.

In the past I have been very judgmental towards people who find themselves in a situation of poverty, drugs, alcoholism and the like. I figured a lot of them brought this on themselves and so let them lie in the bed they made for themselves. The truth is that all of us have taken a wrong turn somewhere. Maybe we quit a job because a boss made us mad and it cost people counting on us, cheated or lied to someone and lost peoples' trust, gambled or drank away money that was needed for living expenses. Those were some of my past failures. You can fill in the blank with your selfish mistakes. Yet in every case someone helped me out of a place that it would have been difficult, if not impossible for me to escape under my own power.

What I am saying is, except for the Grace of God, there goes you and me. If people want and need help out of bad situations they find themselves in, no matter how they got there, we should help. Not to mention that helping the poor and needy is way up there on God's list.

Everyone of us is gifted by God. Each of us is good at doing something good. We each have a skill to make money, or give time to cook, to give medical care, to build shelters, to educate, to transport people, to employ and many other useful tools of rescue. Maybe most of all, to be a friend to encourage and pray for someone in a tough time in their lives.

I used to have a boss on a construction site who would say after lunch or break: "Off your ass and on your feet! Get to work!" So lets not just sit in our comfortable lifestyles with all our gifts in the back of our trucks. Lets back our "gift truck" right up to those in need of these gifts God gave us to share, and pour them out on them. Our gifts might be just what someone needs to be rescued.

Witnesses — December 27

What is the most incredible thing you have ever witnessed? The birth of a child? Someone walking away from a plane crash? An injured or handicapped person being healed?

How about the kid the other day on a church outing who was taken under by the surf. He was under water some twenty minutes before they found him. His lifeless body was brought out of the water and taken to the hospital as his church group prayed for him. They later regained his pulse, but there was fear of severe brain damage if he did survive. Incredibly, a few days later, it seems that he will recover nicely. He is coherent, talking and recovering.

We believe this story because there are many witnesses who can tell us about it. They saw this amazing event and are excited to the point of telling others about it.

Their reasons for telling this story to others may vary. Maybe they are just excited and amazed at the event. Maybe they are happy for the boy's recovery. Maybe they want to show the power of prayer. Whatever their reason, they are all witnesses to the event and we believe it because several witnesses tell us the same story.

Several witnesses tell us another story:

For what I received I passed on to you as of first importance: That Christ died for our sins according to the Scriptures, that he was buried, that he was raised on the third day according to the Scriptures, and that he appeared to Cephas, and then to the Twelve. After that, he appeared to more than five hundred of the brothers and sisters at the same time, most of whom are still living, though some have fallen asleep. Then he appeared to James, then to all the apostles, and last of all he appeared to me also, as to one abnormally born. – I Corinthians 15: 3-7

So there it is. Over 500 witnesses that would tell you, excitedly and with no doubt, that Jesus died, was buried, rose from the dead three days later, and was walking, talking and eating with them. How many witnesses do we need? I think more than 500 do it for me! How many does it take for you to believe?

The Coloring Book   December 28

I remember as a child I wasn't so good with crayons and coloring books. The whole idea of staying inside the lines was a frustration to me. I would give it a shot only to see the blue crayon slip out of the sky into where the grass was supposed to be green! I couldn't erase crayon; it would smear. I couldn't scrape it off. It would tear the page and ruin the the picture. No mistakes allowed!

Staying inside the lines was my feeble attempt at perfection and I had no shot at staying inside those lines. Sometimes a grown up would come along and give me some pointers that would help and I would get better at it for a while, until I got a new coloring book with a higher difficulty factor and I was crossing the line again.

We have lines that we are not supposed to cross both spiritually and in this natural life. Many of our laws (lines) in this life are based on the commands of God: don't steal, kill, and lie, etc. When we cross (color outside) those lines, as we are not supposed to, the picture can turn ugly.

In this life someone may come along and help us to learn to stay inside the lines more consistently but there is not one of us who is able to color this life inside the lines. So every single one of our life's "page in the coloring book" has a smear or a tear in it from "crossing the line."

Yet there is hope for our perfect picture in the Kingdom. First of all we can have a brand new page (life) to color on by just asking Jesus for a new page. This new page offers us a fresh start and He will show us how and will help us to stay inside the lines. You know what though? We will still sometimes color outside the lines (sin), but Jesus has the eraser that cleans up outside the lines!

We should get a new page (life) to color, if you need it. We should ask Jesus to erase the places we crossed the line and live in the peace and assurance of coloring "The Perfect Picture."

Oh, by the way, the new coloring book (life) is free and it comes with the "outside-the-lines crayon" (sin) eraser.

The Fly Over   December 29

Air travel has made the world a smaller place. Sure, TV, the Internet, radio and the telephone have shrunk our world in regards to news, world wide events and communication. However, for purposes of going some great distance in a short amount of time and actually being there, airline travel has made this a small world.

Before I was born, my mom traveled to be with my dad at his station overseas. She was to travel by ship, but due to a medical condition she was afforded airplane travel instead. A trip that could have taken weeks only took a couple of days. Now that trip could even be done in less than a day!

Yet air travel has its down side. On one occasion I remember a landing in Pittsburgh during a terrible storm. We hit the runway so hard, I suspect we did some pretty good damage to the airplane, although the passengers were never told.

On another flight returning from Atlanta, we suddenly banked left like a fighter plane during our landing approach. While we were in this hard banking turn I could see a small plane below us that the pilot had turned to avoid! Moments later Hannah Poo filled the barf bag, along with several other passengers (different bags of course).

During my LAST flight a few months ago, I experienced excruciating ear and head pain during the landings. Yeah, I know, they have medicine for that. Well, it didn't help on the second landing. That's it! I am a ground traveler now.

That said, air line travel has it's place. It is efficient, time saving and allows us to travel long distances in a short amount of time. Although we may occasionally experience a sickness, discomfort or even a scare, it is considered one of the safer ways of travel.

I went a long way to say this. The flip side for me is that my most memorable trips were road trips. I saw beautiful places, met interesting people, did fun things, and built relationships while traveling on the surface rather than in the air.

As a people today we seem to all be in some great hurry as if what we are doing is more important than the people we are "flying over." I think we should slow down and stay grounded while we're here. When you boil it down, our given purpose "on" this earth is relationships! To God and others.

Jesus' mode of transportation? Slow boats and walking with people.

Happy Birthday, Son   December 30

Today we are celebrating the birthday of my oldest son. Ben has grown up in so many ways since his first birthday when I held him in my arms as a baby. Two months ago Ben's first son was born and it just sends me back when I see him holding his son.

He has a wonderful wife that I am proud to call my daughter. Ben also has a beautiful daughter that lights up her "Papa's" world. Ben is a godly man who loves and provides for his family, serves his Lord and raises his children in the way they should go.

As Ben's father I could not be more pleased with the man he has become.

All parents should be willing to make sacrifices for their children. Although we are far from perfect parents, Hannah Pooh and I have made our share of sacrifices of our sons.

I'm sure Ben and Brianna will willingly sacrifice what is necessary for their childrens' good as well.

All children should want and try to please good, loving, caring parents (honor their parents).

God made the ultimate sacrifice for all of us (His children) so that we could have and celebrate our "spiritual birthdays" and thereby have life eternally with Him.

I think the next time I think about my spiritual birthday, I'm going to take a good look and see if I am becoming the kind of "child of God" that pleases my Father. I'll probably need to make some adjustments because I do want to please Him. I want to hear Him say: "I am pleased with you, Son! Happy Birthday!"

Timing   December 31

I once had to change a water pump on a small car. The little engine completely filled the engine compartment so that there was hardly any room to work. I had changed water pumps before and they were a relatively simple replacement as far as engine repairs are concerned. Not this time.

The lack of work area was only the beginning of the struggles. I would have to take everything off of the front of the engine block to get to the water pump. Some of the things that had to be removed included the timing belt. Timing for a motor is essential. Without the proper timing the engine will not fire in the correct sequence and it will not run properly, if at all.

I knew this and was trying to be careful not to move the camshaft or lower gears, but somehow in my hurry, aggravation and impatience, I got the timing off. After I got it all back together it would not run. I had to start all over taking the engine apart again. This took considerable extra effort and time, but without the correct timing it just won't work. The timing has to be right.

This is the same with the will of God. The timing has to be right. When God shows us something, we need to be sure the timing is right. David knew it was God's will for him to be king. David had several opportunities to kill Saul himself and be king immediately, but he knew it was not for him to take God's timing into his own hands.

Maybe Joseph jumped the gun a little by telling his brothers about his dreams of them bowing down to him. It was seventeen years before Joseph became Pharaoh's right hand man.

Yes, God's plan will ultimately come about and often we are shown things that are in His immediate will. However, I believe that His timing is crucial. I believe that in my life things could have come around a lot smoother and sooner if I had obeyed not only what he had for me to do, but waited for Him to show me when to do it.

His will likely involves who, what, when, where and how. Let's not leave out when and how. Let's exercise patient obedience so that we don't have to do it over again.

Also from the May Family

You're just 100 pages from rock bottom!

Hannah May is one of those very rare individuals who truly understands that truth does its own work; you are invited, never coerced.
Alan Ferguson
United Methodist Pastor

MORE FROM ENERGION PUBLICATIONS

Fiction
Covenant	Daniel Martin	$17.99
Megabelt	Nick May	$12.99
Prayer Trilogy	Kimberly Gordon	$9.99
Stories of the Way	Henry Neufeld	$9.99
The Traveler's Advance	Heath Taws	$14.99

Personal Study
Operation Olive Branch	Hannah May	$16.99
The Jesus Paradigm	David Alan Black	$17.99
The Sacred Journey	Chris Surber	$12.99
When People Speak for God	Henry Neufeld	$17.99

Christian Living
Faith in the Public Square	Robert D. Cornwall	$16.99
Grief: Finding the Candle of Light	Jody Neufeld	$8.99
I Want to Pray	Perry M. Dalton	$7.99
Soup Kitchen for the Soul	Renee Crosby	$12.99
Crossing the Street	Robert LaRochelle	$16.99

Bible Study
Learning and Living Scripture	Lentz/Neufeld	$12.99
From Inspiration to Understanding	Edward W. H. Vick	$24.99
Luke: A Participatory Study Guide	Geoffrey Lentz	$8.99
Philippians: A Participatory Study Guide	Bruce Epperly	$9.99
Ephesians: A Participatory Study Guide	Robert D. Cornwall	$9.99

Theology
The Politics of Witness	Allan R. Bevere	$9.99
Ultimate Allegiance	Robert D. Cornwall	$9.99
History and Christian Faith	Edward W. H. Vick	$9.99
The Church Under the Cross	William Powell Tuck	$11.99
Journey to the Undiscovered Country	William Powell tuck	$9.99

Generous Quantity Discounts Available
Dealer Inquiries Welcome
Energion Publications — P.O. Box 841
Gonzalez, FL 32560
Website: http://energionpubs.com
Phone: (850) 525-3916

Printed in the USA
CPSIA information can be obtained
at www.ICGtesting.com
JSHW080035110124
55191JS00001B/14